THE

AMERICAN

MAGAZINE

WRITING

2015

THE BEST AMERICAN MAGAZINE WRITING

2015

Edited by Sid Holt for the American Society of Magazine Editors

Columbia University Press   New York

Columbia University Press
Publishers Since 1893
New York   Chichester, West Sussex
cup.columbia.edu
Copyright © 2015 Columbia University Press
All rights reserved

Library of Congress Cataloging-in-Publication Data
ISSN 1541-0978
ISBN 978-0231-16959-2 (pbk.)

∞

Columbia University Press books are printed on permanent and durable
acid-free paper.
This book is printed on paper with recycled content.
Printed in the United States of America

p 10 9 8 7 6 5 4 3 2 1

COVER DESIGN: CATHERINE CASALINO

References to websites (URLs) were accurate at the time of writing.
Neither the author nor Columbia University Press is responsible for URLs
that may have expired or changed since the manuscript was prepared.

Contents

Evan Ratliff

Introduction

Before you delve into what will no doubt be the final edition of *The Best American Magazine Writing*,[1] let us all pause to memorialize the demise of the great magazine story. Indeed, you may have purchased this volume as a kind of collectors' edition, one to pull down from the shelf one day and regale your kids with tales of a time when quality magazines thrived. Perhaps you hope to later pawn it off on eBay to some Brooklyn hotel proprietor, seeking a touch of classy nostalgia for his lobby.

It's been a good run for magazine writing—at least 150 years, by most calculations. But I've been reading up on the state of the business, and I can report back that the future is dire. The enemy, it turns out, is you and I. Or rather, it is what the demon Internet has done to us, through the Web and the smartphones upon which it is consumed. Always in the pocket, always bleeping its siren call of apps and games, Twitter and Snapchat, and every other flashing distraction—or, as we magazine lovers might

---

1. Full disclosure: This is untrue. The American Society of Magazine Editors would like me to state officially, on the likely chance that you do not read to the end of this introduction, that there will in fact be an edition next year and for the foreseeable years after that.

say, affliction. Always conspiring to eliminate our desire for prose longer than a brunch-photo caption.

So we've been told, at least, in countless articles built on the indelible strength of anecdotal reflections. A few years ago, on that same Web, I chanced upon an infographic from a company called Killian Branding that purported to capture the stark nature of this decline. It purported to chart attention span over time, from 1860 to the present day. Points along the logarithmically sinking line were marked by the famous attention-holding names of the appropriate moments, from the height of Dickens through Hemingway, sixty- and thirty-second TV commercials, YouTube, then Vine, before continuing on an apparently infinite regression toward zero. It perfectly captured modern thinking on the topic of attention spans. Upon closer inspection, it was based upon no actual data.

I don't think data get any clearer than that! In the late nineteenth century, our massive attention spans were primed for serialized Dickens. And now, as it stands, by the year 2020 our attention will hold to little more than five single-syllable words in a sitting. Farewell, *Best American Magazine Writing*; greetings, *Best American Sequences of Five Monosyllabic Words*.

It may comfort you to know, however, that we are not the first generation to witness the death of great magazine writing. That bell began tolling, some would say, as far back as 1911, when a run of unprofitability forced Samuel S. McClure to sell off *McClure's*—founded in 1893, and the birthplace of the muckraking narrative journalism of Ida Tarbell and Lincoln Steffens—to creditors who slowly bled it to death. Sure, the nineteenth century also produced long-running magazines like *National Geographic*, *Harper's*, and *The Atlantic Monthly*. But as avid readers watched the likes of *Munsey's* and the *Century* follow *McClure's* down the hole, the stench of death was already upon us.

The 1920s brought some hope, with the advent of *Time* and *The New Yorker*, which, alongside *The New Republic*, *Fortune*, and *Esquire*, were harbingers of a great century ahead. But when *Vanity Fair* came (in 1913) and went (in 1936), it was only a hint of the carnage that the era of radio would bring. We lost the titanic trio of *Scribner's*, *Forum*, and *Liberty*—you remember them, of course—not to mention *Living Age*. When the *Delineator* went from more than two million subscribers in 1929 to suddenly ceasing publication in 1937, the writing was on the wall.

Wait, you say, what of the famed New Journalism of mid-century? Wonderful, inventive work it was, its novelistic style and immersive reporting coursing through the likes of *Esquire*, *Rolling Stone*, and *New York*. But the 1950s and 1960s also cost us *Collier's* and the *Saturday Evening Post Magazine*, and in the 1970s so went the agenda-setting *Life* and *Look*. New Journalism swashbuckler *Scanlan's* lasted only a year.

By 1985, then *Harper's* editor Lewis Lapham acknowledged the approaching end of great magazine writing in a *Christian Science Monitor* story delineating how television had finally replaced "the durable word as the lingua franca of American thought." "You've got to work with what you've got," Lapham said of America's remaining readers, and what we had, he observed, was a generation raised on "MTV and 'The A-Team.'" It had come time, the *Monitor* concluded, "to kiss long-form journalism goodbye." (Yet the 1980s saw the return of *Vanity Fair*, and the 1990s spawned both *Wired* and *Spy*, the magazine lover's magazine, which burned as brightly as any publication ever has before extinguishing in 1998.)

Now, of course, the Internet has decimated the tattered remains of our attention span. Worse, we're told that it has paradoxically fostered a new scourge for great magazine writing: more of it. In just the last five years, websites and magazines new and old— from *Nautilus* to *BuzzFeed* to *Grantland* to *The Atavist*, which I edit—have engaged in an ambitious resurgence in long, serious magazine writing. While this might seem like a sign of life, critics have explained that in fact such efforts are diminishing this great craft. Terms like "long-form" and hashtags like #longreads—through which readers recommend work they appreciate to other potential readers—only serve to dilute what was once the purview of discriminating enthusiasts alone. "The problem," Jonathan Mahler wrote in the *New York Times* in 2014, "is that long-form stories are too often celebrated simply because they exist." It was bad enough when our capacity to produce and read great stories collapsed. Now it seems we've turned around and loved magazine writing to death.

•   •   •

I don't mean to make light of the real financial and even existential conundrums facing magazines today, of course. I only mean to observe that they have existed as long as magazines themselves. (Except that last one; complaints about *too much* magazine writing, and what we label it, seem to be this century's peculiar, philistines-in-the-country-club anxiety.) In truth, I have my share of worries about the future of serious long-form journalism—who wouldn't, knowing its history? But when it comes to explanations, I'm partial to one from the great Ian Frazier. It appeared in a 2002 essay introducing *The Fish's Eye,* a collection of his writing on fishing, with pieces dating back to the 1970s. In those days, Frazier wrote:

> Magazines regularly ran long nonfiction pieces, ambitious in style and content, that originated in the thoughts of individual writers, in their experiences and sensibilities, and in what they believed was important to say. . . . I'm not sure why this emphasis on writers took hold. Maybe it had to do with the fact that in those years America had recently and unexpectedly come unglued; perhaps people suspected that a writer out walking around in the midst of it would know more of what was going on than an editor behind a desk in New York.

Neither do I know why that writers' era should disappear. But it pretty much has, in magazines at any rate.

Frazier's speculation—that perhaps the role of writers changes in relation to how often a chaotic world forces itself onto editors' desks—strikes me as more believable than most. I would argue that the trend is not linear, however, but cyclical. Just as great magazines have always come and gone, so, too, have the periods where editors were more or less willing and able to assign ambitious stories.

Great magazine pieces, after all, grow out of a simple transaction: an editor saying yes to an idea and, in turn, to a writer. *Yes* to a writer who will risk her time and even safety to venture into the world and return with a story that makes sense of it. *Yes* to a writer brave enough to lay bare her own past as a window into an important issue. *Yes* to a writer who invests her intellect and humor into a fresh perspective on art or culture. (Of course, great magazine writing involves more than *just* saying yes. It involves the editor eventually saying no: *no* to lazy phrasing, *no* to shaky facts, *no* to reporting shortcuts. When long-form writing fails— as it did dangerously in widely discussed incidents in *Grantland* and *Rolling Stone* this past year, it is not because of the names we give it, the hashtags we apply to it, or its word-count ambitions. It fails because an editor declined to say no to facts that weren't checked or to a piece whose ambition had overstepped its humanity.)

Therein lies the explanation for the volume in your hands, filled with work that stands in defiance of the latest doomsaying. What distinguishes the stories in this collection is not just their dedication to in-depth reporting and stylish storytelling. It is the decision of the editors behind them to assume the best of not just their writers but of their readers, in whatever medium those readers would encounter them. Indeed, anyone who takes the time to look at what's behind the online thumbs-upping and recommending finds an audience craving depth and context precisely *because* they are awash in information, an audience begging to be moved *because* of the soulless content we bathe in daily.

This collection also reflects a time when America has, in Frazier's words, "recently and unexpectedly come unglued." A country still blinded to its failure to grapple with its history of racism and oppression requires a writer like Ta-Nehisi Coates in "The Case for Reparations." The pitch to his editor at *The Atlantic*, Coates told me on the Longform Podcast last year, was simple: an argument could be made for reparations not through statistics and nineteenth-century history but through the narrative of those still suffering today from redlining in Chicago. "We really don't even have to go back to slavery," Coates said. "This wouldn't have to be this old, musty thing." An editor trusted him and said yes. And when Coates handed that editor a draft of some 13,000 words, "they came back to me and said: 'We need more.'"

Similarly, the cauldron of hate for women that has erupted on the Internet requires a writer like Amanda Hess, deftly weaving together her personal experience with searing reporting in "Women Aren't Welcome Here." A culture seamlessly blending politics and celebrity is an occasion for Monica Lewinsky to tell her own, forgotten story in *Vanity Fair*. A generation of college students confronting the looming threat of rape on campus demands the thoughtful reflection of Emily Yoffe in *Slate*.

Fourteen years of perpetual war in Afghanistan call for James Verini's "Love and Ruin," a story examining decades of interventions into that country's history through the story of one woman. A nation celebrating its Olympic medal hoard while ignoring the host country's homophobic laws requires the work of a reporter like Jeff Sharlet, who ventured to Moscow and St. Petersburg for *GQ* and returned with a deeply human portrait of the targets of those laws.

America's tendency to ignore and discard its elderly—even as it faces a wave of aging baby boomers—demands Tiffany Stanley's wrenching story, "Jackie's Goodbye," of caring for her aunt with Alzheimer's. And it can do no better than the magical prose of *New Yorker* legend Roger Angell, laying bare the comedy and tragedy of aging, alongside the joy of a life well lived, in "This Old Man."

It's a reality that all of these stories and the institutions behind them—whether renowned ones like *The New Yorker* or upstarts like *Pacific Standard* and *The Atavist*—must now compete in a world saturated with information and distraction. It's true that even the definition of a magazine has been stretched and twisted by a digital world that blows apart tables of contents and deposits them, story by story, on screens the size of a pack of cigarettes. With apologies to the collectors out there, however, this won't be the final edition of *The Best American Magazine Writing.* Great writers will keep finding the wherewithal to chase the bold ideas, and great editors will keep finding ways to say yes.

Even better, the next era of magazine work can be one that is more diverse in the character of its writers and in the form of its work. It can be one in which ambitious experimentation is celebrated alongside tradition, one which encompasses the live shows of *Pop Up Magazine* on the West Coast, the evolving tradition of *National Geographic,* the design serenity of *Nautilus,* the raucous reporting of *Vice.* Perhaps magazines have to die every once in a while so that they may be born again for a new age. "I know people who say they don't have a television," Roger Angell told an interviewer, a few years back. "You better belong to the times you're in."

Sid Holt

Acknowledgments

This edition of *The Best American Magazine Writing* brings together winners and finalists of the 2015 National Magazine Awards. Not all the winners, of course, or even most of the finalists—a book like this could hardly contain finalists from categories like General Excellence, which honors three entire print issues, much less categories like Multimedia and Video. What *BAMW* does do is collect fifteen examples of the best literary journalism published in the United States in the last year.

This year these stories are primarily drawn from the finalists in six Ellie categories: Public Interest, Reporting, Feature Writing, Essays and Criticism, Columns and Commentary, and Fiction. (The National Magazines Awards, it should be noted, are called the Ellies because the trophy presented to winners is modeled on an Alexander Calder stabile called *Elephant*.) The only exception is Jonathan Van Meter's profile of Kate Upton, taken from one of the issues that won *Vogue* the 2015 award for Magazine of the Year.

Most of the magazines represented in this edition of *BAMW* are familiar to aficionados, if such there are, of long-form journalism—magazines like *The Atlantic, Vanity Fair, GQ,* the *New York Times Magazine, New York,* and *The New Yorker.* The smaller magazines (smaller, that is, in audience, not ambition) included here are also well known to admirers of dogged reporting and graceful writing: *Pacific Standard*, *The New Republic*, *Chicago*, and *National Journal*.

What is new to this volume is the solid presence of digital-only publications, among them *Slate*, *The Atavist*, and *Grantland*. Just two years ago, *Slate* became the first online-only magazine to win an Ellie in a traditionally "print" category, Columns and Commentary. This year it was *The Atavist*'s turn when it won one of the most prestigious of the twenty-four National Magazine Awards, the Ellie for Feature Writing.

But it was not these titles alone that turned the 2015 National Magazine Awards into a digital steeplechase: this year, almost twenty of the finalists were either digital-only entries or were pieces—like the Rebecca Traister columns for *The New Republic* included here—first published online. This digital success story may lead some readers to wonder, What makes pixels on a screen a magazine? The answer is the same online as it is in print: editorial vision and readers who share the same interests and passions, not merely the same zip code.

A glib answer to a difficult question does not, however, make the task of the Ellie judges any easier. Every year since the awards were founded in 1966, the number of judges needed to evaluate an ever-expanding tally of longer and more complex entries has grown. This year, 340 judges—magazine editors, art directors, photography editors, journalism educators—gathered on two of the coldest days of the year at the Columbia Journalism School in New York City to read the 1,548 print and digital entries submitted by the 263 magazines that summoned the courage to participate in this, the most competitive of journalism-awards programs.

The judges chose five finalists in each category except in two very popular categories—Reporting and Feature Reporting—in which seven finalists were chosen. After the winners were selected from among those finalists, the judges' decisions were ratified by the National Magazine Awards Board, composed of veteran judges and other industry leaders. One week later the finalists were Twittercast . . . very slowly . . . to an audience mostly composed of magazine journalists—writers and reporters who, in the middle of the day, appeared to be oddly underemployed.

Then at the beginning of February came "the magazine Oscars"—an awards dinner with a special glamour all its own, at least to fans of print and pixel. This year some 600 editors and publishers attended the dinner, hosted by the gracious—and efficient—anchor and managing editor of ABC News's *World News Tonight*, David Muir. The 2015 dinner included the presentation not only of the twenty-four Ellies but also of a lifetime achievement award to the photojournalist James Nachtwey, whose inspiring acceptance speech is posted on the ASME YouTube Channel. And so ended an awards cycle that had begun six months before.

The members of ASME owe both David Muir and James Nachtwey thanks for joining us at the 2015 dinner, but there are many others who deserve gratitude for their work in making the National Magazine Awards possible. First, the judges: many of them sacrifice weekends and holidays to prepare for the judging then travel at their own expense to New York to spend those two days in crowded conference rooms that are either too hot or too cold. What all the judges share is a dedication to the task of identifying and honoring the best work published in American magazines in the preceding year.

Also deserving of thanks is the ASME Board of Directors, especially the 2014–15 president of ASME, Mark Jannot, who in his spare time is the vice president for content of the National Audubon Society. The board not only oversees the administration and presentation of the Ellies but also fiercely protects the integrity of the awards.

Since they were founded a half century ago, the Ellies have been cosponsored by the Columbia Journalism School. ASME thanks Steve Coll, the Pulitzer Prize–winning author who now serves as dean of the journalism school and Henry R. Luce Professor, for his support of the awards. Abi Wright, the executive director of the Alfred I. duPont–Columbia University Awards, also deserves recognition for her help organizing the judging and for her work as a member of the National Magazine Awards Board.

On behalf of ASME, I especially want to thank Evan Ratliff, the cofounder and editor in chief of *The Atavist*, for writing the introduction to this edition of *The Best American Magazine Writing* even as his first child was being born. Evan is also to be congratulated not only on *The Atavist*'s first Ellie—the 2015 National Magazine Award for Feature Writing for "Love and Ruin," by James Verini—but also for the seven other Ellie finalists *The Atavist* has published in the last four years.

As always, the members of ASME are grateful to our agent, David McCormick of McCormick Literary, for his skillful representation of our interests. ASME's editors at Columbia University Press, Philip Leventhal and Michael Haskell, also deserve thanks for their commitment to this series, their enthusiasm for magazine journalism, and, most of all, for their talent and patience.

ASME works closely throughout the year—and especially during the months when ASME functions as the "National Magazine Awards Company"—with the members and staff of MPA, the Association of Magazine Media. I want to express our thanks for their support to the chair of the MPA board of directors, Steve Lacy of Meredith Corporation, and Mary Berner, the president and CEO of MPA. Most deserving of recognition is my ASME colleague Nina Fortuna, who answers every phone call and e-mail with Spartan discipline.

But really, all our thanks belong to the writers and editors who make the Ellies—and this book—possible. Their dedication to the craft of journalism is a not-so-simple gift to every reader.

For more information about the National Magazine Awards, including a searchable database of winners and finalists, visit http://www.magazine.org/asme. To watch the presentation of the 2015 Ellies, go to the ASME YouTube Channel.

THE BEST
AMERICAN
MAGAZINE
WRITING

2015

The Atlantic

FINALIST—ESSAYS AND
CRITICISM

In hindsight, it is clear that the publication of "The Case for Reparations" in the June 2014 issue of The Atlantic *marked the beginning of new era in the way Americans think about race. As the Ellie judges said: "Ta-Nehisi Coates' passionate argument for reparations, based on centuries of injustice that continue into our own time, has changed the national conversation about race and history. His reporting on the impact of racism on individual Chicagoans makes his case all the more convincing." Coates's "Fear of a Black President" won the Ellie for Essays and Criticism in 2013. Founded in 1857,* The Atlantic *is now one of the most innovative of multiplatform publications, reaching nearly 14 million readers every month.*

Ta-Nehisi Coates

The Case for Reparations

And if thy brother, a Hebrew man, or a Hebrew woman, be sold unto thee, and serve thee six years; then in the seventh year thou shalt let him go free from thee. And when thou sendest him out free from thee, thou shalt not let him go away empty: thou shalt furnish him liberally out of thy flock, and out of thy floor, and out of thy winepress: of that wherewith the LORD thy God hath blessed thee thou shalt give unto him. And thou shalt remember that thou wast a bondman in the land of Egypt, and the LORD thy God redeemed thee: therefore I command thee this thing today.

—Deuteronomy 15: 12–15

Besides the crime which consists in violating the law, and varying from the right rule of reason, whereby a man so far becomes degenerate, and declares himself to quit the principles of human nature, and to be a noxious creature, there is commonly injury done to some person or other, and some other man receives damage by his transgression: in which case he who hath received any damage, has, besides the right of punishment common to him with other men, a particular right to seek reparation.

—John Locke, "Second Treatise"

By our unpaid labor and suffering, we have earned the right
to the soil, many times over and over, and now we are determined to have it.

—Anonymous, 1861

I. "So That's Just One of My Losses"

Clyde Ross was born in 1923, the seventh of thirteen children,
near Clarksdale, Mississippi, the home of the blues. Ross's parents
owned and farmed a forty-acre tract of land, flush with cows,
hogs, and mules. Ross's mother would drive to Clarksdale to do
her shopping in a horse and buggy, in which she invested all the
pride one might place in a Cadillac. The family owned another
horse, with a red coat, which they gave to Clyde. The Ross family
wanted for little, save that which all black families in the Deep
South then desperately desired—the protection of the law.

In the 1920s, Jim Crow Mississippi was, in all facets of society, a kleptocracy. The majority of the people in the state were
perpetually robbed of the vote—a hijacking engineered through
the trickery of the poll tax and the muscle of the lynch mob. Between 1882 and 1968, more black people were lynched in Mississippi than in any other state. "You and I know what's the best
way to keep the nigger from voting," blustered Theodore Bilbo, a
Mississippi senator and a proud Klansman. "You do it the night
before the election."

The state's regime partnered robbery of the franchise with
robbery of the purse. Many of Mississippi's black farmers lived in
debt peonage, under the sway of cotton kings who were at once
their landlords, their employers, and their primary merchants.
Tools and necessities were advanced against the return on the
crop, which was determined by the employer. When farmers were
deemed to be in debt—and they often were—the negative balance was then carried over to the next season. A man or woman
who protested this arrangement did so at the risk of grave injury

or death. Refusing to work meant arrest under vagrancy laws and forced labor under the state's penal system.

Well into the twentieth century, black people spoke of their flight from Mississippi in much the same manner as their runagate ancestors had. In her 2010 book, *The Warmth of Other Suns*, Isabel Wilkerson tells the story of Eddie Earvin, a spinach picker who fled Mississippi in 1963, after being made to work at gunpoint. "You didn't talk about it or tell nobody," Earvin said. "You had to sneak away."

When Clyde Ross was still a child, Mississippi authorities claimed his father owed $3,000 in back taxes. The elder Ross could not read. He did not have a lawyer. He did not know anyone at the local courthouse. He could not expect the police to be impartial. Effectively, the Ross family had no way to contest the claim and no protection under the law. The authorities seized the land. They seized the buggy. They took the cows, hogs, and mules. And so for the upkeep of separate but equal, the entire Ross family was reduced to sharecropping.

This was hardly unusual. In 2001, the Associated Press published a three-part investigation into the theft of black-owned land stretching back to the antebellum period. The series documented some 406 victims and 24,000 acres of land valued at tens of millions of dollars. The land was taken through means ranging from legal chicanery to terrorism. "Some of the land taken from black families has become a country club in Virginia," the AP reported, as well as "oil fields in Mississippi" and "a baseball spring training facility in Florida."

Clyde Ross was a smart child. His teacher thought he should attend a more challenging school. There was very little support for educating black people in Mississippi. But Julius Rosenwald, a part owner of Sears, Roebuck, had begun an ambitious effort to build schools for black children throughout the South. Ross's teacher believed he should attend the local Rosenwald school. It was too far for Ross to walk and get back in time to work in the fields. Local white children had a school bus. Clyde Ross did not, and thus lost the chance to better his education.

Then, when Ross was ten years old, a group of white men demanded his only childhood possession—the horse with the red coat. "You can't have this horse. We want it," one of the white men said. They gave Ross's father seventeen dollars.

"I did everything for that horse," Ross told me. "Everything. And they took him. Put him on the racetrack. I never did know what happened to him after that, but I know they didn't bring him back. So that's just one of my losses."

The losses mounted. As sharecroppers, the Ross family saw their wages treated as the landlord's slush fund. Landowners were supposed to split the profits from the cotton fields with sharecroppers. But bales would often disappear during the count, or the split might be altered on a whim. If cotton was selling for fifty cents a pound, the Ross family might get fifteen cents, or only five. One year Ross's mother promised to buy him a seven-dollar suit for a summer program at their church. She ordered the suit by mail. But that year Ross's family was paid only five cents a pound for cotton. The mailman arrived with the suit. The Rosses could not pay. The suit was sent back. Clyde Ross did not go to the church program.

It was in these early years that Ross began to understand himself as an American—he did not live under the blind decree of justice but under the heel of a regime that elevated armed robbery to a governing principle. He thought about fighting. "Just be quiet," his father told him. "Because they'll come and kill us all."

Clyde Ross grew. He was drafted into the army. The draft officials offered him an exemption if he stayed home and worked. He preferred to take his chances with war. He was stationed in California. He found that he could go into stores without being bothered. He could walk the streets without being harassed. He could go into a restaurant and receive service.

Ross was shipped off to Guam. He fought in World War II to save the world from tyranny. But when he returned to Clarksdale, he found that tyranny had followed him home. This was 1947, eight years before Mississippi lynched Emmett Till and tossed his broken body into the Tallahatchie River. The Great Migration, a mass exodus of 6 million African Americans that spanned most of the twentieth century, was now in its second wave. The black pilgrims did not journey north simply seeking better wages and work or bright lights and big adventures. They were fleeing the acquisitive warlords of the South. They were seeking the protection of the law.

Clyde Ross was among them. He came to Chicago in 1947 and took a job as a taster at Campbell's Soup. He made a stable wage. He married. He had children. His paycheck was his own. No Klansmen stripped him of the vote. When he walked down the street, he did not have to move because a white man was walking past. He did not have to take off his hat or avert his gaze. His journey from peonage to full citizenship seemed near-complete. Only one item was missing—a home, that final badge of entry into the sacred order of the American middle class of the Eisenhower years.

In 1961, Ross and his wife bought a house in North Lawndale, a bustling community on Chicago's West Side. North Lawndale had long been a predominantly Jewish neighborhood, but a handful of middle-class African Americans had lived there starting in the 1940s. The community was anchored by the sprawling Sears, Roebuck headquarters. North Lawndale's Jewish People's Institute actively encouraged blacks to move into the neighborhood, seeking to make it a "pilot community for interracial living." In the battle for integration then being fought around the country, North Lawndale seemed to offer promising terrain. But out in the tall grass, highwaymen, nefarious as any Clarksdale kleptocrat, were lying in wait.

Three months after Clyde Ross moved into his house, the boiler blew out. This would normally be a homeowner's responsibility, but in fact, Ross was not really a homeowner. His payments were made to the seller, not the bank. And Ross had not signed a normal mortgage. He'd bought "on contract": a predatory agreement that combined all the responsibilities of homeownership with all the disadvantages of renting—while offering the benefits of neither. Ross had bought his house for $27,500. The seller, not the previous homeowner but a new kind of middleman, had bought it for only $12,000 six months before selling it to Ross. In a contract sale, the seller kept the deed until the contract was paid in full—and, unlike with a normal mortgage, Ross would acquire no equity in the meantime. If he missed a single payment, he would immediately forfeit his $1,000 down payment, all his monthly payments, and the property itself.

The men who peddled contracts in North Lawndale would sell homes at inflated prices and then evict families who could not pay—taking their down payment and their monthly installments as profit. Then they'd bring in another black family, rinse, and repeat. "He loads them up with payments they can't meet," an office secretary told the *Chicago Daily News* of her boss, the speculator Lou Fushanis, in 1963. "Then he takes the property away from them. He's sold some of the buildings three or four times."

Ross had tried to get a legitimate mortgage in another neighborhood but was told by a loan officer that there was no financing available. The truth was that there was no financing for people like Clyde Ross. From the 1930s through the 1960s, black people across the country were largely cut out of the legitimate home-mortgage market through means both legal and extralegal. Chicago whites employed every measure, from "restrictive covenants" to bombings, to keep their neighborhoods segregated.

Their efforts were buttressed by the federal government. In 1934, Congress created the Federal Housing Administration. The FHA insured private mortgages, causing a drop in interest rates and a decline in the size of the down payment required to buy a house. But an insured mortgage was not a possibility for Clyde Ross. The FHA had adopted a system of maps that rated neighborhoods according to their perceived stability. On the maps, green areas, rated "A," indicated "in demand" neighborhoods that, as one appraiser put it, lacked "a single foreigner or Negro." These neighborhoods were considered excellent prospects for insurance. Neighborhoods where black people lived were rated "D" and were usually considered ineligible for FHA backing. They were colored in red. Neither the percentage of black people living there nor their social class mattered. Black people were viewed as a contagion. Redlining went beyond FHA-backed loans and spread to the entire mortgage industry, which was already rife with racism, excluding black people from most legitimate means of obtaining a mortgage.

"A government offering such bounty to builders and lenders could have required compliance with a nondiscrimination policy," Charles Abrams, the urban-studies expert who helped create the New York City Housing Authority, wrote in 1955. "Instead, the FHA adopted a racial policy that could well have been culled from the Nuremberg laws."

The devastating effects are cogently outlined by Melvin L. Oliver and Thomas M. Shapiro in their 1995 book, *Black Wealth/White Wealth*:

> Locked out of the greatest mass-based opportunity for wealth accumulation in American history, African Americans who desired and were able to afford home ownership found themselves consigned to central-city communities where their investments were affected by the "self-fulfilling prophecies" of the FHA appraisers: cut off from sources of new investment[,] their homes and communities deteriorated and lost value in comparison to those homes and communities that FHA appraisers deemed desirable.

In Chicago and across the country, whites looking to achieve the American dream could rely on a legitimate credit system backed by the government. Blacks were herded into the sights of unscrupulous lenders who took them for money and for sport. "It was like people who like to go out and shoot lions in Africa. It was the same thrill," a housing attorney told the historian Beryl Satter in her 2009 book, *Family Properties*. "The thrill of the chase and the kill."

The kill was profitable. At the time of his death, Lou Fushanis owned more than 600 properties, many of them in North Lawndale, and his estate was estimated to be worth $3 million. He'd made much of this money by exploiting the frustrated hopes of black migrants like Clyde Ross. During this period, according to one estimate, 85 percent of all black home buyers who bought in Chicago bought on contract. "If anybody who is well established in this business in Chicago doesn't earn $100,000 a year," a contract seller told the *Saturday Evening Post* in 1962, "he is loafing."

Contract sellers became rich. North Lawndale became a ghetto.

Clyde Ross still lives there. He still owns his home. He is ninety-one, and the emblems of survival are all around him— awards for service in his community, pictures of his children in cap and gown. But when I asked him about his home in North Lawndale, I heard only anarchy.

"We were ashamed. We did not want anyone to know that we were that ignorant," Ross told me. He was sitting at his dining-room table. His glasses were as thick as his Clarksdale drawl. "I'd come out of Mississippi where there was one mess, and come up here and got in another mess. So how dumb am I? I didn't want anyone to know how dumb I was.

"When I found myself caught up in it, I said, 'How? I just left this mess. I just left no laws. And no regard. And then I come here and get cheated wide open.' I would probably want to do some harm to some people, you know, if I had been violent like some of us. I thought, 'Man, I got caught up in this stuff. I can't even take care of my kids.' I didn't have enough for my kids. You could fall through the cracks easy fighting these white people. And no law."

But fight Clyde Ross did. In 1968 he joined the newly formed Contract Buyers League—a collection of black homeowners on Chicago's South and West Sides, all of whom had been locked into the same system of predation. There was Howell Collins, whose contract called for him to pay $25,500 for a house that a speculator had bought for $14,500. There was Ruth Wells, who'd managed to pay out half her contract, expecting a mortgage, only to suddenly see an insurance bill materialize out of thin air—a requirement the seller had added without Wells's knowledge. Contract sellers used every tool at their disposal to pilfer from their clients. They scared white residents into selling low. They lied about properties' compliance with building codes, then left the buyer responsible when city inspectors arrived. They presented themselves as real-estate brokers, when in fact they were the owners. They guided their clients to lawyers who were in on the scheme.

The Contract Buyers League fought back. Members—who would eventually number more than 500—went out to the posh suburbs where the speculators lived and embarrassed them by knocking on their neighbors' doors and informing them of the details of the contract-lending trade. They refused to pay their installments, instead holding monthly payments in an escrow account. Then they brought a suit against the contract sellers, accusing them of buying properties and reselling in such a manner "to reap from members of the Negro race large and unjust profits."

In return for the "deprivations of their rights and privileges under the Thirteenth and Fourteenth Amendments," the league demanded "prayers for relief"—payback of all moneys paid on contracts and all moneys paid for structural improvement of properties, at 6 percent interest minus a "fair, non-discriminatory" rental price for time of occupation. Moreover, the league asked the court to adjudge that the defendants had "acted willfully and maliciously and that malice is the gist of this action."

Ross and the Contract Buyers League were no longer appealing to the government simply for equality. They were no longer fleeing in hopes of a better deal elsewhere. They were charging society with a crime against their community. They wanted the crime publicly ruled as such. They wanted the crime's executors declared to be offensive to society. And they wanted restitution for the great injury brought upon them by said offenders. In 1968, Clyde Ross and the Contract Buyers League were no longer simply seeking the protection of the law. They were seeking reparations.

II. "A Difference of Kind, Not Degree"

According to the most-recent statistics, North Lawndale is now on the wrong end of virtually every socioeconomic indicator. In 1930 its population was 112,000. Today it is 36,000. The halcyon talk of "interracial living" is dead. The neighborhood is 92 percent black. Its homicide rate is 45 per 100,000—triple the rate of the city as a whole. The infant-mortality rate is 14 per 1,000—more than twice the national average. Forty-three percent of the people in North Lawndale live below the poverty line—double Chicago's overall rate. Forty-five percent of all households are on food stamps—nearly three times the rate of the city at large. Sears, Roebuck left the neighborhood in 1987, taking 1,800 jobs with it. Kids in North Lawndale need not be confused about their prospects: Cook County's Juvenile Temporary Detention Center sits directly adjacent to the neighborhood.

North Lawndale is an extreme portrait of the trends that ail black Chicago. Such is the magnitude of these ailments that it can be said that blacks and whites do not inhabit the same city. The average per capita income of Chicago's white neighborhoods is almost three times that of its black neighborhoods. When the Harvard sociologist Robert J. Sampson examined incarceration rates in Chicago in his 2012 book, *Great American City*, he found that a black neighborhood with one of the highest incarceration rates (West Garfield Park) had a rate more than forty times as high as the white neighborhood with the highest rate (Clearing). "This is a staggering differential, even for community-level comparisons," Sampson writes. "A difference of kind, not degree."

In other words, Chicago's impoverished black neighborhoods—characterized by high unemployment and households headed by single parents—are not simply poor; they are "ecologically distinct." This "is not simply the same thing as low economic status," writes Sampson. "In this pattern Chicago is not alone."

The lives of black Americans are better than they were half a century ago. The humiliation of WHITES ONLY signs are gone. Rates of black poverty have decreased. Black teen-pregnancy rates are at record lows—and the gap between black and white teen-pregnancy rates has shrunk significantly. But such progress rests on a shaky foundation, and fault lines are everywhere. The income gap between black and white households is roughly the same today as it was in 1970. Patrick Sharkey, a sociologist at New York University, studied children born from 1955 through 1970 and found that 4 percent of whites and 62 percent of blacks across America had been raised in poor neighborhoods. A generation later, the same study showed, virtually nothing had changed. And whereas whites born into affluent neighborhoods tended to remain in affluent neighborhoods, blacks tended to fall out of them.

This is not surprising. Black families, regardless of income, are significantly less wealthy than white families. The Pew Research Center estimates that white households are worth roughly 20 times as much as black households, and that whereas only 15 percent of whites have zero or negative wealth, more than a third of blacks do. Effectively, the black family in America is working without a safety net. When financial calamity strikes—a medical emergency, divorce, job loss—the fall is precipitous.

And just as black families of all incomes remain handicapped by a lack of wealth, so too do they remain handicapped by their restricted choice of neighborhood. Black people with upper-middle-class incomes do not generally live in upper-middle-class neighborhoods. Sharkey's research shows that black families making $100,000 typically live in the kinds of neighborhoods inhabited by white families making $30,000. "Blacks and whites inhabit such different neighborhoods," Sharkey writes, "that it is not possible to compare the economic outcomes of black and white children."

The implications are chilling. As a rule, poor black people do not work their way out of the ghetto—and those who do often face the horror of watching their children and grandchildren tumble back.

Even seeming evidence of progress withers under harsh light. In 2012, the Manhattan Institute cheerily noted that segregation had declined since the 1960s. And yet African Americans still remained—by far—the most segregated ethnic group in the country.

With segregation, with the isolation of the injured and the robbed, comes the concentration of disadvantage. An unsegregated America might see poverty, and all its effects, spread across the country with no particular bias toward skin color. Instead, the concentration of poverty has been paired with a concentration of melanin. The resulting conflagration has been devastating.

One thread of thinking in the African American community holds that these depressing numbers partially stem from cultural pathologies that can be altered through individual grit and exceptionally good behavior. (In 2011, Philadelphia mayor Michael Nutter, responding to violence among young black males, put the blame on the family: "Too many men making too many babies they don't want to take care of, and then we end up dealing with your children." Nutter turned to those presumably fatherless babies: "Pull your pants up and buy a belt, because no one wants to see your underwear or the crack of your butt.") The thread is as old as black politics itself. It is also wrong. The kind of trenchant racism to which black people have persistently been subjected can never be defeated by making its victims more respectable. The essence of American racism is disrespect. And in the wake of the grim numbers, we see the grim inheritance.

The Contract Buyers League's suit brought by Clyde Ross and his allies took direct aim at this inheritance. The suit was rooted in Chicago's long history of segregation, which had created two housing markets—one legitimate and backed by the government, the other lawless and patrolled by predators. The suit dragged on until 1976, when the league lost a jury trial. Securing the equal protection of the law proved hard; securing reparations proved impossible. If there were any doubts about the mood of the jury, the foreman removed them by saying, when asked about the verdict, that he hoped it would help end "the mess Earl Warren made with *Brown v. Board of Education* and all that nonsense."

The Supreme Court seems to share that sentiment. The past two decades have witnessed a rollback of the progressive legislation of the 1960s. Liberals have found themselves on the defensive. In 2008, when Barack Obama was a candidate for president, he was asked whether his daughters—Malia and Sasha—should benefit from affirmative action. He answered in the negative.

The exchange rested upon an erroneous comparison of the average American white family and the exceptional first family. In the contest of upward mobility, Barack and Michelle Obama have won. But they've won by being twice as good—and enduring twice as much. Malia and Sasha Obama enjoy privileges beyond the average white child's dreams. But that comparison is incomplete. The more telling question is how they compare with Jenna and Barbara Bush—the products of many generations of privilege, not just one. Whatever the Obama children achieve, it will be evidence of their family's singular perseverance, not of broad equality.

III. "We Inherit Our Ample Patrimony"

In 1783, the freedwoman Belinda Royall petitioned the commonwealth of Massachusetts for reparations. Belinda had been born in modern-day Ghana. She was kidnapped as a child and sold into slavery. She endured the Middle Passage and fifty years of enslavement at the hands of Isaac Royall and his son. But the junior Royall, a British loyalist, fled the country during the Revolution. Belinda, now free after half a century of labor, beseeched the nascent Massachusetts legislature:

> The face of your Petitioner, is now marked with the furrows of time, and her frame bending under the oppression of years, while she, by the Laws of the Land, is denied the employment of one morsel of that immense wealth, apart whereof hath been accumilated by her own industry, and the whole augmented by her servitude.
>
> WHEREFORE, casting herself at your feet if your honours, as to a body of men, formed for the extirpation of vassalage, for the reward of Virtue, and the just return of honest industry—she prays, that such allowance may be made her out of the Estate of Colonel Royall, as will prevent her, and her more infirm daughter, from misery in the greatest extreme, and scatter comfort over the short and downward path of their lives.

Belinda Royall was granted a pension of fifteen pounds and twelve shillings, to be paid out of the estate of Isaac Royall—one of the earliest successful attempts to petition for reparations. At the time, black people in America had endured more than 150 years of enslavement, and the idea that they might be owed something in return was, if not the national consensus, at least not outrageous.

"A heavy account lies against us as a civil society for oppressions committed against people who did not injure us," wrote the Quaker John Woolman in 1769, "and that if the particular case of many individuals were fairly stated, it would appear that there was considerable due to them."

As the historian Roy E. Finkenbine has documented, at the dawn of this country, black reparations were actively considered and often effected. Quakers in New York, New England, and Baltimore went so far as to make "membership contingent upon compensating one's former slaves." In 1782, the Quaker Robert Pleasants emancipated his 78 slaves, granted them 350 acres, and later built a school on their property and provided for their education. "The doing of this justice to the injured Africans," wrote Pleasants, "would be an acceptable offering to him who 'Rules in the kingdom of men.'"

Edward Coles, a protégé of Thomas Jefferson who became a slaveholder through inheritance, took many of his slaves north and granted them a plot of land in Illinois. John Randolph, a cousin of Jefferson's, willed that all his slaves be emancipated upon his death, and that all those older than forty be given ten acres of land. "I give and bequeath to all my slaves their freedom," Randolph wrote, "heartily regretting that I have been the owner of one."

In his book *Forever Free*, Eric Foner recounts the story of a disgruntled planter reprimanding a freedman loafing on the job:

PLANTER: "You lazy nigger, I am losing a whole day's labor by you."
FREEDMAN: "Massa, how many days' labor have I lost by you?"

In the twentieth century, the cause of reparations was taken up by a diverse cast that included the Confederate veteran Walter R. Vaughan, who believed that reparations would be a stimulus for the South; the black activist Callie House; black-nationalist leaders like "Queen Mother" Audley Moore; and the civil-rights activist James Forman. The movement coalesced in 1987 under an umbrella organization called the National Coalition of Blacks for Reparations in America (N'COBRA). The NAACP endorsed reparations in 1993. Charles J. Ogletree Jr., a professor at Harvard Law School, has pursued reparations claims in court.

But while the people advocating reparations have changed over time, the response from the country has remained virtually the same. "They have been taught to labor," the *Chicago Tribune* editorialized in 1891. "They have been taught Christian civilization, and to speak the noble English language instead of some African gibberish. The account is square with the ex-slaves."

Not exactly. Having been enslaved for 250 years, black people were not left to their own devices. They were terrorized. In the Deep South, a second slavery ruled. In the North, legislatures, mayors, civic associations, banks, and citizens all colluded to pin black people into ghettos, where they were overcrowded, overcharged, and undereducated. Businesses discriminated against them, awarding them the worst jobs and the worst wages. Police brutalized them in the streets. And the notion that black lives, black bodies, and black wealth were rightful targets remained deeply rooted in the broader society. Now we have half-stepped away from our long centuries of despoilment, promising, "Never again." But still we are haunted. It is as though we have run up a credit-card bill and, having pledged to charge no more, remain befuddled that the balance does not disappear. The effects of that balance, interest accruing daily, are all around us.

Broach the topic of reparations today and a barrage of questions inevitably follows: Who will be paid? How much will they be paid? Who will pay? But if the practicalities, not the justice, of reparations are the true sticking point, there has for some time been the beginnings of a solution. For the past twenty-five years, Congressman John Conyers Jr., who represents the Detroit area, has marked every session of Congress by introducing a bill calling for a congressional study of slavery and its lingering effects as well as recommendations for "appropriate remedies."

A country curious about how reparations might actually work has an easy solution in Conyers's bill, now called HR 40, the Commission to Study Reparation Proposals for African Americans Act. We would support this bill, submit the question to study, and then assess the possible solutions. But we are not interested.

"It's because it's black folks making the claim," Nkechi Taifa, who helped found N'COBRA, says. "People who talk about reparations are considered left lunatics. But all we are talking about is studying [reparations]. As John Conyers has said, we study everything. We study the water, the air. We can't even study the issue? This bill does not authorize one red cent to anyone."

That HR 40 has never—under either Democrats or Republicans—made it to the House floor suggests our concerns are rooted not in the impracticality of reparations but in something more existential. If we conclude that the conditions in North Lawndale and black America are not inexplicable but are instead precisely what you'd expect of a community that for centuries has lived in America's crosshairs, then what are we to make of the world's oldest democracy?

One cannot escape the question by hand-waving at the past, disavowing the acts of one's ancestors, nor by citing a recent date of ancestral immigration. The last slaveholder has been dead for a very long time. The last soldier to endure Valley Forge has been dead much longer. To proudly claim the veteran and disown the slaveholder is patriotism à la carte. A nation outlives its generations. We were not there when Washington crossed the Delaware, but Emanuel Gottlieb Leutze's rendering has meaning to us. We were not there when Woodrow Wilson took us into

World War I, but we are still paying out the pensions. If Thomas Jefferson's genius matters, then so does his taking of Sally Hemings's body. If George Washington's crossing the Delaware matters, so must his ruthless pursuit of the runagate Oney Judge.

In 1909, President William Howard Taft told the country that "intelligent" white southerners were ready to see blacks as "useful members of the community." A week later Joseph Gordon, a black man, was lynched outside Greenwood, Mississippi. The high point of the lynching era has passed. But the memories of those robbed of their lives still live on in the lingering effects. Indeed, in America there is a strange and powerful belief that if you stab a black person ten times, the bleeding stops and the healing begins the moment the assailant drops the knife. We believe white dominance to be a fact of the inert past, a delinquent debt that can be made to disappear if only we don't look.

There has always been another way. "It is in vain to alledge, that *our ancestors* brought them hither, and not we," Yale president Timothy Dwight said in 1810.

> We inherit our ample patrimony with all its incumbrances; and are bound to pay the debts of our ancestors. *This* debt, particularly, we are bound to discharge: and, when the righteous Judge of the Universe comes to reckon with his servants, he will rigidly exact the payment at our hands. To give them liberty, and stop here, is to entail upon them a curse.

IV. "The Ills That Slavery Frees Us From"

America begins in black plunder and white democracy, two features that are not contradictory but complementary. "The men who came together to found the independent United States, dedicated to freedom and equality, either held slaves or were willing to join hands with those who did," the historian Edmund S. Morgan wrote. "None of them felt entirely comfortable about the fact, but neither did they feel responsible for it. Most of them had inherited both their slaves and their attachment to freedom from an earlier generation, and they knew the two were not unconnected."

When enslaved Africans, plundered of their bodies, plundered of their families, and plundered of their labor, were brought to the colony of Virginia in 1619, they did not initially endure the naked racism that would engulf their progeny. Some of them were freed. Some of them intermarried. Still others escaped with the white indentured servants who had suffered as they had. Some even rebelled together, allying under Nathaniel Bacon to torch Jamestown in 1676.

One hundred years later, the idea of slaves and poor whites joining forces would shock the senses, but in the early days of the English colonies, the two groups had much in common. English visitors to Virginia found that its masters "abuse their servantes with intollerable oppression and hard usage." White servants were flogged, tricked into serving beyond their contracts, and traded in much the same manner as slaves.

This "hard usage" originated in a simple fact of the New World—land was boundless but cheap labor was limited. As life spans increased in the colony, the Virginia planters found in the enslaved Africans an even more efficient source of cheap labor. Whereas indentured servants were still legal subjects of the English crown and thus entitled to certain protections, African slaves entered the colonies as aliens. Exempted from the protections of the crown, they became early America's indispensable working class—fit for maximum exploitation, capable of only minimal resistance.

For the next 250 years, American law worked to reduce black people to a class of untouchables and raise all white men to the level of citizens. In 1650, Virginia mandated that "all persons except Negroes" were to carry arms. In 1664, Maryland mandated that any Englishwoman who married a slave must live as a slave of her husband's master. In 1705, the Virginia assembly passed a law allowing for the dismemberment of unruly slaves—but forbidding masters from whipping "a Christian white servant naked, without an order from a justice of the peace." In that same law, the colony mandated that "all horses, cattle, and hogs, now belonging, or that hereafter shall belong to any slave" be seized and sold off by the local church, the profits used to support "the poor of the said parish." At that time, there would have still been people alive who could remember blacks and whites joining to burn down Jamestown only twenty-nine years before. But at the beginning of the eighteenth century, two primary classes were enshrined in America.

"The two great divisions of society are not the rich and poor, but white and black," John C. Calhoun, South Carolina's senior senator, declared on the Senate floor in 1848. "And all the former, the poor as well as the rich, belong to the upper class, and are respected and treated as equals."

In 1860, the majority of people living in South Carolina and Mississippi, almost half of those living in Georgia, and about one-third of all Southerners were on the wrong side of Calhoun's line. The state with the largest number of enslaved Americans was Virginia, where in certain counties some 70 percent of all people labored in chains. Nearly one-fourth of all white Southerners owned slaves, and upon their backs the economic basis of America—and much of the Atlantic world—was erected. In the seven cotton states, one-third of all white income was derived from slavery. By 1840, cotton produced by slave labor constituted 59 percent of the country's exports. The web of this slave society extended north to the looms of New England, and across the Atlantic to Great Britain, where it powered a great economic transformation and altered the trajectory of world history. "Whoever says Industrial Revolution," wrote the historian Eric J. Hobsbawm, "says cotton."

The wealth accorded America by slavery was not just in what the slaves pulled from the land but in the slaves themselves. "In 1860, slaves as an asset were worth more than all of America's manufacturing, all of the railroads, all of the productive capacity of the United States put together," the Yale historian David W. Blight has noted. "Slaves were the single largest, by far, financial asset of property in the entire American economy." The sale of these slaves—"in whose bodies that money congealed," writes Walter Johnson, a Harvard historian—generated even more ancillary wealth. Loans were taken out for purchase, to be repaid with interest. Insurance policies were drafted against the untimely death of a slave and the loss of potential profits. Slave sales were taxed and notarized. The vending of the black body and the sundering of the black family became an economy unto themselves, estimated to have brought in tens of millions of dollars to antebellum America. In 1860 there were more millionaires per capita in the Mississippi Valley than anywhere else in the country.

Beneath the cold numbers lay lives divided. "I had a constant dread that Mrs. Moore, her mistress, would be in want of money and sell my dear wife," a freedman wrote, reflecting on his time in slavery. "We constantly dreaded a final separation. Our affection for each was very strong, and this made us always apprehensive of a cruel parting."

Forced partings were common in the antebellum South. A slave in some parts of the region stood a 30 percent chance of being sold in his or her lifetime. Twenty-five percent of interstate trades destroyed a first marriage and half of them destroyed a nuclear family.

When the wife and children of Henry Brown, a slave in Richmond, Virginia, were to be sold away, Brown searched for a white master who might buy his wife and children to keep the family together. He failed:

> The next day, I stationed myself by the side of the road, along which the slaves, amounting to three hundred and fifty, were to pass. The purchaser of my wife was a Methodist minister, who was about starting for North Carolina. Pretty soon five waggon-loads of little children passed, and looking at the foremost one, what should I see but a little child, pointing its tiny hand towards me, exclaiming, "There's my father; I knew he would come and bid me good-bye." It was my eldest child! Soon the gang approached in which my wife was chained. I looked, and beheld her familiar face; but O, reader, that glance of agony! may God spare me ever again enduring the excruciating horror of that moment! She passed, and came near to where I stood. I seized hold of her hand, intending to bid her farewell; but words failed me; the gift of utterance had fled, and I remained speechless. I followed her for some distance, with her hand grasped in mine, as if to save her from her fate, but I could not speak, and I was obliged to turn away in silence.

In a time when telecommunications were primitive and blacks lacked freedom of movement, the parting of black families was a kind of murder. Here we find the roots of American wealth and democracy—in the for-profit destruction of the most important asset available to any people, the family. The destruction was not incidental to America's rise; it facilitated that rise. By erecting a slave society, America created the economic foundation for its great experiment in democracy. The labor strife that seeded Bacon's rebellion was suppressed. America's indispensable working class existed as property beyond the realm of politics, leaving white Americans free to trumpet their love of freedom and democratic values. Assessing antebellum democracy in Virginia, a visitor from England observed that the state's natives "can profess an unbounded love of liberty and of democracy in consequence of the mass of the people, who in other countries might become mobs, being there nearly altogether composed of their own Negro slaves."

V. The Quiet Plunder

The consequences of 250 years of enslavement, of war upon black families and black people, were profound. Like homeownership today, slave ownership was aspirational, attracting not just those who owned slaves but those who wished to. Much as homeowners today might discuss the addition of a patio or the painting of a living room, slaveholders traded tips on the best methods for breeding workers, exacting labor, and doling out punishment. Just as a homeowner today might subscribe to a magazine like *This Old House*, slaveholders had journals such as *De Bow's Review*, which recommended the best practices for wringing profits from slaves. By the dawn of the Civil War, the enslavement of black America was thought to be so foundational to the country that those who sought to end it were branded heretics worthy of death. Imagine what would happen if a president today came out in favor of taking all American homes from their owners: the reaction might well be violent.

"This country was formed for the *white*, not for the black man," John Wilkes Booth wrote, before killing Abraham Lincoln. "And looking upon *African slavery* from the same standpoint held by those noble framers of our Constitution, I for one have ever considered *it* one of the greatest blessings (both for themselves and us) that God ever bestowed upon a favored nation."

In the aftermath of the Civil War, Radical Republicans attempted to reconstruct the country upon something resembling universal equality—but they were beaten back by a campaign of "Redemption," led by White Liners, Red Shirts, and Klansmen bent on upholding a society "formed for the *white*, not for the black man." A wave of terrorism roiled the South. In his massive history *Reconstruction*, Eric Foner recounts incidents of black people being attacked for not removing their hats; for refusing to hand over a whiskey flask; for disobeying church procedures; for "using insolent language"; for disputing labor contracts; for refusing to be "tied like a slave." Sometimes the attacks were intended simply to "thin out the niggers a little."

Terrorism carried the day. Federal troops withdrew from the South in 1877. The dream of Reconstruction died. For the next century, political violence was visited upon blacks wantonly, with special treatment meted out toward black people of ambition. Black schools and churches were burned to the ground. Black voters and the political candidates who attempted to rally them were intimidated, and some were murdered. At the end of World War I, black veterans returning to their homes were assaulted for daring to wear the American uniform. The demobilization of soldiers after the war, which put white and black veterans into competition for scarce jobs, produced the Red Summer of 1919: a succession of racist pogroms against dozens of cities ranging from Longview, Texas, to Chicago to Washington, D.C. Organized white violence against blacks continued into the 1920s—in 1921 a white mob leveled Tulsa's "Black Wall Street," and in 1923 another one razed the black town of Rosewood, Florida—and virtually no one was punished.

The work of mobs was a rabid and violent rendition of prejudices that extended even into the upper reaches of American government. The New Deal is today remembered as a model for what progressive government should do—cast a broad social safety net that protects the poor and the afflicted while building the middle class. When progressives wish to express their disappointment with Barack Obama, they point to the accomplishments of Franklin Roosevelt. But these progressives rarely note that Roosevelt's New Deal, much like the democracy that produced it, rested on the foundation of Jim Crow.

"The Jim Crow South," writes Ira Katznelson, a history and political-science professor at Columbia, "was the one collaborator America's democracy could not do without." The marks of that collaboration are all over the New Deal. The omnibus programs passed under the Social Security Act in 1935 were crafted in such a way as to protect the southern way of life. Old-age insurance (Social Security proper) and unemployment insurance excluded farmworkers and domestics—jobs heavily occupied by blacks. When President Roosevelt signed Social Security into law in 1935, 65 percent of African Americans nationally and between 70 and 80 percent in the South were ineligible. The NAACP protested, calling the new American safety net "a sieve with holes just big enough for the majority of Negroes to fall through."

The oft-celebrated G.I. Bill similarly failed black Americans, by mirroring the broader country's insistence on a racist housing policy. Though ostensibly color-blind, Title III of the bill, which aimed to give veterans access to low-interest home loans, left black veterans to tangle with white officials at their local Veterans Administration as well as with the same banks that had, for years, refused to grant mortgages to blacks. The historian Kathleen J. Frydl observes in her 2009 book, *The GI Bill*, that so many blacks were disqualified from receiving Title III benefits "that it is more accurate simply to say that blacks could not use this particular title."

In Cold War America, homeownership was seen as a means of instilling patriotism, and as a civilizing and antiradical force. "No man who owns his own house and lot can be a Communist," claimed William Levitt, who pioneered the modern suburb with the development of the various Levittowns, his famous planned communities. "He has too much to do."

But the Levittowns were, with Levitt's willing acquiescence, segregated throughout their early years. Daisy and Bill Myers, the first black family to move into Levittown, Pennsylvania, were greeted with protests and a burning cross. A neighbor who opposed the family said that Bill Myers was "probably a nice guy, but every time I look at him I see $2,000 drop off the value of my house."

The neighbor had good reason to be afraid. Bill and Daisy Myers were from the other side of John C. Calhoun's dual society. If they moved next door, housing policy almost guaranteed that their neighbors' property values would decline.

Whereas shortly before the New Deal, a typical mortgage required a large down payment and full repayment within about ten years, the creation of the Home Owners' Loan Corporation in 1933 and then the Federal Housing Administration the following year allowed banks to offer loans requiring no more than 10 percent down, amortized over twenty to thirty years. "Without federal intervention in the housing market, massive suburbanization would have been impossible," writes Thomas J. Sugrue, a historian at the University of Pennsylvania. "In 1930, only 30 percent of Americans owned their own homes; by 1960, more than 60 percent were home owners. Home ownership became an emblem of American citizenship."

That emblem was not to be awarded to blacks. The American real-estate industry believed segregation to be a moral principle. As late as 1950, the National Association of Real Estate Boards' code of ethics warned that "a Realtor should never be instrumental in introducing into a neighborhood . . . any race or nationality, or any individuals whose presence will clearly be detrimental to property values." A 1943 brochure specified that such potential undesirables might include madams, bootleggers, gangsters—and "a colored man of means who was giving his children a college education and thought they were entitled to live among whites."

The federal government concurred. It was the Home Owners' Loan Corporation, not a private trade association, that pioneered the practice of redlining, selectively granting loans and insisting that any property it insured be covered by a restrictive covenant—a clause in the deed forbidding the sale of the property to anyone other than whites. Millions of dollars flowed from tax coffers into segregated white neighborhoods.

"For perhaps the first time, the federal government embraced the discriminatory attitudes of the marketplace," the historian Kenneth T. Jackson wrote in his 1985 book, *Crabgrass Frontier*, a history of suburbanization. "Previously, prejudices were personalized and individualized; FHA exhorted segregation and enshrined it as public policy. Whole areas of cities were declared ineligible for loan guarantees." Redlining was not officially outlawed until 1968, by the Fair Housing Act. By then the damage was done—and reports of redlining by banks have continued.

The federal government is premised on equal fealty from all its citizens, who in return are to receive equal treatment. But as late as the mid-twentieth century, this bargain was not granted to black people, who repeatedly paid a higher price for citizenship and received less in return. Plunder had been the essential feature of slavery, of the society described by Calhoun. But practically a full century after the end of the Civil War and the abolition of slavery, the plunder—quiet, systemic, submerged—continued even amidst the aims and achievements of New Deal liberals.

VI. Making the Second Ghetto

Today Chicago is one of the most segregated cities in the country, a fact that reflects assiduous planning. In the effort to uphold white supremacy at every level down to the neighborhood, Chicago—a city founded by the black fur trader Jean Baptiste Point du Sable—has long been a pioneer. The efforts began in earnest in 1917, when the Chicago Real Estate Board, horrified by the influx of southern blacks, lobbied to zone the entire city by race. But after the Supreme Court ruled against explicit racial zoning that year, the city was forced to pursue its agenda by more-discreet means.

Like the Home Owners' Loan Corporation, the Federal Housing Administration initially insisted on restrictive covenants, which helped bar blacks and other ethnic undesirables from receiving federally backed home loans. By the 1940s, Chicago led the nation in the use of these restrictive covenants, and about half of all residential neighborhoods in the city were effectively off-limits to blacks.

It is common today to become misty-eyed about the old black ghetto, where doctors and lawyers lived next door to meatpackers and steelworkers, who themselves lived next door to prostitutes and the unemployed. This segregationist nostalgia ignores the actual conditions endured by the people living there—vermin and arson, for instance—and ignores the fact that the old ghetto was premised on denying black people privileges enjoyed by white Americans.

In 1948, when the Supreme Court ruled that restrictive covenants, while permissible, were not enforceable by judicial action, Chicago had other weapons at the ready. The Illinois state legislature had already given Chicago's city council the right to approve—and thus to veto—any public housing in the city's wards. This came in handy in 1949, when a new federal housing act sent millions of tax dollars into Chicago and other cities around the country. Beginning in 1950, site selection for public housing proceeded entirely on the grounds of segregation. By the 1960s, the city had created with its vast housing projects what the historian Arnold R. Hirsch calls a "second ghetto," one larger than the old Black Belt but just as impermeable. More than 98 percent of all the family public-housing units built in Chicago between 1950 and the mid-1960s were built in all-black neighborhoods.

Governmental embrace of segregation was driven by the virulent racism of Chicago's white citizens. White neighborhoods vulnerable to black encroachment formed block associations for the sole purpose of enforcing segregation. They lobbied fellow whites not to sell. They lobbied those blacks who did manage to buy to sell back. In 1949, a group of Englewood Catholics formed block associations intended to "keep up the neighborhood." Translation: keep black people out. And when civic engagement was not enough, when government failed, when private banks could no longer hold the line, Chicago turned to an old tool in the American repertoire—racial violence. "The pattern of terrorism is easily discernible," concluded a Chicago civic group in the 1940s. "It is at the seams of the black ghetto in all directions." On July 1 and 2 of 1946, a mob of thousands assembled in Chicago's Park Manor neighborhood, hoping to eject a black doctor who'd recently moved in. The mob pelted the house with rocks and set the garage on fire. The doctor moved away.

In 1947, after a few black veterans moved into the Fernwood section of Chicago, three nights of rioting broke out; gangs of whites yanked blacks off streetcars and beat them. Two years later, when a union meeting attended by blacks in Englewood triggered rumors that a home was being "sold to niggers," blacks (and whites thought to be sympathetic to them) were beaten in the streets. In 1951, thousands of whites in Cicero, twenty minutes or so west of downtown Chicago, attacked an apartment building that housed a single black family, throwing bricks and firebombs through the windows and setting the apartment on fire. A Cook County grand jury declined to charge the rioters—and instead indicted the family's NAACP attorney, the apartment's white owner, and the owner's attorney and rental agent, charging them with conspiring to lower property values. Two years after that, whites picketed and planted explosives in South Deering, about thirty minutes from downtown Chicago, to force blacks out.

When terrorism ultimately failed, white homeowners simply fled the neighborhood. The traditional terminology, *white flight*, implies a kind of natural expression of preference. In fact, white flight was a triumph of social engineering, orchestrated by the shared racist presumptions of America's public and private sectors. For should any nonracist white families decide that integration might not be so bad as a matter of principle or practicality, they still had to contend with the hard facts of American housing policy: When the mid-twentieth-century white homeowner claimed that the presence of a Bill and Daisy Myers decreased his property value, he was not merely engaging in racist dogma—he was accurately observing the impact of federal policy on market prices. Redlining destroyed the possibility of investment wherever black people lived.

VII. "A Lot of People Fell by the Way"

Speculators in North Lawndale, and at the edge of the black ghettos, knew there was money to be made off white panic. They resorted to "block-busting"—spooking whites into selling cheap before the neighborhood became black. They would hire a black woman to walk up and down the street with a stroller. Or they'd hire someone to call a number in the neighborhood looking for "Johnny Mae." Then they'd cajole whites into selling at low prices, informing them that the more blacks who moved in, the more the value of their homes would decline, so better to sell now. With these white-fled homes in hand, speculators then turned to the masses of black people who had streamed northward as part of the Great Migration, or who were desperate to escape the ghettos: the speculators would take the houses they'd just bought cheap through block-busting and sell them to blacks on contract.

To keep up with his payments and keep his heat on, Clyde Ross took a second job at the post office and then a third job delivering pizza. His wife took a job working at Marshall Field. He had to take some of his children out of private school. He was not able to be at home to supervise his children or help them with their homework. Money and time that Ross wanted to give his children went instead to enrich white speculators.

"The problem was the money," Ross told me. "Without the money, you can't move. You can't educate your kids. You can't give them the right kind of food. Can't make the house look good. They think this neighborhood is where they supposed to be. It changes their outlook. My kids were going to the best schools in this neighborhood, and I couldn't keep them in there."

Mattie Lewis came to Chicago from her native Alabama in the mid-1940s, when she was twenty-one, persuaded by a friend who told her she could get a job as a hairdresser. Instead she was hired by Western Electric, where she worked for forty-one years. I met Lewis in the home of her neighbor Ethel Weatherspoon. Both had owned homes in North Lawndale for more than fifty years. Both had bought their houses on contract. Both had been active with Clyde Ross in the Contract Buyers League's effort to garner restitution from contract sellers who'd operated in North Lawndale, banks who'd backed the scheme, and even the Federal Housing Administration. We were joined by Jack Macnamara, who'd been an organizing force in the Contract Buyers League when it was founded, in 1968. Our gathering had the feel of a reunion, because the writer James Alan McPherson had profiled the Contract Buyers League for *The Atlantic* back in 1972.

Weatherspoon bought her home in 1957. "Most of the whites started moving out," she told me. "'The blacks are coming. The blacks are coming.' They actually said that. They had signs up: DON'T SELL TO BLACKS."

Before moving to North Lawndale, Lewis and her husband tried moving to Cicero after seeing a house advertised for sale there. "Sorry, I just sold it today," the realtor told Lewis's husband. "I told him, 'You know they don't want you in Cicero,'" Lewis recalls. "'They ain't going to let nobody black in Cicero.'"

In 1958, the couple bought a home in North Lawndale on contract. They were not blind to the unfairness. But Lewis, born in the teeth of Jim Crow, considered American piracy—black people keep on making it, white people keep on taking it—a fact of nature. "All I wanted was a house. And that was the only way I could get it. They weren't giving black people loans at that time," she said. "We thought, 'This is the way it is. We going to do it till we die, and they ain't never going to accept us. That's just the way it is.'

"The only way you were going to buy a home was to do it the way they wanted," she continued. "And I was determined to get me a house. If everybody else can have one, I want one too. I had worked for white people in the South. And I saw how these white people were living in the North and I thought, 'One day I'm going to live just like them.' I wanted cabinets and all these things these other people have."

Whenever she visited white coworkers at their homes, she saw the difference. "I could see we were just getting ripped off," she said. "I would see things and I would say, 'I'd like to do this at my house.' And they would say, 'Do it,' but I would think, 'I can't, because it costs us so much more.'"

I asked Lewis and Weatherspoon how they kept up on payments.

"You paid it and kept working," Lewis said of the contract. "When that payment came up, you knew you had to pay it."

"You cut down on the light bill. Cut down on your food bill," Weatherspoon interjected.

"You cut down on things for your child, that was the main thing," said Lewis. "My oldest wanted to be an artist and my other wanted to be a dancer and my other wanted to take music."

Lewis and Weatherspoon, like Ross, were able to keep their homes. The suit did not win them any remuneration. But it forced contract sellers to the table, where they allowed some members of the Contract Buyers League to move into regular mortgages or simply take over their houses outright. By then they'd been bilked for thousands. In talking with Lewis and Weatherspoon, I was seeing only part of the picture—the tiny minority who'd managed to hold on to their homes. But for all our exceptional ones, for every Barack and Michelle Obama, for every Ethel Weatherspoon or Clyde Ross, for every black survivor, there are so many thousands gone.

"A lot of people fell by the way," Lewis told me. "One woman asked me if I would keep all her china. She said, 'They ain't going to set you out.'"

VIII. "Negro Poverty Is Not White Poverty"

On a recent spring afternoon in North Lawndale, I visited Billy Lamar Brooks Sr. Brooks has been an activist since his youth in the Black Panther Party, when he aided the Contract Buyers League. I met him in his office at the Better Boys Foundation, a staple of North Lawndale whose mission is to direct local kids off the streets and into jobs and college. Brooks's work is personal. On June 14, 1991, his nineteen-year-old son, Billy Jr., was shot and killed. "These guys tried to stick him up," Brooks told me. "I suspect he could have been involved in some things . . . He's always on my mind. Every day."

Brooks was not raised in the streets, though in such a neighborhood it is impossible to avoid the influence. "I was in church three or four times a week. That's where the girls were," he said, laughing. "The stark reality is still there. There's no shield from life. You got to go to school. I lived here. I went to Marshall High School. Over here were the Egyptian Cobras. Over there were the Vice Lords."

Brooks has since moved away from Chicago's West Side. But he is still working in North Lawndale. If "you got a nice house, you live in a nice neighborhood, then you are less prone to violence, because your space is not deprived," Brooks said. "You got a security point. You don't need no protection." But if "you grow up in a place like this, housing sucks. When they tore down the projects here, they left the high-rises and came to the neighborhood with that gang mentality. You don't have nothing, so you going to take something, even if it's not real. You don't have no street, but in your mind it's yours."

We walked over to a window behind his desk. A group of young black men were hanging out in front of a giant mural memorializing two black men: In Lovin Memory Quentin aka "Q," July 18, 1974 ❤ March 2, 2012. The name and face of the other man had been spray-painted over by a rival group. The men drank beer. Occasionally a car would cruise past, slow to a crawl, then stop. One of the men would approach the car and make an exchange, then the car would drive off. Brooks had known all of these young men as boys.

"That's their corner," he said.

We watched another car roll through, pause briefly, then drive off. "No respect, no shame," Brooks said. "That's what they do. From that alley to that corner. They don't go no farther than that. See the big brother there? He almost died a couple of years ago. The one drinking the beer back there . . . I know all of them. And the reason they feel safe here is cause of this building, and because they too chickenshit to go anywhere. But that's their mentality. That's their block."

Brooks showed me a picture of a Little League team he had coached. He went down the row of kids, pointing out which ones were in jail, which ones were dead, and which ones were doing all right. And then he pointed out his son—"That's my boy, Billy," Brooks said. Then he wondered aloud if keeping his son with him while working in North Lawndale had hastened his death. "It's a definite connection, because he was part of what I did here. And I think maybe I shouldn't have exposed him. But then, I had to," he said, "because I wanted him with me."

From the White House on down, the myth holds that fatherhood is the great antidote to all that ails black people. But Billy Brooks Jr. had a father. Trayvon Martin had a father. Jordan Davis had a father. Adhering to middle-class norms has never shielded black people from plunder. Adhering to middle-class norms is what made Ethel Weatherspoon a lucrative target for rapacious speculators. Contract sellers did not target the very poor. They targeted black people who had worked hard enough to save a down payment and dreamed of the emblem of American citizenship—homeownership. It was not a tangle of pathology that put a target on Clyde Ross's back. It was not a culture of poverty that singled out Mattie Lewis for "the thrill of the chase and the kill." Some black people always will be twice as good. But they generally find white predation to be thrice as fast.

Liberals today mostly view racism not as an active, distinct evil but as a relative of white poverty and inequality. They ignore the long tradition of this country actively punishing black success—and the elevation of that punishment, in the mid-twentieth century, to federal policy. President Lyndon Johnson may have noted in his historic civil-rights speech at Howard University in 1965 that "Negro poverty is not white poverty." But his advisers and their successors were, and still are, loath to craft any policy that recognizes the difference.

After his speech, Johnson convened a group of civil-rights leaders, including the esteemed A. Philip Randolph and Bayard Rustin, to address the "ancient brutality." In a strategy paper, they agreed with the president that "Negro poverty is a special, and particularly destructive, form of American poverty." But when it came to specifically addressing the "particularly destructive," Rustin's group demurred, preferring to advance programs that addressed "all the poor, black and white."

The urge to use the moral force of the black struggle to address broader inequalities originates in both compassion and pragmatism. But it makes for ambiguous policy. Affirmative action's precise aims, for instance, have always proved elusive. Is it meant to make amends for the crimes heaped upon black people? Not according to the Supreme Court. In its 1978 ruling in *Regents of the University of California v. Bakke*, the Court rejected "societal discrimination" as "an amorphous concept of injury that may be ageless in its reach into the past." Is affirmative action meant to increase "diversity"? If so, it only tangentially relates to the specific problems of black people—the problem of what America has taken from them over several centuries.

This confusion about affirmative action's aims, along with our inability to face up to the particular history of white-imposed black disadvantage, dates back to the policy's origins. "There is no fixed and firm definition of affirmative action," an appointee in Johnson's Department of Labor declared. "Affirmative action is anything that you have to do to get results. But this does not necessarily include preferential treatment."

Yet America was built on the preferential treatment of white people—395 years of it. Vaguely endorsing a cuddly, feel-good diversity does very little to redress this.

Today, progressives are loath to invoke white supremacy as an explanation for anything. On a practical level, the hesitation comes from the dim view the Supreme Court has taken of the reforms of the 1960s. The Voting Rights Act has been gutted. The Fair Housing Act might well be next. Affirmative action is on its last legs. In substituting a broad class struggle for an antiracist struggle, progressives hope to assemble a coalition by changing the subject.

The politics of racial evasion are seductive. But the record is mixed. Aid to Families with Dependent Children was originally written largely to exclude blacks—yet by the 1990s it was perceived as a giveaway to blacks. The Affordable Care Act makes no mention of race, but this did not keep Rush Limbaugh from denouncing it as reparations. Moreover, the act's expansion of Medicaid was effectively made optional, meaning that many poor blacks in the former Confederate states do not benefit from it. The Affordable Care Act, like Social Security, will eventually expand its reach to those left out; in the meantime, black people will be injured.

"All that it would take to sink a new WPA program would be some skillfully packaged footage of black men leaning on shovels smoking cigarettes," the sociologist Douglas S. Massey writes. "Papering over the issue of race makes for bad social theory, bad research, and bad public policy." To ignore the fact that one of the oldest republics in the world was erected on a foundation of white supremacy, to pretend that the problems of a dual society are the same as the problems of unregulated capitalism, is to cover the sin of national plunder with the sin of national lying. The lie ignores the fact that reducing American poverty and ending white supremacy are not the same. The lie ignores the fact that closing the "achievement gap" will do nothing to close the "injury gap," in which black college graduates still suffer higher unemployment rates than white college graduates, and black job applicants without criminal records enjoy roughly the same chance of getting hired as white applicants *with* criminal records.

Chicago, like the country at large, embraced policies that placed black America's most energetic, ambitious, and thrifty countrymen beyond the pale of society and marked them as rightful targets for legal theft. The effects reverberate beyond the families who were robbed to the community that beholds the spectacle. Don't just picture Clyde Ross working three jobs so he could hold on to his home. Think of his North Lawndale neighbors—their children, their nephews and nieces—and consider how watching this affects them. Imagine yourself as a young black child watching your elders play by all the rules only to have their possessions tossed out in the street and to have their most sacred possession—their home—taken from them.

The message the young black boy receives from his country, Billy Brooks says, is "'You ain't shit. You not no good. The only thing you are worth is working for us. You will never own anything. You not going to get an education. We are sending your ass to the penitentiary.' They're telling you no matter how hard you struggle, no matter what you put down, you ain't shit. 'We're going to take what you got. You will never own anything, nigger.'"

IX. Toward a New Country

When Clyde Ross was a child, his older brother Winter had a seizure. He was picked up by the authorities and delivered to Parchman Farm, a 20,000-acre state prison in the Mississippi Delta region.

"He was a gentle person," Clyde Ross says of his brother. "You know, he was good to everybody. And he started having spells, and he couldn't control himself. And they had him picked up, because they thought he was dangerous."

Built at the turn of the century, Parchman was supposed to be a progressive and reformist response to the problem of "Negro crime." In fact it was the gulag of Mississippi, an object of terror to African Americans in the Delta. In the early years of the twentieth century, Mississippi governor James K. Vardaman used to amuse himself by releasing black convicts into the surrounding wilderness and hunting them down with bloodhounds. "Throughout the American South," writes David M. Oshinsky in his book *Worse Than Slavery*, "Parchman Farm is synonymous with punishment and brutality, as well it should be . . . Parchman is the quintessential penal farm, the closest thing to slavery that survived the Civil War."

When the Ross family went to retrieve Winter, the authorities told them that Winter had died. When the Ross family asked for his body, the authorities at Parchman said they had buried him. The family never saw Winter's body.

And this was just one of their losses.

Scholars have long discussed methods by which America might make reparations to those on whose labor and exclusion the country was built. In the 1970s, the Yale Law professor Boris Bittker argued in *The Case for Black Reparations* that a rough price tag for reparations could be determined by multiplying the number of African Americans in the population by the difference in white and black per capita income. That number—$34 billion in 1973, when Bittker wrote his book—could be added to a reparations program each year for a decade or two. Today Charles Ogletree, the Harvard Law School professor, argues for something broader: a program of job training and public works that takes racial justice as its mission but includes the poor of all races.

To celebrate freedom and democracy while forgetting America's origins in a slavery economy is patriotism à la carte.

Perhaps no statistic better illustrates the enduring legacy of our country's shameful history of treating black people as subcitizens, sub-Americans, and subhumans than the wealth gap. Reparations would seek to close this chasm. But as surely as the creation of the wealth gap required the cooperation of every aspect of the society, bridging it will require the same.

Perhaps after a serious discussion and debate—the kind that HR 40 proposes—we may find that the country can never fully repay African Americans. But we stand to discover much about ourselves in such a discussion—and that is perhaps what scares us. The idea of reparations is frightening not simply because we might lack the ability to pay. The idea of reparations threatens something much deeper—America's heritage, history, and standing in the world.

·   ·   ·

The early American economy was built on slave labor. The Capitol and the White House were built by slaves. President James K. Polk traded slaves from the Oval Office. The laments about "black pathology," the criticism of black family structures by pundits and intellectuals, ring hollow in a country whose existence was predicated on the torture of black fathers, on the rape of black mothers, on the sale of black children. An honest assessment of America's relationship to the black family reveals the country to be not its nurturer but its destroyer.

And this destruction did not end with slavery. Discriminatory laws joined the equal burden of citizenship to unequal distribution of its bounty. These laws reached their apex in the mid-twentieth century, when the federal government—through housing policies—engineered the wealth gap, which remains with us to this day. When we think of white supremacy, we picture COLORED ONLY signs, but we should picture pirate flags.

On some level, we have always grasped this.

"Negro poverty is not white poverty," President Johnson said in his historic civil-rights speech.

> Many of its causes and many of its cures are the same. But there are differences—deep, corrosive, obstinate differences—radiating painful roots into the community and into the family, and the nature of the individual. These differences are not racial differences. They are solely and simply the consequence of ancient brutality, past injustice, and present prejudice.

We invoke the words of Jefferson and Lincoln because they say something about our legacy and our traditions. We do this because we recognize our links to the past—at least when they flatter us. But black history does not flatter American democracy; it chastens it. The popular mocking of reparations as a harebrained scheme authored by wild-eyed lefties and intellectually unserious black nationalists is fear masquerading as laughter. Black nationalists have always perceived something unmentionable about America that integrationists dare not acknowledge—that white supremacy is not merely the work of hotheaded demagogues, or a matter of false consciousness, but a force so fundamental to America that it is difficult to imagine the country without it.

And so we must imagine a new country. Reparations—by which I mean the full acceptance of our collective biography and its consequences—is the price we must pay to see ourselves squarely. The recovering alcoholic may well have to live with his illness for the rest of his life. But at least he is not living a drunken lie. Reparations beckons us to reject the intoxication of hubris and see America as it is—the work of fallible humans.

Won't reparations divide us? Not any more than we are already divided. The wealth gap merely puts a number on something we feel but cannot say—that American prosperity was ill-gotten and selective in its distribution. What is needed is an airing of family secrets, a settling with old ghosts. What is needed is a healing of the American psyche and the banishment of white guilt.

What I'm talking about is more than recompense for past injustices—more than a handout, a payoff, hush money, or a reluctant bribe. What I'm talking about is a national reckoning that would lead to spiritual renewal. Reparations would mean the end of scarfing hot dogs on the Fourth of July while denying the facts of our heritage. Reparations would mean the end of yelling "patriotism" while waving a Confederate flag. Reparations would mean a revolution of the American consciousness, a reconciling of our self-image as the great democratizer with the facts of our history.

X. "There Will Be No 'Reparations' from Germany"

We are not the first to be summoned to such a challenge.

In 1952, when West Germany began the process of making amends for the Holocaust, it did so under conditions that should be instructive to us. Resistance was violent. Very few Germans believed that Jews were entitled to anything. Only 5 percent of West Germans surveyed reported feeling guilty about the Holocaust, and only 29 percent believed that Jews were owed restitution from the German people.

"The rest," the historian Tony Judt wrote in his 2005 book, *Postwar*, "were divided between those (some two-fifths of respondents) who thought that only people 'who really committed something' were responsible and should pay, and those (21 percent) who thought 'that the Jews themselves were partly responsible for what happened to them during the Third Reich.'"

Germany's unwillingness to squarely face its history went beyond polls. Movies that suggested a societal responsibility for the Holocaust beyond Hitler were banned. "The German soldier fought bravely and honorably for his homeland," claimed President Eisenhower, endorsing the Teutonic national myth. Judt wrote, "Throughout the fifties West German officialdom encouraged a comfortable view of the German past in which the Wehrmacht was heroic, while Nazis were in a minority and properly punished."

Konrad Adenauer, the postwar German chancellor, was in favor of reparations, but his own party was divided, and he was able to get an agreement passed only with the votes of the Social Democratic opposition.

Among the Jews of Israel, reparations provoked violent and venomous reactions ranging from denunciation to assassination plots. On January 7, 1952, as the Knesset—the Israeli parliament—convened to discuss the prospect of a reparations agreement with West Germany, Menachem Begin, the future prime minister of Israel, stood in front of a large crowd, inveighing against the country that had plundered the lives, labor, and property of his people. Begin claimed that all Germans were Nazis and guilty of murder. His condemnations then spread to his own young state. He urged the crowd to stop paying taxes and claimed that the nascent Israeli nation characterized the fight over whether or not to accept reparations as a "war to the death." When alerted that the police watching the gathering were carrying tear gas, allegedly of German manufacture, Begin yelled, "The same gases that asphyxiated our parents!"

Begin then led the crowd in an oath to never forget the victims of the Shoah, lest "my right hand lose its cunning" and "my tongue cleave to the roof of my mouth." He took the crowd through the streets toward the Knesset. From the rooftops, police repelled the crowd with tear gas and smoke bombs. But the wind shifted, and the gas blew back toward the Knesset, billowing through windows shattered by rocks. In the chaos, Begin and Prime Minister David Ben-Gurion exchanged insults. Two hundred civilians and 140 police officers were wounded. Nearly 400 people were arrested. Knesset business was halted.

Begin then addressed the chamber with a fiery speech condemning the actions the legislature was about to take. "Today you arrested hundreds," he said. "Tomorrow you may arrest thousands. No matter, they will go, they will sit in prison. We will sit there with them. If necessary, we will be killed with them. But there will be no 'reparations' from Germany."

Survivors of the Holocaust feared laundering the reputation of Germany with money and mortgaging the memory of their dead. Beyond that, there was a taste for revenge. "My soul would be at rest if I knew there would be 6 million German dead to match the 6 million Jews," said Meir Dworzecki, who'd survived the concentration camps of Estonia.

Ben-Gurion countered this sentiment, not by repudiating vengeance but with cold calculation: "If I could take German property without sitting down with them for even a minute but go in with jeeps and machine guns to the warehouses and take it, I would do that—if, for instance, we had the ability to send a hundred divisions and tell them, 'Take it.' But we can't do that."

The reparations conversation set off a wave of bomb attempts by Israeli militants. One was aimed at the foreign ministry in Tel Aviv. Another was aimed at Chancellor Adenauer himself. And one was aimed at the port of Haifa, where the goods bought with reparations money were arriving. West Germany ultimately agreed to pay Israel 3.45 billion deutsche marks, or more than $7 billion in today's dollars. Individual reparations claims followed—for psychological trauma, for offense to Jewish honor, for halting law careers, for life insurance, for time spent in concentration camps. Seventeen percent of funds went toward purchasing ships. "By the end of 1961, these reparations vessels constituted two-thirds of the Israeli merchant fleet," writes the Israeli historian Tom Segev in his book *The Seventh Million*. "From 1953 to 1963, the reparations money funded about a third of the total investment in Israel's electrical system, which tripled its capacity, and nearly half the total investment in the railways."

Israel's GNP tripled during the twelve years of the agreement. The Bank of Israel attributed 15 percent of this growth, along with 45,000 jobs, to investments made with reparations money. But Segev argues that the impact went far beyond that. Reparations "had indisputable psychological and political importance," he writes.

Reparations could not make up for the murder perpetrated by the Nazis. But they did launch Germany's reckoning with itself and perhaps provided a road map for how a great civilization might make itself worthy of the name.

Assessing the reparations agreement, David Ben-Gurion said:

> For the first time in the history of relations between people, a precedent has been created by which a great State, as a result of moral pressure alone, takes it upon itself to pay compensation to the victims of the government that preceded it. For the first time in the history of a people that has been persecuted, oppressed, plundered and despoiled for hundreds of years in the countries of Europe, a persecutor and despoiler has been obliged to return part of his spoils and has even undertaken to make collective reparation as partial compensation for material losses.

Something more than moral pressure calls America to reparations. We cannot escape our history. All of our solutions to the great problems of health care, education, housing, and economic inequality are troubled by what must go unspoken. "The reason black people are so far behind now is not because of now," Clyde Ross told me. "It's because of then." In the early 2000s, Charles Ogletree went to Tulsa, Oklahoma, to meet with the survivors of the 1921 race riot that had devastated "Black Wall Street." The past was not the past to them. "It was amazing seeing these black women and men who were crippled, blind, in wheelchairs," Ogletree told me. "I had no idea who they were and why they wanted to see me. They said, 'We want you to represent us in this lawsuit.'"

A commission authorized by the Oklahoma legislature produced a report affirming that the riot, the knowledge of which had been suppressed for years, had happened. But the lawsuit ultimately failed, in 2004. Similar suits pushed against corporations such as Aetna (which insured slaves) and Lehman Brothers (whose cofounding partner owned them) also have thus far failed. These results are dispiriting, but the crime with which reparations activists charge the country implicates more than just a few towns or corporations. The crime indicts the American people themselves, at every level, and in nearly every configuration. A crime that implicates the entire American people deserves its hearing in the legislative body that represents them.

John Conyers's HR 40 is the vehicle for that hearing. No one can know what would come out of such a debate. Perhaps no number can fully capture the multicentury plunder of black people in America. Perhaps the number is so large that it can't be imagined, let alone calculated and dispensed. But I believe that wrestling publicly with these questions matters as much as—if not more than—the specific answers that might be produced. An America that asks what it owes its most vulnerable citizens is improved and humane. An America that looks away is ignoring not just the sins of the past but the sins of the present and the certain sins of the future. More important than any single check cut to any African American, the payment of reparations would represent America's maturation out of the childhood myth of its innocence into a wisdom worthy of its founders.

. . .

In 2010, Jacob S. Rugh, then a doctoral candidate at Princeton, and the sociologist Douglas S. Massey published a study of the recent foreclosure crisis. Among its drivers, they found an old foe: segregation. Black home buyers—even after controlling for factors like creditworthiness—were still more likely than white home buyers to be steered toward subprime loans. Decades of racist housing policies by the American government, along with decades of racist housing practices by American businesses, had conspired to concentrate African Americans in the same neighborhoods. As in North Lawndale half a century earlier, these neighborhoods were filled with people who had been cut off from mainstream financial institutions. When subprime lenders went looking for prey, they found black people waiting like ducks in a pen.

"High levels of segregation create a natural market for subprime lending," Rugh and Massey write, "and cause riskier mortgages, and thus foreclosures, to accumulate disproportionately in racially segregated cities' minority neighborhoods."

Plunder in the past made plunder in the present efficient. The banks of America understood this. In 2005, Wells Fargo promoted a series of Wealth Building Strategies seminars. Dubbing itself "the nation's leading originator of home loans to ethnic minority customers," the bank enrolled black public figures in an ostensible effort to educate blacks on building "generational wealth." But the "wealth building" seminars were a front for wealth theft. In 2010, the Justice Department filed a discrimination suit against Wells Fargo alleging that the bank had shunted blacks into predatory loans regardless of their creditworthiness. This was not magic or coincidence or misfortune. It was racism reifying itself. According to the *New York Times*, affidavits found loan officers referring to their black customers as "mud people" and to their subprime products as "ghetto loans."

"We just went right after them," Beth Jacobson, a former Wells Fargo loan officer, told the *Times*. "Wells Fargo mortgage had an emerging-markets unit that specifically targeted black churches because it figured church leaders had a lot of influence and could convince congregants to take out subprime loans."

In 2011, Bank of America agreed to pay $355 million to settle charges of discrimination against its Countrywide unit. The following year, Wells Fargo settled its discrimination suit for more than $175 million. But the damage had been done. In 2009, half the properties in Baltimore whose owners had been granted loans by Wells Fargo between 2005 and 2008 were vacant; 71 percent of these properties were in predominantly black neighborhoods.

Pacific Standard

Called "brave" and "disturbing" by the judges who awarded it the National Magazine Award for Public Interest, "Women Aren't Welcome Here" forces readers to confront an issue often dismissed as insignificant by both online businesses and law enforcement: the harassment of women on the Internet. But after describing the savage abuse she and others have experienced on the Web, Amanda Hess reminds us that "today's harmless jokes and undue burdens are tomorrow's civil rights agenda." Launched as Miller-McCune in 2008, Pacific Standard is published bimonthly in print and online at psmag.com. Before winning its first Ellie for this story, the magazine was nominated for a General Excellence award in 2014.

Amanda Hess

Women Aren't Welcome Here

I was twelve hours into a summer vacation in Palm Springs when my phone hummed to life, buzzing twice next to me in the dark of my hotel room. I squinted at the screen. It was five-thirty a.m., and a friend was texting me from the opposite coast. "Amanda, this twitter account. Freaking out over here," she wrote. "There is a twitter account that seems to have been set up for the purpose of making death threats to you."

I dragged myself out of bed and opened my laptop. A few hours earlier, someone going by the username "headlessfemalepig" had sent me seven tweets. "I see you are physically not very attractive. Figured," the first said. Then: "You suck a lot of drunk and drug fucked guys cocks." As a female journalist who writes about sex (among other things), none of this feedback was particularly out of the ordinary. But this guy took it to another level: "I am 36 years old, I did 12 years for 'manslaughter', I killed a woman, like you, who decided to make fun of guys cocks." And then: "Happy to say we live in the same state. Im looking you up, and when I find you, im going to rape you and remove your head." There was more, but the final tweet summed it up: "You are going to die and I am the one who is going to kill you. I promise you this."

My fingers paused over the keyboard. I felt disoriented and terrified. Then embarrassed for being scared, and, finally, pissed. On the one hand, it seemed unlikely that I'd soon be defiled and decapitated at the hands of a serial rapist-murderer. On the other hand, headlessfemalepig was clearly a deranged individual with a bizarre fixation on me. I picked up my phone and dialed 911.

Two hours later, a Palm Springs police officer lumbered up the steps to my hotel room, paused on the outdoor threshold, and began questioning me in a steady clip. I wheeled through the relevant background information: I am a journalist; I live in Los Angeles; sometimes, people don't like what I write about women, relationships, or sexuality; this was not the first time that someone had responded to my work by threatening to rape and kill me. The cop anchored his hands on his belt, looked me in the eye, and said, "What is Twitter?"

Staring up at him in the blazing sun, the best answer I could come up with was, "It's like an e-mail, but it's public." What I didn't articulate is that Twitter is the place where I laugh, whine, work, schmooze, procrastinate, and flirt. It sits in my back pocket wherever I go and lies next to me when I fall asleep. And since I first started writing in 2007, it's become just one of the many online spaces where men come to tell me to get out.

The examples are too numerous to recount, but like any good journalist, I keep a running file documenting the most deranged cases. There was the local cable viewer who hunted down my e-mail address after a television appearance to tell me I was "the ugliest woman he had ever seen." And the group of visitors to a "men's rights" site who pored over photographs of me and a prominent feminist activist, then discussed how they'd "spend the night with" us. ("Put em both in a gimp mask and tied to each other 69 so the bitches can't talk or move and go round the world, any old port in a storm, any old hole," one decided.) And the anonymous commenter who weighed in on one of my articles: "Amanda, I'll fucking rape you. How does that feel?"

None of this makes me exceptional. It just makes me a woman with an Internet connection. Here's just a sampling of the noxious online commentary directed at other women in recent years. To Alyssa Royse, a sex and relationships blogger, for saying that she hated *The Dark Knight*: "you are clearly retarded, i hope someone shoots then rapes you." To Kathy Sierra, a technology writer, for blogging about software, coding, and design: "i hope someone slits your throat and cums down your gob." To Lindy West, a writer at the women's website Jezebel, for critiquing a comedian's rape joke: "I just want to rape her with a traffic cone." To Rebecca Watson, an atheist commentator, for blogging about sexism in the skeptic community: "If I lived in Boston I'd put a bullet in your brain." To Catherine Mayer, a journalist at *Time* magazine, for no particular reason: "A BOMB HAS BEEN PLACED OUTSIDE YOUR HOME. IT WILL GO OFF AT EXACTLY 10:47 PM ON A TIMER AND TRIGGER DESTROYING EVERYTHING."

A woman doesn't even need to occupy a professional writing perch at a prominent platform to become a target. According to a 2005 report by the Pew Research Center, which has been tracking the online lives of Americans for more than a decade, women and men have been logging on in equal numbers since 2000, but the vilest communications are still disproportionately lobbed at women. We are more likely to report being stalked and harassed on the Internet—of the 3,787 people who reported harassing incidents from 2000 to 2012 to the volunteer organization Working to Halt Online Abuse, 72.5 percent were female. Sometimes, the abuse can get physical: A Pew survey reported that 5 percent of women who used the Internet said "something happened online" that led them into "physical danger." And it starts young: Teenage girls are significantly more likely to be cyberbullied than boys. Just appearing as a woman online, it seems, can be enough to inspire abuse. In 2006, researchers from the University of Maryland set up a bunch of fake online accounts and then dispatched them into chat rooms. Accounts with feminine usernames incurred an average of 100 sexually explicit or threatening messages a day. Masculine names received 3.7.

There are three federal laws that apply to cyberstalking cases; the first was passed in 1934 to address harassment through the mail, via telegram, and over the telephone, six decades after Alexander Graham Bell's invention. Since the initial passage of the Violence Against Women Act, in 1994, amendments to the law have gradually updated it to apply to new technologies and to stiffen penalties against those who use them to abuse. Thirty-four states have cyberstalking laws on the books; most have expanded long-standing laws against stalking and criminal threats to prosecute crimes carried out online.

But making quick and sick threats has become so easy that many say the abuse has proliferated to the point of meaninglessness and that expressing alarm is foolish. Reporters who take death threats seriously "often give the impression that this is some kind of shocking event for which we should pity the 'victims,'" my colleague Jim Pagels wrote in *Slate* this fall, "but anyone who's spent 10 minutes online knows that these assertions are entirely toothless." On Twitter, he added, "When there's no precedent for physical harm, it's only baseless fear mongering." My friend Jen Doll wrote, at *The Atlantic Wire*, "It seems like that old 'ignoring' tactic your mom taught you could work out to everyone's benefit. . . . These people are bullying, or hope to bully. Which means we shouldn't take the bait." In the epilogue to her book *The End of Men*, Hanna Rosin—an editor at *Slate*—argued that harassment of women online could be seen as a cause for celebration. It shows just how far we've come. Many women on the Internet "are in positions of influence, widely published and widely read; if they sniff out misogyny, I have no doubt they will gleefully skewer the responsible sexist in one of many available online outlets, and get results."

So women who are harassed online are expected to either get over ourselves or feel flattered in response to the threats made against us. We have the choice to keep quiet or respond "gleefully."

But no matter how hard we attempt to ignore it, this type of gendered harassment—and the sheer volume of it—has severe implications for women's status on the Internet. Threats of rape, death, and stalking can overpower our emotional bandwidth, take up our time, and cost us money through legal fees, online protection services, and missed wages. I've spent countless hours over the past four years logging the online activity of one particularly committed cyberstalker, just in case. And as the Internet becomes increasingly central to the human experience, the ability of women to live and work freely online will be shaped, and too often limited, by the technology companies that host these threats, the constellation of local and federal law-enforcement officers who investigate them, and the popular commentators who dismiss them—all arenas that remain dominated by men, many of whom have little personal understanding of what women face online every day.

· · ·

This summer, Caroline Criado-Perez became the English-speaking Internet's most famous recipient of online threats after she petitioned the British government to put more female faces on its bank notes. (When the Bank of England announced its intentions to replace social reformer Elizabeth Fry with Winston Churchill on the five-pound note, Criado-Perez made the modest suggestion that the bank make an effort to feature at least one woman who is not the queen on any of its currency.) Rape and death threats amassed on her Twitter feed too quickly to count, bearing messages like "I will rape you tomorrow at 9 p.m . . . Shall we meet near your house?"

Then, something interesting happened. Instead of logging off, Criado-Perez retweeted the threats, blasting them out to her Twitter followers. She called up police and hounded Twitter for a response. Journalists around the world started writing about the threats. As more and more people heard the story, Criado-Perez's follower count skyrocketed to near 25,000. Her supporters joined in urging British police and Twitter executives to respond.

Under the glare of international criticism, the police and the company spent the next few weeks passing the buck back and forth. Andy Trotter, a communications adviser for the British police, announced that it was Twitter's responsibility to crack down on the messages. Though Britain criminalizes a broader category of offensive speech than the United States does, the sheer volume of threats would be too difficult for "a hard-pressed police service" to investigate, Trotter said. Police "don't want to be in this arena." It diverts their attention from "dealing with something else."

Meanwhile, Twitter issued a blanket statement saying that victims like Criado-Perez could fill out an online form for each abusive tweet; when Criado-Perez supporters hounded Mark Luckie, the company's manager of journalism and news, for a response, he briefly shielded his account, saying that the attention had become "abusive." Twitter's official recommendation to victims of abuse puts the ball squarely in law enforcement's court: "If an interaction has gone beyond the point of name calling and you feel as though you may be in danger," it says, "contact your local authorities so they can accurately assess the validity of the threat and help you resolve the issue offline."

In the weeks after the flare-up, Scotland Yard confirmed the arrest of three men. Twitter—in response to several online petitions calling for action—hastened the rollout of a "report abuse" button that allows users to flag offensive material. And Criado-Perez went on receiving threats. Some real person out there—or rather, hundreds of them—still liked the idea of seeing her raped and killed.

•   •   •

The Internet is a global network, but when you pick up the phone to report an online threat, whether you are in London or Palm Springs, you end up face-to-face with a cop who patrols a comparatively puny jurisdiction. And your cop will probably be a man: According to the U.S. Bureau of Justice Statistics, in 2008, only 6.5 percent of state police officers and 19 percent of FBI agents were women. The numbers get smaller in smaller agencies. And in many locales, police work is still a largely analog affair: 911 calls are immediately routed to the local police force; the closest officer is dispatched to respond; he takes notes with pen and paper.

After Criado-Perez received her hundreds of threats, she says she got conflicting instructions from police on how to report the crimes and was forced to repeatedly "trawl" through the vile messages to preserve the evidence. "I can just about cope with threats," she wrote on Twitter. "What I can't cope with after that is the victim-blaming, the patronising, and the police record-keeping." Last year, the American atheist blogger Rebecca Watson wrote about her experience calling a series of local and national law-enforcement agencies after a man launched a website threatening to kill her. "Because I knew what town [he] lived in, I called his local police department. They told me there was nothing they could do and that I'd have to make a report with my local police department," Watson wrote later. "[I] finally got through to someone who told me that there was nothing they could do but take a report in case one day [he] followed through on his threats, at which point they'd have a pretty good lead."

The first time I reported an online rape threat to police, in 2009, the officer dispatched to my home asked, "Why would anyone bother to do something like that?" and declined to file a report. In Palm Springs, the officer who came to my room said, "This guy could be sitting in a basement in Nebraska for all we know." That my stalker had said that he lived in my state and had plans to seek me out at home was dismissed as just another online ruse.

Of course, some people are investigated and prosecuted for cyberstalking. In 2009, a Florida college student named Patrick Macchione met a girl at school, then threatened to kill her on Twitter, terrorized her with lewd videos posted to YouTube, and made hundreds of calls to her phone. Though his victim filed a restraining order, cops only sprung into action after a county sheriff stopped him for loitering, then reportedly found a video camera in his backpack containing disturbing recordings about his victim. The sheriff's department later worked with the state attorney's office to convict Macchione on nineteen counts, one of which was cyberstalking (he successfully appealed that count on grounds that the law hadn't been enacted when he was arrested); Macchione was sentenced to four years in prison. Consider also a recent high-profile case of cyberstalking investigated by the FBI. In the midst of her affair with General David Petraeus, the biographer Paula Broadwell allegedly created an anonymous e-mail account for the purpose of sending harassing notes to the Florida socialite Jill Kelley. Kelley reported them to the FBI, which sniffed out Broadwell's identity via the account's location-based metadata and obtained a warrant to monitor her e-mail activity.

In theory, appealing to a higher jurisdiction can yield better results. "Local law enforcement will often look the other way," says Dr. Sameer Hinduja, a criminology professor at Florida Atlantic University and codirector of the Cyberbullying Research Center. "They don't have the resources or the personnel to investigate those crimes." County, state, or federal agencies at least have the support to be more responsive: "Usually they have a computer crimes unit, savvy personnel who are familiar with these cases, and established relationships with social media companies so they can quickly send a subpoena to help with the investigation," Hinduja says.

But in my experience and those of my colleagues, these larger law enforcement agencies have little capacity or drive to investigate threats as well. Despite his pattern of abusive online behavior, Macchione was ultimately arrested for an unrelated physical crime. When I called the FBI over headlessfemalepig's threats, a representative told me an agent would get in touch if the bureau was interested in pursuing the case; nobody did. And when Rebecca Watson reported the threats targeted at her to the FBI, she initially connected with a sympathetic agent—but the agent later expressed trouble opening Watson's file of screenshots of the threats, and soon stopped replying to her e-mails. The Broadwell investigation was an uncommon, and possibly unprecedented, exercise for the agency. As the University of Wisconsin–Eau Claire criminal justice professor Justin Patchin told *Wired* at the time: "I'm not aware of any case when the FBI has gotten involved in a case of online harassment."

After I received my most recent round of threats, I asked Jessica Valenti, a prominent feminist writer (and the founder of the blog Feministing), who's been repeatedly targeted with online threats, for her advice, and then I asked her to share her story. "It's not really one story. This has happened a number of times over the past seven years," she told me. When rape and death threats first started pouring into her inbox, she vacated her apartment for a week, changed her bank accounts, and got a new cell number. When the next wave of threats came, she got in touch with law-enforcement officials, who warned her that though the men e-mailing her were unlikely to follow through on their threats, the level of vitriol indicated that she should be vigilant for a far less identifiable threat: silent "hunters" who lurk behind the tweeting "hollerers." The FBI advised Valenti to leave her home until the threats blew over, to never walk outside of her apartment alone, and to keep aware of any cars or men who might show up repeatedly outside her door. "It was totally impossible advice," she says. "You have to be paranoid about everything. You can't just not be in a public place."

And we can't simply be offline either. When the *Time* journalist Catherine Mayer reported the bomb threat lodged against

her, the officers she spoke to—who thought usernames were secret codes and didn't seem to know what an IP address was—
advised her to unplug. "Not one of the officers I've encountered
uses Twitter or understands why anyone would wish to do so,"
she later wrote. "The officers were unanimous in advising me to
take a break from Twitter, assuming, as many people do, that
Twitter is at best a time-wasting narcotic."

All of these online offenses are enough to make a woman *want*
to click away from Twitter, shut her laptop, and power down her
phone. Sometimes, we do withdraw: Pew found that from 2000
to 2005, the percentage of Internet users who participate in online chats and discussion groups dropped from 28 percent to
17 percent, "entirely because of women's fall off in participation."
But for many women, steering clear of the Internet isn't an option.
We use our devices to find supportive communities, make a living,
and construct safety nets. For a woman like me, who lives alone,
the Internet isn't a fun diversion—it is a necessary resource for
work and interfacing with friends, family, and, sometimes, law-
enforcement officers in an effort to feel safer from both online and
offline violence.

The Polish sociologist Zygmunt Bauman draws a distinction
between "tourists" and "vagabonds" in the modern economy.
Privileged tourists move about the world "on purpose," to seek
"new experience" as "the joys of the familiar wear off." Disempow-
ered vagabonds relocate because they have to, pushed and pulled
through mean streets where they could never hope to settle down.
On the Internet, men are tourists and women are vagabonds.
"Telling a woman to shut her laptop is like saying, 'Eh! Just stop
seeing your family,'" says Nathan Jurgenson, a social media sociologist (and a friend) at the University of Maryland.

What does a tourist look like? In 2012, *Gawker* unmasked
"Violentacrez," an anonymous member of the online community
Reddit who was infamous for posting creepy photographs of un-
derage women and creating or moderating subcommunities on

the site with names like "chokeabitch" and "rapebait." Violent-acrez turned out to be a Texas computer programmer named Michael Brusch, who displayed an exceedingly casual attitude toward his online hobbies. "I do my job, go home, watch TV, and go on the Internet. I just like riling people up in my spare time," he told Adrian Chen, the *Gawker* reporter who outed him. "People take things way too seriously around here."

Abusers tend to operate anonymously, or under pseudonyms. But the women they target often write on professional platforms, under their given names, and in the context of their real lives. Victims don't have the luxury of separating themselves from the crime. When it comes to online threats, "one person is feeling the reality of the Internet very viscerally: the person who is being threatened," says Jurgenson. "It's a lot easier for the person who made the threat—and the person who is investigating the threat—to believe that what's happening on the Internet isn't real."

•   •   •

When authorities treat the Internet as a fantasyland, it has profound effects on the investigation and prosecution of online threats. Criminal threat laws largely require that victims feel tangible, immediate, and sustained fear. In my home state of California, a threat must be "unequivocal, unconditional, immediate, and specific" and convey a "gravity of purpose and an immediate prospect of execution of the threat" to be considered a crime. If police don't know whether the harasser lives next door or out in Nebraska, it's easier for them to categorize the threat as nonimmediate. When they treat a threat as a boyish hoax, the implication is that the threat ceases to be a criminal offense.

So the victim faces a psychological dilemma: How should she understand her own fear? Should she, as many advise, dismiss an online threat as a silly game and not bother to inform the cops that someone may want to—ha, ha—rape and kill her? Or should she dutifully report every threat to police, who may well dismiss her concerns? When I received my most recent rape and death threats, one friend told me that I should rest assured that the anonymous tweeter was unlikely to take any physical action against me in real life; another noted that my stalker seemed like the type of person who would fashion a coat from my skin and urged me to take any action necessary to land the stalker in jail.

Danielle Citron, a University of Maryland law professor who focuses on Internet threats, charted the popular response to Internet death and rape threats in a 2009 paper published in the *Michigan Law Review.* She found that Internet harassment is routinely dismissed as "harmless locker-room talk," perpetrators as "juvenile pranksters," and victims as "overly sensitive complainers." Weighing in on one online harassment case, in an interview on National Public Radio, the journalist David Margolick called the threats "juvenile, immature, and obnoxious, but that is all they are . . . frivolous frat-boy rants."

Of course, the frat house has never been a particularly safe space for women. I've been threatened online, but I have also been harassed on the street, groped on the subway, followed home from the 7-Eleven, pinned down on a bed by a drunk boyfriend, and raped on a date. Even if I sign off Twitter, a threat could still be waiting on my stoop.

Today, a legion of anonymous harassers are free to play their "games" and "pranks" under pseudonymous screen names, but for the women they target, the attacks only compound the real fear, discomfort, and stress we experience in our daily lives.

•   •   •

If American police forces are overwhelmingly male, the technology companies that have created the architecture of the online world are, famously, even more so. In 2010, according to the information services firm CB Insights, 92 percent of the founders of fledgling Internet companies were male; 86 percent of their founding teams were exclusively male. While the number of women working across the sciences is generally increasing, the percentage of women working in computer sciences peaked in 2000 and is now on the decline. In 2012, the Bureau of Labor Statistics found, women made up just 22.5 percent of American computer programmers and 19.7 percent of software developers. In a 2012 study of 400 California companies, researchers at the University of California–Davis, found that just 7 percent of the highest-paid executives at Silicon Valley companies were women.

When Twitter announced its initial public offering in October, its filings listed an all-male board. Vijaya Gadde, Twitter's general counsel, was the only woman among its executive officers. When Vivek Wadhwa, a fellow at Stanford's Rock Center for Corporate Governance, suggested that the gender imbalance on Twitter's board was an issue of "elite arrogance" and "male chauvinistic thinking," Twitter CEO Dick Costolo responded with a joking tweet, calling Wadhwa "the Carrot Top of academic sources."

Most executives aren't intentionally boxing women out. But the decisions these men make have serious implications for billions of people. The gender imbalance in their companies compromises their ability to understand the lives of half their users.

Twitter "has a history of saying 'too bad, so sad'" when confronted with concerns about harassment on its platform, says Citron, the University of Maryland law professor who studies the emerging legal implications of online abuse against women. The culture of the platform has typically prioritized freewheeling discussion over zealous speech policing. Unlike Facebook, Twitter doesn't require people to register accounts under their real names. Users are free to enjoy the frivolity—and the protection— that anonymous speech provides. If a user runs afoul of Twitter's terms of service, he's free to create a new account under a fresh handle. And the Communications Decency Act of 1996 protects platforms like Twitter from being held legally responsible for what individuals say on the site.

The advent of the "report abuse" button is a development Citron finds "very heartening." Allowing people to block an abuser's account helps women avoid having to be faced with vile and abusive tweets. But our problems can't all be solved with the click of a button. In some cases, the report-abuse button is just a virtual Band-Aid for a potentially dangerous real-world problem. It can undermine women by erasing the trail of digital evidence. And it does nothing to prevent these same abusers from opening a new account and continuing their crimes.

When I received those seven tweets in Palm Springs, a well-meaning friend reported them as abusive through Twitter's system, hoping that action on the platform's end would help further my case. A few hours later, the tweets were erased from the site without comment (or communication with me). Headlessfemalepig's Twitter feed was replaced with a page noting that the account had been suspended. Luckily, I had taken screenshots of the tweets, but to the cops working with a limited understanding of the platform, their sudden disappearance only confused the issue. The detective assigned to my case asked me to send him links pointing to where the messages lived online—but absent a subpoena of Twitter's records, they were gone from law enforcement's view. If someone had reported the threats before I got a chance to see them, I might not even have been able to indicate their existence at all. Without a proper investigation, I am incapable of knowing whether headlessfemalepig is a one-time offender or the serial stalker who has followed me for many years. Meanwhile, nothing's stopping headlessfemalepig from continuing to tweet away under a new name.

It shouldn't be Twitter's responsibility to hunt down and sanction criminals who use its service—that's what cops are (supposedly) for. Twitter has to balance its interests in addressing abusive behavior with its interests in protecting our private information (or that of, say, political dissidents), which means keeping a tight lid on users' IP addresses and refusing to offer up deleted material to civilians. When I asked how Twitter balances those demands, Nu Wexler, who leads public-policy communications for the company, pointed me to a chart published by the Electronic Frontier Foundation—an advocacy group dedicated to defending the free speech and privacy rights of Internet users—that illustrates the platform's "commitment to user privacy." The chart, titled "Who Has Your Back: Which Companies Help Protect Your Data From the Government?," awards Twitter high marks for fighting for users' privacy rights in court and publishing a transparency report about government data requests.

A high score awarded by the Electronic Frontier Foundation communicates to users that their Internet activity will be safe from overreaching government snoops—and post–Edward Snowden, that concern is more justified than ever. But in some cases, the impulse to protect our privacy can interfere with the law's ability to protect us when we're harassed. Last year, the Electronic Frontier Foundation came out against an amendment to the Violence Against Women Act. Until recently, the law criminalized abusive, threatening, and harassing speech conveyed over a telephone line, provided the abuser placed the call; the new law, passed in March, applies to any electronic harassment targeted at a specific person, whether it's made over the telephone or by another means. Critics of the legislation pulled out the trope that the Internet is less real than other means of communication. As the foundation put it, "a person is free to disregard something said on Twitter in a way far different than a person who is held in constant fear of the persistent ringing of a telephone intruding in their home."

The Electronic Frontier Foundation—and the tech companies that benefit from its ratings—are undoubtedly committed to fighting government First Amendment abuses. But when they focus their efforts on stemming the spread of anti-harassment laws from outdated media, like landline telephones, to modern means like Twitter, their efforts act like a thumb on the scale, favoring some democratic values at the expense of others. "Silicon Valley has the power to shape society to conform to its values, which prioritize openness and connectivity," Jurgenson says. "But why are engineers in California getting to decide what constitutes harassment for people all around the world?"

Tech companies are, of course, fully aware that they need a broad base of users to flourish as billion-dollar businesses. Today women have the bargaining power to draft successful petitions calling for "report abuse" buttons, but our corporate influence is limited, and alternative venues for action are few. Local police departments "have no money," Jurgenson says, and "it feels unlikely that the government is going to do more anytime soon, so we're forced to put more pressure on Twitter." And while an organized user base can influence the decisions of a public, image-conscious company like Twitter, many platforms—like the dedicated "revenge porn" sites that have proliferated on the Web—don't need to appease women to stay popular. "I call this the myth of the market," Citron says. "There's definitely a desire for antisocial behavior. There are eyeballs. And there are users who are providing the content. The market isn't self-correcting, and it's not going to make this go away."

•　　　•　　　•

In a 2009 paper in the *Boston University Law Review*, Citron proposed a new way of framing the legal problem of harassment on the Internet: She argued that online abuse constitutes "discrimination in women's employment opportunities" that ought to be better addressed by the U.S. government itself. Title VII of the Civil Rights Act of 1964, which outlawed discrimination based on race, religion, or gender, was swiftly applied to members of the Ku Klux Klan, who hid behind hoods to harass and intimidate black Louisianans from voting and pursuing work. Anonymous online harassment, Citron argued, similarly discourages women from "writing and earning a living online" on the basis of their gender. "It interferes with their professional lives. It raises their vulnerability to offline sexual violence. It brands them as incompetent workers and inferior sexual objects. The harassment causes considerable emotional distress."

On the Internet, women are overpowered and devalued. We don't always think about our online lives in those terms—after all, our days are filled with work to do, friends to keep up with, Netflix to watch. But when anonymous harassers come along—saying they would like to rape us, or cut off our heads, or scrutinize our bodies in public, or shame us for our sexual habits—they serve to remind us in ways both big and small that we can't be at ease online. It is precisely the banality of Internet harassment, University of Miami law professor Mary Anne Franks has argued, that makes it "both so effective and so harmful, especially as a form of discrimination."

The personal and professional costs of that discrimination manifest themselves in very real ways. Jessica Valenti says she has stopped promoting her speaking events publicly, enlisted security for her public appearances, signed up for a service to periodically scrub the Web of her private information, invested in a post-office box, and begun periodically culling her Facebook friend list in an attempt to filter out readers with ulterior motives. Those efforts require a clear investment of money and time, but the emotional fallout is less directly quantifiable. "When people say you should be raped and killed for years on end, it takes a toll on your soul," she says. Whenever a male stranger approaches her at a public event, "the hairs on the back of my neck stand up." Every time we call the police, head to court to file a civil protection order, or get sucked into a mental hole by the threats that have been made against us, zeroes drop from our annual incomes. Says Jurgenson, "It's a monetary penalty for being a woman."

Citron has planted the seed of an emerging debate over the possibility of applying civil rights laws to ensure equal opportunities for women on the Internet. "There's no silver bullet for addressing this problem," Citron says. But existing legislation has laid the groundwork for potential future reforms. Federal civil rights law can punish "force or threat[s] of force" that interfere with a person's employment on the basis of race, religion, or national origin. That protection, though, doesn't currently extend to threats targeted at a person's gender. However, other parts of the Civil Rights Act frame workplace sexual harassment as discriminatory, and requires employers to implement policies to both prevent and remedy discrimination in the office. And Title IX of the Education Amendments of 1972 puts the onus on educational institutions to take action against discrimination toward women. Because Internet harassment affects the employment and educational opportunities of women, laws could conceivably be amended to allow women to bring claims against individuals.

But it's hard to get there from here. As Citron notes, the Internet is not a school or a workplace, but a vast and diffuse universe that often lacks any clear locus of accountability. Even if online threats are considered a civil rights violation, who would we sue? Anonymous tweeters lack the institutional affiliation to make monetary claims worthwhile. And there is the mobbing problem: One person can send just one horrible tweet, but then many others may pile on. A single vicious tweet may not clear the hurdle of discriminatory harassment (or repetitive abuse). And while a mob of individuals each lobbing a few attacks clearly looks and feels like harassment, there is no organized group to take legal action against. Bringing separate claims against individual abusers would be laborious, expensive, and unlikely to reap financial benefits. At the same time, amending the Communications Decency Act to put the onus on Internet platforms to police themselves could have a serious chilling effect on all types of speech, discriminatory or otherwise.

Citron admits that passing new civil rights legislation that applies to a new venue—the Internet—is a potentially Sisyphean task. But she says that by expanding existing civil rights laws to recognize the gendered nature of Internet threats, lawmakers could put more pressure on law-enforcement agencies to take those crimes seriously. "We have the tools already," Citron says. "Do we use them? Not really." Prosecuting online threats as bias-motivated crimes would mean that offenders would face stronger penalties, law-enforcement agencies would be better incentivized to investigate these higher-level crimes—and hopefully, the Internet's legions of anonymous abusers would begin to see the downside of mouthing off.

Our laws have always found a way to address new harms while balancing long-standing rights, even if they do it very slowly. Opponents of the Civil Rights Act of 1964 characterized its workplace protections as unconstitutional and bad for business. Before workplace sexual harassment was reframed as discriminatory under Title VII, it was written off as harmless flirting. When Title IX was first proposed to address gender discrimination in education, a Senate discussion on the issue ended in laughter when one senator cracked a coed football joke. Until domestic violence became a national policy priority, abuse was dismissed as a lovers' quarrel. Today's harmless jokes and undue burdens are tomorrow's civil rights agenda.

·　　·　　·

My serial cyberstalker began following me in 2009. I was on the staff of an alt-weekly when a minicontroversy flared up on a blog. One of the blog's writers had developed a pattern of airing his rape fantasies on the site; I interviewed him and the site's other contributors and published a story. Then I started receiving rape threats of my own. Their author posted a photo of me on his blog and wrote, "Oh, sure, you might say she's pretty. Or you might say she looks sweet or innocent. But don't let looks fool you. This woman is pure evil." (To some harassers, you're physically not very attractive; to others, you're beautiful.) "I thought I'd describe her on my blog as 'rape-worthy,' but ultimately decided against it," he added. "Oops! I've committed another thought crime!"

In the comments section below the article, threats popped up under a dozen fake names and several phony IP addresses—which usually point to a device's precise location, but can be easily faked if you have the right software. "Amanda, I'll fucking rape you," one said. "How's that feel? Like that? What's my IP address, bitch?" On his Twitter account, my stalker wrote that he planned to buy a gun—apparently intending to defend his First Amendment rights by exercising the Second.

Then, one night when my boyfriend and I were in our apartment, my cell phone started ringing incessantly. I received a series of voicemails, escalating in tone from a stern "You cut the shit right fucking now" to a slurred "You fucking dyke . . . I will fuck you up." For the first time ever, I called the police. When an officer arrived at my house, I described the pattern of abuse. He expressed befuddlement at the "virtual" crime, handed me his card, and told me to call if anyone came to my house—but he declined to take a report.

Without police support, I opted to file a civil protection order in family court. I posted a photograph of my stalker at my office's front desk. When the local sheriff's department failed to serve him court papers, I paid one hundred dollars for a private investigator to get the job done. It took me five visits to court, waiting for my case to be called up while sitting quietly across the aisle from him in the gallery as dozens of other local citizens told a domestic violence judge about the boyfriends and fathers and ex-wives who had threatened and abused them. These people were seeking protection from crowbar-wielding exes and gun-flashing acquaintances—more real crimes the justice system had failed to prosecute. By the time the judge finally called up my protection order for review, I had missed a half-dozen days of work pursuing the case. I was lucky to have a full-time job and an understanding boss—even if he didn't understand the threats on the same level I did. And because my case was filed under new antistalking protections—protections designed for cases like mine, in which I was harassed by someone I didn't have a personal relationship with—I was lucky to get a court-appointed lawyer, too. Most victims don't.

My harasser finally acquiesced to the protection order when my lawyer showed him that we knew the blog comments were coming from his computer—he had made a valiant attempt to obscure his comments, but he'd slipped up in a couple of instances, and we could prove the rape threats were his. When the judge approved the order, she instructed my harasser that he was not allowed to contact me in any way—not by e-mail, Twitter, phone, blog comment, or by hiring a hot air balloon to float over my house with a message, she said. And he had to stay at least one hundred feet away from me at all times. The restraining order would last one year.

Soon after the order expired, he sent an e-mail to my new workplace. Every once in a while, he reestablishes contact. Last summer, he waded into the comments section of an article I wrote about sex website creator Cindy Gallop, to say, "I would not sacrifice the physiological pleasure of ejaculating inside the woman for a lesser psychological pleasure. . . . There is a reason it feels better to do it the right way and you don't see others in the ape world practicing this behavior." A few months later, he reached out via LinkedIn. ("Your stalker would like to add you to his professional network.") A few days before I received the threats in Palm Springs, he sent me a link via Twitter to a story he wrote about another woman who had been abused online. Occasionally, he sends his tweets directly my way—a little reminder that his "game" is back on.

It's been four years, but I still carry the case files with me. I record every tweet he sends me in a Word document, forward his e-mails to a dedicated account, then print them out to ensure I'll have them ready for police in analog form if he ever threatens me again (or worse). Whenever I have business travel to the city where he lives, I cart my old protection order along, even though the words are beginning to blur after a dozen photocopies. The stacks of paper are filed neatly in my apartment. My anxieties are harder to organize.

Slate

FINALIST—PUBLIC
INTEREST

"The College Rape Overcorrection" asks whether colleges and universities, in their effort to protect women from sexual assault, are abrogating the rights of the men accused of rape. The Ellie judges said the story was "original and provocative," and Slate's readers agreed, posting nearly 6,000 comments on the website and sharing the story more than 25,000 times on Facebook and Twitter. Emily Yoffe is a regular contributor to Slate and also writes its "Dear Prudence" advice column. Founded in 1996 by the ASME Hall of Famer Michael Kinsley, Slate is the most honored digital-only publication in the history of the National Magazine Awards, having garnered twenty-four nominations and three Ellies, including two for General Excellence."

Emily Yoffe

The College Rape Overcorrection

1. An Accusation

Drew Sterrett couldn't know that when his friend slipped into his bottom bunk late one night in March of his freshman year, she was setting off a series of events that would end his college education. It was 2012, and Sterrett was an engineering student at the University of Michigan. The young woman, CB, lived down the hall. A group of students had been hanging out in the dorm on a Friday evening—there was drinking, but no one was incapacitated—when CB told Sterrett that her roommate had family members staying in their room and she needed a place to spend the night. Sterrett loaned her a shirt to sleep in and assumed she'd crash on the mat he and his roommate kept for visitors. Instead, CB came and lay down next to him on his bed. The two had made out in the past but had no serious romantic interest in each other.

They talked quietly, started kissing, and then things escalated, as they often do when two teenagers are in bed together. When it became clear they were going to have intercourse, CB asked Sterrett about a condom, and he retrieved one from a drawer. Their sex became so loud and went on for so long that Sterrett's roommate, unable to sleep in the upper bunk, sent Sterrett a Facebook message around 3 a.m.: "Dude, you and [CB] are being abnoxtiously [*sic*] loud and inconsiderate, so expect to pay back in full tomorrow . . ."

The two finally finished and went to sleep. The next morning, Sterrett says CB told him that she wanted to keep their interlude private. He thought she was embarrassed that she'd had sex with a friend and agreed not to talk to others about it. They saw each other frequently in the dorm until the school year ended.

Sterrett was home in New York for the summer when he was contacted by a university official, Heather Cowan, program manager of the Office of Student Conflict Resolution, and told to make himself available for a Skype interview with her and another administrator. No reason was given.

As the interview got under way, Sterrett realized that CB must have told Cowan something disturbing about their one-time assignation. Becoming concerned about the tenor of the questions, he asked the administrators if he should consult a lawyer. He says they told him that if he ended the interview in order to seek counsel that fact would be reported to the university and the investigation would continue without his input. He kept talking. He told Cowan that he and CB had had a consensual encounter while his roommate was only a few feet away. As the interview was coming to a close, Sterrett says the administrators told him this matter was confidential—though he'd still not been explicitly told what the matter was—and that he should not talk to anyone about it, especially not fellow students who might be witnesses on his behalf.

Later, Sterrett would consult a lawyer and file a lawsuit against the university alleging he'd been deprived of his constitutional right to due process. This account is drawn from the legal filings in that ongoing case. These include Sterrett's case against the university, affidavits from witnesses sworn on Sterrett's behalf, the university's response, and a deposition of CB taken by Sterrett's lawyer. (Through his lawyer, Sterrett declined to speak to me. A Michigan spokesman said the university cannot comment on a pending case. CB has remained anonymous in court filings. I contacted her lawyer, Joshua Sheffer, who sent the following statement: "While we strongly disagree with Plaintiff's description of the night in question, we do not feel that it should be played out in the press." It continued: "This lawsuit is between Plaintiff and the University of Michigan; my client wishes only to put this traumatic event behind her and move forward with her education and life.")

Cowan told Sterrett over Skype that there would be restrictions placed on him when he returned to campus for his sophomore year. Sterrett and CB were part of a special program called the Michigan Research Community, and members lived together in a residence hall. Although Sterrett and CB had continued to live on the same floor until the end of the school year, and she hadn't complained about his presence, Cowan told Sterrett that he would be removed from the dorm. He was also told that he could not be in the vicinity of CB, which meant he was in effect barred from entering the dorm, cutting him off from most of his friends.

The events that prompted the university to take these actions against Sterrett are detailed in an affidavit sworn on Sterrett's behalf by LC, a friend of CB's and her sophomore year roommate. LC stated that in July she received a call from an "emotionally upset" CB who explained that her mother had found her diary. LC recalled that CB explained that the diary "contained descriptions of romantic and sexual experiences, drug use, and drinking." (CB confirmed the contents of the diary in her own deposition.) During the phone call, CB asked LC if she remembered the night CB had sex with Sterrett. LC didn't, because CB had never mentioned it. Now CB told her, "I said no, no, and then I gave in." Eventually, as described in CB's deposition, CB's mother called the university to report that CB would be making a complaint against Sterrett. CB's mother drove her to campus, and CB met with Heather Cowan.

2. An Overcorrection

We are told that one of the most dangerous places for a young woman in America today is a college campus. As President Obama said at a White House event in September, where he announced a campaign to address campus violence, "An estimated one in five women has been sexually assaulted during her college years—one in five." (At an earlier White House event on the issue, the president declared of sexual violence, "It threatens our families, it threatens our communities; ultimately, it threatens the entire country.") In recent weeks, *Rolling Stone*'s lurid account of a premeditated gang rape at the University of Virginia has made the issue of campus sexual violence front-page news. (The reporting and the allegations in the article have since been called into question, and *Rolling Stone* has issued a statement acknowledging that the magazine failed to properly investigate and corroborate the story.)

Sexual assault at colleges and universities is indeed a serious problem. The attention it's receiving today—on campus, at the White House, in the media—is a direct result of the often callous and dismissive treatment of victims. For too long, women who were assaulted on campus and came forward were doubted or dismissed, and the men responsible were given a mild rebuke or none at all. Those who commit serious sexual crimes on campus must be held to account.

In recent years, young activists, many of them women angry about their treatment after reporting an assault, have created new organizations and networks in an effort to reform the way colleges handle sexual violence. They recognized they had a powerful weapon in that fight: Title IX, the federal law that protects against discrimination in education. Schools are legally required by that law to address sexual harassment and violence on campus, and these activists filed complaints with the federal government about what they describe as lax enforcement by schools. The current administration has taken up the cause—the *Chronicle of Higher Education* describes it as "a marquee issue for the Obama administration"—and praised these young women for spurring political action. "A new generation of student activists is effectively pressing for change," read a statement this spring announcing new policies to address campus violence. The Department of Education has drafted new rules to address women's safety, some of which have been enshrined into law by Congress, with more legislation likely on the way.

Unfortunately, under the worthy mandate of protecting victims of sexual assault, procedures are being put in place at colleges that presume the guilt of the accused. Colleges, encouraged by federal officials, are instituting solutions to sexual violence against women that abrogate the civil rights of men. Schools that hold hearings to adjudicate claims of sexual misconduct allow the accuser and the accused to be accompanied by legal counsel. But as Judith Shulevitz noted in the *New Republic* in October, many schools ban lawyers from speaking to their clients (only notes can be passed). During these proceedings, the two parties are not supposed to question or cross-examine each other, a prohibition recommended by the federal government in order to protect the accuser. And by federal requirement, students can be found guilty under the lowest standard of proof: preponderance of the evidence, meaning just a 51 percent certainty is all that's needed for a finding that can permanently alter the life of the accused.

More than two dozen Harvard Law School professors recently wrote a statement protesting the university's new rules for handling sexual assault claims. "Harvard has adopted procedures for deciding cases of alleged sexual misconduct which lack the most basic elements of fairness and due process," they wrote. The professors note that the new rules call for a Title IX compliance officer who will be in charge of "investigation, prosecution, fact-finding, and appellate review." Under the new system, there will be no hearing for the accused and thus no opportunity to question witnesses and mount a defense. Harvard University, the professors wrote, is "jettisoning balance and fairness in the rush to appease certain federal administrative officials." But to push back against Department of Education edicts means potentially putting a school's federal funding in jeopardy, and no college, not even Harvard, the country's richest, is willing to do that.

Hard-line policies like Harvard's are necessary, government officials say, because undergraduate women are in unique peril. Often-cited studies of sexual violence at colleges describe an epidemic. But each of these studies has serious methodological limitations. In some cases, the studies make sensational assertions that are not supported by the underlying data. In others, the experiences of one or two campuses have been made to stand in for the entirety of America's higher education system.

Sen. Kirsten Gillibrand (D–New York), is a cosponsor of the bipartisan Campus Accountability and Safety Act, or CASA, expected to be voted on next year. The legislation would, among other things, require all colleges provide a confidential adviser to guide victims through the entire process of bringing an accusation while no guidance or assistance is mandated for the accused. Gillibrand said in announcing the legislation, "We should never accept the fact that women are at a greater risk of sexual assault as soon as they step onto a college campus. But today they are."

This is one of the frequently made assertions about campus violence, but the evidence to back it up is lacking. Being young does make people more vulnerable to serious violent crime, including sexual assault; according to government statistics those aged eighteen to twenty-four have the highest rates of such victimization. But most studies don't compare the victimization rates of students to nonstudents of the same age. One recent paper that does make that comparison, "Violence Against College Women" by Callie Marie Rennison and Lynn Addington, compares the crime experienced by college students and their peers who are not in college, using data from the National Crime Victimization Survey. What the researchers found was the opposite of what Gillibrand says about the dangers of campuses: "Non-student females are victims of violence at rates 1.7 times greater than are college females," the authors wrote, and this greater victimization holds true for sex crimes: "Even if the definition of violence were limited to sexual assaults, these crimes are more pervasive for young adult women who are not in college."

Rennison, an associate professor at the School of Public Affairs at the University of Colorado Denver, recognized in an interview that her study goes against a lot of received wisdom. "Maybe that's not a really popular thing to say," she said, adding, "I hate the notion that people think sending kids off to college is sending them to be victimized."

Any woman who is raped, on campus or off, deserves a fair and thorough investigation of her claim, and those found guilty should be punished. But the new rules—rules often put in place hastily and in response to the idea of a rape epidemic on campus—have left some young men saying *they* are the ones who have been victimized. They are starting to push back. In the past three years, men found responsible for sexual assault on campus have filed more than three dozen cases against schools. They argue that their due process rights have been violated and say they have been victims of gender discrimination under Title IX. Their complaints are starting to cost universities. The higher education insurance group United Educators did a study of the 262 insurance claims it paid to students between 2006 and 2010 because of campus sexual assault, at a cost to the group of $36 million. The vast majority of the payouts, 72 percent, went to the accused—young men who protested their treatment by universities.

Assertions of injustice by young men are infuriating to some. Caroline Heldman, an associate professor of politics at Occidental College and cofounder of End Rape on Campus, said of the men who are turning to the courts, "These lawsuits are an incredible display of entitlement, the same entitlement that drove them to rape." Sen. Claire McCaskill (D-Missouri), a cosponsor of the CASA bill, said to the *Washington Post* of these suits, "I don't think we are anywhere near a tipping point where the people accused of this are somehow being treated unfairly."

I've read through the court filings and investigative reports of a number of these cases, and it's clear to me that many of the accused are indeed being treated unfairly. Government officials and campus administrators are attempting to legislate the bedroom behavior of students with rules and requirements that would be comic if their effects weren't frequently so tragic. The legal filings in the cases brought by young men accused of sexual violence often begin like a script for a college sex farce but end with the protagonist finding himself in a Soviet-style show trial. Or, as in the case of Drew Sterrett, punished with no trial at all.

3. The Punishment

At the beginning of his sophomore year, Drew Sterrett was in limbo. He did not know whether he would face further disciplinary action as a result of the accusation against him, and indeed no formal written charge was ever issued. The single, cryptic Skype interrogation—the one that blindsided Sterrett over his summer vacation—was to be his sole hearing with campus administrators. He never met them in person. Sterrett's suit against the university accuses it of violating his constitutional right to due process. But as he waited out the fall, often there didn't seem to be any process.

Through September and October, he heard nothing further about the charge. Unbeknownst to him, CB was having second thoughts, as she explained in a deposition taken as a result of Sterrett's case against the university, because she wasn't sure she wanted Sterrett to be able to read her statement against him. The only word he received from school administrators during this period was a warning e-mail from Cowan, in October. One day Sterrett was walking with a friend who was putting his bike away at Sterrett's old dorm. CB saw him near her residence and contacted Cowan, who informed Sterrett that the visit gave an appearance of "retaliatory contact." He replied to Cowan and said it was troubling that his mere presence near a residence hall was considered an act of impropriety and asked that the investigation be finished "as quickly and compassionately as possible for everyone involved."

On November 9, 2012, Sterrett was given a one-page document titled "Summary of Witness Testimony and Review of Other Evidence." It consisted primarily of summaries of statements from anonymous witnesses. For example, it stated: "Two witnesses stated the Complainant reported to them that she tried to push the Respondent off her." (CB didn't know who these two witnesses were. She confirmed in her deposition that in her original statement to Cowan, she never said that she had tried to push Sterrett off her.) It also stated: "[A] witness reported that the Respondent told them that he engaged in penetration with the Complainant and 'she was saying 'no,' and that it was just—it was 'just like a second,' and then he stopped, and then the Complainant left.' " (In her deposition, CB acknowledged this was not how their sexual encounter transpired, although she maintained that at some point she said "no.")

The document made clear to Sterrett that CB was claiming that she had said "no" during their encounter. He put together a lengthy rebuttal. Of CB's claim, he wrote, "I cannot state it more clearly that this is untrue. I asked her if she wanted to have sex; she said 'yes.' " (CB's assertion was also challenged later by an affidavit sworn on Sterrett's behalf by his freshman-year roommate, the one in the upper bunk. The roommate said that he saw CB get into Sterrett's bed of her own volition and that his bed and Sterrett's were so close that he would have heard if she had exclaimed "no" or "stop." He stated that he was annoyed that their sex was keeping him awake and that as a friend of both he would have intervened if he felt something untoward was happening.)

Sterrett's rebuttal also noted that Cowan's document failed to mention the role CB's mother played in bringing the accusation against him after she found her daughter's diary. CB's roommate, LC, in an affidavit sworn on behalf of Sterrett, said that over the summer CB's mother had called her repeatedly warning her not to talk to Sterrett and to take CB's side in all proceedings. LC stated that she never saw any change in CB's behavior from the time of the alleged assault until the end of freshman year. But, she said, CB's personality changed dramatically after her mother found her diary and the fall semester began. In her affidavit, LC said it pained her to speak against her friend, but she stated: "It is my belief, based on my personal observations and conversations with CB, that it is possible CB manufactured a story about a sexual assault in response to the conflict CB described occurring between her and her mother in the summer of 2012."

On November 30, Sterrett received Cowan's final "Sexual Misconduct Investigation Report." His lawsuit states that the final report failed to take note of anything he had written in his rebuttal. The final report was longer than Cowan's previous one and included further allegations that either CB herself did not corroborate or appeared unsupported by the available evidence. For example, it stated: "The Complainant framed the events in question as a sexual assault to witnesses the day following the event." In her deposition, CB acknowledged that she didn't do that, that in fact she'd never used the words "sexual assault" to describe what happened. The report said that Sterrett's roommate was asleep during the entire sexual encounter. This was contradicted by the time-stamped Facebook message complaining that he was being kept awake.

The report also said that Sterrett had confessed to his roommate that he'd had a nonconsensual encounter with CB. When

Cowan interviewed the roommate—who says she never told him the purpose of her investigation—he had mentioned that Sterrett said he regretted the encounter with CB. In Cowan's report, that statement is described as a confession of sexual violation. But as the roommate clarified in his affidavit, Sterrett was not expressing "that he had done anything morally or legally or ethically wrong." He was expressing regret for sleeping with someone in their group of friends.

The final report came to this conclusion: "[I]t is determined that the Respondent engaged in sexual intercourse with the Complainant without her consent and that that activity is so severe as to create a hostile environment." His punishment was that he was suspended from college until July 2016—after CB graduated. In order for the university to consider reinstating him, he would have to agree that he had engaged in sexual misconduct. Whether or not he returned, the finding would stay on his permanent record. Sterrett's lawsuit says a university official acknowledged to him that these sanctions would "limit his educational, employment and career opportunities."

With the help of a lawyer, Sterrett filed an appeal to the Office of Student Conflict Resolution. He included affidavits from classmates who said their words had been misconstrued and even falsified, and included the statement by Sterrett's roommate that CB was a willing participant and that the roommate would have heard and intervened if CB had said no. The university's response was to stand by its finding that Sterrett was responsible for sexual misconduct but to change the reason. Now Cowan issued an addendum stating that Sterrett had committed sexual misconduct because CB was too drunk to consent. (In her deposition, CB acknowledged that while she had been drinking, she was not incapacitated.)

Upholding the finding that he committed sexual misconduct required Sterrett to leave the university. But he had already decided not to return to school after winter break of his sophomore year. His lawyer explained in an e-mail that Sterrett felt the restrictions put on his movements in order to avoid running into CB—he could be expelled if she saw him and felt his presence was "retaliatory"—made it impossible for him to be at school. Sterrett filed another appeal, this one to Michigan's university Appeals Board. In July 2013, it upheld the sexual misconduct finding, though it agreed to place Sterrett on disciplinary probation instead of suspension. The probation, however, came with onerous conditions, according to his lawyer: He would now be barred from any university housing and was prohibited from enrolling in any class in which CB was enrolled (and thus prohibited from registering and enrolling in classes until CB had finalized her schedule). He declined to return.

In April of this year, Sterrett filed suit against the university. The suit states that the public university violated his Fourteenth Amendment rights of due process and that Michigan contravened its own procedures for disciplinary hearings, which call for written notice of allegations against a student, sufficient time to prepare for an arbitration or other meeting (Sterrett says there was no arbitration or meeting), knowledge of the names of witnesses, the opportunity to pose questions to the complainant or other witnesses, and more. As a result of these violations, his suit says, he was subjected to a process that was "capricious, reckless, incomplete, [and] lacked fundamental fairness."

Michigan has asked the United States District Court for the Eastern District of Michigan to dismiss Sterrett's suit. Its motion to dismiss outlines the university's version of events. Michigan asserts Sterrett was given fair notice of the charges against him, citing the fact that Sterrett's own suit stated that he "gleaned" that he was being accused of sexual assault from his Skype interrogation. The motion states that Sterrett was given several opportunities to file his rebuttals and appeals, concluding, "That's not lack of due process. It's abundant process." It also noted that Sterrett decided to file a lawsuit rather than return to the university under the sanctions and restrictions it offered. The statement issued by CB's lawyer noted, "The University of Michigan thoroughly investigated the matter. Plaintiff and my client each had an opportunity to present evidence. Plaintiff was found responsible; he appealed that decision, and it was upheld."

I spoke to Sterrett's lawyer, Deborah L. Gordon. She said that like many similarly accused young men, Sterrett believed that once a responsible investigation was undertaken, everything would be straightened out. "He had no idea he was on his way out no matter what he said or what the facts were," she said. She hopes to get the case to a jury, but she says the university is making every legal effort to delay. Sterrett should be graduating from college next spring, but the sexual misconduct charge against him has made it virtually impossible for him to be accepted as a transfer student elsewhere. He was accepted to one well-regarded university, but the offer was rescinded when the school heard of his disciplinary finding at Michigan. Now twenty-two, he's hoping that if his suit is successful, he will be able to finish his education—some day.

4. The Numbers

One campus rape is one too many. But the severe new policies championed by the White House, the Department of Education, and members of Congress are responding to the idea that colleges are in the grips of an epidemic—and the studies suggesting this epidemic don't hold up to scrutiny. Bad policy is being made on the back of problematic research and will continue to be unless we bring some healthy *skepticism* to the hard work of putting a number on the prevalence of campus rape.

It is exceedingly difficult to get a numerical handle on a crime that is usually committed in private and the victims of which—all the studies agree—frequently decline to report. A further complication is that because researchers are asking about intimate subjects, there is no consensus on the best way to phrase sensitive questions in order to get the most accurate answers. A 2008 National Institute of Justice paper on campus sexual assault explained some of the challenges: "Unfortunately, researchers have been unable to determine the precise incidence of sexual assault on American campuses because the incidence found depends on how the questions are worded and the context of the survey." Take the National Crime Victimization Survey, the nationally representative sample conducted by the federal government to find rates of reported and unreported crime. For the years 1995 to 2011, as the University of Colorado Denver's Rennison explained to me, it found that an estimated 0.8 percent of noncollege females age eighteen to twenty-four revealed that they were victims of threatened, attempted, or completed rape/sexual assault. Of the college females that age during that same time period, approximately 0.6 percent reported they experienced such attempted or completed crime.

That finding diverges wildly from the notion that one in five college women will be sexually assaulted by the time they graduate. That's the number most often used to suggest there is overwhelming sexual violence on America's college campuses. It comes from a 2007 study funded by the National Institute of Justice, called the "Campus Sexual Assault Study," or CSA. (I cited it last year in a story on campus drinking and sexual assault.) The study asked 5,466 female college students at two public universities, one in the Midwest and one in the South, to answer an online survey about their experiences with sexual assault. The survey defined sexual assault as everything from nonconsensual sexual intercourse to such unwanted activities as "forced kissing," "fondling," and "rubbing up against you in a sexual way, even if it is over your clothes."

There are approximately 12 million female college students in the United States (There are about 9 million males.) I asked the lead author of the study, Christopher Krebs, whether the CSA represents the experience of those millions of female students. His answer was unequivocal: "We don't think one in five is a nationally representative statistic." It couldn't be, he said, because his team sampled only two schools. "In no way does that make our results nationally representative," Krebs said. And yet President Obama used this number to make the case for his sweeping changes in national policy.

The Sexual Victimization of College Women, a 2000 study commissioned by the U.S. Department of Justice, is the basis for another widely cited statistic, even grimmer than the finding of CSA: that one in four college women will be raped. (An activist organization, One in Four, takes its name from the finding.) The study itself, however, found a completed rape rate among its respondents of 1.7 percent. How does a study that finds less than 2 percent of college women in a given year are raped become a 25 percent likelihood? In addition to the 1.7 percent of victims of completed rape, the survey found that another 1.1 percent experienced attempted rape. As the authors wrote, "One might conclude that the risk of rape victimization for college women is not high; 'only' about 1 in 36 college women (2.8 percent) experience a completed rape or attempted rape in an academic year."

But the authors go on to make several assumptions that ratchet up the risk. The study was carried out during the spring and asked women to describe any assaults experienced during that academic year. The researchers decided to double the numbers they received from their subjects, in order to extrapolate their findings over an entire calendar year even as they acknowledged that this was "problematic," as students rarely attend school for twelve months. That calculation brought the incidence figure to nearly 5 percent. Although college is designed to be a four-year experience, the authors note that it takes students "an average" of five years, so they then multiplied their newly-arrived-at 5 percent of student victims by five years, and thus they conclude: "The percentage of completed or attempted rape victimization among women in higher educational institutions might climb to between one-fifth and one-quarter."

In a footnote, the authors acknowledge that asserting that one-quarter of college students "might" be raped is not based on actual evidence: "These projections are suggestive. To assess accurately the victimization risk for women throughout a college career, longitudinal research following a cohort of female students across time is needed." The one-fifth to one-quarter assertion would mean that young American college women are raped at a rate similar to women in Congo, where rape has been used as a weapon of war.

No one disputes that only a percentage of sexual assaults get reported, but the studies that have tried to capture the incidence of unreported rape are miles apart. As Christopher Krebs observed, "Some [surveys] I think create high numbers that are difficult to defend. Some create artificially low numbers that are impossible to defend." We do have hard numbers on actual reports of sexual assault on campus thanks to the Clery Act, the federal law that requires colleges to report their crime rates. But even these figures are controversial. Minuscule sexual assault numbers have long been a consistent feature of Clery Act reporting. Victim advocates say administrators deliberately suppress their numbers in order to make the schools look safer. (Unsurprisingly, schools deny this.) In July, the *Washington Post* published the Clery number for 2012: There were just over 3,900 forcible sexual offenses, with most schools reporting single or low double-digit numbers. (Under the Clery Act a "forcible sexual offense" does not require the use of actual physical force, it can simply be an act against someone's will. Offenses include everything from rape to fondling.) Given the approximately 12 million female college students, that's a reported sexual assault rate of 0.03 percent.

Reported sexual assaults have been rising on campus in recent years, at a time when other campus crime is declining. (The nation as a whole has experienced a dramatic drop in all violent crime over the past few decades, including sexual assault, which is down more than 60 percent since 1995.) The rise of reporting on campus sexual assault is generally described by security experts as a function of a greater willingness on the part of women to make complaints, not an increase in incidence. Despite reports of "soaring" sexual assault rates on campus, the raw numbers remain low. At the University of Chicago, the jump from 2011 to 2013 was 83 percent: an increase from six reports to eleven, which represents 0.4 percent of the university's undergraduate women. Carnegie Mellon went up 220 percent, from five cases to sixteen, or 0.6 percent of the university's undergraduate women. President Obama has asserted that only about 12 percent of sexual assault victims make a report to authorities. If he is correct, and we extrapolate from the Clery numbers, that would suggest there were 32,500 assaults in 2012, reported and not, or a 0.27 percent incidence.

.   .   .

A widely held belief about a college man accused of sexual assault is that he is likely a serial predator. This is a result of the work of David Lisak, one of the most influential experts on sexual assault in the country. "College presidents don't like to hear this, but these are sex offenders," Lisak said at an event at Harvard in 2013. "Every report should be viewed and treated as an opportunity to identify a serial rapist."

Lisak retired not long ago after more than two decades of teaching psychology at the University of Massachusetts Boston. He remains a consultant to universities, the military, and other institutions on sexual assault. His 2002 paper, "Repeat Rape and Multiple Offending Among Undetected Rapists," is a foundational study in the movement to curb campus sexual assault. It's cited endlessly, by everyone from President Obama to college faculty members to student activists. It's even cited by critics of the new campus sexual assault policies.

Lisak told me that he meets understandable resistance when delivering his message to college administrators. "It's hard to think of any of your students as a sex offender," he said. "But the data are pretty clear. They're not a large group. It's a fairly small percentage, but their behavior is really consistent with everything we know about sex offenders."

In a 2011 article in *Sexual Assault Report*, Lisak disparaged "the widely-held view that sexual assaults committed on university campuses are typically the result of a basically 'decent' young man who, were it not for too much alcohol and too little communication, would never do such a thing." (He concedes that "some campus sexual assaults do fit this more benign view.") Instead, he asserts that the vast majority of sexual assaults on campus, more than 90 percent of them, are perpetrated by serial offenders. His work, he says, shows that these offenders are relentless, averaging six rape victims each. "They've perfected ways of identifying who on campus, for example, are most vulnerable." In the 2011 article, he wrote that these "predators" were "serial and multi-faceted offenders" who "plan and premeditate their attacks" and that various prevention education programs are unlikely to be effective because "it is extremely difficult to change the behavior of a serial predator even when you incarcerate him and subject him to an intensive, multi-year treatment program."

For the 2002 study, Lisak found 120 men, or 6.4 percent of respondents, "met criteria for rape or attempted rape," with 80 percent of that group admitting that they took advantage of an unwilling partner's intoxication. Of the 120, about one-third said they'd committed a single rape, and 76 men, or 63 percent, admitted to multiple offenses. Lisak calculated an average of 5.8 rapes each for these repeat offenders.

Based on these findings, Lisak says it's likely that any young man who is accused of sexual misconduct on campus is a serial predator. He told me he arrived at this conclusion by calculating the number of rapes the self-admitted serial attackers said they perpetrated. Those rapes represented 90 percent of the total acknowledged rapes in his study.

The 2002 study is now frequently used to portray college students, some still teenagers, as among society's most ruthless and sadistic predators. And yet the limitations of the study are such that it cannot fairly be said to describe the behavior of the majority of young men who find themselves accused. To start, though the study was of college men, it was not of *college-age* men (who are traditionally ages 18 to 24). Lisak's participants ranged in age from 18 to 71. The average age of his respondents was 26.5, and more than 20 percent were older than 30. How does a study of men in college include so many older men? Lisak recruited people from where he taught, the University of Massachusetts Boston, an urban commuter school with no campus housing. Many students are older working people returning to or just starting college. Currently, 30 percent of its students attend part time and the school's four-year graduation rate is 15 percent. By comparison, at the state's flagship university in Amherst, 7 percent of students are enrolled part time and its four-year graduation rate is 60 percent.

I spoke with James J. Cochran, professor of applied statistics at the University of Alabama. He said that because the population of male students at UMass Boston may differ in important ways from the population of male college students across all universities, we must be careful in generalizing results from the UMass Boston sample to the population of male college students across all universities. People tend to think that a single study is definitive, Cochran told me. But generally what a single study tells you, he said, is that we have "evidence of something interesting, let's study it more." (The "Campus Sexual Assault Study" also attempted to identify male perpetrators. Lead author Christopher Krebs said a "shockingly low" number of college-age men in his study acknowledged committing sexual assault. The researchers surveyed 1,375 male students and 34, or 2.5 percent, "reported perpetrating any type of sexual assault," the majority involving incapacitation.)

Lisak conducted the study between 1991 to 1998, at several-year intervals, setting up tables on campus, where he offered men three or four dollars to complete a study on "childhood experiences and adult functioning." In all, Lisak and his coauthor recruited 1,882 participants (the school had a total of about 5,800 male students during this period). Lisak and his coauthor wrote: "Because of the non-random nature of the sampling procedures, the reported data cannot be interpreted as estimates of the prevalence of sexual and other acts of violence." I asked Lisak about this caveat in an interview and he said, "That's a standard disclaimer for any study." But he also acknowledged that the only way to find out if his population differed from the usual typical student population would be to replicate his study at a more traditional campus.

Lisak deserves credit for identifying a type of stealthy predator who evades law enforcement. Such men exist, are dangerous, and should be prosecuted for their crimes. But describing such people does not mean that they constitute the entire universe of college men who find themselves accused of sexual misconduct. That, however, is how his work and his public comments are frequently used. Here's Yale Law professor Jed Rubenfeld, writing last month on campus sexual assault in the *New York Times*: "Research suggests that more than 90 percent of campus rapes are committed by a relatively small percentage of college men—possibly as few as 4 percent—who rape repeatedly, averaging six victims each."

Lisak told me he continues to dispute the view, held by some college administrators, that the majority of campus sexual assault disputes are the result of drunken miscommunication. I asked Lisak what percentage of reported sexual misconduct is of this less predatory type. "There's no way I can answer," he said. "Not that it never occurs; it does. I think a lot of college administrators think that is the norm. That's what I really dispute."

I asked Lisak whether it was fair to presume any given accused student is a serial predator. He said such a supposition would be "sloppy thinking." He went on: "You have to investigate the assault and who the individual is. Everything hinges on the investigation." He also said that a major problem with adjudicating campus sexual assault is how ill equipped universities are to conduct such investigations.

.   .   .

The potential for misuse of Lisak's study can be seen in the 2013 case of the Occidental College student "John Doe," who brought a suit against the school after he was expelled for a sexual encounter with "Jane Doe," in September of his freshman year. The *Los Angeles Times* summed up the events: "The college's investigative report, performed by an outside firm, said both parties agreed on the following facts: Both had been drinking, she went to his room, took off her shirt while dancing, made out with him and returned to his room later for sex, asking if he had a condom. When friends stopped by the room to ask if she was OK, she told them yes." Prior to their encounter, the two exchanged texts about their planned assignation, and Jane texted another friend to announce she was going to have sex. Later, when Jane came to see the incident as rape, she reported it to the Los Angeles Police Department. A female LAPD officer investigated and a female deputy district attorney declined to pursue the case. She wrote, "Witnesses were interviewed and agreed that the victim and suspect were both drunk, however, that they were both willing participants exercising bad judgment." Her report further found that Jane was capable of resisting and that John had reasonably concluded that her communications and actions conveyed consent.

But Jane ended up being convinced that John fit the pattern of the kind of serial predator Lisak describes. John had the misfortune of being accused of sexual misconduct following the filing, by attorney Gloria Allred, of a Title IX violation complaint against the school, charging lax punishment for serial offenders. And Jane ended up being counseled by the assistant professor of sociology Danielle Dirks, a prime mover behind the Title IX filing and a nationally prominent activist on campus sexual assault.

Jane lost her virginity that night, and when she sobered up and realized what happened, in distress she went to a faculty adviser who referred her to Dirks. An eighty-two-page investigative report prepared for the school by the firm Public Interest Investigations shows it was Dirks, in her first phone conversation with Jane, who introduced Jane to the idea that she had been raped. Jane told the professor, "Oh, I am not calling it rape yet." Over many hours of conversation, Dirks helped move Jane from what the professor described as Jane's "strong state of denial" about what happened.

The report notes that Jane "stated that she has learned that 90 percent of rapes are done by repeat offenders." (John was a freshman, on campus for a few weeks, with no complaints against him.) Jane told Dirks that John had expressed regret that she lost her virginity that way—he hadn't known she was a virgin—and when she was absent from a class they took together, he texted to make sure she was all right. The professor had a skeptical view of his behavior. All this was "disingenuous," said Dirks, according to the report: It was typical of rapists who, she said, try to control, dominate, manage, and manipulate. Strikingly, it was Dirks herself who initiated proceedings to get John removed from campus, explaining, "I know how jarring it is for me to see him on campus, so how is it for Jane?" (An Occidental spokesman said he could not comment on a pending lawsuit. Dirks said in an e-mail that the report "contains factual errors regarding my involvement in the case." However, beyond disputing a statement attributed to her by Jane and not quoted here, she declined to elaborate on what the errors are.)

Occidental hired an outside attorney to review the investigative report and make a recommendation about John. Here's the conclusion of the attorney, as reported by the *Los Angeles Times*: "The attorney, Marilou F. Mirkovich, found that the young man did not know that his classmate was too drunk to consent because he, too, was inebriated. But, citing the college's policy that does not allow alcohol or drug consumption to excuse sexual misconduct, Mirkovich found that he should have known and was responsible for the assault." After only a few months as a college student, John was expelled. He told the *Los Angeles Times* the whole experience has been "soul-crushing." John has since been unable to enroll in another college.

5. The Federal Government Steps Up

Much of what's happening on campuses today regarding the handling of sexual assault is due to the rise of a small, once-obscure arm of the federal government. The Department of Education's Office for Civil Rights dictates to colleges the procedures they must follow in regard to campus sexual complaints. It also examines schools for violations of Title IX, the law that forbids discrimination in education on the basis of sex. In recent years, OCR has used Title IX, best known for tackling imbalances in athletics, as a tool to address sexual violence. When OCR issues findings against a school, if the school declines to admit wrongdoing, the office has the power, as yet unexercised, to essentially shut the school down.

In 2011, OCR released what's come to be known as the "Dear Colleague" letter. It called for new procedures to be put in place for handling sexual assault allegations at colleges and universities receiving federal funds (virtually all of them). The federal office had to act, it said, because "the likelihood that [female students] will be assaulted by the time they graduate is significant." It asserted the process should be equitable and impartial. But it laid out procedures that privilege the rights of victims over those of the accused. It recommended schools provide "comprehensive, holistic victim services including medical, counseling and academic support services, such as tutoring" for the accuser, without describing any services that should be available to help the accused navigate a pervasively adversarial process. If a school allowed the accused to appeal a verdict of responsibility for sexual misconduct, then an accuser *also* got to appeal if the accused was found not responsible. This provision meant someone accused of a campus sexual assault could find himself sitting through a second tribunal on the same charge.

Among the most significant changes described by the Dear Colleague letter was the requirement that schools lower the standard by which they judge whether a student is responsible for sexual assault. (There is no uniform definition of sexual assault on campus. Because these are civil, not criminal proceedings, what constitutes sexual misconduct can vary widely from campus to campus.) Colleges were told to adopt a "preponderance of evidence" standard when evaluating whether a student was to be found responsible for an allegation. This is the lowest evidentiary standard, only requiring a smidge more than 50 percent certainty. Because the punishment for such infractions can be severe—from suspension to expulsion—many schools had previously used the "clear and convincing evidence" standard, a significantly higher burden of proof, though still below the "beyond a reasonable doubt" standard used in criminal proceedings. (The University of Michigan, in its legal motion to dismiss Drew Sterrett's case, specifically noted the findings against Sterrett met the preponderance of evidence standard.)

Legal protections granted students at public and private institutions are somewhat different. A public university, as a government entity, must provide certain due process rights. Students at private schools do not have this protection, but they do have contractual rights, and virtually all students are covered by Title IX. To head off concerns about significantly lowering evidentiary standards, the OCR asserted that because a campus tribunal's worst punishment is expulsion, not imprisonment, "the same procedural protections and legal standards are not required" as in a criminal case.

"Not Alone," billed as "The First Report of the White House Task Force to Protect Students From Sexual Assault," was released to great fanfare at the White House in April, and it outlined how OCR would help implement the report's stated goals. "Not Alone" encouraged schools to consider adopting a "single-investigator" model—as Harvard has done—in which a sole administrator is tasked with being investigator, prosecutor, judge, and jury in sexual assault cases. Since that person would work at the school's Title IX office, which is tasked with keeping the school off the list of those being scrutinized by the federal government, impartiality may not be that person's first imperative.

Being investigated by OCR for a Title IX violation places a college on a growing federal list of shame, now eighty-eight schools long. Even more disastrous is standing up to OCR. The agency has the power to pull a school's federal funding, essentially putting a school out of business—ask Tufts University if they're willing to use it. A female Tufts student had accused a former boyfriend of rape, and after he was cleared (and the female student sanctioned for misleading campus authorities in the course of their investigation), she brought a Title IX complaint against the school. OCR's mandate was to look at Tufts's procedural deficiencies, not the finding in the case, and it criticized Tufts at length. The university agreed to make all the OCR's recommended changes: to improve its protections for accusers and speed up its resolution process, among other things. The school also agreed to give a monetary settlement to the female student. But Tufts balked at signing off on OCR's finding that the school was a Title

IX violator. It issued a statement saying the school "could not, in good faith, allow our community to believe that we are not in compliance with such an important law." In response, OCR told Tufts it would pull the university's federal funds, a threat, the *Boston Globe* wrote, that was "so catastrophic that it virtually required Tufts to reach some understanding with the government." It took only a few days for Tufts to cave.

6. The New Rules of Engagement

To punish the alleged perpetrators of sexual violence, colleges have put in place systems that are heavy-handed and unfair. Efforts to *prevent* sexual violence from occurring are unfortunately no more enlightened. College students today are increasingly treated as a special sexual caste, who unlike their peers out in the working world can't be relied upon to have sex without convoluted regulations that treat lovemaking as if it were a contract negotiation. Often, they are governed by a regimen called "affirmative consent," an attempt by legislators and administrators to remove all ambiguity from sex.

The federal government has so far not mandated affirmative consent as a national standard, but states have been enthusiastically embracing the idea. Andrew Cuomo, governor of New York, recently enacted an affirmative consent standard for all State University of New York schools, calling the statistics on sexual assault "breathtaking." California just became the first state to write the practice into law for all public *and* private colleges. The precise rules vary from place to place, but the point is to systematize the progression of a sexual encounter. Consent can't be presumed—even between members of an established couple. It must be affirmatively given—for each and every sexual encounter and for every sex act.

At Ohio State University, two young people who want to engage in sexual congress might be well advised to first consult with the philosophy department and the law school. The university's consent guidelines state, in part: "Consent is a knowing and voluntary verbal or non-verbal agreement between both parties to participate in each and every sexual act." "Effective consent can be given by words or actions so long as the words or actions create a mutual understanding between both parties regarding the conditions of the sexual activity—ask, 'do both of us understand and agree regarding the who, what, where, when, why, and how this sexual activity will take place?'" "Regardless of past experiences with other partners or your current partner, consent must be obtained. Consent can never be assumed, even in the context of a relationship."

The Foundation for Individual Rights in Education is a civil-liberties group dedicated to defending constitutional rights on campus, and Joseph Cohn is its legislative and policy director. The group says affirmative consent is both unnecessary and potentially pernicious. "Our laws already make sexual activity without consent illegal," Cohn says. Affirmative consent, he says, makes sexual activity that is lawful off campus a punishable offense on it.

Advocates of affirmative consent argue that these regulations won't lead to frivolous accusations. They say only women who truly haven't given consent will ever bring a charge. But under an affirmative consent regime, a young man can be threatened with expulsion even if his sexual partner doesn't say no.

The *Yale Daily News* recently reported on a sexual assault case that illuminates what can now be considered an offense worthy of punishment and the elaborate investigative and hearing processes now in place to adjudicate who agreed to what. A male and female who were sometime lovers hooked up one night after she had been drinking and they had been sending flirty texts. (She wrote to him, "Don't let me try to seduce you though. Because that is a distinct possibility.") She eventually invited him to her room, where she says she capitulated to his desire for sex because in the past when she refused him he would scream and cry, which she found overwhelming. His version was that upon arrival she grabbed him, kissed him, they each took off their clothes, and then had sex twice that evening and once in the morning. Although she was sober by the time of the morning encounter, she later told Yale officials that all of the sex was nonconsensual because she was too drunk during the evening to consent, and in the morning, the *Yale Daily News* reports, "she did not resist because she felt refusal would be too emotionally exhausting." A full year after the encounter, she brought a sexual assault charge against the young man, hoping to get him expelled. There was an investigation by an "impartial fact-finder," a written report, then a three-and-a-half-hour hearing. The tribunal found that the young man did not violate Yale's sexual misconduct policy.

It might easily have gone the other way, given the capaciousness of Yale's consent standard: "Yale's definition of consent reflects the University's high expectations and permits discipline for behavior that does not meet a criminal standard," reads Yale's Title IX FAQ. Yale "may find that an encounter took place without coercion, force, or threat of force (criteria often associated with the term 'rape') but still deem it to have lacked the unambiguous ongoing agreement that constitutes consent under the Yale standard."

Carol Tavris is a social psychologist and author of the feminist classic *The Mismeasure of Woman* and, with Elliot Aronson, *Mistakes Were Made (but Not by Me)*. She says she is troubled by the blurring of distinctions between rape (notably by predatory males), unwanted sex (where one party agrees to sex not out of desire but to please or placate the partner), and the kind of consensual sex where both parties are so drunk they can barely remember what happened—and one of them later regrets it. She says, "Calling all of these kinds of sexual encounters 'rape' or 'sexual assault' doesn't teach young women how to learn what they want sexually, let alone how to communicate what they want, or don't want. It doesn't teach them to take responsibility for their decisions, for their reluctance to speak up. Sexual communication is really hard—you don't learn how to do it in a few weekends."

Tavris also believes holding only men responsible for their sexual behavior has pernicious effects on women because it supports a victim identity that is already too prevalent in our society. "It's so much easier to be a victim than to admit culpability, admit your own involvement, admit that you made a mistake," she says. "It's much easier to say it's all his fault. Look, sometimes it *is* all his fault. That's called rape. But ambiguities and unexpected decisions are part of many encounters, especially sexual ones."

7. The Alcohol Taboo

Government officials and campus administrators are paying more attention to what's going on between the sheets in dorm rooms than ever before. Despite all their newfound efforts to curtail sexual violence on campus, however, they're willfully ignoring the most important single factor running through accounts of such violence: alcohol.

It's a surprisingly loaded subject, given the widely acknowledged prevalence of drinking on American campuses. Last year, I wrote about drinking and sexual assault in a *Slate* piece titled, "College Women: Stop Getting Drunk." I said that binge drinking was bad for everyone but that it presented a particular danger for young women because it made them more vulnerable to sexual assault—I described sober predators who specifically targeted intoxicated women. I was widely denounced for "victim-blaming." This year, I was disinvited to speak at a West Coast college after board members of a student organization that had invited me decided my presence would make student victims "feel unsafe."

In the White House report "Not Alone," the Obama administration promises to develop new prevention strategies for campus sexual assault. But that's going to be difficult if it continues to refuse to address drinking. Raynard Kington, president of

Grinnell College and former director of the National Institute on Alcohol Abuse and Alcoholism, wrote in *Inside Higher Ed* in response to the report, "As a public health physician, I was surprised and disappointed that the word 'alcohol' literally does not appear anywhere in the chapter on prevention." He said he understood the concern about blaming the victim when discussing alcohol, but in tackling sexual assault at Grinnell he realized "we would never address the problem unless we also addressed the issue of excessive drinking."

A September article in the *Chronicle of Higher Education* noted that for the past fifteen years, Department of Justice grants to study campus sexual assault prevention have specifically excluded focusing on alcohol. Why? Because DOJ didn't want any emphasis on "changing victim behavior." The *Chronicle* article quoted a coordinator for Partners in Prevention, a higher-education substance-abuse program, who said, "What we steer our campuses away from is anything that says someone experienced gender violence because they had been drinking. Even if a student is sitting in a residence-hall room, gender violence can happen to them."

It is simply misleading to tell young women they have as great a chance of being sexually assaulted while in their dorm studying at one p.m. as they do at a drunken frat party at one a.m. There are patterns to victimization. The "Campus Sexual Assault Study" found the majority of victims were freshmen and sophomores, the most common time of year to be assaulted is when school begins in the fall, the most common days were Friday and Saturday, the most common time was after midnight. People who had been previously assaulted were at far greater risk of revictimization. Alcohol was overwhelmingly an element. The United Educators study of insurance payouts for sexual assault found that "alcohol was a significant factor in nearly all of the claims studied."

And it's not just about conveying to young women the dangers of drinking. It's equally important to tell young men about the jeopardy they face when having an alcohol-fueled sexual encounter at college. While women's consumption is often considered a mitigating factor at campus tribunals, men's consumption generally is not. This disparity is sex discrimination, says Brett Sokolow, president of the National Center for Higher Education Risk Management. Sokolow has long fought for harsh penalties for accused men on campus. But in an open letter titled "Sex and Booze," he writes: "If both are intoxicated they both did the same thing to each other. Why should only the male be charged if both students behave in ways defined as prohibited by the policy?" He has been called in to consult on cases in which schools have suspended or expelled the young man when both students were equally intoxicated. Schools that are doing so, he says, are creating male "Title IX plaintiffs."

Sokolow also says schools err when they adhere to an unrealistic standard that consumption of alcohol renders consent moot. Criminal statutes generally require that for sex to be nonconsensual due to alcohol or drugs, the accuser be not just intoxicated but incapacitated. Having had a few drinks does not mean people, even young people, lack the capacity to make decisions about their actions, however poor those decisions may look in retrospect. Sokolow notes, however, that at some colleges "boards and panels can't tell the difference between drunk sex and a policy violation."

To the extent the Obama administration *has* addressed the role of alcohol in sexual assault, it's done so in a way that suggests it has not thought carefully about this potentially complicated issue. When the president announced in "Not Alone" that his administration was committed to "putting an end" to sexual violence on campus, the first step he suggested was to have every college student take a survey. (The CASA bill would make this survey taking mandatory.) The administration released a "toolkit," a sample survey. Creating a national sexual assault census might seem to solve the problem of unrepresentative studies, though it is concerning that the federal government would require students to answer invasive questions about their sexual experiences, even anonymously. (One question asks respondents whether they've experienced, against their will, "someone putting their finger or an object like a bottle or candle in your vagina or anus.")

But some sections of the toolkit seem less interested in gathering data than in promoting a black-and-white view of situations that are notoriously murky. One section, titled "Rape Myth Acceptance," lists what it describes as myths about drinking and rape. These include, "If both people are drunk, it can't be rape" and "It shouldn't be considered rape if a guy is drunk and didn't realize what he was doing." It is obviously incorrect to say that if both parties are drunk, it *can't* be rape or to suggest that being drunk could ever be an *excuse* for rape. But this exercise in supposed myth busting doesn't allow for the ambiguity of these often bedeviling situations, and it fails to acknowledge that when both people are drunk, sometimes they both make regrettable decisions and have genuinely divergent views about what happened the next morning.

K. C. Johnson, of the Manhattan Institute's *Minding the Campus* blog, has compiled a list of top-ranked institutions, including Columbia, Duke, and Stanford, whose policies could lead to a young man being found responsible for a sexual offense simply if the complainant establishes that she had any degree of intoxication. Johnson notes that at Brown if two people were drinking and later an accusation is made, the disparate treatment is stark. The policy states: "A charged student's use of any drug, including alcohol, judged to be related to an offense will be considered an exacerbating rather than a mitigating circumstance."

8. A Matter for Prosecutors, Not Professors

The names Hannah Graham and Morgan Harrington, two Virginia college students who were kidnapped, raped, and murdered, are powerful testimony to the need to get campus sexual assault right. Jesse Matthew, thirty-two, being held for Graham's murder, has also been linked to Harrington's and will be tried for the rape of a third woman who managed to get away. When he was a college student, Matthew was expelled from two consecutive schools, Liberty University and Christopher Newport University, after accusations of rape. Tragically, neither case ended up in the criminal justice system. It is precisely because serial predators of the kind Lisak describes do exist that we should recognize adjudicating rape is not the job of college administrators but of law enforcement. Expelling a predator only sends him out into society to attack again.

Consider the *Rolling Stone* article about the alleged gang rape at the University of Virginia, which reignited a heated national debate about the treatment of victims on campus. The article is now unraveling, with both Sabrina Rubin Erdely's journalism and her source's account called into question. But the story did raise legitimate concerns about reporting requirements on campuses. Let's assume that the alleged victim, Jackie, did tell a dean at the university that she had been the victim of a gruesome attack, as Erdely wrote in her story. How could an allegation of a clearly criminal act not be reported directly to law enforcement? As my colleague Dahlia Lithwick has explained, the federal government mandates that schools offer a "noncriminal, survivor-centered, confidential response" to victims. This means not reporting a crime to the police if the victim prefers not to. (Erdely wrote that Jackie had been told by the dean that she *could* make a criminal complaint, but had declined to do so.) Respecting the feelings of victims is important, and crucial to encouraging more women to report violence. But elevating the psychological comfort of victims over society's need to punish criminals will only let perpetrators go free.

The critiques of how the criminal justice system treats victims are many and justified, but that's an argument for further reform and for finding ways to reduce the trauma to victims, not for asking schools to take over the role of law enforcement. (To its credit, the proposed Campus Accountability and Safety Act does recognize the important role the criminal justice system should play in campus sexual assault and calls for standardizing co-operation between colleges and local law enforcement so that more perpetrators are investigated by trained law-enforcement professionals.)

FIRE's Joseph Cohn says the unfortunate but pervasive message students get is that law enforcement is not there to help. "It's not perfect. But that's not the argument for seeking justice outside it." If victims don't go to the police, he adds, "the conviction rate is zero." He says when students are getting sexual assault education, administrators must emphasize the importance of procedures to protect evidence and must tell them about going to the hospital to get a timely rape kit—it has to be done within seventy-two hours. Doing so doesn't mean a student is committing to a criminal charge. But without such steps, it can be futile to later try to bring one.

9. The Way Forward

What is to be done? How can the government and institutions of higher education address sexual assault, support victims, identify predators, and not unfairly punish innocent students?

A good place to start would be scaling back the powers of the Department of Education's Office for Civil Rights, which has overstepped its bounds in micromanaging university policies and enforcing draconian rules that infringe on the rights of the accused. And before making policy based on alarming statistics, officials should ponder a study's limitations and read all the footnotes.

Rather than creating a separate (and unfair) system of justice, we should ensure the safety of college students the same way we ensure the safety of those who aren't in college. Instead of universities writing expansive and elaborate sexual conduct rules, they should rely on the narrower statutes that govern criminal sexual assault and civil sexual harassment. "Affirmative consent" regulations should be struck. These rules dictate how young adults in college make love, and that's both ridiculous and quixotic. (There's a vast difference between telling people how to conduct their sex lives and having laws that punish those who perpetrate sex crimes.) When universities do take action against a student for sexual misconduct, if the definition of misconduct is narrower, and if there is a return to a standard of "clear and convincing evidence," as there should be, there will be fewer miscarriages of justice.

Any student who feels she has been sexually victimized should be able to turn to campus counselors who are sensitive listeners and not crusaders. Students who have had a distressing sexual experience need supportive people to help them figure out their next steps. Maybe a potential criminal violation took place and the student needs an escort to the hospital, so that whatever her ultimate decision, crucial evidence is collected. Maybe it was simply a distressing encounter and counseling is the best path. The adults who help these young people should be able to recognize the difference between the two and not default to calling for the accused's head.

The prohibition about discussing the connection between alcohol and sexual assault should be lifted. We don't live in a perfect world, and while school administrators should do their best to provide safe environments, it is up to each individual to make wise decisions. Getting incapacitated has no upside for young men or women. Administrators ignore the role of alcohol in sexual assault at their peril, and at the peril of their students, men and women.

We also need to change the culture of discourse around sexual assault on campuses. To stand up for the rights of the accused is not to attack victims or women. Our colleges, like the rest of our society, must be places where you are innocent until proven guilty. The day after graduation, young men and women will be thrown into a world where there is no Gender-Based Misconduct Office. They will have to live by the rules of society at large. Higher education should ready our students for this reality, not shield them from it.

The New Republic

FINALIST—COLUMNS AND
COMMENTARY

*When they nominated Rebecca
Traister's work for* The New
Republic *for the National
Magazine Award for Columns and
Commentary, the Ellie judges
used phrases like "thoughtful
and wide ranging"; "fresh, often
unexpected analysis"; and
"desperately needed feminist
perspective" to describe it. The
topics here range from young
women's often complicated,
sometimes dangerous friendships
to the ugly, tangled history of sex
and race in America. (Magazine
journalism also takes it on the chin
a couple of times.) Traister joined*
The New Republic *in 2014 after
working at* Salon *and the* New
York Observer. *Founded in 1914
by leaders of the Progressive
movement,* The New Republic
*has been owned since 2012 by
Chris Hughes, cofounder of
Facebook.*

Rebecca Traister

When Michael Dunn Compared Himself to a Rape Victim, He Was Following an Old, Racist Script *and* I Don't Care If You Like It *and* The Slenderman Stabbing Shows Girls Will Be Girls, Too

When Michael Dunn Compared Himself to a Rape Victim, He Was Following an Old, Racist Script

In 2012, when Michael Dunn shot and killed a black seventeen-year-old who he thought was playing music too loud, the news was quickly situated in several ugly American storylines: about senseless gun culture, about racially motivated violence, about the impact of Florida's Stand Your Ground law.

On February 15, when a jury failed to convict Dunn of murdering Jordan Davis in a convenience store parking lot, Dunn became further entwined in an even older and possibly still more shameful American tale: the one in which white men are not forced to pay for the taking of black life.

And last Tuesday—when it was revealed that Dunn, a man who emptied ten rounds into a car full of unarmed teenagers, had compared his own situation to that of an imagined female rape victim—he became emblematic of a pathology that is even more particularly American, if less immediately discernible to modern news consumers: the summoning of the specter of black-on-white sexual assault as a justification for white-on-black violence.

"It's not quite the same, but it made me think of the old TV shows and movies, how the police used to think when a chick got raped, 'Oh, it's her fault because of the way she dressed,'" Dunn laughingly told his girlfriend in a jailhouse phone call released last week. He would not play the rape victim, Dunn continued. And so he fought back.

In making this analogy, Dunn shed contemporary light on America's perpetually warped racial psyche and tapped into some of its most chilling history.

It's a history that stretches back deep into Reconstruction, the period after the Civil War, when the increased civic and political power of formerly enslaved men, who could now vote and hold office, created a threat to exclusive white power. That increased public power got translated, in the white imagination, to a sexual threat.

Crystal Feimster, the Yale historian and author *of Southern Horrors: Women and the Politics of Rape and Lynching*, explained it this way by phone: "There's a long narrative in which white men who feel threatened by black men, in terms of economic power, political power, or even feeling that they might be physically assaulted—whether that feeling is real or imagined—link that black male power to sexuality because black men have always been demonized as sexually bestialized figures."

.   .   .

In the years following the Civil War, rumors of black sexual advances on white women spurred white mobs to destroy towns where African Americans had built up any sort of power. In 1898, in Wilmington, North Carolina, a town in which African Americans were thriving in business and government, whispers about sexual assaults on white women were used to incite a riot, in which murderous white-supremacist insurgents burned down the black newspaper building and overthrew the legitimately elected multiracial city government, in this country's only coup d'etat.

The protection of white bodies from black sexual advance often served as the excuse for lynchings, which were so common that, according to a 1933 volume cited the by historian Isabel Wilkerson, "someone was hanged or burned alive across the South every four days from 1889–1929."

That rape was being used as a metaphor for other kinds of incursions on white dominance was not lost on antilynching activists, including Ida B. Wells and Frederick Douglass, who would write (not quite accurately) that "in slaveholding times no one heard of any such crime [rape of a white woman] by a Negro," and that "it is only since the Negro has become a citizen and a voter that this charge has been made."

It was a charge that never stopped being made, with horrific repercussions. In 1923, Wilkerson has recalled, a white mob burned a black town in Florida after a white woman claimed to have been attacked by a black man; "anything that was black or looked black was killed," one survivor said. In 1934, a twenty-three-year-old black field hand accused of the rape and murder of a white woman was castrated, tortured, and hung from an oak tree. No one was ever charged in the man's murder. In 1955, four-teen-year-old Emmett Till was beaten and killed in Mississippi after allegedly making a pass at a white woman; his killers were never convicted.

This is the history Michael Dunn summoned in drawing an apparently light-hearted comparison between his own reaction to the black boys he shot and the experience of a rape victim.

Dunn certainly isn't the only contemporary white man to con-tinue to lean on this rhetoric. We've been knee-deep in it ever since our first African American president took office in 2009. That's the year Rush Limbaugh said "We are being told that we have to . . . bend over, grab the ankles, bend over forward, backward, whichever, because his father was black, because this is the first black president." In 2010, the actor Jon Voight went on Mike Huckabee's FOX News show and read an anti-Obama letter in which he argued that with his "socialistic, Marxist teaching," President Obama "rapes this nation." Last year, Tea Party Nation president Judson Philips promoted a piece about the Affordable Care Act that included an extended rape metaphor and the ar-gument that "the Obama Regime" has a simple message, "Lie back and quit fighting and eventually you will enjoy the experience." Around the same time, a conservative group funded by the Koch brothers aired an anti-Obamacare ad depicting a masked Uncle Sam emerging from between the stirruped legs of a woman get-ting a pelvic exam. So popular is the image of Barack Obama as rapist that it's possible to buy a variety of bumper stickers bear-ing slogans like, "Bend Over, Here Comes YOUR President."

·　　　·　　　·

What's revealed by these kinds of constructions is the degree to which white America sees the sharing of space or power with nonsubservient African Americans—presidential, economic, po-litical, social, even the sharing of a convenience-store parking lot—as a physical assault on a body, a national body, still presumed to be white.

Never mind the irony, that the history of forced physical incursion operates largely in reverse of the white-rape-victim narrative, that in fact, it was whites who forcibly moved black bodies to this country, who bought and sold and raped enslaved African Americans. Never mind that it was white mobs who lynched men and burnt towns and tortured and assaulted black women throughout the end of the nineteenth and early twentieth centuries or that it was white-run government agencies and economic institutions that physically cut off African Americans from civic and economic participation later in the twentieth century by redlining and building highways through black neighborhoods.

That history of white violence against blacks gets reversed—or at least imaginatively explained away—as soon as a man like Dunn redraws the picture, suggesting that it was he who was the victim, the white body in danger of sexual violation. Never mind that Dunn himself faced *no* physical violation, sexual or otherwise.

Because tangled in Dunn's allusion is another, gendered inconsistency: the diminishment of the experience of rape as it experienced by actual people. It's telling that the rape victim summoned by Dunn is fictional, a television character, that she's not a woman, but a "chick," and that even as he puts himself, imaginatively, in her position, he still leaves room to blame her for the crime committed against her. She is a "chick [who] got raped." In his formulation, she is the actor in the situation, the one who "got" herself violated.

The minimizing of real assault against women in service of a narrative that explains white male violence also fits a larger historical pattern. While much of the Reconstruction and Progressive-era mob violence was committed in the name of protecting white women, the men committing the crimes had little respect for those women's bodies. They used them as an excuse to sack black towns and kill and torture black men and women, but as Feimster points out, nineteenth-century law didn't even treat rape as a "crime against a woman, but against her husband, her brother, the men whose property had been violated."

The historian Martha Hodes has shown how often, the very women used as the excuse for retribution against blacks were themselves assaulted by the same mobs, especially if they were poor. She cites a Reconstruction-era case in Georgia in which a black man was castrated by members of the Ku Klux Klan for living with a white woman; Klansmen then "took the woman, laid her down on the ground, then cut a slit on each side of her orifice, put a large padlock in it, locked it up, and threw away the key." Hodes also cites a more recent example of a similar phenomenon: in 1989, when sixteen-year-old African American Yusuf Hawkins was killed in New York City by a mob of white men who believed him to be dating a white woman, the young woman in question was denigrated by some neighbors with more ferocity than was directed at Hawkins' killers.

This inconsistency—the use of and disregard for women in these formulations—finds its contemporary equivalent with the right-wingers who fight against Obamacare with an image of a predatory Uncle Sam and who fret over being anally violated by a black president and who are also enthusiastic about mandatory transvaginal ultrasounds. They're the same guys who can't seem to be convinced that the literal rape—of actual human beings, many of whom are women—is a serious crime, unless it can be proven to be "honest" "real, genuine" or "legitimate."

Michael Dunn was not honestly, really, genuinely, legitimately raped by anyone. He was not assaulted by anyone or even threatened by anyone. He is the one who killed another human being.

And yet this country has given him a script. Not just the one he remembers from old television shows and movies, but one that has played out in real life again and again over centuries. It's a script that tells him that his crimes are justified, will be forgiven and, yes, forgotten, if he can only successfully call forth the image of the "chick [who] got raped."

I Don't Care If You Like It

Last week, I got into a fight on Twitter with *New York* magazine's Jonathan Chait, whose work I respect, and it wasn't about anything that either of us had written; rather, we were tussling over the merits of a piece written by Tom Junod, for *Esquire*, about how today's forty-two-year-old women are hotter than ever before.

There's no need to linger over our differences: I thought the article was a piece of sexist tripe, celebrating a handful of Pilates-toned, famous, white-plus–Maya Rudolph women as having improved on the apparently dismal aesthetics of previous generations; my primary objections to the piece have been ably laid out by other critics. Chait tweeted that he viewed the piece as a "mostly laudable" sign of progress: a critique not of earlier iterations of forty-two-year-old womanhood, but rather of the old sexist beauty standards that did not celebrate those women; he saw it as an acknowledgment of maturing male attitudes toward women's value.

The truth is, had Chait been correct about it being a thoughtful piece laying into the entrenched short-sightedness and sexist cruelty of male-controlled media, I might have hated it *more*. Then I would have felt obligated to feel grateful for it, grateful in the same way I'm supposed to feel grateful toward, say, Marvel Comics for making Thor a woman or toward Harry Reid for challenging Mitch McConnell on some typically boorish and inane statement how women have achieved workforce equality. In its actual form, I didn't have to consider thinking *Yay, thanks* for some crumbs of enlightened thinking, for some slightly nuanced improvements in the daily, punishing business of publicly evaluating and then reevaluating women's worth.

Instead, I've been thinking about an anecdote in Tina Fey's *Bossypants*. Amy Poehler, then new to *Saturday Night Live*, was engaging in some loud and unladylike vulgarity in the writers' room when the show's then-star Jimmy Fallon jokingly told her to cut it out, saying, "It's not cute! I don't like it!" In Fey's retelling, Poehler "went black in the eyes for a second, and wheeled around on him," forcefully informing him: "I don't fucking care if you like it."

I don't think I'm alone in feeling this way. Just this week, the journalist Megan Carpentier wrote a piece about the evolving public appraisals of Hillary Clinton's facial expressions that concluded with her suggestion that we get over the idea of 2014 being "the year of the strong female politician" and aim instead for "the year of the strong female politician who doesn't give a fuck if you think she's pretty."

Carpentier doesn't care if you like it. Neither does the Buzzfeed writer Arianna Rebolini, who wrote this week about the video for John Legend's song "You and I," about the diverse beauty of women. Rebolini dutifully *yay-thanks*-ed the fact that it's "uplifting to see these women—of all ages, sizes, ethnicities—in the spotlight" before confessing her discomfort with how the song's lyrics fall into the well-worn pop tradition of celebrating the beauty of women who don't know they're beautiful. "These songs, which presume to assure women that they are attractive (and, by extension, worthwhile)," Rebolini writes, "assume that the singer's relationship to our bodies overrules *our* relationship with them."

Arianna Rebolini doesn't care if you like it. "Don't tell us we don't know we're beautiful," she concludes. "And certainly don't tell us that our ignorance to this fact is our best quality. We're good."

I suspect that a lot of this irritation over the small stuff right now is directly related to the fact that we're mired in a moment at which lots and lots of women are *not good*, for reasons far graver than anything having to do with *Esquire*, Jimmy Fallon, John Legend, or Hillary Clinton's Bitchy Resting Face.

Stacia Brown recently wrote a lyrical, sad piece in *Gawker* that began with a description of some raucous young men outside her sleeping daughter's window, speculating about whether a woman they knew had HIV. She described those boys as "negotiating [the woman's] worth to them. . . . It isn't clear to me if they even know that it is moot to denigrate a woman for contracting a disease that she has likely gotten for a man. . . . [But] in 2014, only women are called 'loose' in voices that carry." These days, Brown went on, "casting lots about a young girl's sexual history, while walking in the summer night under the neighbors' open windows, is practically innocuous. . . . At least they are not bragging about having roofied her."

But Brown doesn't emphasize her gratitude that these men were not doing something worse, largely because her essay is actually about Jada, the sixteen-year-old Houston girl who last week told the story of how she was drugged and sexually assaulted at a party; images of her naked, limp body were shared—and mocked—on social media.

Jada's story recalls too many other recent headlines but happens to have come out at the same time as last weekend's lengthy *New York Times* investigation of Hobart & William Smith's handling of charges that football players sexually assaulted a freshman girl. The *Times* story was about a lot of things—differences between campus and police investigations, a heightened public awareness about the frequency of coerced or violent sexual encounters on college campuses. But at its heart, it was a story about how women are assessed: by disciplinary committees, police departments, their friends, the public, and by the people they identify as their assailants. It was about how female availability and consent and intoxication are appraised based on how women look, dance, dress, and act, even when those appraisals are at odds with medical evidence, eyewitness accounts, inconsistent stories from accused parties, and certainly with the woman's own interpretation of her experience or intentions.

This comfort with group assessment of femininity in turn reminds me of the ease with which women's choices regarding their bodies, futures, health, sex, and family life are up for public evaluation. Women are labeled as good or bad, as moral or immoral, by major religions and "closely held corporations," whose rights to allow those estimations to dictate their corporate obligations are upheld over the rights of the women themselves by high courts.

It has lately been made perfectly clear, for example, that while in many places women should not be allowed—and increasingly *are* not allowed—to run their own independent calculations about whether or not to get abortions, other people, unspecified people standing outside clinics, should be allowed—*are* now allowed—to get in those women's faces and publicly render *their* judgments and voice *their* opinions about those women and their circumstances.

These days, law enforcement can comfortably deem a Tennessee mother unfit and jail her for having taken methamphetamine while pregnant. Authorities can condemn—by arrest and the removal of her child to foster care—South Carolina mother Debra Harrell, who allowed her nine-year-old daughter to play at the park while she worked at McDonald's. It's such a comfortable pose, gathering around women and deciding what we think of them—hot or not, alluring or tragic, moral or immoral, responsible or irresponsible, capable of consent or incapable of consent, maternal or neglectful.

The problem isn't so simple as a man-versus-woman frame. Examples of this evaluative pattern are rarely as easy to parse as when a men's magazine writer treats some women as steaks who've gotten tastier with age, Pilates, and feminism. After all, women ran the disciplinary committee that was so quick to dismiss rape charges at Hobart & William Smith. On Tuesday, the Tennessee representative Marsha Blackburn and other female antichoice activists testified against the Women's Health Protection Act, a bill that would ban onerous restrictions on abortion rights and that was sponsored by senators Tammy Baldwin and Richard Blumenthal, a man. Meanwhile, a bill to reverse the Hobby Lobby decision was cosponsored by senators Patty Murray and Mark Udall, another man. Many of the sharpest take-downs of Junod's piece came from men, and I want to note that my Twitter-sparrer Jonathan Chait yesterday wrote one of the finest and most astute pieces about the injustice of Harrell's arrest.

Yay, thanks! No, really, I mean it.

But what all these issues, no matter how gigantically separated an *Esquire* puff piece and a Tennessee mother's jailing for meth may seem, reflect back at us: How, in this country, every barometer by which female worth is measured—from the superficial to the life-altering, the appreciative to the punitive—has long been calibrated to "dude," whether or not those measurements are actually being taken by dudes. Men still run, or at bare minimum have shaped and codified the attitudes of, the churches, the courts, the universities, the police departments, the corporations that so freely determine women's worth. As Beyoncé observed last year, "Money gives men power to run the show. It gives men the power to define value. They define what's sexy. And men define what's feminine. It's ridiculous."

It *is* ridiculous, and I wish we could all tell them how little it matters what they think. Except that of course most women, those who bear the brunt of these assessments, aren't Beyoncé or Amy Poehler—who, not coincidentally, was on Junod's list of newly untragic forty-two-year-olds. Instead, they are women who may not be able to pay for Pilates, let alone for day care or contraceptives, who may need but not be able to afford drug treatment, who

Esquire would likely still rate as not-hot or more likely not rate at all, but whose fates nonetheless rest in the hands of empowered committees on the general value and status of womanhood in America.

I wish it were different. I wish that every woman whose actions and worth are parsed and restricted, congratulated and condemned in this country might just once get to wheel around—on the committee that doesn't believe their medically corroborated story of assault, or on the protesters who tell them that termination is a sin they will regret, or on the boss who tells them he doesn't believe in their sexual choices, or on the midfifties man who congratulates them, or himself, on finding them appealing deep into their dotage—and go black in the eyes and say, "I don't fucking care if you like it."

The Slenderman Stabbing Shows Girls Will Be Girls, Too

News of youthful violence is all too familiar to us: the shootings, stabbings, bombings perpetrated by young people are the stuff we—necessarily—analyze, search for patterns, try to make sense of, as we did two weeks ago in the wake of Elliot Rodger's massacre in Isla Vista.

But this week came a different kind of story, about two twelve-year-old neighbors from the Milwaukee suburb of Waukesha, Wisconsin, who stabbed one of their friends nearly to death in the woods. According to reports, one of the assailants pushed the victim down and told the other, "Go ballistic. Go crazy," before the other did as instructed, stabbing the girl nineteen times as she cried, "I hate you. I trusted you." The stabbing victim survived and crawled to the edge of the woods for help; her two attackers were arrested. One of them reportedly told police, "It was weird that I didn't feel remorse," while the other described a more torn reaction: "The bad part of me wanted her to die. The good part of me wanted her to live."

The press and local authorities promptly glommed on to the admittedly shivery detail of the story: that the stabbers claimed to have acted in an effort to appease "Slenderman," a fictional child-stalker whose spectral presence has been created, spread, and improvised upon by scores of chat-room users, filmmakers, and online storytellers.

There are three particularly defining elements to this story: that authorities want to prosecute these preteens, who may have acted based on a fictionalized belief system, as adults; that the assailants are young women who do not fit the description of disaffected masculinity that has become so horrifyingly linked to instances of youthful violence; and that everyone immediately decided that this was a story about the evils of Internet technology. "Unmonitored and unrestricted access to the Internet by children is a growing and alarming problem," said Waukesha police chief Russell Jack in a press conference on Monday. "This should be a wake-up call for parents. Parents are strongly encouraged to restrict and monitor their children's Internet usage."

But what's interesting about the case, or at least the little we know about it so far, is not that it's an example of a new and looming online threat. Rather, it appears to echo patterns of behavior—belief in culturally supported fantasies, tightly cathected bonds between young women, an intensity of connection that has occasionally led to violence—that have occurred repeatedly, in various forms, throughout history and around the world. And they happen outside the heterosexual framework we use to understand Rodgers's misogynistic rampage. This crime is one that reminds us of the central role that homosocial bonding plays in the lives of the many young women who spend their adolescent years battling, and occasionally "seeing," their own demons.

If the two Wisconsin assailants were indeed motivated by their belief in a fantasy figure of Slenderman—and I hasten to add that it's possible this is just an agreed-upon excuse designed to appeal to Internet-paranoid parents—they are not the first young women to have confused socially crafted fictions with reality.

Joan of Arc was estimated to have been about twelve years old in 1424 when she first saw the Archangel Michael and Saints Margaret and Catherine in her father's garden in Domrémy, France, a vision that inspired her to lead an army to drive the English from France. Four centuries later, fourteen-year-old Bernadette Soubirous, an asthmatic shepherdess who'd been shuttled between her home and a set of foster parents, saw a vision of the Virgin Mary in a grotto in Lourdes, France. Her vision had less militaristic consequences than Joan's; Lourdes remains a spiritual destination to this day. In the early 1980s, during a period of building aggressions between the Hutus and the Tutsis, a group of young women at Kibeho College in southern Rwanda claimed to experience visions of the Virgin Mary, urging them to prevent the oncoming bloodshed that would be the Rwandan genocide. Less spiritual were the convictions of nineteenth-century female readers who wept by the Trinity churchyard gravesite of Charlotte Temple, the fictional heroine of Susanna Rowson's eponymous 1791 novel of seduction and abandonment.

Writing this, I think even of the hours and months my high school best friend and I spent obsessing over fictional characters on soap operas. None of which led us to stab anyone, but which was certainly symptomatic of how powerful and intoxicating escapist fantasy from the sometimes scary world of female adolescence, especially in thrilling tandem with another person, can be.

Indeed, for all the time we spend wringing our hands over the deleterious impact of popular culture on young people, we spend far too little considering the impact that young people can have on each other.

The intensity of bonds between young women have gone especially underexamined in recent years. For generations, it was accepted that adolescent girls might form highly emotional, deeply felt relationships with each other, kind of proto-marriages. For periods of American history, adolescent and teen schoolgirls regularly shared beds, openly expressed their adoration and devotion to each other, and were sometimes said to be "smashed"—entwined in committed partnerships. But in the early twentieth century, as heterosexual marriage came to be seen as a relationship based on emotion and mutual desire, female partnerships began to be seen as competitive and suspect. Young women were encouraged to train their attentions on young men; a dating culture emerged, and we have not spent nearly enough time since acknowledging the powerful influence that adolescent girls continue to have on each other.

Not that that influence is usually murderous! But popular narrative—and the historical record—does contain some connections between female alliance and violent action. Sometimes, female friendships have been depicted as the basis of strength from which women can exact revenge on men who have abused or taken advantage of them, as in movies like *Thelma and Louise* and *9 to 5*.

The 1994 movie *Heavenly Creatures* is an example of a different kind of arc: in which female friendship is so intense that it results in the murder of another woman. The film was based on the true story of New Zealand sixteen-year-olds Pauline Parker and Juliet Hulme, best friends from Christchurch who bludgeoned Parker's mother to death in Victoria Park in 1954. Parker and Hulme had bonded over illnesses they'd suffered as children, but through their friendship began to build an active fantasy life, with characters and stories they'd create and act out together. When their parents—worried that their bond was homosexual—tried to separate them, the girls conspired to kill Parker's mother.

They were tried as juveniles and spent five years in prison; Hulme went on to become a mystery novelist published under the name Anne Perry.

2012 brought a recent case of intra-gender violence, the murder of sixteen-year-old West Virginia student Skylar Neese by her two best friends, Rachel Shoaf and Shelia Eddy. The trio had apparently had a falling out, with Neese tweeting, in the days before her death, "you doing shit like that is why I will NEVER completely *trust* you." After the eventual confessions of Eddy and Shoaf, it was revealed that the two assailants offered only one explanation for their crime—that they had stopped liking their friend—and that the murder had involved a degree of synchronicity: they had agreed to count to three before stabbing Neese. As Eddy would later tweet, horribly, "we really did go on three," a sentiment that seems to marvel at the mirroring connection she had with her co-murderer.

And, of course, there was the witchcraft panic of Salem, Massachusetts, in early 1692 and 1693, in which a series of accusations—made first by a collection of pubescent and teenaged girls who were experiencing muscular spasms, tics, and fits—led to the prosecution of 144 people and the execution of 20 convicted of witchcraft.

There are many conflicting theories about psychological, political, and social explanations for the Salem witchhunts. Some historians blame the rise of mercantile capitalism and economic tensions between Salem Village and Salem Town; some cite the boredom of and inattention to young women in the town. What is certainly true is that the panic began when a group of socially affiliated girls began exhibiting physical symptoms and describing spectral visions.

The historian Mary Beth Norton, who argued in her book *In the Devil's Snare* that the witchcraft crisis stemmed from anxieties over the French and Indian war, border disputes over Maine, and a series of violent attacks on Puritans by natives, said by phone that while court records don't leave us with detailed evidence of how close the young accusers' relationships were to each other, she could think of at least one tight alliance: between twelve-year-old Ann Putnam Jr. and Mercy Lewis, an eighteen-year-old Maine native whose entire family had been killed in an Indian raid and had been placed as a servant in the Putnam household. Despite their age difference, Norton said, the girls were very close, and, she guessed, likely shared a bed or at least a sleeping loft, as per the domestic arrangements of the time. She also noted that it was likely that the interpretation of the girls' fits and visions was guided by Puritan beliefs that Native Americans were devil worshippers and that, in the midst of bloody conflict between native and Puritan populations, translating the physical tics and social confusions of young women into a widespread campaign against fellow Puritans permitted some fantasy of control, since "if you can't defeat the Indians in the woods, you can defeat witches in the courtroom."

Norton drew a connection between Salem and the more recent, nonviolent case of cheerleaders in Le Roy, New York, a suburb of Rochester, who exhibited physical symptoms that strongly echoed those displayed by Salem girls. In 2011, a group of these Le Roy students, many of them cheerleaders, began to suffer from tics and stutters, humming, and involuntary muscle spasms.

And while our cultural lens wasn't trained on demonic possession anymore, nearly every other contemporary interpretation was brought to bear: therapists, activists, and journalists attributed the outbreak to everything from environmental toxins to the postmanufacturing economy, social, familial, and academic stresses to absent fathers and mass hysteria.

As the reporter Susan Dominus reported in her excellent piece on Le Roy, the case appeared to come down to "two equally poorly understood phenomena: conversion disorder and mass psychogenic illness." As Dominus reported, "Half of mass psychogenic illnesses occur in schools, and they are far more common in young women than in any other category." In her piece, Dominus also explored the ways in which many of the sufferers in Le Roy seemed to entail social mirroring, the unconscious sharing of symptoms and affliction. Psychogenic illness, she wrote, "seems deeply connected to empathy and to a longing for what social psychologists call affiliation: belonging."

Of course, that's not to say that any of this may have anything to do with what happened in Waukesha, Wisconsin. But what is true is that adolescent intensity, obsession, fantasy, derangement, illness, and, yes, sometimes violence, are not the exclusive domain of boys. To consider the kinds of complicated relationships girls have with each other, we need to move beyond the (hetero) sexual framework we've come to accept as the defining norm of adolescence. We must acknowledge that there is a universe of female communication, commitment, and confusion that looms large for many and that can, in rare instances, have dire consequences.

Vanity Fair

FINALIST—ESSAYS AND
CRITICISM

*Quoting from the story itself,
the Ellie judges said this about
"Shame and Survival": "Monica
Lewinsky writes with authority
and conviction about an Internet-
driven culture 'that not only
encourages and revels in
Schadenfreude but also rewards
those who humiliate others.'
This deeply touching essay
accomplished precisely what its
writer set out to achieve. Lewinsky
was no longer seen as a punchline
but as a woman determined to live
her own life." Relaunched in 1983
(an earlier* Vanity Fair *ceased
publication in 1936),* Vanity Fair
*has been edited since 1992 by
ASME Hall of Famer Graydon
Carter. Justly celebrated for its
entertainment coverage and
celebrity portraits, the magazine
has earned Ellie recognition for its
literary journalism more than
three dozen times since Carter
became editor.*

Monica Lewinsky

Shame and Survival

"How does it feel to be America's premier blow-job queen?"

It was early 2001. I was sitting on the stage of New York's Cooper Union in the middle of taping a Q&A for an HBO documentary. I was the subject. And I was thunderstruck.

Hundreds of people in the audience, mostly students, were staring at me, many with their mouths agape, wondering if I would dare to answer this question.

The main reason I had agreed to participate in the program was not to rehash or revise the story line of Interngate but to try to shift the focus to meaningful issues. Many troubling political and judicial questions had been brought to light by the investigation and impeachment of President Bill Clinton. But the most egregious had been generally ignored. People seemed indifferent to the deeper matters at hand, such as the erosion of private life in the public sphere, the balance of power and gender inequality in politics and media, and the erosion of legal protections to ensure that neither a parent nor a child should ever have to testify against each other.

How naïve I was.

There were gasps and sputters from the audience. Numerous blurred, faceless people called out, *"Don't answer it!"*

"It's hurtful and it's insulting," I said, attempting to gather my wits. "And as insulting as it is to me, it's even more insulting to my family. I don't actually know why this whole story became about oral sex. I don't. It was a mutual relationship. . . . The fact that it did is maybe a result of a male-dominated society."

The audience laughed. Maybe they were surprised to hear these words coming from me.

I looked straight at the smirking guy who had asked the question. "You might be better poised to answer that." After a pause, I added, "That's probably cost me another year of therapy."

You could argue that in agreeing to participate in an HBO documentary called *Monica in Black and White* I had signed up to be shamed and publicly humiliated yet again. You might even think I would have been inured to humiliation. This encounter at Cooper Union, after all, paled in comparison with the 445-page Starr Report, which was the culmination of independent counsel Kenneth Starr's four-year investigation of the Clinton White House. It included chapter and verse about my intimate sexual activities, along with transcripts of audiotapes that chronicled many of my private conversations. But the "BJ Queen" question—which was included in the show when it aired on HBO in 2002—sat with me for a long time after the audience left and the taping wrapped.

True, this wasn't the first time I'd been stigmatized for my affair with Bill Clinton. But never had I been so directly confronted, one-on-one, with such a crass characterization. One of the unintended consequences of my agreeing to put myself out there and to try to tell the truth had been that shame would once again be hung around my neck like a scarlet-*A* albatross. Believe me, once it's on, it is a bitch to take off.

Had that awkward moment at Cooper Union aired only a few years later, with the advent of social media, the humiliation would have been even more devastating. That clip would have gone viral on Twitter, YouTube, Facebook, *TMZ*, *Gawker*. It would have become a meme of its own on Tumblr. The viralness itself would have merited mention on the *Daily Beast* and *Huffington Post*. As it was, it was viral enough, and, thanks to the all-encompassing nature of the Web, you can, twelve years later, watch it all day long on YouTube if you want to (but I really hope you have better things to do with your time).

I know I'm not alone when it comes to public humiliation. No one, it seems, can escape the unforgiving gaze of the Internet, where gossip, half-truths, and lies take root and fester. We have created, to borrow a term from the historian Nicolaus Mills, a "culture of humiliation" that not only encourages and revels in Schadenfreude but also rewards those who humiliate others, from the ranks of the paparazzi to the gossip bloggers, the late-night comedians, and the Web "entrepreneurs" who profit from clandestine videos.

Yes, we're all connected now. We can tweet a revolution in the streets or chronicle achievements large and small. But we're also caught in a feedback loop of defame and shame, one in which we have become both perps and victims. We may not have become a crueler society—although it sure feels as if we have—but the Internet has seismically shifted the tone of our interactions. The ease, the speed, and the distance that our electronic devices afford us can also make us colder, more glib, and less concerned about the consequences of our pranks and prejudice. Having lived humiliation in the most intimate possible way, I marvel at how willingly we have all signed on to this new way of being.

In my own case, each easy click of that YouTube link reinforces the archetype, despite my efforts to parry it away: Me, America's BJ Queen. That Intern. That Vixen. Or, in the inescapable phrase of our forty-second president, "That Woman."

It may surprise you to learn that I'm actually a person.

· · ·

In 1998, when news of my affair with Bill Clinton broke, I was arguably the most humiliated person in the world. Thanks to the *Drudge Report*, I was also possibly the first person whose global humiliation was driven by the Internet.

For several years I tried my hand in the fashion-accessory business and became involved in various media projects, including the HBO documentary. Then I lay low for the most part. (The last major interview I granted was ten years ago.) After all, not lying low had exposed me to criticism for trying to "capitalize" on my "notoriety." Apparently, others talking about me is OK; me speaking out for myself is not. I turned down offers that would have earned me more than $10 million because they didn't feel like the right thing to do. Over time, the media circus quieted down, but it never quite moved on, even as I attempted to move on.

Meanwhile, I watched my friends' lives move forward. Marriages. Kids. Degrees. (Second marriages. More kids. More degrees.) I decided to turn over a new leaf and attend grad school.

I moved to England to study, to challenge myself, to escape scrutiny, and to reimagine my identity. My professors and fellow students at the London School of Economics were wonderful—welcoming and respectful. I had more anonymity in London, perhaps due to the fact that I spent most of my waking hours in class or buried in the library. In 2006, I graduated with a master's in social psychology. My master's thesis examined social bias in the courtroom and was titled "In Search of the Impartial Juror: An Exploration of Pretrial Publicity and the Third Person Effect." I liked to joke that I was trading the blue dress for blue stockings, and the degree provided new scaffolding to hang my life experiences on. It would also prove, so I hoped, to be a gateway to a more normal life.

I moved between London, Los Angeles, New York, and Portland, Oregon, interviewing for a variety of jobs that fell under the umbrella of "creative communication" and "branding," with an emphasis on charity campaigns. Yet, because of what potential employers so tactfully referred to as my "history," I was never "quite right" for the position. In some cases, I was right for all the wrong reasons, as in, "Of course, your job would require you to attend our events." And, *of course*, these would be events at which press would be in attendance.

In one promising job interview that took place during the run-up to the 2008 primary season, the conversation took an interesting turn. "So here's the thing, Monica," the interviewer said. "You're clearly a bright young woman and affable, but for us—and probably any other organization that relies on grants and other government funding—it's risky. We would first need a letter of indemnification from the Clintons. After all, there is a 25 percent chance that Mrs. Clinton will be the next president." I gave a fake smile and said, "I understand."

Another job interview, this one typical: walked into the stark, terminally cool reception area of a hip-yet-prestigious advertising agency in Los Angeles, my hometown. As always, I put on my best "I'm friendly, not a diva" smile. "Hi. Monica Lewinsky here to see So-and-So."

The twenty-something receptionist pushed her black-rimmed hipster frames up her nose. "Monica *who?*"

Before I could answer, another twenty-something, in skinny jeans, plaid shirt, and bow tie, rushed over and interrupted: "*Ms. Lewinsky.*" Like a maître d', he continued, "*Pleasure to have you here.* I'll let So-and-So know you've arrived. Soy latte? Green tea? Filtered water?"

I found myself sitting at a small round table, face-to-face with So-and-So, the agency's head of strategy and planning. We talked. She kept wincing. This was not going well. I tried to keep myself from getting flustered. Now she was not only wincing but also clearing her throat. Was that perspiration on her brow? It hit me: *she* was nervous, in full-tic mode.

I've had to become adept at handling any number of reactions in social situations and job interviews. I get it: it must be disconcerting to sit across from "That Woman." Needless to say, I didn't get the position.

I eventually came to realize that traditional employment might not be an option for me. I've managed to get by (barely, at times) with my own projects, usually with start-ups that I have participated in or with loans from friends and family.

In another job interview I was asked, "If you were a brand, which brand would you be?" Let me tell you, when you're Monica Lewinsky, that is one loaded question.

In September of 2010, the culmination of these experiences began to snap into a broader context for me. A phone conversation with my mother shifted the lens through which I viewed my world. We were discussing the tragic death of Tyler Clementi. Tyler, you will recall, was an eighteen-year-old Rutgers freshman who was secretly streamed via Webcam kissing another man. Days later, after being derided and humiliated on social media, he committed suicide by jumping off the George Washington Bridge.

My mom wept. Sobbing, she kept repeating over and over, "How his parents must feel . . . his poor parents."

It was an unbearably tragic event, and while hearing of it brought me to tears, too, I couldn't quite grasp why my mom was so distraught. And then it dawned on me: she was reliving 1998, when she wouldn't let me out of her sight. She was replaying those weeks when she stayed by my bed, night after night, because I, too, was suicidal. The shame, the scorn, and the fear that had been thrown at her daughter left her afraid that I would take my own life—a fear that I would be literally humiliated to death. (I have never actually attempted suicide, but I had strong suicidal temptations several times during the investigations and during one or two periods after.)

I would never be so presumptuous as to equate my own story with Tyler Clementi's. After all, my public humiliation had been the result of my involvement with a world-renowned public figure—that is, a consequence of my own poor choices. But in that moment, when I felt the depths of my mother's anguish, I wished I could have had a chance to have spoken to Tyler about how my love life, my sex life, my most private moments, my most sensitive secrets, had been broadcast around the globe. I wished I had been able to say to him that I knew a little of how it might have felt for him to be exposed before the world. And, as hard as it is to imagine surviving it, it is possible.

In the wake of Tyler's tragedy, my own suffering took on a different meaning. Perhaps by sharing my story, I reasoned, I might be able to help others in their darkest moments of humiliation. The question became: How do I find and give a purpose to my past? It was my Prufrockian moment: "Do I dare / Disturb the universe?" Or, in my case, the Clinton universe.

·　　·　　·

Despite a decade of self-imposed silence, I have been periodically resuscitated as part of the national conversation, almost always in connection with the Clintons. For instance, in January and February of this year, Rand Paul, the Kentucky senator and a possible 2016 Republican presidential aspirant, managed to drag me into the preelection muck. He fought back against the Democrats' charges of a GOP "war on women" by arguing that Bill Clinton had committed workplace "violence" and acted in a "predatory" manner against "a twenty-year-old girl who was there from college."

Sure, my boss took advantage of me, but I will always remain firm on this point: it was a consensual relationship. Any "abuse" came in the aftermath, when I was made a scapegoat in order to protect his powerful position.

So, trying to disappear has not kept me out of the fray. I am, for better or for worse, presumed to be a known quantity. Every day I am recognized. *Every day.* Sometimes a person will walk past me again and again, as if I wouldn't notice. (Thankfully, 99.9 percent of the time when strangers do say something to me they are supportive and respectful.) Every day someone mentions me in a tweet or a blog post and not altogether kindly. Every day, it seems, my name shows up in an op-ed column or a press clip or two—mentioned in passing in articles on subjects as disparate as millennials, *Scandal,* and French president François Hollande's love life. Miley Cyrus references me in her twerking stage act, Eminem raps about me, and Beyoncé's latest hit gives me a shout-out. Thanks, Beyoncé, but if we're verbing, I think you meant "Bill Clinton'd all on my gown," not "Monica Lewinsky'd."

With every man I date (*yes,* I date!), I go through some degree of 1998 whiplash. I need to be extremely circumspect about what it means to be "public" with someone. In the early years postimpeachment, I once left a front-row seat along the third-base line at a Yankees game when I learned that my date—a guy whose company I thoroughly enjoyed—was actually in another relationship. It was only a green-card marriage, but I freaked that we could be photographed together and someone might call the gossip rags. I've become adept at figuring out when men are interested in me for the wrong reason. Thankfully, those have been few and far between. But every man that has been special to me over the past sixteen years has helped me find another piece of myself—the self that was shattered in 1998. And so, no matter the heartbreak, tears, or disenchantment, I'll always be grateful to them.

.   .   .

In February of this year, around the same time Senator Paul put me back into the unwanted spotlight, I became the "narcissistic loony toon," the latest twist on Me as Archetype.

A snapshot of a scenario I've grown all too accustomed to, even as I attempt to move on with my life: A shrill ring interrupts the rhythms of my day. The call—from the doorman of the apartment building where I'm staying in New York—leads me to an exasperated "*What? Again?*" They've reappeared: the paparazzi, like swallows, have returned to the sidewalk outside, pacing and circling and pacing some more.

I hit the computer. Time for a little self-Google. (Oh, dear reader, please do not judge.) My heart sinks. There's an explosion on Google News. I know what this means. Whatever day I've planned has been jettisoned. To leave the house—and risk a photo—only ensures that the story will stay alive.

The cameras have returned because of the headlines: a conservative website has gone poking around the University of Arkansas archive of one of Hillary Clinton's closest friends and admirers, Diane Blair, and has unearthed a cache of memos from the 1990s. In some of them, Blair, who died in 2000, quotes the former first lady about her husband's relationship with me. Though Hillary, according to Blair's notes, claimed to find her husband's "lapse" inexcusable, she praised him for trying to "manage someone who was clearly a 'narcissistic loony toon.'"

My first thought, as I was getting up to speed: If that's the *worst* thing she said, I should be so lucky. Mrs. Clinton, I read, had supposedly confided to Blair that, in part, she blamed *herself* for her husband's affair (by being emotionally neglectful) and seemed to forgive him. Although she regarded Bill as having engaged in "gross inappropriate behavior," the affair was, nonetheless, "consensual (was not a power relationship)."

I field the usual calls from friends who lend moral support whenever these volcanic media stories erupt. They diffuse the tension with good-natured teasing: "So, are we changing your monogram to NLT?" I try to ignore the former first lady's long-buried comments. Given my experiences with Linda Tripp, I know better than anyone what it's like to have a conversation with a girlfriend exposed and scrutinized, taken out of context. But, even so, it begins to gnaw at me. I realize that Hillary Clinton was—unlike me when Tripp was prying loose my innermost secrets and insecurities and recording them surreptitiously—fully aware of this documentation: she's the one who, according to the memos, asked Blair to keep a record or diary of their discussions for archival purposes.

Yes, I get it. Hillary Clinton wanted it on record that she was lashing out at her husband's mistress. She may have faulted her husband for being inappropriate, but I find her impulse to blame the Woman—not only me, but herself—troubling. And all too familiar: with every marital indiscretion that finds its way into the public sphere—many of which involve male politicians—it always seems like the woman conveniently takes the fall. Sure, the Anthony Weiners and Eliot Spitzers do what they need to do to look humiliated on cable news. They bow out of public life for a while, but they inevitably return, having put it all behind them. The women in these imbroglios return to lives that are not so easily repaired.

But there is another layer here that is making me bristle: *Narcissist? Loony?*

You might remember that just five days before the world had ever heard my name the FBI—after my friend Linda Tripp approached Special Prosecutor Kenneth Starr's office with information about my affair with the president—entrapped me in a terrifying "sting" in the Pentagon City mall. At age twenty-four, cornered in a hotel room on January 16, 1998, with mainly male interrogators taking orders from Starr, I was discouraged from contacting my attorney and threatened with twenty-seven years in jail for filing an affidavit denying the affair with Clinton, among other alleged crimes. I was offered immunity from that threat if I agreed to place monitored calls and wear a wire in conversations with two of the president's confidants and possibly the president himself. I refused. Confiding in Linda Tripp turned into an unintended betrayal. But this? The mother of all betrayals. That, I couldn't do. Courageous or foolish, maybe, but narcissistic and loony?

.   .   .

These sixteen-year-old descriptions of me triggered memories of past anguish, particularly in the area of women lobbing derision at one another. So where, you might be wondering, were the feminists back then?

It's a question that troubles me to this day.

I sorely wished for some sign of understanding from the feminist camp. Some good, old-fashioned, girl-on-girl support was much in need. None came. Given the issues at play—gender politics, sex in the workplace—you'd think they would have spoken up. They didn't. I understood their dilemma: Bill Clinton had been a president "friendly" to women's causes.

It also didn't help that my case was not one of conventional "sexual harassment"; *that* charge against Bill Clinton had been made by Paula Jones, who brought a colossal lawsuit against him. My name surfaced only because, thanks to newly won advances by feminists, investigations of such cases were now allowed to cast a wider net. The Jones case became a stick that the right wing used to strike back at the Clinton-supporting feminists: *Why wouldn't they enthusiastically support an investigation into a case of sexual harassment? What if the president had been a Republican?* Charges of hypocrisy flew.

A handful of representatives of the modern feminist movement did chime in, obliquely. Yet instead of any meaningful engagement, we got this: January 30, 1998. Day nine of the scandal. Cocktails at Le Bernardin, in Manhattan. In attendance: writers Erica Jong, Nancy Friday, Katie Roiphe, and Elizabeth Benedict; *Saturday Night Live* writer Patricia Marx; Marisa Bowe, the editor of *Word*, an online magazine; fashion designer Nicole Miller;

former dominatrix Susan Shellogg; and their host, Le Bernardin co-owner Maguy Le Coze. The *New York Observer* brought this coven together to trade Interngate insights, to be recorded by Francine Prose. (Sadly, the gal who would really make this coven complete is missing: Maureen Dowd, or Moremean Dowdy, as I used to refer to her. Today, I'd meet her for a drink.)

Oh, to have been at that cocktail party:

MARISA BOWE: His whole life is about having to be in control and really intelligent all the time. And his wife is really intelligent and in control all the time. And the idea of just having stupid sex with some not-brilliant woman in the Oval Office, I can see the appeal in that.

IMAGINARY ME: I'm not saying I'm brilliant, but how do you know I'm not? My first job out of college was at the White House.

SUSAN SHELLOGG: And do you think it's tremendously selfish? Selfish and demanding, having oral sex and not reciprocating? I mean . . . she didn't say, "Well, you know he satisfied me."

ME: And where exactly "didn't" I say this? In which public statement that I didn't make? In which testimony that's not been released?

KATIE ROIPHE: I think what people are outraged about is the way that [Monica Lewinsky] looks, which is interesting. Because we like to think of our presidents as sort of godlike, and so if JFK has an affair with Marilyn Monroe, it's all in the realm of the demigods. . . . I mean, the thing I kept hearing over and over again was Monica Lewinsky's not that pretty.

ME: Well, thanks. The first picture that surfaced was a passport photo. Would you like to have a passport photo splattered across publications around the world as the picture that defines you?

> *What you are also saying here is that the primary
> quality that would qualify a woman to have an intimate
> relationship with a powerful man is physical attractive-
> ness. If that's not setting the movement back, I don't know
> what is.*

ERICA JONG: My dental hygienist pointed out that she had
third-stage gum disease.

SHELLOGG: What do you think will happen to [her]? I mean,
she'll just fade out quietly or write a book? Or people will
forget about her six months from now?

NANCY FRIDAY: She can rent out her mouth.

ME: (Speechless.)

JONG: But, you know, men do like to get close to the mouth
that has been close to power. Think of the fantasy in the
man's mind as she's going down on him and he's thinking, "Oh my God."

ELIZABETH BENEDICT: Do for me what you did to the
president. Do that.

ME: (Still speechless.)

JONG: I think it's a tribute to how far we've come that we're
not trashing Monica Lewinsky.

The catty confab appeared under the headline "Supergals Love
That Naughty Prez." (Writing in *Vanity Fair*, Marjorie Williams
called it "the most embarrassing thing I had read in a long time.")
To me, it illustrates a perplexing aspect of the culture of humiliation, one that Phyllis Chesler recognized in her book *Woman's
Inhumanity to Woman*: that women themselves are not immune
to certain kinds of misogyny. We see it today in how the "mean
girls" at school lurk on the modern playground of the Web (or
around a pundit's roundtable on TV or at a French restaurant), ever
eager to pile on.

I still have deep respect for feminism and am thankful for the
great strides the movement has made in advancing women's rights

over the past few decades. But, given my experience of being passed around like gender-politics cocktail food, I don't identify myself as a Feminist, capital *F*. The movement's leaders failed in articulating a position that was not essentially antiwoman during the witch hunt of 1998. In the case of the New York Supergals, it should not have been that hard for them to swoon over the president without attacking and shaming me. Instead, they joined the humiliation derby.

· · ·

I, myself, deeply regret what happened between me and President Clinton. Let me say it again: I. Myself. Deeply. Regret. What. Happened. At the time—at least from my point of view—it was an authentic connection, with emotional intimacy, frequent visits, plans made, phone calls and gifts exchanged. In my early twenties, I was too young to understand the real-life consequences, and too young to see that I would be sacrificed for political expediency. I look back now, shake my head in disbelief, and wonder: what was I—what were we—thinking? I would give anything to go back and rewind the tape.

· · ·

Like many other Americans, I've been thinking about Hillary Clinton. What might happen, I've wondered, if she does run in 2016? And what if she wins—and then wins a second term?

But when I think about these matters, there's a dimension at play for me other than just the fact that we might finally have a woman in the White House. We all remember the second-wave feminist rallying cry *The personal is political.* Many people (myself included) proclaimed that my relationship with Bill Clinton was a personal matter, not one to be used in a high-stakes political war. When I hear of Hillary's prospective candidacy, I cannot help but fear the next wave of paparazzi, the next wave of "Where is she now?" stories, the next reference to me in Fox News's coverage of the primaries. I've begun to find it debilitating to plot out the cycle of my life based, to some degree, on the political calendar. For me, it's a scenario in which the personal and the political are impossible to separate.

In 2008, when Hillary was running for president, I remained virtually reclusive, despite being inundated with press requests. I put off announcing several media projects in 2012 until after the election. (They were subsequently canceled—and, no, I wasn't offered $12 million for a salacious tell-all book, contrary to press reports.) And recently I've found myself gun-shy yet again, fearful of "becoming an issue" should she decide to ramp up her campaign. But should I put my life on hold for *another* eight to ten years?

Being a conscientious Democrat—and aware that I could be used as a tool for the left or the right—I have remained silent for ten years. So silent, in fact, that the buzz in some circles has been that the Clintons must have paid me off; why *else* would I have refrained from speaking out? I can assure you that nothing could be further from the truth.

So why speak now? Because it is time.

I turned forty last year, and it is time to stop tiptoeing around my past—and other people's futures. I am determined to have a different ending to my story. I've decided, finally, to stick my head above the parapet so that I can take back my narrative and give a purpose to my past. (What this will cost me, I will soon find out.) Despite what some headlines will falsely report about this piece, this is *not* about Me versus the Clintons. Their lives have moved on; they occupy important and powerful places on the global stage. I wish them no ill. And I fully understand that what has happened to me and the issue of my future do not matter to either of them.

It also goes back to the personal and the political. I have lived many of the questions that have become central to our national discourse since 1998. How far should we allow the government into our bedrooms? How do we reconcile the right to privacy with the need to expose sexual indiscretion? How do we guard against an overzealous government demanding our private data and information? And, most important to me personally, how do we cope with the shame game as it's played in the Internet Age? (My current goal is to get involved with efforts on behalf of victims of online humiliation and harassment and to start speaking on this topic in public forums.)

•   •   •

So far, That Woman has never been able to escape the shadow of that first depiction. I was the Unstable Stalker (a phrase disseminated by the Clinton White House), the Dimwit Floozy, the Poor Innocent who didn't know any better. The Clinton administration, the special prosecutor's minions, the political operatives on both sides of the aisle, and the media were able to brand me. And that brand stuck, in part because it was imbued with power. I became a social representation, a social canvas on which anybody could project their confusion about women, sex, infidelity, politics, and body issues.

Unlike the other parties involved, I was so young that I had no established identity to which I could return. I didn't "let this define" me—I simply hadn't had the life experience to establish my own identity in 1998. If you haven't figured out who you are, it's hard not to accept the horrible image of you created by others. (Thus, my compassion for young people who find themselves shamed on the Web.) Despite much self-searching and therapy and exploring of different paths, I remained "stuck" for far too many years.

No longer. It's time to burn the beret and bury the blue dress. And move forward.

GQ

The judges who awarded "Inside the Iron Closet" the Ellie for Reporting described this story about the perilous lives of Russian gays and lesbians—outlawed by their own government and subject to violent attack by thuggish homophobes—as "courageous" and "timely." Since Jim Nelson was named editor of GQ in 2003, the magazine has received fifty-six Ellie nominations and eight awards. GQ also won the Ellie for Reporting in 2013 for Chris Heath's "18 Tigers, 17 Lions, 8 Bears, 3 Cougars, 2 Wolves, 1 Baboon, 1 Macaque, and 1 Mad Dead in Ohio."

Jeff Sharlet

Inside the Iron Closet

What It's Like to Be Gay in Putin's Russia

Strangers at the Gate

Sunday nights in St. Petersburg are Rainbow Tea Party time. If you're young and queer and hopeful, it's the happiest way to end a weekend. An actual tea party. There are also cookies and—at LaSky, the HIV-awareness center that often hosts the event—more brightly colored giant beanbags than chairs, plus a lot of posters of hunky bare-chested men with floppy hair. There are many, many rainbows, on stickers and pins and brochures, and a rainbow curtain covering a strange little door in the corner.

The door leads to a club called Bunker, which is really a maze, twisting through the rest of the building's vast basement. It's dark; you have to feel your way through. The men who go to Bunker—many or maybe most of them "straight" men, married men, says the bartender—are looking for bodies, not faces. They don't want to see or be seen, only to touch and to be touched in a place where nobody knows them.

Those are the choices: light or dark, tea or poppers, a well-lit game of charades or a grope in the dungeon. Sweet or sordid, it doesn't matter: In Russia now—in the throes of a fever stoked by the Kremlin—both must be hidden. They are not hidden well enough.

One evening in November—the city center like a bowl of pastel candies, Orthodox onion-domes rising above it like spun sugar—two strangers found their way to LaSky. They walked down a long street between a busy road and a canal until they came to an arch in a building. They went through the arch and down a dark alley before they arrived at an unlit empty parking lot, blacktop crumbling. Here they may have stopped to put on their masks. They crossed the lot toward a stand of scrub trees and weeds and took a left down a narrow path, then down an even darker set of uneven stairs to an unmarked steel door. The strangers stood at the threshold.

It was Rainbow Tea Party night. A woman named Anna asked who was there. "We're looking for our friend!" replied one of the strangers. They shoved past her. In the hall, a man named Dmitry Chizhevsky was looking for his jacket. Behind him was a girl I'll call Rose, a few weeks shy of her eighteenth birthday. Rose glanced toward the door: two men wearing ski masks. "Then," she says, "they started shooting." Chizhevsky: "The first bullet came into my eye. The first, the very first." Rose: "I had a thought in my head—maybe I should do something, maybe I should scream." Chizhevsky: "I can remember more closely what was audio." *Pop, pop, pop, pop, pop,* he recalls hearing. Five, he thinks. He says he remembers the sound of the bullet hitting his eye.

Dmitry went down, and Rose ran, and Dmitry crawled. The men followed, kicking. One of them had a bat, "a baseball bat, yes," says Dmitry. They were screaming. "Faggot, faggot, faggot." The bat came down. And then the faggots in the other room charged the men with the gun and the bat and the masks, and the men ran away. Dmitry and Anna, who'd been shot in the back, inspected their wounds. An air gun, they determined. Thank God.

They say you can shoot an eye out with an air gun, but that's not exactly what happened. The pellet, a round metal ball, lodged *behind* Dmitry's eye.

"They tried with a magnet to take it out," says Dmitry. "But, uh, they failed."

What did they try next?

"A hook."

The doctors told him he was lucky; a little farther, it would have entered his brain. All he'd lose would be his vision.

. . .

I went to Moscow and St. Petersburg for two weeks in November because the Olympics were coming to Russia, and for a brief moment it seemed possible that the outside world was interested in the unraveling of civil society in one of the most powerful countries on the globe. Books are being banned—Burroughs and Baudelaire and Huxley's *Brave New World*—immigrants hunted; journalists killed; a riot-grrrl band, Pussy Riot, imprisoned for almost two years for playing a "Punk Prayer" in a Moscow cathedral; blasphemy is now illegal. Civil society isn't just coming undone; it's imploding. I wanted to visit the bottom of the heap. The *golubye*. The blues, which in Russia is another word for queer—any way of being other than "Russian," which, under President Vladimir Putin, has become a kind of sexual orientation. I wanted to see what ordinary LGBT life was like in a nation whose leaders have decided that "homosexualism" is a threat to its "sexual sovereignty," that "genderless tolerance," in Putin's words, is a disease of the West that Russia will cure. The medicine is that of "traditional values," a phrase, ironically, imported from the West, grafted onto a deeply conformist strain of nationalism. In Russia, that means silence and violence, censorship, and, in its shadow, much worse.

One of the first men I met was Alex, a gay police officer who'd recently quit his job rather than enforce Russia's new antigay law. He wasn't always so principled: One of Alex's early assignments on the force was snooping through a fellow officer's computer for evidence of homosexuality. "I was just lucky it wasn't *my* computer," Alex said one night at a café on Arbat Street, Moscow's main thoroughfare of consumer hipsterism.

His boyfriend wasn't as glib: "It's Germany in the thirties," he declared. "Hush, hush," Alex said. "Not so loud." It's not Germany in the thirties, he said; it's Russia now. And that's a subtler problem.

Yes, there are killings. In May, a twenty-three-year-old man in Volgograd allegedly came out to a group of friends, who raped him with beer bottles and smashed his skull in with a stone, and in June a group of friends in Kamchatka kicked and stabbed to death a thirty-nine-year-old gay man then burned the body. There's a national network called Occupy Pedophilia, whose members torture gay men and post hugely popular videos of their "interrogations" online. There are countless smaller, bristling movements, with names presumptuous (God's Will) or absurd (Homophobic Wolf). There are babushkas who throw stones and priests who bless the stones and police who arrest their victims.

But such people exist everywhere, said Alex. The difference in Russia now is who's standing behind them.

The Russian closet has always been deep, but since last June, when the Duma began passing laws designed to shove Russia's tiny out population back into it, the closet has been getting darker. The first law banned gay "propaganda," but it was written so as to leave the definition vague. It's a mechanism of thought control, its target not so much gays as anybody the state declares gay; a virtual resurrection of Article 70 from the old Soviet system, forbidding "anti-Soviet agitation and propaganda." Then, as now, nobody knew exactly what "propaganda" was. The new law explicitly forbids any suggestion that queer love is equal to that of heterosexuals, but what constitutes such a suggestion? One man was charged for holding up a sign that said BEING GAY IS OK. Pride parades are out of the question, a pink triangle enough to get you arrested, if not beaten. A couple holding hands could be accused of propaganda if they do so where a minor might see them; the law, as framed, is all about protecting the children. Yelena Mizulina, chair of the Duma Committee on Family, Women, and Children's Affairs and the author of the bill, says that it's too late to save adult "homosexualists," as they're called, but Russia still has a chance to raise a pure generation.

Mizulina's dream isn't old-fashioned; it is, as one fascist supporter told me, "utopian." He meant that as praise. And the Russian dream is not alone. Liberal Americans imagine LGBT rights as slowly but surely marching forward. But queer rights don't advance along a straight line. In Russia and throughout Eastern Europe—and in India and in Australia, in a belt across Central Africa—antigay crusaders are developing new laws and sharpening old ones. The ideas, meanwhile, are American: the rhetoric of "family values" churned out by right-wing American think tanks, bizarre statistics to prove that evil is a fact, its face a gay one. This hatred is old venom, but its weaponization by nations as a means with which to fight "globalization"—not the economic kind, the human-rights kind—is a new terror.

In Russia, the process is accelerating. In 2006, a bill similar to the law was laughed out of the Duma, dismissed by the then deputy prime minister as "a row of mistakes." In June it passed, 436–0. Alex the cop says 2010 was the best year, a new club or café opening every other weekend. New LGBT groups were forming all over. "It was like a party," one activist told me. What happened between then and now has as much to do with the unstable price of oil and Putin's eroding popular support as it does with actual queer people. The less prosperity Putin can deliver, the more he speaks of holy Russian empire, language to which the Russian Orthodox Church thrills. Putin, says Patriarch Kirill, the church's leader, is a living "act of God." Forget about the price of bread and what you can't afford. Putin has come to save the Russian soul.

Article 6.21, the law's official designation, has proven to be the Duma's most popular social initiative of the year; according to one poll, only 7 percent of Russians firmly oppose it. Another new law requiring nonprofits that receive support outside Russia to register as foreign agents has been used to justify police raids on the country's leading LGBT organizations. In July, Putin signed a law banning the adoption of Russian children by gay parents abroad.

And in October, the Duma started to take up a law to remove children from LGBT parents in Russia. It's been put on hold, but it's expected to return once the Olympics and international scrutiny have passed.

"The problem is bigger than laws," a gay activist named Igor Iasine told me, tracing a line through his beard where neo-Nazis had broken his jaw. "The law is icing on the cake."

For Dmitry Kiselyov, the director of Russia's massive new state media corporation—created in December to swallow up state media entities that show any hint of autonomy—laws are not enough. He's concerned about organ donors, the possibility of a queer heart beating in a straight body.

When homosexuals die, he says, "their hearts should be burned."

·   ·   ·

"I haven't heard of these laws, but I think it's fine," a kid named Kirill tells me at a hidden gay club called Secrets. "We don't need gay pride here. Why do we need to show our orientation?" He shrugs. He has heard of the torture videos popular online, the gangs that kidnap gays, the police that arrest gays, the babushkas with their eggs and their stones. But he hasn't seen them. He prefers not to. "Everybody wants to emigrate, but not me." He shrugs again; it's like a tic. "I love Russia. This is their experience, not mine." He says he does not know what the word *closet* means.

"Something Is Coming"

In an upper-middle-class neighborhood close to Moscow's city center, two apartments face each other. Two families, two daughters. They leave the doors open to allow easy access from one to the other.

Pavel met Irina not long after he moved to Moscow twelve years ago, and almost immediately he knew that someday he'd start a family with her.[1] Irina felt it, too. They agreed on it one night over vodka, after a night of clubbing. The party had moved back to an apartment, where they kept drinking, Irina teasing Pavel, Pavel marveling at Irina's bold friends. She was a Muscovite; Pavel had come from one of those distant eastern cities, 4,000 miles from Moscow. Irina was six years younger, but she was his teacher, teaching him how to be silly and modern and free. They drank and danced, Pavel discovering his hips, until they both collapsed around a kitchen table and, over more vodka, Pavel tried to be funny and Irina thought he was, so she said, "Someday I would like to have a child with you." Pavel said, "I feel the same."

Suddenly they were sober, giddy but clear: They knew it was true. But they had to wait. *To have children is a great responsibility*, Pavel thought. *You have to have a place to live. You have to earn. You have to have a partner you can rely on.* In 2010, they were ready. Their best friends, Nik and Zoya, were having a baby, too, and they lived right next door. Their children would grow up together. Two little girls: Nik and Zoya's Kristina, and then Pavel and Irina's Emma.

Now they are one big happy family, inseparable. Pavel has always been great with kids. He likes to read the girls Russian fairy

1. The names in this section have been changed.

tales, and he buys DVDs of old Russian cartoons, the ones he was raised on. They watch them together. The girls toddle between the apartments through the open doors. Pavel thinks little blonde Kristina looks like an angel. Emma's darker, serious like her father. Both girls call him Papa. The children share a nanny, too, who helps the parents with light cleaning, dishes, and dusting, making sure all the family pictures are in place.

"Nobody would suspect us," Pavel says. Not even the nanny.

Pavel's secret isn't that he's gay. It's that they all are, the adults: Pavel and Nik and Irina and Zoya. Both girls have two mothers, two fathers; they have beds in both apartments. Their life together was, until recently, the fulfillment of all that Pavel had wanted, an ambition that had come to him at almost the same moment he'd realized he was gay: to be "normal." If he were normal, he thought, then he could be a father. "That," he tells me, "has been my precious dream."

．　　　．　　　．

Pavel agrees to talk to me because soon, he fears, the laws that have passed and the laws to come may make it impossible to hide. I'm told to meet him at a metro station. When I arrive—with my translator, Zhenya, a gay activist—no one is there. A phone call from a mutual friend directs us through the empty station, around a corner, and down some stairs to a basement restaurant, Georgian cuisine, a man in a corner with a bottle of white wine. Is this—? Yes. He smiles. We sit down.

"Something is coming," says Pavel. What it will be, he's not sure. He's worried about "special departments" in local police stations, dedicated to removing children from gay homes. He's worried about a coworker discovering him. He is worried about blackmail. He is worried, and he does not know what else to do. He wishes he could fight, but he doesn't know how. Sign a petition? March in a parade? Pavel would never do that now. "My children," he murmurs.

"This law," he says, referring to the ban on "propaganda." "If something happens, it touches only me. And I can protect myself." But the next law: "This is about my child. My baby." If the next law passes, they will leave. The two women are doctors and Nik works in higher education, careers that will require new certification. Which means that only Pavel, a manager for the state oil company, will be able to work right away. They will be poor, but they will leave. They might have to separate, Pavel and Irina and Emma to Israel, where Irina can become a citizen, Nik and Zoya and Kristina to any country that will take them. They might have to become the couples they pretend to be. For now, they are staying. "We're going to teach them," he says of his two little girls, Emma and Kristina. "How to protect themselves. How to keep silence."

This is how the law really works: It's the little things that break first. Like a child who wants to call her father Papa. "Father can be only one," Pavel tells Kristina. She can never call him Papa again. If someone overheard her . . . No, not even at home. She must forget that was ever his name. "I can be anybody but Father," he tells the girl he used to call daughter.

A Dangerous Pride

In 2006, an activist named Nikolai Alekseyev organized Russia's first pride parade. Moscow's mayor forbade it; he called for "concrete measures" to stop it. On May 27, Alekseyev and a few comrades approached Russia's Tomb of the Unknown Soldier with flowers. The tomb is a memorial to the millions of Soviet troops killed in what Russians call the "war against fascism."

The little group found the gate closed. Before it stood a line of police and squads of the OMON, elite riot cops in boots and blue camo and black berets. And a crowd, chanting, "Russia without faggots!" One man, in a fit of apparent generosity, screamed, "You have your nightclubs!" Another began shouting about his grandfather, who had fought in the war. Alekseyev shouted back that his own grandfather died fighting. Then the police arrested Alekseyev, and the crowd took the others, and the Tomb was preserved, safe from gay roses.

In 2007, about three dozen pride marchers tried to deliver a letter signed by more than forty members of the European Parliament to the mayor of Moscow, asking for permission to hold the parade. The mayor called it a "work of Satan." Among those beaten was an Italian parliamentarian.

In 2008, activists applied to hold marches across the city, all denied, and then assembled as a flash mob for moments in front of a statue of Tchaikovsky.

They tried the same trick in 2009, but the police were ready.

2010: Success! Thirty marchers marched for ten minutes before they were captured.

2011: Three minutes, maybe four.

2012: Moscow officially banned gay-pride parades for one hundred years.

Last year: The police were waiting. They brought trucks fitted with metal cages.

•   •   •

At Bunker one night, a fat man named Yuri, pink-cheeked and furry-chested, leans in close, over my notebook. Not threatening; frightened. "No more parades!" he says. "No more marches!" Yes, he would like to have rights. "But this is Russia!" He's shaking an open palm on either side of my face, making sure I write this down: "I will be beaten!" He points to a teenager. "He will be beaten. All of us will be beaten! And we will go to the police, and they will just smile."

.   .   .

Elena Kostyuchenko knew she would be beaten. It was how hard she went down that surprised her. Not immediately. When the fist connected with her skull, she fell, yes, but then she stood again and raised her rainbow flag. The crowd was silent. Their mouths were open as if screaming, but there was no sound. Her hearing was gone. Then the police grabbed her, and Elena's first gay-pride parade was over.

Elena is twenty-seven. "I'm not very tall; I weigh fifty kilos. I can't overthrow this world," she says. But she is trying. It took months, hospitalizations, five medications "to widen the veins in my brain," but most of her hearing is back now, and there's an app on her computer that allows her to jack movies up to 150 percent of what you might consider tolerable volume. She wears her hair in a short black shag with high spiky bangs, and she has big pale blue eyes that lighten in to the pupils. Her voice is droll, her manner deadpan, her presence at first unassuming; I talked to her for a couple of hours before I learned how much violence she's endured since that first pride event in 2011, and she never did get around to telling me that when she was nine she was given up for dead, warehoused in a cancer ward for kids her provincial hospital deemed "unlikely" to survive.

She and Zhenya and I meet at a dull little café near her metro station. Grayish pink walls, two TV screens playing Western pop videos from the eighties and nineties—there's a lot of Wham!— and a fluorescent-lit smog of cigarette smoke. Elena's a reporter, hard-nosed. "Prostitutes, addicts, these are my people," she says. She has fainting spells, but she wills herself to keep standing: "A journalist shouldn't faint." In the nine years she's been working for her paper, *Novaya Gazeta*—the last major opposition publication— three of its reporters have been murdered, including Anna Politkovskaya, shot four times in her apartment elevator in 2006, the killer still unknown. "I'm lucky," Elena says. She means alive.

She knows some English, but she speaks mostly in Russian. Explaining her view of Russia's rising homophobia, she dictates to Zhenya: "Putin needs external enemies and internal enemies. The external enemies are the U.S. and Europe. Internal enemies, they had to think about. The ethnic topic is dangerous. Two wars in the Caucasus, a third one, nobody knows how it would end. Jews? After Hitler, it's not kosher. We—" she waves a hand at herself and Zhenya—"are the ideal. We are everywhere. We don't look different, but we are." She inhales. She's one of those smokers who hold your eyes when they're smoking. Cigarettes disappear into her lungs. She says, in English: "It's our turn. Just our turn." She exhales. She has a pleasant smile.

She met her girlfriend four and a half years ago, at a lesbian movie night in a club. The movie was *Lost and Delirious*, translated into Russian as *They're Not Gonna Get You*. Mischa Barton, prep-school lesbians. They both thought it was a little childish. Elena liked Anya's seriousness and her broad grin; she liked her earnestness and her calm. Their love was quick and deep and strong. Soon Elena was thinking about a home together. "Then I was thinking, 'I have health issues. I'm hospitalized once in a while. I can be unconscious—who will come and make medical decisions for me?' Then, at one moment, I realize Anya is the one I want to have my children with." That's when she got scared. "Before that, I didn't feel like I was discriminated against. Then Anya appeared."

She'd reported on pride events in 2009. She found it pitiful: a handful of queers. "Why does nobody want to defend *my* rights?" she'd ask. "Why does nobody want to fight for *my* happy future?"

The morning of the pride demonstrations in 2011, Elena wrote a post on her blog that would, in the days that followed, go viral. It was very simple: "Why I Am Going to Gay Pride." She was going for Anya. They would wear silly T-shirts—I LOVE HER, with arrows. Elena made a sign that said HATE IS BORING. She put on a black raincoat, Anya an olive green one, to hide their shirts until they got there. "I was scared that at the moment I wouldn't be able to unzip my raincoat, that people would somehow feel we were lesbians, that we would be beaten before raising the flag."

There is video of the man attacking Elena. His name is Roman Lisunov. Not an activist—a family man. "Just a simple Russian guy," as homophobes here like to say. Elena's flag flickers, and then hurtling from behind comes Lisunov's fist, taking Elena's skull flat across his knuckles, just above her left ear. In his defense, he will tell the police that he is baptized. That's it. Good enough! The detective assigned to the case will ask her lawyer, "Why would she go to the street? What protection does she want now?"

·   ·   ·

They caught Anya on the metro. "They know our faces really well," says Elena. They know all the activists. "They know Anya is my girlfriend." Three surrounded her on the escalator going down. One put Anya in a headlock to hold her still, then smashed his fist up into her face once, twice, three times, four, five. Anya counted.

This was after a kiss-in protest at the Duma last winter. It wasn't like they hadn't been warned. Some neo-Nazis had posted instructions online: "The guys, we beat them until they can't stand up anymore. The women, we break their faces." But the men in the metro weren't Nazis. Their leader seemed to be a man named Dmitry Enteo, a one-man would-be Pussy Riot of the right who leads an "action art" group called God's Will, linked to the Russian Orthodox Church. Like performance art, Enteo will tell me later, only, you know, more real. He's kind of a hipster.

The kiss-ins were Elena's idea. She'd been complaining to a friend. "I am tired of standing there with a poster," she said. Well, said her friend, what would you rather be doing? Easy question! "Kissing Anya."

Announcing the event on her blog, she wrote: "A kiss only concerns two people. . . . It does not need permission from deputies of the Duma." And: "How long should you kiss? However long you like."

Anyone was invited to join them. "I don't like being an activist," she says. But what choice does she have? "It's a long time until there will be some kind of magical Russian Harvey Milk who will defend my rights. I have been waiting, but he is not coming."

The LGBT movement splits along two philosophical lines, she says. "One of them says we need to work through education and enlightenment. The other says we should stop trying to get everyone to like us. I respect the educational approach. It takes a lot of time. I don't have so much time. We want to have children. I need my rights now." Her demands are modest: marriage, kids, a mortgage. Also, if possible, she would like not to be murdered. She doesn't want to be Harvey Milk: "Harvey Milk was killed!"

"Take a plane," her mother begs her. Emigrate. "Two hours, you will be in another world, where you will be loved and needed." But Elena can't leave. So now her mother calls her after every action. "Are you in a police van?" she asks. "If I say yes, she says, 'Thank God.'" Better a jailed daughter than a dead one.

•   •   •

The day of the fourth and last kiss-in, the day the law passed, June 2013, the haters tried a new weapon. It gives even Elena pause. She stubs out a cigarette, starts a fresh one, and begins to speak. Zhenya listens. "The homophobes . . . ," he says, starting his translation. Then he stops. "Zhenya?" I ask. Elena continues. Zhenya is nodding, but he says nothing. His face is flushing.

He's twenty-six, grew up in Vladivostok, was beaten, saw his straight friends beaten for trying to protect him. He became an exile at the first chance, living abroad for five years. He worked for a human-rights organization, writing reports on the escalating violence in Russia. It wasn't enough. After the law passed, he came home. "To fight," he says.

"Zhenya?" I say again. He's staring at the wall. Elena says, "He is crying."

He composes himself and continues the translation of the story that overwhelmed him. On the day of the last kiss-in, the mob tried something new. They brought their children. Action art. A mockery. A lesson. Not rocks; the children were their weapon. Who would hit a child? Adolescent boys, twelve, thirteen, moved in packs from activist to activist, one by one, throwing fists, kicking. It was a day of beatings.

It takes me a moment. "Their kids?"

Elena smiles. "Yeah."

"We *couldn't* fight them," says Zhenya, finishing his translation. He moans and starts to shake. And that's it; now he's broken. Because everybody knows twelve-year-old boys can be real shits, these are the same fights they have with one another in the schoolyard, but the hope is that they'll grow up, that their parents will teach them. The hope is always that it will get better.

•   •   •

At a club called Ice, I befriend a long-necked hustler with bright green eyes, wearing a white NYPD cap. His name is Nikolai. He says he kissed his first boy at fourteen but that it took him until he was seventeen to realize he was gay. He was small in school and he fought often, but he was perhaps a little slow to grasp his social condition; he didn't understand why other boys beat him. By the time he got it, he'd learned how to beat them. Such was his coming-out story.

He was happy being gay, though. He liked knowing what he wanted. The problem was his mother. Gay she could handle, but she wanted grandkids. She made him a deal: an apartment in exchange for grandchildren. Plural. Minimum two.

So Nikolai did what he had to do: "I married a woman. I am a father!" He beams. He has delivered the goods: a girl, one and a half years old; a boy, four months. His mother rewarded him with the apartment, and he came out to his wife.

"I don't think there is homophobia in Russia," he says, "because I always carry a gun."

The logic takes me a moment. He means they can't hurt him, because he will hurt them first. His father, a "criminal," he says, found Nikolai on a Grindr-like app once. He said he was coming to kill Nikolai. Nikolai wrote back: "I'm waiting for you." His father never came. Nikolai is waiting. He taps one side of his head and then the other, to show the path of the bullet he'll put through his father's skull.

"Violence Is Acceptable"

There are three faces of homophobia in Russia: that of the state, that of the Orthodox Church, that of the fringe. And yet they're one—a kind of Trinity. The state passes laws; the church blesses them; the fringe puts them into action. The state is the mind of hate, the church, now, its heart; the fringe is made up of its many hands. Some use the courts; some use fists. There are street fighters, and there are polished men and women who attend international conferences on "family values."

Timur Isaev uses cameras. He likes to watch.

That's how his activism began, he tells me one night in St. Petersburg. As young men, he and his friends liked to hunt and beat gays. "For fun," he says. But then he became a father. Like many parents, he worried about the Internet. Late at night, he studied it. He watched YouTube. "Girls," he says, "young girls, undressing themselves." Using a special "tool for developers," he says, he was able to discern that the other people watching these videos at two a.m. were homosexual men. "The analysis of their accounts," he says, "showed that they also watched young boys." That's when Timur realized he must become an activist. For the children.

Timur bought a video camera, a very good one. He began documenting LGBT life. At first, demonstrations; then he began idling outside activists' offices, filming and photographing people coming and going. He showed me one of his galleries: dozens, maybe hundreds of faces. Some he has photographed himself, others he finds online. He is a great policeman of VK, Russia's version of Facebook. These days he stays up late at night searching for homosexual teachers. It's kind of his specialty.

I've sought Timur out to confirm a story I'd been told the night before at LaSky, from a former schoolteacher named Olga Bakhaeva. She said she'd lost her job because Timur, posing as a concerned mother, had outed her.

"Is Olga's story true?" I ask Timur.

"Yes!" he says, flattered. In fact, he is working on another teacher now. She's going to be fired next week, he hopes. "We usually fire good shots—good *informational* shots," he says. Olga was his sixth. He takes out his tablet to shows me the others. He loves social media. He poses for a picture, holding up a photograph of Olga he found online. It's a trophy.

How does he do it? He has connections. In my notebook he scribbles a list of names and numbers, a who's who of right-wing St. Petersburg, including Vitaly Milonov, the author of the city's antigay legislation. Timur makes calls when he senses something suspicious. Just last night he had another success. There was a support group for LGBT families. He'd been stalking it online. He had information that there would be a minor there. He'd arranged a raid.

It was true. As it happens, I had been at that meeting. The police had been right outside the door, held at bay because they didn't have the right warrant. Inside, there was a seventeen-year-old boy talking about coming out to his mother. For this, we all could have gone to prison.

In America, I'd dismiss Timur as a crank. In Russia, he seems everywhere to be at the center of events. He scrolls through his photos to show me something special—LaSky, the site of Dmitry Chizhevsky's shooting, with multiple views of the area outside. Timur says the gays did it to themselves. To make Russia look bad. See, he says, "thirteen surveillance cameras." He has documented them. "Here," he says, pointing to a picture, "there is a very good camera. You couldn't have gone unnoticed." He points to another. "Can't get past this camera . . ." It is impossible, he says. "No sane person would go there with a gun. You would have to go there without a mask and put it on there." Which is what happened. He knows how it could have been done: "I have blueprints of the building."

He moves on, showing more pictures. He slides the tablet across to me, reaching over and flicking through the images, talking about men "who are not worthy of the nationalist name. People like this . . ." He looks down at the tablet. It is not a picture of a person; it is a picture of an air gun, a pistol, still in the box, on top of it a jar of little metal balls. "Ah," he says. He didn't mean to show that one. I'm just as stunned. "A gift for my son," he says quickly, searching for photographs of the boy. He wants to prove the innocence of the gun.

Timur knows what I'm thinking. He says, "If I wanted to shoot someone, I would think of *my* safety first." Proof, he claims, that he is not the man who shot Dmitry Chizhevsky in the eye. Too risky.

Besides, says Timur, he is a peaceful man now. He giggles.

•　　•　　•

At St. Petersburg's biggest gay club, I meet a bartender in tight jean shorts and a skimpy turquoise tank top who whispers to me,

"I'm not gay." He pretends, for the job. In fact, he says, "I'm a homophobe." He struggles not to hit his customers. But he wishes he could change. "I don't want to hate anymore," he says. He glances at a man who's been giving him the eye. He shudders. "It's not working."

·　　·　　·

We are walking down a long dark street on the outskirts of St. Petersburg on our way to a meeting Timur has arranged with Anatoly Artyukh—pronounced "R-2." Artyukh is the big man in Timur's circles, the founder of the St. Petersburg branch of Narodny Sobor—"People's Council"—a national umbrella group for hundreds of organizations dedicated to preserving Russia's "traditional values." It accepts all kinds: skinheads, Cossacks, veterans, Orthodox crusaders, scary squadrons of angry mothers, and more than a few politicians—Artyukh himself is an "aide" to Vitaly Milonov.

When we get to the backdoor apartment-block address we've been given, we're taken into the basement, a rec room that is filling up for a meeting. On the agenda: developing "new tools" to defeat the homosexualists. A lot of old guys, sour with broad pickled faces. Some young guys in track pants; a couple of babushkas in leather. There's a man dressed like a Cossack, like an extra from the big pogrom number in *Fiddler on the Roof.* One of the last to arrive is Artyukh, a gray-black widow's-peaked buzz cut squaring off a face like Sean Connery plus fifty pounds. Leather jacket, shoulders padded, black suit beneath, black shirt unbuttoned to air out a few iron curls. He says this is a private club but he'll receive us upstairs.

Two floors up, Artyukh settles behind a giant desk. One of Artyukh's lieutenants, exceedingly friendly despite the boss's open hostility, directs us to our seats.

Artyukh leans back, fat fingers knitted across his stomach. Over his right shoulder there's the double-headed-eagle flag of czarist Russia; on his desk there's a bouquet of four flags from the old Confederacy. "Gift from American friends," he says. "We consider them brothers." In fact, many of the People's Council's initiatives—including the "research" in which the antipropaganda law is rooted—are taken from the curdled theories of the American right. "When people read it, they are shocked! They understand the gays are not some harmless people."

Artyukh says he is afraid blood will be shed. That's why he's for the full criminalization of homosexuality: "to protect the people from being hurt. The homosexual people." They have a choice: let the law walk them back into the closet, or war. He will accept either. "When there is war, you can see the enemy."

Violence is justified?

"Yes, of course violence is acceptable."

"What about actions like Timur's?" I mention the incident at LaSky. "You know about this?"

He does a perfect Tony Soprano, that little pressed-lip half smile with a head nod. "Yes," he says.

"Was it the right way to fight?"

Artyukh glances at his lieutenant and arches an eyebrow. "Timur is Muslim," he says. "Muslim people are heated guys." He thumps his chest. "Fire in their hearts. Cruel men."

He nods. He feels he has said it well. "I only pray for him not to cross the line of the law. I would not want to have to get him out of jail. But we support his activities."

"This confrontation," I say, referring to the shooting, "is that crossing the line?"

"It is," says Artyukh. But only slightly. "If the government doesn't act, other methods will be used. There are going to be fists, and then there are going to be shots."

•   •   •

The last man we talk to that night is the Cossack. Or rather, we listen. Artyukh's lieutenant fetches him for us. He's a big man with sallow eyes and a mighty mustache, his head shaved on the sides and a sweep of black hair falling over his shoulders in a style traditional to Cossacks for hundreds of years before Canadians invented the mullet. His uniform is black with red piping, cinched at the cuffs and above his big black boots.

"Homosexualism is a war against Cossacks," he tells us. So by rights homosexuals should be slaughtered. He recounts some of the ways Cossacks murder homosexuals. Historically speaking. "Of course, I cannot say this officially." He cracks his first smile. "Cossacks," he says, "are known for their humor." For instance, gay men "like to put their cocks in the ass, so we put the shit on their cocks for them." In fact, he says, sometimes they hold a man down and smear shit over his whole body. He chortles, waits for me to laugh. Do I not think this is funny?

"Tell me about your outfit," I say brightly. He shows me his whip, weighted with a sharp lead block. He puts its thick wooden grip in my hand. "Feel," he says. He unsheathes a wide black blade as long as my forearm. He says nothing about the handgun at his side.

"What kind of gun is that?" I ask.

"A good one," he says. He releases the clip to show me it's loaded. He pushes the clip back in. He points the gun at me. Very casual. Just in my direction. Cossack humor. Do I not think this is funny? I lift my notebook off the table. It's time to go. He reaches across and thumps it down. "*Pishi*," he says. "Write."

The Future, Vandalized

In Russia, things are not falling apart, they're coming together, isolated attacks developing into a pattern, the id of the street ever more in line with the Kremlin's growing ego. My last day in Russia began with the news that Cossacks had vandalized two theaters in the night, neither of them gay but guilty of showing plays with homosexual characters. One got graffiti; the other got a bloody pig's head at its door. Humor. Russia's first queer film festival was to open that night—Gus Van Sant was coming to show *Milk*—but it was shut down by a bomb threat. In the afternoon, Artyukh just happened to be having a coffee at a café next to the theater. He got into an argument with a gay activist. Artyukh ripped out the man's earring.

By then I was with Timur again, pressing him about the picture of the gun and about Artyukh's words. Were they true? Was he a "heated man"? Timur was furious. He called Artyukh and put him on speaker phone. Artyukh declared Timur innocent. He declared me a liar. He said he had never heard of the attack at LaSky. Timur grew angrier. What right did I have to dispute him? "Whoever did this"—shooting Dmitry—"it's not your place to judge!" He said I was a guest in his country; he said I have no rights. A warning. My flight was midmorning, but I left and went back to my hotel and packed and went to the airport. It was four a.m.

I tried not to think about Timur. Instead, I thought about a boy I'll call Peter. He's eight years old, the son of a lesbian activist, Sasha, and her partner, Ksenia. I'd met Sasha at the LGBT organization where she worked. Peter was watching a cartoon, waiting for his mother. He invited me home with them. Peter's skinny and pale, with rosy lips and big bright eyes, and he does not like to stop moving. As we walked, he bounced back and forth between us, a game he called "white blood cell."

He was born HIV-positive. He's healthy, but when Sasha met him, volunteering at an orphanage, he weighed half as much as a three-and-a-half-year-old boy should, and his hair was falling out. The only word he knew was Russian for "Don't do that." The nurses told Sasha not to touch him. Not because of the HIV. It was love they were concerned with. If he received any, he'd want more, and none would be forthcoming. He was aging out of the ward, and now they were going to send him to another one, more hopeless still, where he would be thrown in with lost causes of all ages. And there he would remain, as long as he remained.

So Sasha took him. She lied to the orphanage, claimed she was single, and took him home to Ksenia, and they hugged him and told him they would love him, even though they didn't know him. Six months later, he said the second word of his life: his name. He has a name. It breaks my heart that I can't tell it to you.

My last day, in between the pig's head and the bomb threat, I met Sasha and Peter at the park, where Sasha told me about growing up in a city without a name, one of the Soviet Union's secret closed military cities, left off the map and known only by a number. Sasha is built like an elf, with freckles and red hair pulled back in a ponytail. She was a shy and dutiful girl until she saw Ksenia on the day of her college exams. They marveled over each other. Neither of them knew what to call this feeling. They had never heard of lesbians. Literally—they did not know the word. When they kissed, Sasha wondered if they were inventing something new and wonderful. They knew they could tell no one.

But Sasha's mother confronted her one night. "What do you have with this girl?" Sasha, who had never defied her parents, who had never defied anyone, was speechless for a moment. She had no words. Then she found one. "Everything."

Peter knows his mothers are lesbians. What he does not know is that people hate them. Soon, says Sasha, they will have to tell him. Maybe sooner than they had planned. One law has passed; another is coming. They are thinking about Finland, so they can stay close to Russia. They are thinking about Russia, and about how they don't want to leave.

Peter is thinking about faraway places. Over dinner, he asks me if I'll send him a card from America. I can do better than that—how about a present? "Yes!" he says. He knows what he wants. He asks if he can borrow my notebook. He'll draw it for me.

It's an airplane. A big one, so there's room for his whole family. Everyone who loves him, he says happily, drawing the wings.

The Atavist

WINNER—FEATURE WRITING

"Love and Ruin" is, according to the Ellie judges, "an astonishing profile of a woman who played a remarkable role in preserving the archaeological legacy of Afghanistan," written in prose that is "both restrained and beautiful." This is also the first story published by a digital-only publication to win the National Magazine Award for Feature Writing. Another 2014 piece by James Verini, National Geographic's "Should the United Nations Wage War to Keep Peace?"—about the conflict in the Democratic Republic of Congo—won the sixty-sixth annual George Polk Award for Magazine Reporting. A media and software company founded in 2009, The Atavist has earned eight Ellie nominations in the last four years.

James Verini

Love and Ruin

Prologue

It has no official number in the archaeological record, nor an agreed-upon name. Some curators at the National Museum of Afghanistan in Kabul, where it resides, have called it the Limestone Head. Others call it the Carved Pebble. Still others call it simply the Head, and while there is no question that the artifact they're talking about depicts a head, the answer to the question of just whose head it depicts—which person or deity its unyielding eyes and screwed mouth reflect—is lost, like so much else in Afghanistan is lost, to some insolently mute vault of time.

The Head is carved into a limestone pebble two and a half inches high by one and a quarter inches wide. It dates from around 10,000 BCE, placing it in the Upper Paleolithic and making it one of the oldest pieces of sculpture ever found on the Asian continent. We know that it turned up in a gorge near the village of Aq Kupruk, in the northern foothills of the Hindu Kush. Beyond that we know nothing. The best that the most thorough scholarly paper written about the Head—published by the American Philosophical Society in 1972, seven years after it was discovered—can say for its subject is that it is "apparently humanoid." Was it devotional, decorative, whimsical? "Was the head made for a onetime limited use or was it intended for long-term retention and repeated use? . . . Since it will not stand, was it intended to be carried about?" The Head won't say.

But its dumbness beckons. The Head's sculptor was far cleverer than an artist living 12,000 years ago had any call to be. The eyes are not crude circles (all you'd really need in the Upper Paleolithic, you'd think), but composed of a series of subtle line strokes, as though they are contemplating us wearily. The nose, the American Philosophical Society paper observes, "begins with a wide angular cleft rather like that of the nose cavity in a skull and seems almost to be intentionally 'unrealistic,'" while the "deeply engraved line of the mouth itself apparently arcs upward in what seems to be a smile." The paper concludes that the Head does not come from an "individual or cultural 'infantilism.'" Yet the overall effect, millennia later, is a kind of infancy. It's somehow fetal looking, the Head. Some observers see on its face a smile, others a frown, and still others that inscrutable expression, neither frown nor smile, that a wise child makes when he peers into you.

The archaeologist who unearthed the Head, who might have had the most questions about it, had the fewest. Louis Dupree was certain it depicted a woman—and, furthermore, that it had been carved by one. "What else?" Dupree said to a *New York Times* reporter, rather tauntingly, in 1968, when he brought the relic to the American Museum of Natural History. "Women ruled the hearth and the world then. The men were away hunting." *Of course* it was a woman.

That was how Louis Dupree talked—to *Times* writers, to fellow archeologists, presidents, statesmen, interrogators, spies. He even talked that way to his wife, Nancy, who, when asked whether it was true her husband swore like sailor (and a sailor he had been before becoming an archaeologist), would sometimes sigh longingly and reply, "Worse."

Dupree's personal correspondence is full of letters from nervous museum administrators asking after unaccounted-for expenses and unpaid salaries. In the field he worked casually. In 1962, he carried out the first major excavation at Aq Kupruk, an immensely important site, essentially by himself. For the follow-up dig, three years later, when he discovered the Head, he splurged and brought along as diggers and assistants a pair of graduate students, a pair of precocious high schoolers, and his cook.

"We were very, very careful with it," Charles Kolb, one of the graduate students, recalled of the Head. Except for Dupree, that is. Although it was very possibly the most important find of his career, he never properly catalogued it (thus its lack of a single name or record number). Then, in Kabul, he took it home with him, where Nancy, a writer of guidebooks and an amateur scholar, came to adore it as much as he did. Dupree's daughter took a shine to it, too, and called it Daddy's Head. The name stuck.

The Afghan official who granted Dupree permission to take Daddy's Head to New York told him, "If you lose it, you'll owe us half a million dollars." The careful procedure Dupree employed to transport it overseas involved putting it in his jacket pocket, folding the jacket, and stuffing the jacket into the overhead shelf on the plane. Nancy spent the flight looking up nervously at the bundle.

Upon its return from the United States, Daddy's Head was installed at the National Museum in Kabul. Between their excavations, research trips, lecture tours, and teaching stints abroad, Louis and Nancy would visit it there. They'd stare at it for what seemed like hours, talking about the history it must have witnessed. One photograph of the couple shows them sitting at a table, gazing at the artifact as Louis holds it in his fingers (gingerly, but on equal terms). They appear mesmerized, as though Daddy's Head is almost physically drawing them back in time. The photo was taken in 1971, as they were falling more deeply in love with one another, and, together, with Afghanistan. They peered into the country's wondrous, terrible, unknowable past. Daddy's Head, they liked to think, was opening its vault of secrets.

In 1978, a communist cabal seized power in Afghanistan. Louis was imprisoned and deported. The next year the Soviet Union invaded. Its troops pulverized the country, reducing much of its history—the unearthed chapters and those still buried—to rubble. Louis helped the Afghan resistance while Nancy worked with refugees. The struggle against the Soviets gave way to civil war, and their beloved National Museum was in the crossfire.

Nancy and others tried to save the artifacts in the collection. But she didn't find Daddy's Head. The Taliban ended the civil war, but followed that by closing schools, ransacking libraries, and destroying much of what was left of the collection. She wondered if all of the work she and Louis had done to preserve Afghan culture had been in vain. She assumed she would never see Daddy's Head again.

One

I first encountered Nancy Dupree in a ghostly sort of a way. On a Tuesday night in 2003, while soldiers my age were in Afghanistan fighting the Taliban, I was sitting in a theater in Los Angeles, watching a production of Tony Kushner's *Homebody/Kabul*. The play's first scene is given over entirely to a monologue spoken by a Mrs. Dalloway–type character. Why she is addressing us, and from where, she leaves unspoken, as she does her identity—she does not name herself and is known in the program only as the Homebody—but we're aware from the Homebody's first words that the central fact about this woman is that she is deeply taken by, even lost to, Afghanistan. She speaks about the country with passionate eloquence, yet it seems her knowledge of the place has left her understanding less about it, not more. In the convolutions of her speech and mind, the Homebody is wise and helpless, composed and scattered, ancient and infantile. "Our story begins at the very dawn of history, circa 3,000 BC," she begins, as the lights come up, but interrupts herself at once to explain, "I am reading from an outdated guidebook about the city of Kabul."

The Homebody's monologue is brilliant but tortuous, almost infuriatingly so. She departs the narrative of Afghan history for jags about party etiquette and antidepressants, uses words no audience member could be expected to know and then apologizes for them. She is, in other words, very human. So much so, it's clear—or anyway was to me that night—that she must be based on a real woman.

Curious, I eventually contacted Kushner and learned her back story. In the 1990s, he was browsing the stacks at the New York University library, looking for material about Afghanistan, when he stumbled across a volume titled *An Historical Guide to Kabul*. He opened the book and didn't close it until he'd read to the end; the Homebody and the play had emerged. The guidebook's author's name was Nancy Hatch Dupree.

I started asking around about her.

"If the Afghans ever go back to deities, she'll be one," the former American ambassador to Afghanistan Ryan Crocker told me of Dupree. "They all know what she's gone through with them and on their behalf."

Ashraf Ghani, the Afghan intellectual and presidential candidate, described her as "a grandmother figure and mother figure in Afghanistan. Somebody who's given us our cultural heritage. Someone who's played a living witness to our history."

Kushner, who since writing the play has become friends with Dupree and serves on the advisory council of her foundation, called her a woman of "dazzling erudition." (Nancy has never seen *Homebody/Kabul*. "I hear it's good," she tells people.)

The Grandmother of Afghanistan—that is not original to Ghani. It is what Afghans call Dupree, aware that she is technically American. In fact, if she could be said to have any single vocation, this may be it: She is a self-appointed but also widely acknowledged guardian of Afghan culture, the country's bluffest and most beloved expatriate busybody. Among other things, she is the author of dozens of books and scholarly articles on Afghanistan's history, architecture, politics, music, literature, and art; a founder of the Society for the Preservation of Afghanistan's Cultural Heritage; the creator of a library extension service that distributes books to schools and government bodies around the country; the creator of the most extensive digital archive of Afghan historical materials; an occasional adviser to ministers and generals; and an advocate for Afghan women's and children's rights.

Natives and foreigners alike have been trading stories and legends of her ever since she first arrived in Afghanistan over a half-century ago. There was the episode in the 1960s, for instance, when Nancy saved Bagh-e-Bala, the onetime summer palace of the emirs, from destruction, partly out of scholarly devotion to the building and partly so she could host her wedding there. In the 1980s, a young Saudi man approached her, looking for help bringing in equipment to dig tunnels where mujahideen fighters could hide between attacks on Soviet troops. Dupree was not an official, he was aware, but he had heard that she knew everyone of importance in Afghanistan, and that she had the rind to get what she wanted from any one of them. Nancy was too busy to help him, but she recalls the man, who went by the name Osama bin Laden, being "very shy and polite."

More recently, while ordering lumber for a construction project, Nancy ran up against a moratorium on logging that Hamid Karzai had instated. After she called him and made her frustrations known, Karzai ordered the moratorium lifted temporarily. "He was just a little nobody when I first met him," she told me of the president of the Islamic Republic of Afghanistan.

Karzai had other reasons to be helpful. The lumber was for a library Dupree was building at Kabul University, for which he'd already helped raise $2.5 million. The project that could most properly be called her life's work, she has been planning the library and collecting its contents for thirty years. Those contents represent one of the most comprehensive, if not the most comprehensive, archives of post-1979 Afghan historical documents and scholarship anywhere. The library is the more impressive because it is a repository of knowledge about a time during which knowledge was concertedly destroyed in Afghanistan—a memory bank for a generation of Afghans whose clearest personal memories are of exile. She sees it as her greatest gift to her adopted home, as well as her last attempt to save Afghanistan's past, as it were, from itself.

Like other Americans, in the years after 9/11 I read and thought a lot about Afghanistan, that country—in the Homebody's words—"so at the heart of the world the world has forgotten it." After learning of Dupree's collection, I found myself thinking a lot about it, too. I tried to picture its old books and photographs. I wondered what they had to say about this place that has so changed the course of my own country's history, this place where so many Americans have gone to die, but about which America still knows so little. In the fall of 2012, I heard that Dupree's library was, after so many years in the making, finally scheduled to open. I also heard that her health was failing. I called her and told her I wanted to come to Afghanistan. She wasn't overly excited at the prospect, but neither did she exactly object. I booked a ticket for Kabul.

Two

On a hot September morning, I stepped from one of Kabul's loud, dusty streets to the Kabul University gate. The guard refused to let me in. "I'm here to see Nancy Dupree," I told him, reckoning the Grandmother of Afghanistan must be known to all. His expression underwent no change. "The Afghanistan Center at Kabul University?" Nothing. Finally, losing interest, he waved me through.

Dark episodes in recent Afghan history originated on the university campus. It was here that communists and Islamists first did battle in the ideological skirmishes that led up to the Soviet invasion, here that the warlords who would destroy the country—and who still run much of it—first rubbed shoulders. Ashraf Ghani told me that when he came to the university, "people were literally killing each other there. There were warring student gangs." One of his first acts as chancellor was to remove forty-three tons of scrap metal from the school, he said, most of it pieces of blown-up tanks. The tanks have been replaced by a lot of healthy-looking trees, and fewer, less-healthy-looking buildings. Today the campus has a liberal vibe that contrasts with the rest of the country. Female students wear cursory headscarves or none at all; they and their male classmates look at and sometimes even talk to each other.

Twenty feet from the gate I got lost. Dupree had anticipated this, apparently: Soon a silver sedan pulled alongside me. The silhouette of what might have been a child appeared in a back window. I'd never met Dupree, only spoken with her on the phone. Her avian voice hadn't prepared me for the diminutive woman I found. A collapsing robin's nest of gray hair didn't quite get her to five feet, and she couldn't have weighed more in pounds than her age in years, eighty-six at the time. Her eyes were sunken, her face a topography of wrinkles. (I was reminded of the Homebody's description of an Afghan whose "skin is broken by webs of lines inscribed by hardships, siroccos, and strife.") But her cheeks were girlish and full, her mouth small and coy.

Hidden inside a light blue *salwar kameez* and a long scarf, Dupree seemed already to be in mid-conversation when I settled next to her in the backseat. That morning had produced a dustup over fabrics that she wanted for the library, she was saying, and "people just do not realize you don't accomplish things overnight here. They come from somewhere else and expect everything to fall into place. But it takes so much bloody time." Looking out the window, she added, "That's why everything here is kind of . . . half-assed."

We drove to her temporary office, which she'd been working out of for years, in a converted garage. With a cough, she eased into a chair behind the old dining room table that serves as her desk. Her staff, at small desks around the room, greeted her as Nancy Jan. (*Jan* is a Dari diminutive that means, roughly, "dear.") They were all Afghan, all in their twenties or thirties, and all, I noticed, men.

"Oh, I'm notorious," she said when I asked her to square this with her advocacy for Afghan women. "In Peshawar, I tried to have women, and I discovered that they're not reliable. In this society, you get somebody trained and then the father says, 'We're moving from Peshawar to Islamabad,' and off they go. Or they get married. Or they've got children and, you know, they don't turn up because their child's got diarrhea."

A cook brought out plates of rice pilau from the kitchen (a closet with a hot plate) as the library's designers arrived to discuss the fabric situation. Dupree had been informed there was not enough of the red pattern she'd ordered long before for all the upholstery and curtains in the library and now was, she announced, "really browned off. We could have done this six months ago!"

"Two years ago," said Dupree's executive director, Waheed Wafa, a tall, warm-voiced man whose face exuded beleaguerment. Like many educated Kabulis, Wafa grew up with the Duprees' books. Also like many educated Kabulis, he was beaten by the Taliban. When the U.S.-led coalition invaded, in 2001, he became a fixer for the *New York Times*, then a reporter. Dupree hired him in 2011.

Wafa produced a fan of swatches, potential replacements, and held up a reddish one. "That's dullsville," Dupree said, waving a hand dismissively. She jumped to the issue of acoustics. Without enough good fabric to absorb sound, the library would be too loud.

"What about urns?" Waheed suggested. Knowing Dupree's mood could be improved by a story of Afghan ingenuity, he told one: During the Taliban years, he said, his friends in the Kabul underground used to hold meetings in a room they thought was secure. But one day they realized Talibs were listening outside. So they lined the walls of the room with large urns, to muffle their voices.

"Oh yes, yes!" Dupree said, getting into the story, and smiling for the first time since I'd met her. A cordial South African designer stepped into the office and joined the conversation. "See how everything in Afghanistan has to be negotiated?" he whispered to me.

After some gentle cajoling from Wafa and the others, Dupree agreed on potential vendors. "OK, that's done. Decision made. Bang!" she said, slapping her hand on the table. Her staff looked up from their desks hopefully. A date was set to go to the market, and the group left. "He's writing a book," Dupree said of the South African designer once he had gone. "*Everybody's* writing a book." I asked if she ever thought of writing another book. "No. I don't know enough. I don't *care* enough."

Later, Wafa told me the new library was still months from completion. Since Dupree was relying on the Afghan government to pay for much of it, she was also relying on the government to pay the workers who were supposed to be finishing it. It hadn't been, and they weren't. I asked him when it might open. "God knows," Waheed said, dragging on a Marlboro. He'd recently upped from a half-pack to a whole pack per day, he confided.

Three

A few days later, Dupree and a thickset, bearded man in his mid-thirties named Mashall, who manages her box-library program, drove to Charikar, a town about forty miles north of Kabul, to check in on a provincial council and a few schools. As we were departing, I asked if it was safe in Charikar. "We don't ask questions like that," she said. "If you think about that you'll go nowhere. And that's why the Americans don't go anywhere." Not just Americans but foreigners generally are seen by Afghans mostly as they make their way in chauffeured cars between fortified homes, fortified offices, fortified hotels, and fortified restaurants. Dupree is known for going anywhere she likes and for despising fortification.

On Kabul's outskirts, we drove past mile after mile of new cinderblock homes and roadside shops fashioned from steel shipping containers. "What you're going through now, this place used to be desert, complete desert, just ten years ago," she said. "It just shows that when Afghans decide to do something, they're not slackers, they get at it and they do!" Then she pondered. Her mood turned. "But it's not organized. It's all . . . *personal.* I suppose they tax all this, but do they pay the taxes? Who knows. It's higgledy-piggledy."

"It's not sketched, Nancy Jan," Mashall said.

Like many Afghans, Mashall has come to know Afghanistan only in adulthood. Before that he lived in Pakistan, where he'd moved as a child after his village was bombed in the Soviet war. He grew up in Peshawar, where he met Dupree in 1999. "When people see Nancy on the TV," he said, "they say, 'She's still working, she's still here.' We say to our women, 'Look at Nancy Dupree, she's eighty and still working.'"

Dupree waved a hand. "When people see me they say, 'Good God, that woman is still alive?'"

She looked from the window onto a magnificent view. In the distance were the "skirts of the mountains," as a Persian poet once called the foothills of the Hindu Kush, and before them the Shomali Plain, a mine-ridden flatland once alive with vegetables and grapevines. We passed a cinderblock sprawl that had been a meadow, the site of a cavalry battle in the First Anglo-Afghan war, in the early 1840s. Dupree recounted how she and a friend used to ride horses there and reenact the fighting. "I swear there must be people in that village who tell stories about these two crazy women who rode around charging at each other."

We passed Bagh-e-Bala, the domed hilltop palace that the emir Abdur Rahman built to escape the heat of the Kabul Valley at the end of the nineteenth century. "That's where Louis and I were married," she said.

Four

Nancy Hatch was born in Cooperstown, New York, in 1926, and raised in Travancore, a small feudal kingdom on the southern tip of India, during the last gasps of the Raj. Her mother, a onetime stage actress, studied traditional Indian theater and wrote a guidebook to Travancore. Her father, who'd fought in the First World War with the British, worked on education projects for UNESCO around Asia. "He taught me a tremendous amount," Dupree said. "One thing was, if you hold on to something too long, it fails."

Living in India in the 1930s and 1940s, she told me, "was like growing up on a movie set. The maharaja was very fond of my father. I was the same age as the maharaja's brother. Every time there was a new birth of leopards or tigers at the zoo, they'd bring the cubs to the palace, and I'd go to the palace with my little white gloves and big hat." She left to study at Barnard College and after graduating performed as a harpist. She gave that up to enroll in the Chinese and Japanese Studies Department at Columbia University and then returned to Asia, following her father into UNESCO, where she worked as an adviser to the governments of India and Ceylon (now Sri Lanka).

At Columbia, she met an aspiring diplomat named Alan Wolfe, a suave and capable product of Manhattan wealth. They married in Ceylon. The match was not ideal, according to some friends. Wolfe was "definitely not Nancy's type," said one of them, Mary

MacMakin. "Though the fact that he was in the Foreign Service was such a draw for her. I think that's why she married him." According to MacMakin, Nancy was "a party girl" but "a brain, too."

Wolfe joined the Foreign Service after the war. He was posted to Iraq, where Nancy edited a news bulletin for American embassy staff, and then transferred to Pakistan. One day they were gazing toward the Khyber Pass, the entrance to the Hindu Kush and Afghanistan, and she suggested a trip there. "He couldn't think of anything worse," she told me. But, to her delight, Wolfe was assigned to the Kabul embassy in 1962. "He wasn't happy. I was very happy." Though on paper Wolfe was a cultural attaché, in truth Afghan culture was of only secondary interest to him. That was because, off the books, he was the Central Intelligence Agency's new chief of station in Kabul.

A rising star in the agency, Wolfe was, if not the best-liked operative in the Clandestine Services, surely among its most ambitious. An underling once described him to a journalist as "the kind of guy who only speaks to Cabots, Lodges, and God." Duane Clarridge, a former CIA agent who worked under Wolfe, writes in his memoir that Wolfe "constantly measured [his superior's] chair for size" and had "a low threshold for the dim-witted." Another former agent who worked under him described to me his first meeting with Wolfe. "Wolfe was dressed in a very good suit, Brooks Brothers I'm sure," he said. He walked around the room, making a point to look at his pocket watch every few minutes. "I'm expecting a call from Kissinger," Wolfe kept saying.

Soon after they moved to Kabul, Alan and Nancy met Louis Dupree. Born in 1925 to descendants of French Huguenots on the family tobacco farm at Dupree's Crossroads, North Carolina, as a boy Dupree thought he would become a Presbyterian preacher. He also believed in integration, and the two were immiscible in the Jim Crow South. As a youth leader in the church, said Nancy—with the air of hagiography that characterizes much of her recollection of Louis—he invited a black boy to a service, and "when the church elders told him he couldn't do that, he said, 'Fuck you.'

"This was way before Martin Luther King," she added.

With the outbreak of World War II, Dupree dropped out of school to attend the Coast Guard Academy, then joined the merchant marine. At sea he read everything he could. In 1944, he joined the army, trained as a paratrooper, and was dispatched to the Pacific, where his most challenging mission, according to stories he would later tell, found him dropping behind enemy lines in the Philippines to recruit Bontoc Igorot natives to fight the Japanese. The Bontoc, renowned headhunters, didn't require much training. "Louis would tell us how they'd come back from raids with bags, sometimes, of Japanese heads," Charles Kolb, the archaeologist who worked with Dupree at Aq Kupruk, recalled. Dupree was awarded a Purple Heart and a Bronze Star.

After the war, he won a scholarship contest for veterans and, with no high school diploma, was admitted to Harvard, where in eight years he completed bachelor's, master's, and doctorate degrees in anthropology. The Harvard archaeologist Carleton Coon took Dupree under his wing. One of the last great American academic generalists, Coon was, like Dupree, interested primarily in prehistoric Asian archaeology, but he convinced his pupil that to really understand the world, he must be versed in not only archaeology but also history, geography, biology, linguistics, ethnomusicology, political science, and whatever else he had time for. Dupree agreed. His dissertation, on Paleolithic tools, took up two volumes.

Early on, he displayed a knack for portentous finds. At an excavation in Iran, he and Coon discovered skeletal remains that helped debunk the theory, dominant in archaeology at the time, that humanity's origins lay in the Far East. On an expedition in France, he unearthed a stone carved with animal images dating from 25,000 BCE, at the time the oldest piece of moveable sculpture ever found. Then Dupree—the church youth leader had grown into a master schmoozer—convinced the French government to let his team take it back to Harvard.

In the summer of 1949, he and a friend were sent by the Museum of Natural History to carry out the first American dig in Afghanistan. French and German archaeologists had long been active in the country, but their interest was in its Buddhist past. The remnants of prehistory lay mostly untouched. Within a few months, Dupree and a colleague had found the medieval city of Peshawarun, long thought vanished, in Afghanistan's southwestern desert. They stumbled upon it while searching for a drink of water, they explained. Later Dupree found the oldest human remains ever discovered in Afghanistan, dated to 30,000 BCE, and the oldest tools, dated to 100,000 BCE.

Dupree and his colleagues were regularly written up in newspapers, but they were anachronisms; the swashbuckling era of archaeology was ending. Coon's generation had relied on their vast stores of personal knowledge to arrive at grand theories. Dupree's contemporaries, by contrast, were scientific specialists who employed new technologies and meticulous record keeping—all of which bored Dupree no end. "He wasn't really up on the Paleolithic literature or the most recent anthropological theories," said Rick Davis, an archaeologist who worked for Dupree. "He kind of painted with a broad brush." Charles Kolb said the handling of the Aq Kupruk artifacts was shambolic: When it came time to divide the excavation's yield—including Daddy's Head—among the Afghan and American partners, they simply laid out the thousands of pieces they'd found and commenced haggling.

What Dupree lacked in punctiliousness, however, he compensated for with toil, good cheer, and a leonine confidence. He had the aura of a bygone age about him, at once domineering and gracious. "He was a real commander [and] was very direct," said

Davis. "He facilitated and encouraged so many people who came to Afghanistan, even people with the most slender credentials. He'd introduce these wayfaring scholars to these local people." He added: "He worked very hard and liked to have a drink after six o'clock."

Ashraf Ghani was one of many young Afghan scholars whom Dupree helped and encouraged. "He was an incredibly gracious man," Ghani said. "It was the openness of his mind. He exemplified a tolerance for critique, for ideas."

Dupree signed off letters with the Latinism "Summum Bonum." Originally an Aristotelian notion translated as "the highest good," he meant it more as Cicero had, as something like "happiness is to be found in the highest pursuits." Depending on the day, he embodied this ideal or its opposite or both simultaneously.

He was "a very profane character," the American ambassador to Afghanistan in the mid-1970s, Ted Eliot, said. The first time Eliot's wife dined at Dupree's home in Kabul, a high-ranking Afghan official was also present. Eliot's wife privately expressed her worry to Dupree that the Afghan regime was spoiling for a war with Pakistan. Dupree, well into his cups, brought the official over to Mrs. Eliot. "So what about it?" Dupree asked him. "Are you going to start a fucking war with Pakistan?"

"That was typical," Eliot said.

In the list of Dupree's published works for 1967—this is on his official résumé—one finds an entry for an article entitled "The Relationship of Religious Ritual to Orgasm Frequency Among the Tribal Women of Fungoolistan: A Humping and Gathering Society."

Such impieties aside, by the 1960s Dupree was, by general consent, the leading Western expert on Afghanistan's history. Some said *the* leading expert. His "knowledge of the country was extraordinary," Kolb said. "He understood it from the prehistoric era through the current political situation."

Five

Abdur Rahman, the builder of Bagh-e-Bala, liked to call his country Yaghistan: Land of Insolence. And, indeed, while there was much about Afghanistan to attract the polymath bon vivant Dupree, its chief appeal to his rebellious nature may have been precisely that. "The insolence of the Afghan, however, is not the frustrated insolence of urbanized, dehumanized man in western society," Dupree would write in the introduction to his most important book, *Afghanistan*. "But insolence without arrogance, the insolence of harsh freedoms set against a backdrop of rough mountains and deserts, the insolence of equality felt and practiced (with an occasional touch of superiority), the insolence of bravery past and bravery anticipated."

Afghans like to claim that Cain and Abel founded Kabul, and that Cain is buried there. If so, he was only the first of many murderous dynasty builders to arrive. He was followed by the Aryans, the Kushans, the Persians, Alexander the Great and the Greeks, the White Huns, the Arabs, Tamurlane and the Mongols, the Ghaznavids, and yet more Persians. Afghanistan emerged as a loose coalition of territories under a monarchy only in the mid-1700s, and its boundaries were not formally delineated until the 1880s, when they were decided on by British and Russian cartographers. Seeing the country as a mutually beneficial stretch of insulation between the Raj and the Tsar, they gave little thought to the myriad cultures and faiths that unwittingly found themselves inside the new borders: Pashtuns, Turkmen, Tajiks, Uzbeks, Hazaras, and Baluchis, who variously practiced Sunni, Sufi, and Shiite Islam, Buddhism, and even some Zoroastrianism, along with expert grudge-holding and famously bloody battles over succession. The colonially minded American historian Theophilus Rodenbough, writing in 1885, observed that "the love of war is felt much more among Afghans then by other eastern peoples." Commenting on local dress, he noted, "Weapons are borne by all."

Britain and Russia spent much of the nineteenth century vying for control of Central and South Asia in the sadistic enterprise known as the Great Game. Rodenbough proudly related that during the First Anglo-Afghan War, "Kabul and other towns were leveled with the ground; [Afghan] troops were blown from guns, and the people were collected together and destroyed like worms." However, the Afghans had one elusive advantage over their would-be occupiers: Unlike the Britons and the Russians, they were not, had never been, a feudal people. Afghan political life was arranged around complex authority-sharing conclaves known as *jirgas* and *shuras*. When trouble arose, elders, chiefs, and religious leaders would act together to protect their territories. In this way, they had rebuffed one attempted conquest after another. Uninterested in cohering in peacetime, in war Afghans were something to watch; the British may have blown their enemy from cannons, but eventually they left in humiliation.

In the 1930s, Afghanistan—for as long as anyone could remember, a byword for exotic isolation—began opening up to the world. On the eve of World War II, King Mohammed Zahir Shah aligned Afghanistan with the Axis powers and then, seeing which way the wind was blowing, switched to the Allies, thus avoiding being drawn into actual conflict by either. The Dari term for this is *bi-tarafi*, or "without sides." Some observers called it self-preservation, others a way of playing world powers off each other, still others plain deceit. The Westerners, like Dupree, who understood Afghanistan best understood that *bi-tarafi* is all those things. Dupree admired the Afghans' ability to stay out of fights just as much as their willingness to get into them. He liked to call his adopted home the Switzerland of Asia, where "spies swapped lies and information and played cat-and-mouse with counter-agents and counter-counter-agents."

By the time Dupree settled in Kabul, in the 1950s, its upper classes were dressing in Savile Row suits and sending their sons to Oxford. In 1958, the prime minister, Mohammed Daoud, became the first Afghan leader to visit Washington, and the next year Dwight Eisenhower returned the favor, the first American president to venture to the Afghan capital. Embassies opened. Diplomats, academics, archaeologists, and explorers arrived. Kabul University expanded. The Peace Corps set up shop. Kabul became a spur on the Hippie Trail, the path of enlightenment and drug tourism that snaked from Europe to India.

Dupree was in the middle of it all. When not out on a dig, he taught courses and lectured about Afghanistan, compiled reports, advised governments and corporations, filmed documentaries, and wrote or edited scholarly articles and books (some 218 of the former and 22 of the latter by the end of his career). In between he socialized endlessly. "He knew everybody, whether they were Americans, Afghans, French, Russians, East Germans, West Germans, civilians, military," Kolb said. "You name them, he seemed to know them."

More than any other foreigner, Dupree knew Afghans, all kinds of Afghans; he was as charmed by goatherds as he was by the royal family. They all had something to teach him, he felt. He assumed that Afghans found him charming, too, and indeed many did. What Dupree failed to see—what other Americans who knew and loved the country less did see—was that while Afghans liked him, that didn't mean they trusted him. "Afghans were very cautious with Americans," Ted Eliot, the former ambassador, said. "Their long history with foreigners taught them that you never knew who would be in charge next."

Six

Louis Dupree and Alan Wolfe were the only Americans in Kabul who could match one another cocktail for cocktail and tale for tale, and by the mid-1960s they had become good friends. "He was very smooth," Mary MacMakin said of Wolfe. "A good talker, a good dancer, a good drinker—drinking especially."

And Dupree, who had a connection at customs and brought in liquor by the crate, seemed "impervious to alcohol." Wolfe relished drinking martinis with Dupree and listening to stories of the Bontoc headhunters.

To much of the rest of the world, as to the country's more cosmopolitan citizens, the opening of Afghanistan was an encouragement, proof that the Cold War could be avoided in certain corners of the globe. Dupree's social calendar seemed proof of this: On a given night, he might be found dining in the company of the American ambassador or the Russian one. But to Wolfe—a gentleman spy in the classical mold who spoke seven languages and thought a great deal about meaning in history—Afghanistan wasn't just another front in the Cold War; it was a deceptively important one, and one to which Washington wasn't paying sufficient attention, he believed.

And, to a degree, he was right. Russia's preoccupation with Afghanistan had persisted through the fall of the Romanovs and the October Revolution. "The road to Paris and London might lead through Kabul," Leon Trotsky remarked, to the agreement of his boss, V. I. Lenin, who said, "The East will help us to conquer the West. Let us turn our faces toward Asia." For a time, the Afghan royal family was receptive to the Kremlin's overtures, particularly after Lenin wrote the king a pandering letter in which he expressed his conviction that Afghanistan had been chosen by history for a "great and historic task," namely to "unite all the enslaved Muslim peoples." Afghanistan was the first country to recognize Soviet Russia, in 1917, and two years later the USSR was the first nation to recognize an independent Afghanistan.

But the Afghans perceived, rightly, that the atheist Moscow regime was out to topple Islam along with all other religions. They also suspected that the Bolsheviks' intentions for Afghanistan weren't all that different from what the old regime's had been: where the Tsars saw Afghanistan as the passageway to a larger empire, the Bolsheviks saw it as the means to further revolution.

Neither much appealed. This suspicion was confirmed when Lenin backed a plan to recruit an army of disaffected Muslims and use Afghanistan as a staging ground to attack British India. Relations soured further in the 1930s, when Stalin ordered the Muslim leadership in Soviet Central Asia decimated and instituted forced collectivization, sending hordes of refugees into Afghanistan.

The Afghan government wanted help in modernizing, however, and during the Cold War help came from one of two places. Finding American requests to sign mutual-security pacts and contain "communist aggression" too demanding, Kabul turned to Moscow. Beginning in the 1950s, Soviet arms, advisers, and economic aid came rushing in. Afghans traveled to the USSR for academic and military training. Washington countered with projects and weapons of its own, but it never caught up.

Wolfe was acutely aware of all this. How much he privately told Dupree about his work was known only to the two friends. Publicly, they were at the center of Kabul's international social scene. This being the 1960s, that scene was characterized not only by heavy boozing but by adultery. Afghan officials bedded foreign diplomats' wives; foreign diplomats bedded Afghan officials' wives; wives bedded wives. Nancy and Annie Dupree, Louis's wife, rebuffed any number of offers. In the midst of it the two women, who were very different—Nancy was childless and famously flirtatious, Annie more traditional and shy, with three children—bonded. It was with Annie that Nancy reenacted the battles on horseback in the meadow.

Soon after arriving in Afghanistan, Nancy accompanied the American ambassador to see the giant Buddhas at Bamiyan. Appointed to act as an unofficial historian for the trip, she attempted to read up on the statues, but was appalled to find that no guidebooks to Bamiyan existed. At a cocktail party upon their return, she cornered the Afghan minister for tourism, Abdul Tarzi. She recalled the encounter this way: "Now, instead of being a diplomat's wife, I said, 'Mr. Tarzi, it's a scandal. That is one of the wonders of the world and you don't have a proper guide, you don't have anything.' And in typical Afghan style, this Mr. Tarzi drew himself up, and he said, 'You're quite right, why don't you do something about it?' A French archaeologist who was part of the discussion said, 'Madam, do you like ladies' coffee parties?' I said, 'Not really.' He said, 'Do you play bridge, Madam?' I said, 'That's a waste of time.' 'Then,' he says, 'I suggest you take up this challenge of Mr. Tarzi's.'"

She did. Tarzi liked the manuscript for *The Valley of Bamiyan* so much, he had the tourism ministry publish it. She went on to write guides to Balkh, Herat, and the National Museum. The books were increasingly handsome; Afghanistan was becoming a tourist destination, and, as Nancy put it to me, "They needed to be printed in some kind of form that these rich bitches would take notice of." *An Historical Guide to Kabul*, the book that thirty years later would possess Tony Kushner, was published in 1965. Annie proofread it. In the acknowledgments, Nancy wrote, "I owe her for more than these labors, for her understanding of and sympathy for the city has been a constant guide since my arrival."

What happened next is still obscured by mystery and rumor. No two people tell the story the same way. Finally, the one fact that can be verified is the only essential one: At some point, the couples switched partners.

Seven

Some friends of the Duprees and Wolfes believe Annie and Alan fell in love first, leaving Louis and Nancy to do the same. Others maintain that it was the reverse. Charles Kolb had long suspected that Louis and Nancy were having an affair. She visited the camp at Aq Kupruk for no apparent practical reason. Kolb recalls flying into Kabul in 1966 to resume work at Aq Kupruk. Louis picked him up at the airport and, with his customary bluntness, announced, "I've divorced Annie and married Nancy."

"That's all he said about it," Kolb told me. "I said, 'OK.'"

When I asked Nancy about it, she did what she usually did when she didn't want to discuss something—she recalled the most famous and most anodyne episode from the affair and then abruptly ended the conversation. When she finished writing *The Valley of Bamiyan*, she told me, she sent the manuscript to Dupree for fact-checking. For some time she heard nothing back. Finally, he summoned her. When she arrived at his home, he was sitting behind a large desk in a room full of plants that had been moved inside for winter storage. He handed her the manuscript without looking at her. At the top of the first page he'd written, "Adequate, but nothing original."

"After a curt riposte, I turned on my heel and stomped off," she recalled. "I got to the door and he said, 'Come back here.' So I went back. And I never left."

They were married in the winter of 1966, in a blizzard. Minister Tarzi stood in for her father during the negotiation of the bride price, which Louis set at 10,000 sheep. "Even in a situation like that," she told me, "he was a joker."

Alan and Annie Wolfe left Kabul, and Louis and Nancy Dupree became its expat nucleus. They lived in a compound in the modern Shar-e-Nau district. Nancy worked in the main house, Louis in a building in the courtyard. So many visitors stopped by that they had to instruct their guards not to admit anyone who hadn't made an appointment. In the evenings, they hosted a recurring cocktail party known as the Five O'clock Follies. "An amazing troupe of people would come by: Americans, Europeans, Japanese, Afghans," the archaeologist Rick Davis remembered. "He and Nancy were terrific, they were inseparable." Everybody, he said, "wanted to be around them."

Otherwise, the Duprees could be found traveling Afghanistan's rough mountains and deserts in Louis's red Land Rover.

"He was always looking for new caves. And I was always happy to go along because I might see something. And if there was something I needed for the guidebooks he was always happy to go along, because he might find another cave," Nancy said. "Every time one of us would finish an article, he'd open a bottle of champagne. It was real companionship." Together they fell in thrall to a country where, in the Homebody's words, "one might seek in submission the unanswered need."

"I was happy then," Nancy told me. "Going around and learning everything new with Louis Jan. So enthusiastic, like a teenager."

In 1973, Louis published his magnum opus, *Afghanistan*, the culmination of a quarter-century of work and travel. It's still the definitive survey text on the country. For all his lack of sentimentality and his admiration of Afghan insolence, Dupree was an optimist, and the book's keynote is one of hope for the country's future. *Bi-tarafi* had allowed the Afghans not only to stay neutral in the Cold War, Dupree argued, but also to coax mortal enemies into cooperating. In their efforts to use Afghanistan as a proxy battlefield, the United States and the Soviet Union had ended up helping it. "The Soviets assisted the Afghans in building roads from the north, the U.S. from the south," he wrote. "The Soviets helped construct the landing strips and buildings for the new International Airport at Kabul; the Americans installed the electrical and communications equipment."

"But since the West and the Soviet Union are both interested in winning, the question of 'Who's winning, the Americans or the Russians?' should be considered," he went on. "In all honesty, one must answer 'Neither—the Afghans are winning.'"

Nancy likes to deny what everyone knows, which is that she was essential to the research and composition of *Afghanistan*. She claims she merely transcribed it. "You've seen his book?" she asked me one day. I said yes, I'd read it. "Alright, and it's a thick one. I typed that dumb thing three times over—on a manual typewriter! Three times, and I was happy to do it."

The false modesty of this claim was demonstrated when her *An Historical Guide to Afghanistan* was published. Where *Afghanistan* is a monument to fact, her book is an exercise in style and wit, and it's still an indispensable guide for diehard Afghanophiles, who—like Kushner—don't read it so much for the information as for her voice. ("We were totally committed to her guidebooks as we traveled around the country," Ted Eliot, the former ambassador, told me.) In the acknowledgments she wrote, "From my husband, Louis Dupree, I draw a constant charge of excitement and enthusiasm for this land and its people. Together we find new depths and new values. I shall be well pleased if this book succeeds in conveying our continuing affection for Afghanistan."

Eight

After the two hour-long drive north, Nancy, Mashall, and I arrived in Charikar in the late morning. From Western news coverage one can get the idea that, twelve years after the American invasion, the Taliban is still confined to Afghanistan's peripheries. This isn't the case. The Taliban controls much of the countryside, it's true, but it also wields influence and fear in just about every city and major town, including Kabul. Nancy's first stop was at the offices of the provincial council in Charikar, which had been attacked recently. They sit behind blast-shielding berms and a pair of guards whose faces suggest they don't expect to be much help when the next bomb explodes.

For years, Dupree has been sending books, thousands of them, to provincial councils—on history, administration, farming science, public health, and anything else she can have printed—in the hopes that local officials will use them to better govern.

"Mr. Karzai and the government, they don't like it, because it takes away from their own power," she says. "But until the people get a voice, Afghanistan's not going anywhere." After three and a half decades of war, however, the country is still mostly run by small groups of old men, many of them illiterate.

She and Mashall were led into a narrow, dark room lined with overstuffed green felt chairs and coffee tables. A policeman with a limp put out bowls of pistachios and poured tea as provincial officials, all of them old and hirsute—*reesh safeda*, or whitebeards, they're called—shuffled in. Without greeting Nancy, they sank into chairs. She has forgotten most of her Dari, so she asked them questions through an interpreter.

"Is Kabul listening to you?"

Murmurs.

"Are you getting the money for the projects you want to do?"

Fewer murmurs.

"Do you listen to the women and get them money?"

Silence.

The whitebeards knew who she was, perhaps they even appreciated her help, but they couldn't have been less interested in her presence. Dupree elicited somewhat more adamant murmuring when she asked about the recent murder of a local woman. An official spoke to the interpreter, who turned to Dupree and said, "They are totally against the things which are bad." Dupree frowned. The official was now talking into his phone. The meeting was over.

As the officials shuffled out, a younger man introduced himself as the secretary. In precise English, he explained that the council valued her books. They had tried to set up a public library, as she'd requested, but people borrowed the books and neglected to return them. So he'd moved them into a locked office. Now officials neglected to return them.

As he and Dupree talked, he unburdened himself. "The problem in Afghanistan is everything is based on theory," he told her.

The council had no money. He hadn't been paid a salary in a year and half. A local merchant had donated the big green chairs. Dupree listened intently, made suggestions. She said she wanted him to connect the council to her organization online, so she could distribute the newsletter he wrote and send him materials. He looked at the floor. "We don't have Internet."

"This is so typical," she said to Mashall as they left. "He's got the spirit. He wants to do something, not for himself, but for other people. But he can't break out."

"It's true, Nancy Jan."

.   .   .

Some days later, Nancy and Mashall visited a boys' school in an impoverished village on Kabul's fringe. Its mud-brick homes were not old, but the Afghan summers and winters and dust had left them looking like ruins. In the school's drab courtyard, makeshift classrooms were set up under plastic tarps. A geography teacher led them around. Nancy asked him what he could use. "Maps," he said. He taught geography, but there were no maps.

The teacher brought them to the library, a disheartening sight. It was doing double-duty as a storeroom for an old generator and for laboratory equipment that some foreign government had donated, which might have been useful if the school had a laboratory. "They don't have a card catalogue, they don't have a computer. How do they know what's here?" she asked Mashall between coughs. He pointed to a handwritten list of books taped to the side of a cabinet.

An English teacher who spoke very little English brought me to his classroom. Boys sat on windowsills, on top of one another. There were no books, no paper, no pencils. "Most students don't know what books are here," he told me. But they were unbelievably disciplined and, their eyes suggested, dying to learn something, anything. I asked if they liked to read.

"Yes!" they shouted in unison. I asked what they liked to read. "Histories!" one boy said.

His name was Saddiq, and he obviously took school quite seriously. Though he looked no more than thirteen, he was wearing a pink dress shirt and a frayed brown blazer. Saddiq loved Dupree's library, the teacher said. He was borrowing books all the time. I asked Saddiq what period of Afghan history he liked to read about. "The Ghaznavids," he said, referring to the Turkic dynasty that ruled much of what would become Afghanistan in the tenth through twelfth centuries. Many Afghans regard the period as the high point of their history. When I asked whether he didn't want to learn about more recent events, about the time in which he lived, he considered the question. "No," Saddiq said. "It's all war."

In the car on the way back to Kabul, Dupree looked out the window silently and sank lower and lower into her seat. A friend of hers had told me that, left to herself, her thoughts always drifted back to Louis. "If you just watch her body language," he'd said, "it's very distressing." He was right. As we drove by a hillside blooming with redbud, she muttered, "Redbud . . . I wanted redbud for Louis's memorial service, but I couldn't get it. Protected species."

Nine

In 1973, in *Afghanistan*, Louis had expressed great hope for the country's future—too much, as it turned out. He didn't mention that radical communism and radical Islamism were on the rise, nor that the halting attempts at modernization and religious and social reforms undertaken by Mohammed Daoud—who'd been removed from the prime ministership by his cousin, King Zahir Shah, nearly a decade earlier—hadn't made it out of the cities. The gaps between the increasingly secular urban elite and the poor, illiterate, and devout peasantry were more glaring than ever. In 1972, when the country was overcome by famine and hundreds of thousands died, an official remarked, "If the peasants eat grass, it's hardly grave. They're beasts. They're used to it." The next year, after Dupree had completed his book, Daoud staged a palace coup and took back control of the government.

Louis knew the autocratic but generous-spirited Daoud as well as any foreigner did. "You must understand one thing in the beginning: Afghanistan is a backward country," he'd once told Dupree during an interview. "We accept this. We know that we must do something about it or die as a nation." Daoud wanted America to support Afghanistan, he said, but not at the price of its independence. "We first turned to the Unites States for aid, because we believe in the American ideology. The idea of freedom for all is the idea that we have for Afghanistan . . . but any aid which any country gives to us must be with no strings attached."

Daoud delivered the same message, with less tact, to Soviet premier Leonid Brezhnev. By the late 1970s, Moscow was largely keeping Daoud's government afloat, but still he liked to "light Soviet cigarettes with American matches," as one KGB officer put it. "We will never allow you to dictate to us how to run our country," Daoud reportedly told Brezhnev, dispensing with the subtleties of *bi-tarafi*, after the Kremlin had instructed him to expel workers from NATO countries. "Afghanistan shall remain poor, if necessary, but free in its acts and decisions."

In 1978, Afghan Marxists murdered Daoud and his family. Mayhem of the sort not seen since the Anglo-Afghan wars ensued. Officials, academics, businessmen, landowners, journalists, religious leaders, and anyone else deemed a threat to the socialist revolution were rounded up, tortured, and executed.

Louis, of course, knew the Marxist cabal well, including the new president, Nur Mohammed Taraki, a sadistic KGB provocateur of long standing. Taraki, a firm believer in terror, liked to say, "Lenin taught us to be merciless towards the enemies of the revolution." Despite this, Dupree was at first sanguine about his intentions—or startlingly naïve, depending on whom one asked. A month after the coup, Dupree wrote a letter to the *New York Times* emphasizing the nationalist character of Taraki's regime. "One may deplore the bloodshed which accompanied the revolution and feel remorse for the dead, but an enlightened press should avoid the loose use of the term 'Communist,'" he wrote. Ted Eliot recalled Dupree telling him, "These communists are friends from way back." Eliot was amazed. "I said, 'Louis, this is different. It's the *Soviet* communists.'"

Dupree's delusional attitude derived in part from experience, one suspects, and in part from pride, but more than either from his love of the Afghans. He similarly assumed he wouldn't be targeted, regardless of the persistent rumors about him, because so many Afghans loved him. "Louis's conviction was that every Afghan knew he was a friend of Afghanistan and they wouldn't hurt him," Eliot said.

One day in November 1978, Louis and Nancy went to the National Museum to pay a visit to Daddy's Head. That afternoon, after Louis had returned to the hotel suite where they were staying at the time, secret policemen knocked on the door. An Afghan translator Dupree worked with had been arrested and, after being tortured, had identified Dupree as a spy. Others followed suit—maybe to save their skins, maybe because they knew something.

In Kabul, it had long been suspected that Dupree's relationship with Alan Wolfe extended beyond friendship and the eventual exchange of spouses. During the Cold War, it was common for American scholars to gather information for the CIA, and Dupree was a perfect candidate for recruitment: three Harvard degrees, military experience, unparalleled knowledge of the country. He'd been surrounded by spies of one type or another for much of his life. (Carleton Coon, his mentor at Harvard, had been an agent in the Office of Strategic Services, the CIA's precursor.)

And Dupree never really left military service. He always considered himself a soldier at heart. Before moving to Kabul, he'd worked as a researcher in troop behavior for the air force, writing field manuals and course curricula, and later taught at West Point. He didn't officially retire from the army until 1967.

It would have surprised no one, in other words, if Dupree had worked with the CIA. He always denied the rumors—adamantly, sometimes angrily. According to some people who knew him well, however, that may have been a front.

As Kabul station chief, Wolfe had been tasked with providing the CIA with intelligence on the Russian-made hardware being used by the Afghan military. Most of it was in the north of the country, as is Aq Kupruk. The archaeologist Charles Kolb said that on their way to and from the excavation site, Dupree and he took detailed notes on the Russian equipment they saw. Dupree photographed it with a high-speed camera. Kolb believes he was doing this for Wolfe and that Wolfe or the CIA may have funded Dupree's work in some capacity. "We were always looking for military installations," Kolb told me. "He was working with Alan and providing information to Alan directly." He also believes Dupree's popular parties were a means for the pair to gather intelligence. His "soirees were very eye-opening, because you got people together who were theoretically political enemies, but in that environment they would talk. It was very good for Louis to learn what was going on and for Alan Wolfe to get what he needed."

Ten

"Dupree, the biggest CIA agent!" the interrogator called out when the police brought the archaeologist to a seized government building. On a desk, while Dupree was questioned, sat a Kalashnikov, its barrel pointed at him. He was moved to another building, where a man took calls, calmly tabulating political assassinations, as two guards smiled at Dupree and drew their fingers across their necks.

The next day he was interrogated for nine hours. He was instructed to make a list of all the Afghan intellectuals he knew. Suspecting it would be used as a kill list, he refused, telling his captors, "I know practically everyone." He was told instead to make a list of all the Kabulis he knew. He consented, and the first name he wrote down was that of Nur Mohammed Taraki, the new president and possibly the man who'd ordered him arrested. No more lists were requested. Asked what he would say if someone accused him of working for the CIA, Dupree replied, "If you want to accuse me of working for the CIA, don't go through this God damn nonsense," according to an account of his incarceration that he later dictated to Nancy. "Just go ahead and accuse me."

The translator who fingered him was brought in. The man was shaking, and according to Dupree "his face was not his face, it had about a month or more of growth of beard. It was totally misshapen, his eyes were not his own, his lips were swollen and almost dropping down to his lower jaw, he could hardly talk."

An interrogator questioned the translator in front of Dupree.

"Is Dupree CIA?" he demanded.

"Yes, everybody knows Dupree is CIA," the translator whimpered.

Uninvited, Dupree jumped in.

"*Did I ever tell you I was CIA?*" he asked. The translator said no. "Did I ever try to recruit you for CIA?" No again.

The next night, Dupree was made to watch as a cellmate was beaten by a guard. "He just picked him up with one hand and started slapping the bejesus out of him," he told Nancy. "One kicked him in the balls and the other one hit him in the stomach." Then a guard brought in an electrical device with wires hanging out of it, "wiggling like the tentacles of a Medusa trying to escape." The cellmate "just went to pieces."

Through it all, Dupree managed to keep his sense of humor. "I made friends with the cop who brought the food around," he recounted. He found he liked the jail bread. "I always insisted on the end piece, being an old Southern boy, I love the end piece of bread and it's much better to make spoons out of." His attempts to go to sleep were thwarted by "some noises of human beings in distress that occasionally came through the walls and naturally this did not improve my frame of mind at the time." And "little buggies," he went on, "were busy chewing my ass off all the night." The next morning: "No one brought me bed tea; highly pissed off." At one point in the transcript of Dupree's account is the following aside: "Interruption now, because it is 5 o'clock and time for delicious martinis."

After five days, Dupree was brought to the Ministry of Interior. Women demanding to know where their husbands and sons had been taken were being thrown around by their burkas. An official recognized Dupree and, forgetting himself for a moment, shook his hand. Then he stiffened and handed Dupree a statement to sign. "You are hereby informed that you are ordered out of the country never to return," it read. "If you ever do return to Afghanistan, you will be responsible for the consequences." Dupree signed it, but not before appending a statement of his own in the margin: "I would like to add that I have great love and affection for the people of Afghanistan and I hope that eventually a true experiment in socialism will succeed in Afghanistan for the benefit of all the people."

He found Nancy, who'd somehow kept it together during his incarceration. They drove in the red Land Rover to the border. There they were officially expelled from Afghanistan.

To this day, she maintains that none of the rumors about Louis had any basis in fact—that he'd never been connected with the CIA in any way. The translator and others named him, she said, because he was a gossiped-about American and because they didn't want to die. "Some of these characters, I've run into them," she said. "It takes them a long time, but eventually they'll get me into a room all by ourselves, and they'll let it all spill out. They feel so guilty because they turned him in. But it was life or death for them. They were killing people all over the place."

Eleven

Louis and Nancy drove over the Khyber Pass to Peshawar, where other expatriate and Afghan friends who'd made it out were gathering. They moved into Dean's, a Victorian hotel, a hangout for people with information about what was happening in Afghanistan. Their rooms came to be known as the Dupree Suite. They tried to approximate their old life, confident that soon enough everything would calm down and they'd return.

But the Afghanistan they'd known was disappearing. In February 1979, the American ambassador was kidnapped by Islamic extremists and later killed in a shootout. Washington began supplying anticommunist rebels. In September, Taraki's prime minister had him strangled in his bed and took power. The next month Afghans went into open revolt against the Moscow-backed regime and its heavy-handed religious and social reforms. Officials, Soviet advisers, and their families were tortured and murdered, their bodies paraded on pikes in the streets. On Christmas Day, the Soviets invaded.

From its start, the invasion's brutality was matched by its clumsiness. (A Soviet general staff officer remarked that "no one ever actually ordered the invasion of Afghanistan.") The Kremlin promised a months-long operation; a ten-year occupation followed. In that time, over 600,000 Russian troops would be sent to Afghanistan. Fourteen thousand of them would be killed, according to official estimates (unofficial estimates go as high as 75,000) and 400,000 injured or taken ill. Roughly a million and a half Afghans—most of them civilians—would die, and numberless villages and towns would be leveled.

All of it was in vain. It was not long before Russians were referring to the war in Af-*gavni*-stan: Afshitstan. The Afghans simply would not submit. Calling on the old traditions of the *jirgas* and the *shuras*, they created an endlessly brave and hugely effective network of resistance, joined by deserters from the Afghan army and fighters from around the Muslim world. At first they fought with nineteenth-century muskets and WWII-era Lee Enfield rifles and made bullets by hand from spent shell casings. One Afghan attempted a suicide attack by setting himself on fire and rushing at a Russian tank. Eventually, a disorderly coalition of world powers and adversaries that included the United States, China, Pakistan, Israel, Britain, Egypt, and Saudi Arabia provided the mujahideen, as they called themselves—warriors of God—with serious weaponry. Decades worth of grudges against the USSR were avenged on television screens around the world as grainy footage of shoulder-launched rockets turning Russian helicopters into fireballs emerged from the Hindu Kush.

American support for the resistance was run out of CIA headquarters. Among its choreographers there was Alan Wolfe, who had moved to Washington with Annie. By now he was the chief of the Near East Division, known as its Grand Old Man. Shortly after the 1978 coup, Wolfe flew to Islamabad to confer with agents. He told them a story. "I came home the other day, and my wife and I were having our evening martini, and the *Washington Post* was on the coffee table," Wolfe said. "The photo on the front page was of the new Afghan flag being raised in Kabul. I picked it up and showed it to my wife. 'They're fucking with our country, dear!' I can't have that. I am going to change that fucking government, toss those commie bastards out on their asses."

"I sat there looking at Wolfe as he spoke," the agent who worked under him told me. "It was clear to me that this was one of those moments that you hear about but rarely are lucky enough to witness." Years later he bumped into Wolfe, and they reminisced about the meeting. "I reminded him that he had indeed started the process that removed the communist regime. He looked at me like I was from outer space. 'Of course I did. Did you think that I wouldn't succeed?'"

On the ground, the Afghan resistance was run by Pakistani intelligence from Peshawar, where armies of refugees, many eager to fight, were massing. Nancy worked in the overflowing refugee camps, while back at Dean's, rebel leaders conferred with Louis, whose understanding of guerilla warfare and connections with influential leaders across Afghanistan were invaluable. He no longer harbored any illusions about the communists. Word spread. One day someone walked into the hotel with a copy of the *Los Angeles Times*. In it was an op-ed, by a Russian political commentator, entitled "CIA Perfidy Necessitated Rescue by Soviet Union." It read: "In May, 1979, the American intelligence men in Pakistan who were engaged in training Afghan rebels were led by the well-known CIA operative Louis Dupree."

Twelve

There is no evidence Dupree led a rebel army, much as he probably would have liked to, but he did much else to assist the mujahideen. He had known most of its field commanders since they were young men. He snuck into Afghanistan to advise and fight with them. "Actually," claims Nancy, "it was Louis who taught them how to make a Molotov cocktail."

When he wasn't with the rebels or in Peshawar, Dupree traveled to American universities and think tanks to lecture about the war and urge people to get involved; cofounded groups to support the fighters and refugees; and wrote reports and op-eds. He always stressed that this was not a proxy fight between capitalism and communism, that Afghanistan was not a "client" of the West—a position offered with increasing bluster as the mujahideen became celebrities in Georgetown sitting rooms. Afghanistan was its own country fighting for its own future, Dupree reminded his audiences.

In 1981, he was in a near fatal car accident. In the hospital for a year, he underwent two brain surgeries. Still partially paralyzed after being discharged, he went to Washington to urge lawmakers to send the rebels more weapons. Testifying before the Senate, he said, "This is, in my opinion, the most important political and moral issue that faces us at this time and is probably the most important since the Second World War."

In Dupree's personal papers, one finds dozens of letters he sent—to politicians, employers, deans—on behalf of Afghan exiles. More poignant, however, are the letters written to him by the exiles themselves. "Since the year that the Russian took over Afghanistan, many people have been died and many were slaughtered by Russians army," wrote a student turned fighter named Hafizullah who'd fled to Iran. "I was charged for the crime that [I] worked for and with Americans in Kabul. Now I am in Tehran have no passport and I am eager to come over to USA for my further studies or if not possible to take refugee there at that part of the world."

Life got worse for the Duprees, too. Still suspected of being a spy, Louis was expelled from Pakistan in 1979. "I have been followed, harassed and hounded by various elements in the Pakistani government," he wrote in a letter of complaint to (who else?) Pakistani president Muhammed Zia-ul-Haq. "Somewhere in the bowels of the Pakistani bureaucracy exists a hard-core belief that I am a CIA agent." Eventually, he was readmitted.

Although Louis had taken up a professorship at Duke University, he and Nancy never entertained the thought of moving permanently to North Carolina. When I asked her why, she said, "These people were in trouble. Refugees were coming in. It never occurred to me leave. They had given us so much." She choked up. "How could you turn your back on them at that time?"

•   •   •

By 1985, the year Mikhail Gorbachev became general secretary of the Soviet Communist Party, two things were obvious. The first was that the USSR had lost the war in Afghanistan. Though the conflict wouldn't officially end for another four years, withdrawal talks were already under way. The second was that Afghanistan was, in a more profound sense, lost. Five and a half million people—one-third of the population—would flee the country by the end of the decade, and another two million would be displaced internally. Louis called it a "migratory genocide."

If the human toll wasn't enough, there was the cost to Afghan history. As the White Hun and Mongol invaders had tried to do centuries earlier, the Soviets seemed to want to punish Afghanistan for its resistance by trying to make the world forget there had ever been indigenous culture there. The policy was known, with the Russian flair for bloody-minded understatement, as "rubblization." Whole swaths of the country were laid waste; mosques, libraries, schools, museums, and archaeological sites were razed. It was as though some horrible wind had swept in from the north and erased epochs.

As the crisis worsened, so did Louis. Still disabled from the car accident, he was diagnosed with lung cancer. He remained the final authority on Afghan history, however, so when a consortium of charity organizations dealing with the preservation of Afghan culture needed to assemble a bibliography of scholarship on the country, he was the obvious choice. No sooner had he submitted the bibliography, however, than he convinced the consortium it wasn't what they wanted. What they wanted, he said, was the stuff produced during the war: the underground newspapers, the home footage of fighting, the testimonies of Russian defectors, and so on—the documents that would tell a generation living in exile what their country was like while they were gone. "In the camps around Peshawar, they had an unprecedented phenomenon—

Afghans from all over the country, populations that had never interacted with each other, gathering in one place," Nancy said. "The possibilities to create a legacy of learning for when they repatriated were enormous." She and Louis began collecting. It was the start of her library.

Louis was always sure the refugees would repatriate and reclaim their country from the Soviets. "He had every faith," said Nancy. "He said, 'The Afghans will throw them out.'" In January of 1989, as he lay dying in Durham, North Carolina, the last Soviet tanks rolled out of Afghanistan. The mujahideen had captured everything except Kabul.

"Well, darling, you were right," she told him.

Louis looked up at her. "The problems are just beginning."

.   .   .

People traveled from around the world to attend the memorial service at Duke. Dupree's eulogy, read by the director of its Islamic and Arabian Development Studies Department, Ralph Braibanti, was entitled "Tribute to a Mujahid." Louis and Nancy, he told the mourners, had "appeared in a moment in history when the culture they so admired was in crisis. It was this transmigration of their spiritual being that enabled each of them to preserve some part of the national character which now became part of their persona."

In the service program was printed a photograph of Louis taken a few years before, during a mission with the mujahideen. He's wearing large, professorial eyeglasses, an Afghan vest, and a traditional *pakol* cap, gray hair flowing from its brim. He looks haggard but highly pissed off. Aged but eager. A boyish mischievousness dances across his face, halfway between a smile and a frown. "I know a lot," his unyielding eyes and pursed mouth seem to say, "but I'm not going to tell you a fucking thing."

Thirteen

After Louis died, Nancy wound up his affairs, taught his classes through the end of the term, and broke down. She considered "joining Louis"—i.e., killing herself. It didn't help that there were Afghan exiles living in America who could help her mourn. "The Afghans have a terrible habit," she told me. "I mean, it's a lovely habit, but it's awful. When somebody loses a husband or a wife, they come and they sit and they tell you all about how wonderful they were. You say thank you and you cry and you cry and you cry. That's the whole point I suppose."

But she didn't just miss Louis; she missed Afghanistan. They had been her two greatest loves. So when she was invited to return to Peshawar to head an Afghan cultural organization, she thought it might be an opportunity to carry on his work, and she accepted before she could refuse.

Civil war persisted for seven years after the Soviet departure. Kabul, which had made it out of the occupation mostly unscathed, was torn apart. The rebel leaders Louis had helped were now warlords. They battled block by block for control of the city while the last Soviet-backed president, Muhammed Najibullah, tried in vain to hold on to power. Rockets slammed into the National Museum, and soldiers and militiamen looted the collection. In 1993, Nancy traveled to Kabul to assess the damage for the United Nations. "Artifacts [were] strewn among the rubble, and filing cabinets of museum records and catalogs indiscriminately dumped," she later recounted in an article. "Hasps had been unscrewed and locks ripped off steel storage boxes, and drawers and crates had been methodically emptied onto the floor." It was rumored that thieves were using her guidebook to the museum to value stolen pieces. Seventy percent of the collection, she estimated, was gone. Among the missing pieces, it appeared, was Daddy's Head.

In 1996, the warlords were swept from Kabul by the Taliban, which at first was more respectful than anyone had dared hope.

The Taliban leader, Muhammad Omar, appointed a cultural minister and decreed the smuggling of relics illegal. He allowed the UN to repair part of the museum. But in 2001 he changed course, ordering the Bamiyan Buddhas—the subject of Nancy's first guidebook—destroyed. When footage of Talibs blowing up the statues was broadcast around the world, it became clear that hardliners loyal to the polite Saudi she'd met years before, Osama bin Laden, had taken control. Next, Omar ordered what remained of the museum's collection destroyed. Heavies from the Ministry for the Propagation of Virtue and the Prevention of Vice arrived, hammers in hand.

When Dupree went to the museum afterward, "there were pieces no bigger than this," she told me, holding up her thumb and index finger close to each other. "And the rest was all dust. I stood there watching the museum staff collecting these pieces, including the dust. They were sweeping it up, putting it in bags, and I thought, God, you know, what do you think the Taliban is going to do to us?"

Later that year, however, the United States invaded. In 2004, the museum reopened. The curators returned to work. They took the salvaged artifacts from their hiding places and began the slow process of recataloguing them. Nancy, who had been splitting her time between Peshawar and North Carolina, began the process of moving back to Kabul the same year. One day, she received an e-mail from a curator who had "found a remarkable little bundle wrapped in brown paper," Dupree said, recounting the message. "She tore off the paper only to come to another layer of paper, newspaper. She continued peeling the bundle, and under the newspaper she found toilet paper and then tissue paper."

Inside the tissue paper was a small, very old rock. There were markings carved into it. The features were faint.

"Daddy's Head," Dupree said to herself.

Fourteen

After Louis died, one of the things Nancy did to keep her mind off him was continue the collection they'd started during the war. She scoured bazaars and antiques stores and book stalls in Pakistan and Afghanistan. She visited old mujahideen and exiles and aid workers to see what they had. She hired unemployed men to help her. She stored the old books, reports, pamphlets, newspapers and magazines, tracts, treatises, photos, film reels, and slides she gathered in Peshawar. "If it had Afghanistan in the title, it wasn't safe around me," she said.

Of course, it didn't work. In every new find, there was something to remind her of Louis. "Louis would have liked this," she would say to herself, handling a book, or, reading an account of a particular battle, "Louis would have disagreed with that." Finally, she admitted to herself that the collection was her way not of moving on from Louis but of remembering him. More than that, of memorializing him and his love of Afghanistan.

While her new library awaited completion in late 2012, her collection sat in Kabul University's main library, a sad affair in the middle of campus. Most of the materials were stored in locked, fragrant cedar cabinets. In the back of the building was the small, stuffy archiving room. On the days I visited, young male archivists (and one woman) could be found studying and scanning, copying and uploading, unbinding and rebinding. One day I looked over the shoulder of an archivist as he paged through a Taliban propaganda newspaper from 1996 whose headline read "Congratulations to the People of Afghanistan About the Capture of Kabul by the Taliban." Another archivist was at a computer, going through scans of photographs taken by an aid worker. "When people die and their estates don't know what to do with their goddamn things," Nancy said, "they call us."

Operations were overseen by Rahim, a dour, wiry man whom Dupree hired in Peshawar. He and a group of helpers smuggled the collection into Afghanistan. They stuffed about 30,000 items into sacks and loaded them onto the backs of horses and men for the trek over the Khyber Pass. It took six months. Rahim said it was worth it. "We learn many things from Nancy," he told me. "Many information about Afghanistan we get from Nancy." Now they have about 90,000 items.

In 2005, when he was university chancellor, Ashraf Ghani donated a plot of land on the campus to Dupree to house the collection. When I asked him why, he told me the collection "represents the proposition that to overcome the past we need to understand it. The past is haunting Afghanistan. We have too much history—history that has not become historical. History that lives. Our perceptions of history are clouding our future. We've done horrible things to each other, and those things need to be put to rest, and this collection is part of that."

Browsing the cabinets one day, I found myself thinking of a line from the Homebody's monologue:

> My research is moth-like. Impassioned, fluttery, doomed. A subject strikes my fancy: Kabul, you will see why, that's the tale I'm telling—but then, I can't help myself, it's almost perverse, in libraries, in secondhand bookshops, I invariably seek out not the source but all that which was dropped by the wayside on the way to the source. . . . Old magazines, hysterical political treatises written by an advocate of some long-since defeated or abandoned or transmuted cause; and I find these irrelevant and irresistible, ghostly, dreamy, the knowing what *was* known before the more that has since become known overwhelms.

·   ·   ·

One day in the archiving room, I overheard Nancy speaking with a young Englishman who'd been volunteering his time. He had just told her that he would have to come in less.

"So you're leaving us?" she said to him in a plaintive voice.

"No, Nancy," he said, trying to be as gentle as possible. "I'm not leaving. I'll just be able to come in less than I have."

"You'll leave, I suppose," she said. "Everybody leaves eventually."

Maybe sensing he'd stay if she offered him some compensation, she added, "You know, we're out of money. We're broke, completely."

She wasn't exaggerating. It had been obvious enough to me, watching it at work, that her organization was inefficient. Her staff was well intentioned but poorly trained and overly worshipful of her. Nancy herself was Homebody-like, unable to focus on any single task or line of thought for very long. Just how inefficient I learned on my last days in Kabul. Wafa, her executive director, admitted to me that the organization was, indeed, broke. Nancy had blown through a $3 million grant from the State Department a year ahead of schedule. The Norwegian government had stepped in with a bridge loan, but now that was nearly gone, too.

An auditor hired by the grant administrator to assess Dupree's organization told me she "is completely exhausted and wants to let go, and she's trying to hand it over, but her board can't be bothered." The whole thing was being held together, barely, on the strength of her legend, he believed. "The American government has spent $3 million supporting the cult of an old lady." An employee of hers told me the organization "will collapse when Nancy is gone," a contention with which the auditor agreed. Indeed, many of the people around her seemed to believe this.

Penury nagged at her. Grasping deans at the university were making noises about commandeering her new library. She worried that Karzai, having paid for some of it, might use it for his own purposes. After trips such as the one to Charikar, she suspected that Afghans were indifferent to her projects. She seemed to become sicker and more impatient by the day. Her coughing fits grew deeper and longer, her outbursts more plangent and scattershot; it was as though everyone reminded her of how little time she had left and, thus, everyone was a waste of time. Americans took the worst of it. Around them she became annoyed before they'd had a chance to open their mouths. It wasn't long before she was blowing up at me when I walked into her office each morning. She would lapse into the first person plural, as though she were yelling at herself, too. "You don't seem to be interested in the things we are doing!" she said one day. "What are we doing here? Why?! What's our purpose?"

Fifteen

For weeks I had been bothering Dupree to take me to the National Museum. I wanted to see Daddy's Head with her. Finally, she relented, and I could see as soon as we arrived why she hadn't wanted to come. The museum still pains her. Everything in it reminds her of Afghanistan's past, of her past, of Louis.

At the entranceway stands a second-century marble relief of the Kushan king Kinishka that is particularly close to her heart. She likes to call Kinishka, a scholar and arts patron, her hero. The statue's head is gone, smashed by a Talib. "This poor little fella," she said as we walked by him. Inside we passed a damaged Buddha. "I, ah—" she said, then turned away, on the brink of tears.

Upstairs, after looking at a display of gold coins ("I kept telling Louis to find me some gold," she joked), we emerged from the gallery to find burly military contractors with assault rifles taking up positions on the staircase. They looked as though they expected the statues to come to life. Nancy didn't flinch. Nor did she betray interest when their charge—an official, clearly American, in a baggy suit, moustache, bad haircut—bounded up the stairs. He introduced himself as a deputy ambassador of something.

"Another ambassador?" she said.

"There are so many of us," he replied gamely.

The ambassador's wife introduced herself with an eagerness that made it clear she'd wanted to meet Dupree for some time. "Yes, yes," Nancy said, waving a hand and pushing past.

As I was about to ask about Daddy's Head, the museum director, Omara Massoudi, approached. Old friends, he and Dupree used to comb the bazaars in Peshawar together, looking for stolen artifacts. In the Taliban years, he sold potatoes on the street.

"Nancy Jan, will you have a cup of tea with me?" Massoudi asked.

"You're very kind," she said. "Do you really want me to?" The ambassador and his wife and their aides joined them in Massoudi's large, barren office. After business cards had been exchanged, she asked the ambassador, "But anyway, how do you find our poor museum?"

"It's mixed emotions," he said. "It's so impressive and so gorgeous what you see, and heartbreaking to think of what was lost. But I think it is a tribute to—"

"You have to have been here," she said, cutting him off. "Mr. Massoudi and I, we've gone through a lot. You see, he's such a gentleman. Impeccably dressed. Can you imagine him with a beard down to here?" she said, gesturing at her knees. Everyone laughed, and she was off. "And he used to turn up in Peshawar and—those were hard times. But! It was even harder times for the museum, because a rocket had hit the roof and flames all over the place. The roof had fallen onto these precious Islamic bronzes, and they were all melted together. There was no electricity, no water, no nothing. No heat. And the walls were all covered with soot and grime and dust. We went like that for many, many months. So I cannot believe it when I come here, to see this sparkling, beautiful building. It's a miracle.

"I'm building a very small building, but it's taken a long time," she went on. "You must come and see my center."

"I'd love to," the ambassador said. He attempted to make his farewells, but Dupree kept talking. More about the museum, musings on the promise of Afghan youth; then her monologue became mothlike, impassioned, fluttery, doomed. I was sitting next to the Homebody.

"The other day I went to a music concert," she told the ambassador. "Modern classical music. John Cage and all that. You know John Cage?"

"Yeah," the ambassador said, almost hiding his confusion.

"*Ping, bonk, henk, hah*, all that?"

"Yeah."

"Well he used to be my neighbor. And I didn't think much of his music then. And so these people were doing a fantastic job with the cello and the saxophone and the—but all modern. I thought it was quite pleasant. Then they played one with John Cage's concept that there is music in everything. *All noise has music*. Got it? So these three or four people on the stage, they each had a radio. And one by one they each turned the radio to static. *Chek-wawa-kchaea*. This is supposed to be music? I'm sorry. It didn't catch me then and it doesn't catch me now.

"I went out after that," she continued, "and I saw the cellist. She had been overworked, and I gave her a big hug and I said, 'Beautifully done, except that last thing left me cold.' 'Oh,' she said, 'we did that because it's his hundredth anniversary.' My neighbor? Hundredth anniversary? And they were all so embarrassed because I'm nearly a hundred. They didn't mean it that way, but it came out that way."

Nervous laughter.

"Well," the ambassador said, getting up, his moustache hairs seeming to bristle with alarm, or maybe pity. "Anyway the, the— I want to thank you all for the opportunity to visit this museum. It's a real privilege and honor to do it. And I feel much, ah, richer for the experience."

Sixteen

Afterward, I asked Nancy what she thought of him. "He's an ambassador," she said. By this I took her to mean: My patience for my countrymen, and their preposterous exertions in this doomed place that I love so much, is at an end. And it was a position for which I could hardly blame her. On the contrary, the ignorance and futility—there is no other term for it: *the abject failure*—of the American adventure in Afghanistan is obvious as soon as one sets foot in the country. Our attempts to rebuild institutions and infrastructure have come to little; hugely expensive projects sit skeletal and looted, the countryside poor and benighted; Karzai's ministers live like pashas in Kabul. This is to say nothing of a reinvigorated Taliban or of the daily bombings, maimings, beheadings. All of it at the expense of the American taxpayer, America's reputation, and, worst of all, everyday Afghans, the people whom Dupree has been trying to help for most of her adult life.

"We have really destroyed this very sensitive characteristic of the Afghan character, which is self-sufficiency," she told me one day. "They used to be proud of the fact that they did things for themselves. But now they've had so much money thrown at them, they've had so many advisers telling them what to do, that from the village on up, these young people don't want to think for themselves. *Let the foreigners do it.*"

Dupree feels this failure deeply, and as an American adopted by Afghans, it takes a double toll on her, embarrassing and infuriating her in equal measure. She knows that she is part of this failure; that, as the quintessential expat do-gooder in Kabul, she somehow embodies it. On her good days, she also remembers that she is separate from it, that Afghans love her, perhaps even need her. She remembers that, if the glories of Afghanistan's past can only be imagined, she can imagine them better than anyone and help others in the imagining. But on her bad days, she carries this failure on her face, in her bones, like a walking broken promise.

She worries that one or the other of her homelands might blithely do away with her legacy. Her library finally opened in March of last year, several months after my visit. But even as the building's completion approached, she spoke of it as a tenuous thing. "It would only take one mullah with a match or one American daisy cutter," she told me, "and it would be finished."

．　　　．　　　．

Dupree had reluctantly agreed to speak with me one last time. Shortly after I got to her office, however, so did a young Afghan American woman, two hours late for an appointment. Dupree had been yelling about her—"Where the hell is this person? God damn it, damn it, damn it!"—but when the woman finally arrived, apologizing profusely, Dupree issued a contrition-banishing wave of the hand and invited her to sit down.

It was her first time in Kabul, the woman explained, and she'd gotten lost. She was a graduate student, about to begin research near Kandahar. She had nothing pressing to ask of Dupree, nothing to offer her, but Dupree put aside what she was doing—and me—to speak with her, about nothing much. Soon they were trading stories and laughing. She took the woman out to tour the campus. When I returned to the office, three hours later, they were having lunch. Dupree was talking about Louis. It was the happiest I'd seen her. I left quietly.

On my way off campus, I stopped at the new library, recalling something the auditor had said about it. "She wanted to make sense of what her legacy would be," he'd said, "so she's become obsessed with the building." He was probably right—and the obsession had paid off. It was a beautiful building. Its granite walls and stolid wooden beams and flagstone portico were somehow already perfectly weathered. Inside, there was no furniture, no curtains, no books. It felt new and old at the same time. It knew a lot but would say nothing. Students were already walking by it as though it had been there forever, and soon enough, none will remember its provenance. Though it is Nancy's monument to Louis, to their love of Afghanistan, she has refused to put their name on it. It is called, simply, the Afghanistan Center at Kabul University.

I walked into the interior courtyard. A solitary worker was cleaning a new windowpane. Nearby his young son was sitting with a neat pile of tattered textbooks. The school year had started, and he wanted them to last through the long winter ahead. He was carefully wrapping each cover in brown paper.

New York Times Magazine

FINALIST—FEATURE WRITING

The judges who nominated "The Ballad of Geeshie and Elvie" for the National Magazine Award for Feature Writing said that John Jeremiah Sullivan's story about his search for two nearly forgotten blues singers "leads the reader on an unconventional tour of American roots music, introduces us to its obsessive collectors and charts the outer limits of historical memory." In fact, the outer limits of American culture is where Sullivan lives, as evidenced by the extraordinary series of stories that have earned his work two Ellie awards and five additional nominations since 2003, on topics ranging from horse racing and Disneyworld to Christian rock and David Foster Wallace.

John Jeremiah Sullivan

The Ballad of Geeshie and Elvie

I n the world of early-twentieth-century African American music and people obsessed by it, who can appear from one angle like a clique of pale and misanthropic scholar-gatherers and from another like a sizable chunk of the human population, there exist no ghosts more vexing than a couple of women identified on three ultrarare records made in 1930 and 1931 as Elvie Thomas and Geeshie Wiley. There are musicians as obscure as Wiley and Thomas, and musicians as great, but in none does the Venn diagram of greatness and lostness reveal such vast and bewildering coextent. In the spring of 1930, in a damp and dimly lit studio, in a small Wisconsin village on the western shore of Lake Michigan, the duo recorded a batch of songs that for more than half a century have been numbered among the masterpieces of prewar American music, in particular two, Elvie's "Motherless Child Blues" and Geeshie's "Last Kind Words Blues," twin Alps of their tiny oeuvre, inspiring essays and novels and films and cover versions, a classical arrangement.

Yet despite more than fifty years of researchers' efforts to learn who the two women were or where they came from, we have remained ignorant of even their legal names. The sketchy memories of one or two ancient Mississippians, gathered many decades ago, seemed to point to the southern half of that state, yet none led to anything solid. A few people thought they heard hints of Louisiana or Texas in the guitar playing or in the pronunciation of a lyric. We know that the word "Geechee," with a *c*, can refer to a person born into the heavily African-inflected Gullah culture centered on the coastal islands off Georgia and the Carolinas. But nothing turned up there either. Or anywhere. No grave site, no photograph. Forget that—no anecdotes. This is what set Geeshie and Elvie apart even from the rest of an innermost group of phantom geniuses of the twenties and thirties. Their myth was they didn't have anything you could so much as hang a myth on. The objects themselves—the fewer than ten surviving copies, total, of their three known Paramount releases, a handful of heavy, black, scratch-riven shellac platters, all in private hands—these were the whole of the file on Geeshie and Elvie, and even these had come within a second thought of vanishing, within, say, a woman's decision in cleaning her parents' attic to go against some idle advice that she throw out a box of old records and instead to find out what the junk shop gives. When she decides otherwise, when the shop isn't on the way home, there goes the music, there go the souls, ash flakes up the flue, to flutter about with the Edison cylinder of Buddy Bolden's band and the phonautograph of Lincoln's voice.

I have been fascinated by this music since first experiencing it, like a lot of other people in my generation, in Terry Zwigoff's 1994 documentary *Crumb*, on the life of the artist Robert Crumb, which used "Last Kind Words" for a particularly vivid montage sequence. And I have closely followed the search for them over the years; drawn along in part by the sheer History Channel mysteriousness of it but mainly—the reason it never got boring—by their music.

Outside any bullyingly hyperbolical attempts to describe the technical beauty of the songs themselves, there's another facet to them, one that deepens their fascination, namely a certain time-capsule dimension. The year 1930 seems long ago enough now, perhaps, but older songs and singers can be heard to blow through this music, strains in the American songbook that we know were there, from before the Civil War, but can't hear very well or at all. There's a song, Geeshie's "Last Kind Words," a kind of pre-blues or not-yet-blues, a doomy, minor-key lament that calls up droning banjo songs from long before the cheap-guitar era, with a strange thumping rhythm on the bass string. "If I get killed," Geeshie sings, "if I get killed, please don't bury my soul." There's a blues, "Motherless Child," with sixteen-bar, four-line stanzas, that begins by repeating the same line four times, "My mother told me just before she died," AAAA, no variation, just moaning the words, each time with achingly subtle microvariations, notes blue enough to flirt with tonal chaos. Generations of spirituals pass through "Motherless Child," field melodies and work songs drift through it, and, above everything, the playing brims with unfalsifiable sophistication. Elvie's notes float. She sends them out like little sailboats onto a pond. "Motherless Child" is her only song, the only one of the six on which she takes lead to my ears—there are people who think it's also her on "Over to My House." On the other songs she's behind Geeshie, albeit contributing hugely. The famous Joe Bussard (pronounced "buzzard"), one of the world's foremost collectors of prewar 78s, found one of two known copies of "Motherless Child" in an antique store in Baltimore, near the waterfront, in the mid-1960s. The story goes that Bussard used to have people over to his house to play for them the first note of "Motherless Child," just the first few seconds, again and again, an E that Elvie plucks and lets hang. It sounds like nothing and then, after several listens, like nothing else. "Baby, now she's dead, she's six feet in the ground," she sings. "And I'm a child, and I am drifting 'round."

Before there could be the minor miracle of these discs' having survived, there had to be an earlier, major one: that of people like Geeshie and Elvie ever being recorded. To understand how that happened it's needful to know about race records, a commercial field that flourished between the world wars, and specifically the

Paramount company, a major competitor in that game throughout the 1920s.

A furniture company, that's how it started. The Wisconsin Chair Company. They got into making phonograph cabinets. If people had records they liked, they would want phonographs to play them on, and if they had phonographs, they would want cabinets to keep them in. The discs were even sold, especially at first, in furniture shops. They were literally accessories. Toys, you could say. In fact, the first disc "records" were manufactured to go with a long-horned gramophone distributed by a German toy company. So we must imagine, it's as if a subgenre of major American art had been preserved only on vintage View-Master slides.

In 1920, when the white-owned OKeh label shocked even itself by selling hundreds of thousands of copies of Mamie Smith's "Crazy Blues" (the first blues recorded by an African American female vocalist), the furniture-phonograph complex spied a chance. Two populations were forming or achieving critical mass, whites willing to pay for recordings of black music and blacks able to afford phonographs, and together they made a new market. It's around then that the actual phrase "race records" enters the vernacular. In 1926, Paramount had game-changing luck on a string of 78s showcasing the virtuosic Texas songster Blind Lemon Jefferson—his "Long Lonesome Blues" sold into the six figures—and, as in Mamie Smith's case, he touched off a frantic search among labels to find performers in a similar vein. The "country blues" was born, though not yet known by that name. It was men, for the most part, but with an important female minority, a "vital feminizing force," in the words of Don Kent, the influential collector and poet of liner notes.

For the preserving of that force we have to thank not the foresight of those recording companies but their ignorance and even philistinism when it came to black culture. They knew next to nothing about the music and even less about what new trends in it might appeal to consumers. Nowhere was this truer than at Paramount. These were businessmen, Northern and Midwestern, former salesmen. Their notions of what was a hit and what was not were a Magic Eight Ball. So, when the mid-1920s arrived, and Paramount went looking farther afield for new acts, they compensated by recording everything and waiting to see what sold. Not everything, but a lot. A long swath of everything. The result was an unprecedented, never-to-be-repeated, all-but-unconscious survey of America's musical culture, a sonic X ray of it, taken at a moment when the full kaleidoscopic variety of pre-recording-era transracial forms hadn't yet contracted. Hundreds of singers, more thousands of songs. Some of the greatest musicians ever born in this country were netted only there. It was a slapdash and profit-driven documentary project that in some respects dwarfed what the most ambitious and well intentioned ethnomusicologists could hope to achieve (deformed in all sorts of ways by capitalism, but we take what we can get).

Among the first to wake up to these riches was, as it happens, the most prominent of those great ethnomusicologists, Alan Lomax. He had been traveling the back roads with his father, John A. Lomax, making field recordings for the Library of Congress's Archive of American Folk Song, and he had seen firsthand that all of this culture, which had endured mouth-to-ear for centuries, was giving way, proving not quite powerful enough to resist the radio waves and movies. In the late 1930s, Lomax was record hunting one day and came across a large cache of old Paramount discs in a store. At the time they were a mere ten or fifteen years old and couldn't have appeared less valuable to a casual picker. Lomax listened, transfixed by an increasing realization that Paramount offered him an earhole into the past, into the decade just before he joined his father on the song-collecting scene, an enormous commercial complement to what the two of them had been doing under intellectual auspices with their field-recording. Lomax started digging. In 1940 he created a list, with the title "American Folk Songs on Commercial Records," and circulated it in the folklore community.

This list is a very precious little document in twentieth-century American cultural history. It was published in only a limited library report, but copies were passed around. It marked the first time someone had publicly recognized these commercial recordings as something other than detritus. Most important, it made space for, even emphasized, the more obscure blues singers.

To grasp the significance of that, you have to bear in mind how fantastically few record collectors possessed such an interest at the end of the 1930s. Early jazz was a thing in certain hip circles, but only a few true freaks were into the country blues. There was twitchy, rail-thin Jim McKune, a postal worker from Long Island City, Queens, who famously maintained precisely 300 of the choicest records under his bed at the YMCA Had to keep the volume low to avoid complaints. He referred to his listening sessions as séances. Summoning weird old voices from the South, the ethereal falsetto of Crying Sam Collins. Or the whine of Isaiah Nettles, the Mississippi Moaner. Did McKune listen to Geeshie and Elvie? It's unknowable. His records were already gone when he died—murdered in 1971, in a hotel room. Another early explorer? The writer Paul Bowles. The Paul Bowles, believe it or not, who started collecting blues records as an ether-huffing undergraduate in Charlottesville, Va., in the late 1920s, "at second-hand furniture stores in the black quarter." Out West there was Harry Smith, who went on to create the *Anthology of American Folk Music* for Folkways Records, the first "box set," of which it can be compactly if inadequately said: No *Anthology*, no Woodstock. Wee, owlish Smith. He and McKune came to know each other. No less important, they both came to know Alan Lomax's list, which galvanized their passion for this particular chamber of the recorded past, giving shape to their "want lists."

In the 1950s McKune would become a sort of salon master to the so-called Blues Mafia, the initial cell of mainly Northeastern 78-pursuers who evolved, some of them, into the label owners and managers and taste-arbiters of the folk-blues revival. An all-white men's club, several of whom were or grew wealthy, the Blues Mafia doesn't always come off heroically in recent—and vital—revisionist histories of the field, more of them being written by women (including two forthcoming books by Daphne Brooks and Amanda Petrusich). Still, no one who seriously cares about the music would pretend that the cultural debt we owe the Blues Mafia isn't past accounting. It's not just all they found and documented that marks their contribution. It's equally what they spawned, whether they would claim it or not. Dylan didn't listen to 78s, after all, on the floors of those pads he was crashing at in Greenwich Village, but to the early reissue LPs. By Dylan I mean the sixties. But also Dylan. "If I hadn't heard the Robert Johnson record when I did," he wrote ten years ago, "there probably would have been hundreds of lines of mine that would have been shut down."

. . .

There was, in those early days, another individual, one less easily slotted into the Wikipedia story line of blues history. A young man named Robert McCormick, who went by "Mack." In Ohio as a teenager, he fell under the wizardry of jazz, listening to the bands at a nearby amusement park. The musicians, he learned, were invariably curious about the availability of certain species of contraband; he knew where to get it and found that this could put him pretty much anywhere, into any room. He had a mind bent in the direction of curating undervalued things. In his teens, he went to burlesque shows, presumably the only one in the audience with a notebook, and wrote down accounts of the comedy skits, stock bits with vulgar names, the Pickle Caper, things no one would have thought to remember, and possibly no one did, but they're in McCormick's files.

From the musicians, he got the idea that if you wanted the realest jazz, you had to go to New Orleans, so when he wound up in East Texas after the war and found himself within hitchhiking distance of the city, he started making trips there. He became a regular at a place called the New Orleans Record Shop, on Baronne Street, run by a journalist and pioneering discographer named Orin Blackstone. Blackstone knew that McCormick was going back and forth to Texas, so he asked him to keep his eyes peeled for old records there. Before the war, they made recordings in Texas, he said, in "field studios," hotels, warehouses. He showed him the labels to be on watch for, what they looked like. He dubbed McCormick the first-ever Texas editor to the *Index to Jazz*. It was 1946.

That unofficial knighting launched one of the postwar period's most storied careers in American cultural fieldwork. Searching for records led to searching for the people who made them, and McCormick had natural gifts when it came to approaching strangers and getting them to talk or, if they could, to sing and play. He had a likable, approachable face, with pronounced ears and intelligent eyes. He took a job with the census, expressly requesting that he be assigned the Fourth Ward, the historic African American neighborhood in Houston settled by freed slaves who migrated there from all parts of the South, where he knew he would find records and lots of musicians, going house to house. The fables of his research are legion. He drove unthinkable miles. At one point he started traveling county by county or, rather, he started moving in a pattern of counties, from east to west, marking a horizontal band that overlapped the spread of slavery west from the Atlantic colonies. He investigated 888 counties before he was finished. He asked about everything, not just music but recipes, dances, games, ghost stories, and in his note taking, he realized that the county itself, as an organizing geographical principle, had some reality beyond a shape on the map, that it retained in some much-diminished but not quite extinguished sense, the old contours of the premodern world, the world of the commons, how in one county you would have dozens of fiddle players, but in the very next county, none—there everyone played banjo. He began to intuit a theory of "clusters," that this was how culture worked, emanating outward from vortices where craft making and art making suddenly rise, under a confluence of various pressures, to higher levels. Elaborating that theory would be his great work, or part of it.

He never elaborated the theory. It's frank, but I don't think unfair, to say that he won't. He's in his mideighties; his health is shaky. His archive of tapes and transcripts is a labyrinth even to him. He calls it the Monster. He has been open, too, about a lifetime's battles against psychological obstacles, specifically a sometimes paralyzing bipolar disorder. The mania that drove him to those superhuman exploits of cultural questing could turn on him and shut him down when it came time for the drudgery of organizing facts and notes. You can find a very moving "open letter" from him, published in *Blues Unlimited* in 1976, saying, essentially, "Help"; saying, "I've gathered this material, this data, and it has swallowed me." In one letter he mentions having been made aware, at a recent meeting of the American Folklore Society, that certain people in the community were upset with him because he was hoarding so much knowledge. He'd uncovered more than almost anyone about this music they worshiped, yet he had published less than almost anyone. It was holding them back, holding the discipline back. But what did they want him to do? Give it away? It was his work.

He has given a lot away over the years, most famously in the case of Robert Johnson. You know Johnson: hellhounds, crossroads, death by poison. Have you heard of a man who has a picture of Johnson no one has ever seen? That's McCormick. The story goes that they're in a safe place in Mexico, where McCormick lived for a period. Peter Guralnick, whose *Searching for Robert Johnson* has a permanent place on the high shelf of writing about the blues, saw the pictures. McCormick let him.

Guralnick very openly and graciously makes clear in the notes to his book that it draws deeply on McCormick's research and was meant, in fact, to lay the groundwork for what McCormick had gathered and put together about the singer's life. Guralnick sent a copy of the book to McCormick when it was published, with an inscription that said, in a gentle way, "Here's my book, now it's time for yours."

Guralnick's book came out twenty-five years ago. McCormick, needless to say, hasn't finished his own. He is on record (in one of two or three notably good profiles done on him over the years) as saying that the subject of Johnson has gone dead on him. And he has said since that part of him wishes he hadn't let that one singer, that riddle of a man, consume him. Which is a human thing to feel . . . except for when you happen to know more than anyone on earth about a subject that loads of people in several countries want to know more about. Then your inability to produce becomes not just a personal problem but a cultural one. It's plausible that the scope of research finally got too large for any one mind, even a uniquely brilliant one, to hold in orbit. The point here is not to accuse or defend him but rather to point out that even his footnotes, even the fragments from his research that have landed in other scholars' pages, have been enough to place him among the two or three most important figures in this field. He's one of those people whose influence starts to show up everywhere once you're sensitized to it.

Field Work

When I first corresponded a couple of years ago with McCormick, who is still living in the same modest ranch house in northwest Houston where he has been for decades, he began by asking if I could help him find out what happened to Orin Blackstone. They'd lost touch, evidently, and McCormick feared that somehow his mentor had come to an unhappy end. I rooted around some and eventually found an article from *The International Association of Jazz Record Collectors Journal*, paying tribute to Blackstone, who died in Louisiana in 1980. One source quoted in the article said that later in life, Blackstone "had become very bitter." McCormick's response to the news was muted. "Thanks for the Orin Blackstone article, which answers my questions about him," he wrote. I told him I would be in Houston in a few months, and we arranged a visit.

I arrived at his house on a small, silent street after midnight. I had been at an event downtown all evening, but McCormick had told me he routinely stays up until four a.m., that these were decent receiving hours for him. I approached his front door in the dark. A yellow light came on. A little sign read, "If it isn't one o'clock, don't knock."

He opened the door from his wheelchair, then rolled backward and let me in, saying that he could walk some, but with difficulty, and that it had become hard for him to get out of bed. He used a kind of swinging harness apparatus to do it. But his handshake was firm, and his half-smile was full of the reputed charm. He seemed completely there.

We sat up for several hours, drinking screwdrivers. There was a black-and-white movie on, something from the 1940s. He had a fat little dog named Charles, who has since died, that he loved very much. Charles would drink your screwdriver, if you set it on the floor, and McCormick kept having to remind me to put my notepad or a book on top of the glass, so Charles couldn't get to the drink. Now and then McCormick would pause and send me to locate a binder or folder. Mostly he talked, not tediously but spell-bindingly. His recall was encyclopedic, though he frequently cursed his memory, saying he had suffered a small stroke. Yet he roamed through years and names, stopping to ask if you had heard of some person, carrying on heedlessly whether you said yes or no.

He had said he didn't want to talk about Robert Johnson, for personal reasons and on principle. But his talk spiraled inexorably toward Johnson anyway. The singer loomed over his memory as he had over his career. What he told me took me aback. McCormick said that what he realized, in the quarter century since Guralnick's book came out, was that most of what we think we know about Robert Johnson—which is to say, most of what McCormick thought he knew—was highly unstable. We're not even sure, McCormick said, that the man in the pictures we have, the smiling man with long fingers, holding the guitar, is Robert Johnson. Or that he is, as McCormick put it, "the guy who made the records." He is a Robert Johnson. But according to McCormick, the more he has lived with the evidence, the more he doubts. Of the people he interviewed so long ago, more than one of those who had met Johnson and been present at one of his two sessions in Texas told McCormick, when they were shown the famous photograph, "That's not the guy." It didn't look like him, they said. Not everyone said that, but a few.

What about the death certificate, discovered by the mad Mississippi 78-hound and prolific blues researcher Gayle Dean Wardlow (much as McCormick took a job with the census, Wardlow took one in pest control)? There were problems with the death certificate, McCormick said. You had to look at the back of it. The Robert Johnson identified there was a banjo player. It says, "banjo." He added that you had to remember how many men were called Robert Johnson, and how ready to hand it would have been for a singer who needed a professional name. There were other historical proofs (or supposed proofs) I offered—David (Honeyboy) Edwards's testimony, for example—and each one he dismantled with a detailed exegesis. He was saying that we didn't know how little we knew. Could be him in the pictures. Couldn't prove that it wasn't. But McCormick didn't think so. There were weaknesses in his argument, too, and he didn't try to conceal them. They bothered him, which made what he was saying more compelling and more startling.

I'm not a Johnson expert by even the most forgiving definition, and it was not always easy to follow McCormick's verbal hypertext. At times, too, I experienced queasy flashes of suspicion, partly because it seemed impossible that everyone could be wrong about a figure so central to the tradition. Was this a form of subconscious sabotage on McCormick's part? A narrative: He hadn't written his Johnson book; others' books on Johnson would have the last word . . . unless, that is, he could pull the rug out from under the whole field. He still comes out master of the chase. His unwritten Johnson book would enact some Borgesian supersession of the ones that had been written.

My gut said it wasn't that, though. He seemed too unhappy about it all. His tone said he wished he could skip saying these things. A tone not of ironically regretful satisfaction but closer, maybe, to embarrassment. Was that the reason he hadn't said this on the record before? Perhaps he felt he had misled us all? And again, just to be clear, he wasn't saying that everything we thought we knew was flat wrong, only that our faith in it needed to be downgraded by a more-than-symbolic percentage. In the end, the most we could hope for was a kind of less-ignorant fog into which the guy who made the records receded.

This is all to say that my mind had already been Rubik's Cubed around by McCormick, when he abruptly picked up a sheaf of papers, four or five pages, and held them out to me. "I found these," he said. "They should interest you."

I don't remember if we had talked about Geeshie and Elvie or if he knew I had an interest in them. I wrote some pages on them once, on having worked as the fact-checker for an essay about Geeshie that Greil Marcus published fifteen years ago. If McCormick had read my article, he didn't mention it. We must have discussed them.

He bent forward in his recliner, elbows on his knees. I looked down at the papers. These were apparently photocopies of notes and letters. But the originals that had been photocopied were themselves old, typewritten, from the early 1960s. One was a transcript of an interview with a musician identified as Leon Benton. At the top of the notes, in a header, it said that McCormick had located him in the Acres Homes section of Houston. It was 1961, the year after Mack worked the census in the Fourth Ward, and he was following leads generated there. "And during this same period in the early 1930s," Benton was saying, "there was a woman guitar player named L. V. Thomas who also lives out here in Acres Homes now. I worked with her a good deal. In fact for a time we had a group with two guitars and a violin—that was myself, Leroy Johnson and L. V. Thomas. She put out some records. She was as good as any man with that guitar."

L. V.

Down another paragraph: "L. V. Thomas has done just like me, she's joined the church and doesn't fool with music any longer. That's a bad life. I like to hear music but it pulls you in the wrong direction. It's sporting life and helling around and sure trouble coming with it."

At some point I looked up. McCormick was sipping his screwdriver, twinkling a bit. Savoring my speechlessness. "Keep reading," he said.

The next page was a copy of a letter addressed to Paul Oliver, the much-esteemed English blues historian, who is McCormick's longest and most important collaborator. Oliver's book *Songsters and Saints* was the first serious work on prewar black music that I ever read and still one of the most illuminating. Pretty much everything Oliver wrote on the subject is, by definition, essential. "Paul," it began. "I got a live one! A 70-year-old woman blues guitarist and singer—who recorded for Paramount. She is L. V. Thomas who recorded solo and with her partner Lillie Mae 'Geetchie' Wiley in 4 days at Milwaukee, Wis." In the margin, McCormick had written in black marker, "Prob. Grafton, Wis.?" It continued: "Miss (?) Thomas is old and could be—if she will—a most valuable informant. She is a sweet old lady but is reluctant to talk about blues or music. . . . Anyhow she's been playing guitar since she was eleven years old—in 1902! And working, earning money since 1908. Thus everything has to [be] pried out of her most gently else she decide I'm the devil incarnate."

It was two in the morning. I'd never spent much time in Texas, and the overcast spring night outside pressed enormously on the roof and windows. I scanned back up the page and found the name again. Lillie Mae. The true name of Geeshie Wiley. A thing I'd wondered about more than half my life but had never allowed myself to imagine anyone would ever actually see or know. McCormick had known it for more than fifty years.

And "Elvie" was L. V.? Or was it instead the case that McCormick hadn't known who she was when he found her, hadn't heard her records yet (none of them had been reissued by 1961) and so wrote her name as "L. V.," when in fact she meant "Elvie"?

I said several sputtery things. He expressed mild surprise at my overreaction. He seemed unaware that Geeshie and Elvie had developed a following. I asked if he had seen *Crumb*. He said he didn't know it. Twenty years, I suppose, was not a significant number for a man who had been chasing these ghosts for almost seventy. The Monster was boxed and shelved in the room directly behind him. It could be full of revelations like these, for all anybody knows. For McCormick, my overly narrow preoccupations on certain singers hinted of amateurism (correct). He didn't fetishize. He didn't go in for that. It was about bigger things. The clusters. He had allowed himself to become consumed like that once, with Robert Johnson, "carried away with some kind of peculiar enthusiasm," he said, and look what happened. He wasn't going to get worked up about a couple of minor blues women whom some wannabes had decided to build a shrine around.

Still, McCormick couldn't have been unaware, or at least not stayed unaware, for such a long time (*half a century*), that people were identifying Geeshie and Elvie with Mississippi, which has long possessed a unique aura in the blues world. Nor was it dilettantes doing the identifying but some of the most notable curators and reissuers of that music. Songs by Geeshie and Elvie show up on multiple Mississippi-themed compilations, among them *Mississippi Blues* (Belzona, 1968), *Mississippi Girls* (Document, 1988), and *Mississippi Masters* (Yazoo, 1994). There are researchers—I know one of them from my time living in Mississippi—who have spent thousands of hours crisscrossing the state, looking for the smallest bent twig left behind by the two women. There are even, it should be added, a few whose ears were sharp enough to hear betraying hints of Texas in the music—figures like Don Kent, who argued years ago that the guitar in "Last Kind Words" employs "a riff normally associated with Texas artists," or the collector Chris King, in Virginia, who one night was "listening to some interviews/recordings of convicts in a work camp from around Huntsville, Tex.," and noticed that their unusual pronunciation of the word "depot," as DAY-poe, matched Geeshie's own.

What was Mack thinking, during all that time? Was he laughing? Was he taking a dark satisfaction in watching the errors pile up, errors that he knew he would one day sweep away? Maybe he just didn't know what to do, what to say.

The Collectors

It's funny to think that Mack, the person who found them, or preserved the information of who they were, alone encountered them with absolutely no mystique. When Leon Benton told him about this woman in Acres Homes who could play guitar but had given it up for the church, that's all Mack knew, and that's the woman who was in his head all those years while the rest of us were constructing a faceless ideal. He met L. V. She even showed him a picture, that first day, of herself when she was young. "Very nice-looking at that period," he recalled.

Did he have anything else? Had he made a transcription of those interviews?

Yes, he said, he knew he had it somewhere. But he couldn't find it. His papers looked organized, from the outside, they weren't messy, but there were tens of thousands of pages. And photographs? Thousands of them, scattered through which are images of people we have no other images of. Multiple clashing archival code systems had been brought to bear over the decades, but then half or partly finished, and now they existed in skeins on top of one another. The entrance to the labyrinth had been walled up, closed even to the one who had the clue.

·   ·   ·

For some months, I kept in sporadic contact with McCormick, and through a friend in Arkansas, got in touch with a young woman, a twenty-one-year-old undergraduate, curious about the old music, who said she was willing to drop out of school for a year to help Mack. She came complete with the made-up-seeming name of Caitlin Rose Love. With the blessing of her school, she packed her bags and moved to Houston.

It didn't work out between Mack and Caitlin. I won't go into why; it's their business. Nothing unseemly. She had "ideas" about what they should accomplish, and he needed someone who would sit there and do what he said. Fair enough. She, for her part, may have felt there was a lot of storytelling time for a project she had changed her life to help move forward. Didn't he understand the urgency, after all? But a person couldn't bring that up. Didn't need to. Hadn't he written himself, in that open letter in 1976, addressing his writer's block and the singular problem it presented for the field—namely that you couldn't tell the story of the blues without Mack McCormick, and you couldn't tell it because of him—"a related problem that may help explain my personal conflict is the pressure of death and the passage of time." He fired her.

He lost a beloved wife to cancer when she was still young. He has a daughter, who is married and comfortable. She's not interested in the blues and perhaps can't help resenting it for all the times it took her father away, but she loves the man, as I learned the hard way when I called her in an attempt to get her to reason with him. It was the last straw for Mack. He didn't like that, my calling his daughter. He wrote me a letter saying thanks for trying, then stopped communicating.

A night came when Caitlin was sitting on the balcony of her apartment in Houston. It was too late to go back to school. She felt judged and rejected in some unarticulated way, and instead of having jumped a few spaces on the board of life, she had been forced to put the game on pause. I tried to help her see that whatever had played into Mack's decision making had little or nothing to do with her, that it was larger than that. At some point I asked if she'd ever seen, in the time she worked with Mack, anything with the name "L. V. Thomas" on it?

She had, yes. A folder.

Good sense said it was the letters he'd already shown me and to breathe.

No, it was notes. It was a couple of interviews. There was also a tape box, one of those boxes that says "Scotch," with her name on it.

Did she remember anything about the notes?

"I took pictures of them."

I asked him about the fate of those pages a dozen times since that first night at his house, to a degree that in hindsight was pushy. Had he deliberately left these papers in the open in order to test her? Still, it was hard not to feel that he arranged for this little disclosure, even if the pea was very many mattresses down in his psyche.

Minutes later, scans were coming through of old yellowed pages. Typescript, ring-binder holes in the left margin. "L. V.

Thomas . . . Interviewed June 20, 1961." It was late and everyone else in the house was asleep. L. V. Thomas spoke. He found her, in Acres Homes, and approached her gate, and she let him in. He was thirty, she was about to turn seventy. He found her "dried up and shrunken," such that the next time he visited, five months later, he was at first surprised that she was still alive. She told him she was born in August 1891, in Houston. "I was born right down here at 3116 Washington Avenue," she said.

She continues: "I started playing guitar when I was about 11 years old. There were blues even back then. It wasn't so big a part of music as later but there were blues. I can't hardly name them— I don't know that those songs had a name. One song was, 'Oh, My Babe Take Me Back,' and another was 'Jack O' Diamonds.' There was a lot of set pieces, stuff that'd be called for dancing, that everybody learned. . . .

"But in 1937 I joined the church so I gave up all I ever did know about music. I joined the Master and followed after him and gave up all my music since 1937 and I hate for you to ask me about my sinful days. I'm a member of the Mount Pleasant Baptist Church out here in Acres Homes and that's the only place I do any singing anymore."

The two interviews went on for four single-spaced pages. They silently vacuumed out the story of Geeshie and Elvie as it had existed and been accruing conjectural details in my head for twenty years and replaced it with something utterly different. L. V. spent her whole life in Houston. Born into a large family, she says, she was at first the only one interested in music. Some neighborhood boys she ran around with, "They had guitars and liked to fool with them, so I guess they kinda got me started."

Among my first thoughts while reading the transcripts was: this could be fake. Not even in the sense of a forgery but in the sense of a joke. Maybe Mack decided he didn't like me and figured he would detonate my cerebellum for fun before going back to the seven books he has in the works. Or maybe it was even more complicated than that. Maybe it was a *History of the Siege of Lisbon*–like thing; maybe he was tinkering with the machinery of reality because he could or to settle some balance. Other major blues people I spoke with warned me of the same. "I'd be very careful," one said. Another said, "that sounds like fantasy."

The only way to know if the documents were real was to check them against reality. And we had this lucky situation, a catastrophic situation that might be turned to good use. Caitlin was stranded in Houston. I'd still never met her, but the photorealistic detail of her dispatches from inside the Monster had been enjoyable to follow, and I admired the bravery of her act of quasi theft, feeling strongly that it was the right thing to do. You're not allowed to sit on these things for half a century, not when the culture has decided they matter. I know he didn't want to sit on them—he was trapped with them. I give us both a pass. Caitlin had no job. Mack had been her job. But we had these pages, a grand total of nine, the letters and the transcripts. And we had a full-time, on-the-ground researcher/reporter in Houston, whom fate happened to be catching smack in the midst of her own budding Geeshie-and-L. V. enthusiasm. If Mack wouldn't talk to us anymore, we would do this as an assignment for him, we would follow his leads. Caitlin started barnstorming government offices, where old records are kept. Libraries and archives. Back-office experts she was referred to, small-town historical societies, basements with open shelves. It was jealousy inducing—I'd always dreamed of doing blues research like this, the way they did it back in the 1950s, the way Mack had done it. I knew what he meant now when he said that what he did wasn't research, it was search. She was searching. And after some weeks, she started finding things; L. V.'s will, some tax records. And after more weeks, we had enough data between us to start crossing the streams of what Mack had given us (or withheld from us), and not only did everything that McCormick had claimed to hear in 1961 check out; it started to multiply.

The year 1891: the Mauve Decade. Benjamin Harrison is in the White House. Famine in Russia, civil war in Chile. Oscar Wilde is writing *Salome* in Paris. August 7, the day L. V. Thomas is born: Walt Whitman is alive but depressed and eating a bowl of ice cream that he later decides was too much for him. He'll die in about half a year. An old German woman is attacked with a razor blade on a street in London, causing people to fear that the Ripper has returned, but it emerges that she had been trying to fake her own murder, so that her son could collect insurance money. The *Knoxville Journal* reports that the coming Grocer's Association Picnic will involve, as no. 13 in its list of entertainments, "Throwing eggs at Negro's head." The *Cincinnati Enquirer* reports that a Dr. Ege of Pennsylvania has "succeeded in transplanting the skin of a Negro to the arm of a white person." The *Charlotte Democrat* reports that the Rev. Dr. Ebenezer Judkins of Houston, Stonewall Jackson's brother-in-law, has fallen dead on a railroad train, and on Washington Avenue, at some unknown hour, L. V. is born.

The house she was born in is listed as "vacant" in the city directory, which adds that her family was living in the "rear." It's most probable that her father was a man named Peter Grant, and that her name at birth was L. V. Grant. The name Thomas seems to have come from a short-lived marriage very early in her life, in her early teens, to a man who in the absence of a marriage license eludes us.

So, L. V. Thomas was first L. V. Grant; her mother, evidently a woman named Cora. We know only a few things about her childhood: that she left school after the fifth grade and that around the same time, at the age of eleven or so, she started playing the guitar. At some point L. V.'s mother, whether or not she was ever married to her father, married a man named Chris King, who "played all the string instruments," she says. "Mandoline mostly, but guitar and banjo, too. He didn't go out to the country suppers but mostly played in saloons here in Houston."

The country suppers: Mack had written about them, in his notes to the *Treasury of Field Recordings* liner notes, 1960, the year before he met L. V. They were picnics on Saturdays that would last all day and night. "I guess I was about 17"—it was 1908 or '09—"when I started going out playing at country suppers," L. V. says.

Something goes wrong. A 1910 census taker finds her an inmate in the Harris County Jail. For a serious crime? If you were black in Houston in 1910, it was not hard to get arrested for doing nothing. She was working as a dishwasher, the census says. Any records related to the arrest or any trial that took place are gone.

When she gets out—after years or a day—she's still playing music, and not just that, but she's playing with someone major, a singer whose name figures highly in any serious effort to get back through the veil of early recording and hear what the blues might have sounded like on the other side, Alger (Texas) Alexander. "One time Texas Alexander wanted me to go out to West Texas with him, but I didn't like to be away," she says. "I used to play for Texas sometimes down on West Dallas Street or go out to suppers with him." Alexander: small, dark, and handsome, with a voice that could fill a noisy barroom or a canyon, as occasion demanded. Musicologists consider him precious because his singing was very close to the fields. He didn't play an instrument, just sang, beautiful wavering songs, and he did with tempo what he wanted. When the race-record people found him and recorded him, starting in 1927, they supposedly had to work to find accompanists who could handle playing in "Alexander time." Texas Alexander: My God, L. V. had backed him? In two sentences she leapt from the edges of the tradition to the center. All of a sudden at the country supper in my mind, Texas Alexander walked through. Which meant that so did Blind Lemon Jefferson (they worked together). The little boy leading Blind Lemon by the hand and passing the cup for him is T-Bone Walker. We are here in this meadow. It's an environment where any kind of hybridization could happen.

"I remember one night was a big party," L. V. says, "when Sippie Wallace came back to town and all the songsters came together. It was like a contest of a kind. Everyone sang a number, and the audience would call for who they wanted to hear some more and I remember they pulled everyone out but me. Seem like they wanted to hear me most of all."

The ghost had shown up at a singing contest and outsung Sippie Wallace. And L. V. was not a bragging woman. "I was out in the world when I made those records, but now I don't want to talk about it," she says. He asks her about "Last Kind Words Blues," which he'd never heard, at that point; all that had transpired, Geeshie and Elvie–wise, in 1961, is that they were name-checked six years earlier in *Jazz Monthly*, and the Blues Mafiosi had heard them, become interested in them. But Oliver sent McCormick a manuscript of some kind that included the lyrics, and Mack read them to her. "I guess it could have been one of my songs," L. V. said. "Lots of them I made up."

On no subject did her guardedness frustrate him more than on that of Geeshie, her partner. "One thing," he had written to Oliver in those first letters he gave me, "it appears there was some trouble between she [*sic*] and Geeshie Wiley and the story here would be quite a tale I suspect, if it can [be] unearthed." He went on, "Most aggravating of all is the fact that L. V. Thomas apparently know[s] something more of [Geeshie's] present whereabouts than she will offer."

L. V. did give him some scraps on Geeshie during those two afternoons at her house. "The way I came to make records," she said, "was that I went around a lot with a girl named Lillie Mae Wiley. She was called Geetchie Wiley.

"Mr. Laibly of the Paramount record company came to her house one time, and she carried him on over to see me. He listened to me play, and he listened to her, and then he said he'd like for us to go up North and make some records. We knew about his company. I think we both had some Paramount records, and we'd heard of others going up there. I was the older. I was about 38 or so then, so I said all right."

Arthur Laibly. A peripatetic salesman who worked his way up in the company and often gets a bad rap for having essentially presided over Paramount's implosion, though he couldn't really help the Depression.

McCormick asks how Laibly found her and Geeshie. "I don't know how Mr. Laibly heard of her," she says. "I suppose someone down at the music distributing house told about us. We had a pretty good name as two girls to hire for music."

I got in touch with Alex van der Tuuk, a generous and much-esteemed Dutch blues historian, who knows as much about Laibly as anyone alive. He said that Laibly would regularly pack up his car with fresh Paramounts and go on long trips through the South, visiting the record "houses" that sold race records. In one of those stores he must have asked, "Who's good, who's worth recording?" And the guy at the counter says, "You need to check out these two girls, Geeshie and L. V." The guy must have sung their praises. They're the only musicians Laibly recruits during this trip to Houston, that we know of. It's doubtful anyone would have turned him down. He sets out for Geeshie's house, 1205 Saulnier Street, the house where she must have written or at least worked on "Last Kind Words Blues."

Lillie Mae (Geeshie) Wiley. For the first time her silhouette holds steady in front of the lens for a moment. Sharing a house with her husband, a man named Thornton Wiley, who worked at a metal shop around the corner. She was young, twenty-one or twenty-two, no children. Laibly knocks on her door.

"At the very first I started going out alone," L. V. says. "I played all by myself. Then my first partner was Lillie Mae."

That was in the early 1920s. They may have met at one of the country suppers, where they couldn't have missed each other's playing. "When I first met up with her, she was all alone," L. V. says. "She was from some country place"—one census document says Louisiana, born there around 1908—"and living here in Houston when we got together."

In the rooming house on Ruthven Street where L. V. lives, they sit and play for Laibly. Their best stuff, no doubt. The lovely and sinister "Skinny Leg Blues."

> I got little bitty legs, keep up these noble thighs,
> I got little bitty legs, keep up these noble thighs,
> Aah, keep up these noble thighs.
> I got something underneath, and it works like a boar
> hog's eye.

Laibly puts them on the train. "Lillie Mae and I went up there to Milwaukee," L. V. says, where their train ride would have ended. You had to go by car or tram the extra twenty or so miles north to Grafton, where the studio and pressing plant were.

The year 1930. Segregated cars. April: wildflowers in the fields. Seeing the first true cities they've ever seen. The front page of the *Chicago Daily Tribune* reads, "Bull Gets Blues." The true crash of the Depression is underway.

I asked Alex van der Tuuk to help me reconstruct their arrival in Wisconsin, what would have been most likely to happen, when they got off the train. How close could we get to a little movie, sticking to only what we know?

It was cold, about as cold as they'd ever felt. Ice floes had jammed the Milwaukee River, causing a flood in Grafton, where they were scheduled to record the next afternoon. It's possible that they had to wait a few days until it thawed.

They would have most likely taken the tram to the recording studio and been driven back by a man named Alfred Schultz, the pressing foreman at the Paramount plant. Schultz was a young, narrow-faced man who had worked his way up at the company over a decade. Van der Tuuk wrote a very good minibiography of him for *Vintage Jazz Mart* some years back, based on interviews with his daughter. He was well liked, and the company noticed he got along easily with the singers from the South.

Paramount didn't usually keep the black musicians in Grafton. It was an all-white town of mostly European immigrants. The company often housed them instead at a boardinghouse in Brewer's Hill in Milwaukee. They go up the next day by tram, up the Lake Michigan shore, with glittering blue-glass views of the lake to the right as they rode.

They pull into a tiny town with a water wheel on the river, to power the plant.

The studio building was a reddish structure, described by everyone who saw it as "like a barn." There are no photographs of the studio interior, but Van der Tuuk, in *Paramount's Rise and Fall*, skillfully layers the memories of musicians who remembered it. The space is divided into two rooms, the control room and the performance space. There's a wall between them with a door and window in it and a red light that comes on when the artists are recording. There's an upright baby grand piano. The room is cold and damp. The windows were "draped with burlap and blankets" to reduce the reverberation. Thick carpets on the floors. A dark, furred box. A horrible place to record.

They would have been offered illegal liquor, but not too much, just enough to limber them up.

The recording equipment itself, as reconstituted by Van der Tuuk, was a strange liminal beast that probably should have never lived. It was electrical, but it looked acoustical. You sat and sang into a giant wooden horn that was two feet wide at the mouth and eight feet long. The horn was meant to focus and direct the sound toward an electrical microphone. We may be able to hear the eccentricities of the weights and pulleys in the way the speed seems to change slightly about two-thirds of the way through "Motherless Child Blues."

Another nice detail: Schultz's daughter, Janet, not yet four, is impossible to keep out of the studio. The Schultz house is nearby.

She has learned "very quickly to be quiet so I could be with my dad." So, there's a little girl in the corner when Geeshie and Elvie record "Motherless Child Blues" (though not, you would hope, when they record "Skinny Leg Blues," with its earthy exhortation, "Squat low, papa, let your mama see, / I wanna see that old business keeps on a-worrying me").

There they sit. Two guitars. Laibley's there. Schultz is there. The light comes on.

That fearsome A minor. Buzzards circle. Dark clouds form in the little muffled cave. Mack McCormick is in the womb.

They recorded on four consecutive afternoons. L. V. remembered "dozens of songs," but that was probably high. Certainly more than six. After each session Schultz would take the records to a "test room," where he sat and listened to the songs. After each record, he wrote the name and song title on a white label, adding terse reviews.

L. V.'s thumb, thumping on her bass string. "She'd sing one, I'd sing one," she told McCormick, "and each of us would bass for the other." She uses "bass" as a verb like that. It has caused me to hear the six songs in a new way, to know that this is how they conceived of their arrangement; it's part of what makes their sound so distinctive.

"I didn't hear too much back" from Paramount, L. V. tells Mc-Cormick. "We never did get any royalty money or anything from those records. Just what they paid then."

Something minuscule but determining occurs: Laibly, or Laibly and Schultz, one or both of them, changes the spelling of L. V.'s name. "It's just the letters L. V.," she says, "that's all the name I got but he made it out 'Elvie' someway." Maybe he wanted to make sure customers knew it was a woman on the song; two women playing guitars (unusual).

As he writes the five letters, he presses a long, invisible blade down between two destinies, hard enough to cut them off from each other for eighty years. There will be Elvie, a singer, who lives nowhere, and L. V., a woman, at her house in Houston. They call her song "Motherless Child Blues," even though it doesn't have those words anywhere in it and the woman singing, in the song, is not an orphan, so that when thirty-one years later Mack finds her and asks about that song, she doesn't know what he's talking about, she never had a song called "Motherless Child Blues."

And Geeshie? Where did that name come from? "I called her Geetchie," L. V. says, "and that's the name Mr. Laibly decided to put on the records. I was the one started calling her Geetchie—I just picked that for her name." An affectionate way of calling her a hayseed, more or less? Blacks in parts of the South still use it that way. Maybe Lillie Mae talked funny, being from the country, from somewhere in Louisiana.

"I haven't seen her since 1933. I left her in Chico, Okla. Something like Choco . . . Chico. We'd gone out playing around together, traveling, and I left her up there and came on back."

McCormick has penciled in the margins, "Checotah, Okla.! South of Muskogee."

You can tell from the transcript that he keeps asking about Geeshie, where she could be.

"Last I heard of Lillie Mae was about four or five years ago," L. V. says. "She was supposed to be in West Texas then."

So, L. V. was still aware of her, almost thirty years after she'd seen her last.

What about her name, before she married this man, Thornton Wiley? How was she born? Lillie Mae something. Lillie Mae what? "I can't think of her name before she was married," L. V. says.

She tells McCormick that she has bread in the oven, and is "anxious" for him to "leave her alone."

He has acquired tape recordings of the songs since the first time he's seen her, maybe through Oliver, and wants to play them for her, wants her to hear their music again, to see if it jogs anything.

"All that's gone out of my mind and I don't want to bring it back."

.   .   .

I got a text from Caitlin at about 5 in the evening that said "!!!!!!!" Then another one that said, "Check your email."

She was digging around at the genealogical library out there. Houston has a very good one.

I opened the message and the attachment. It was an official form, like a birth certificate. No, a death certificate. State of Texas. Thornton Wiley. Not that exciting. Not "!!!!!!!" Of course he died. Wait, though—it was from 1931, just a year after she was living with him on Saulnier Street in the Fourth Ward. Not long after they made the records. He died young. That was sad. Maybe she loved him, despite L. V.'s seeming distaste for his character. Maybe she is thinking of him in "Last Kind Words" when she sings, "What you do to me, baby, it never gets out of me / I believe I'll see you after I cross the deep blue sea." I'm reading down through the crowded handwriting. "Inquest." "Homicide." He had been murdered.

Manner of injury: "Stab wound in between collarbone and neck."

His brother is listed as the informant. He told the police what happened, or a version of what happened. They were out in Fort Bend County, outside Houston, on a farm near a place called Fulshear, maybe at a country supper. But he's listed as single, so he and Geeshie had recently split.

Then the form got to the cause of death. "Knife wound inflicted by Lillie Mae Scott."

Six months of work to learn more about the murder came to nothing. There wasn't a scrap of paper. The inquest records are lost. I communicated with a lawyer in East Texas who'd worked on similar cases, murders of husbands by wives, not this long ago but fifty years ago. He said that very often, the police were so in-different to the reason a particular black male had been killed, they would happily accept a self-defense theory, if one were put forward. Easier night. Let 'em stab each other. On the other hand, this was a particularly violent one, the knife from above, into the neck at an angle, one cut and deep enough the first time to kill. Also, the brother had been the informant to the police, so it's doubtful they received a sympathetic account of her reasons for killing him. Maybe they did arrest Lillie Mae. Or maybe they tried to arrest her, and she ran away, with L. V., to Oklahoma. And maybe she stayed away.

Up in Grafton, on "Skinny Leg Blues":

I'm gonna cut your throat, baby,
Gonna look down in your face.
I'm gonna let some lonesome graveyard
Be your resting place.

Lillie Mae's trail seemed to end there, or with L. V.'s vague "out West." She had slipped away again, replacing one ghost with another. There are graves of Lillie Mae Scotts in Texas and Oklahoma, and Lily May Scotts, and Lilly M. Scotts, and maybe one of them is hers, and maybe none of them are. Maybe she changed her name completely, or maybe she kept the name Wiley. She could be alive. She'd be about 106; it happens. Maybe you are reading this and you have a great-grandmother named Lillie Mae who told you once that she used to sing and make records. Or maybe nothing. That might be best. That she stay Geeshie, but more so. Lillie Mae of Louisiana was better than myth; she was a mystery. She was the one who had ghosts.

"Skinny Leg Blues"

Just as we were thinking the research had reached a natural plateau, L. V.'s did something we hadn't expected, climbing out of the file cabinet and into the world. Caitlin was talking to people who'd known her. Looking back, I know this shouldn't have been earth-shattering, I don't know why we hadn't hoped for it. If she were alive today, she would be 122. Maybe she seemed too remote. And in McCormick's interviews, you got the sense that she knew or saw very few people and was isolated.

But there was also that one sentence, in the transcripts, suggestive of tethers to a community: "I'm member of the Mount Pleasant Baptist Church out here in Acres Homes, and that's the only place I do any singing anymore."

Acres Homes is a remarkable part of Houston, a big flat area in the northwest part of the city, unincorporated forever, and has historically had a mostly African American population. It's like a big patch of rural land that the city in its expansion oozed around amoeba-style. When I visited there later, it was startling to see guys going past in full urban hip-hop gear, caps and braids, low-slung pants and new sneakers, cell phones out, only they were seated on chestnut mares, with their girlfriends behind them, trotting by.

Mount Pleasant Missionary Baptist Church still stands there, in a building within sight of the spot where it was when L. V. attended. Caitlin started going regularly. The people were exceptionally welcoming, well beyond what the code of Southern interracial church politesse demands. The women called her Sister Love. When the time for announcing visitors came, that first day, the pastor, Calvin Randle, recognized her presence and asked her to introduce herself. She gave a very touching unprepared speech that I listened to on MP3 the same night.

It turned out there were several people at the church who remembered "Sister L. V. Thomas"—or "Mama Thomas," as others called her—beginning with Randle, who alone of the people we've managed to contact knew her in the Fourth Ward, from after her conversion but before she left the neighborhood where she and Lillie Mae played blues together.

Randle remembered her voice. Everyone remembered her voice.

Sister Thomas

L. V. lived near the church. A fiercely independent woman. One of her former neighbors said: "You know how some women gotta have some help, have a man around? She didn't have to have one."

Another thing people at Mount Pleasant talked about consistently were her clothes. Her bulky, orthopedic-style shoes. It didn't seem like a thing to notice, necessarily, about an elderly lady, but there was something that came along with it, a vibe, with how often people brought it up. We got stray physical details from other people. Dark colors. Long skirts, sometimes, but more often, pants. Hair always "kind of pulled back." A "very plain" brown hat. She was short, "maybe about five feet tall."

Sometime later, we went to her grave. It was easy to find, once you had her death certificate. We called the cemetery, still in business. They looked up her name. The directions to her grave were these: "Cemetery Beautiful, Avenue Love, Row Paradise." A simple stone, almost level to the ground. Her name and dates written across an engraving of an open book. And beneath, "The Lord is my light and salvation."

.   .   .

There was one small memory that people in Acres Homes had that nagged us for some reason: That L. V. used to bring a little boy to church. No one remembered his name or knew who he was, only that he would come with her and sit there next to her.

Months went by, and Caitlin added to her pile of interviews, but we kept wondering about this boy. A couple of people thought he might have been family somehow. Eventually, Caitlin reached a Sister White, who didn't want to talk to us, but did say that L. V. had surviving family. No one else in the church had mentioned this. She even had a name: Robin, in California. She gave us a number.

Robin Wartell, in Los Angeles. A singer. Sang backup for P-Funk and is currently singing backup for Lakeside, of "Fantastic Voyage" fame ("Slide, slide, slippety slide . . . "). There's a video of him, shot on Skid Row, in which he discusses his struggles with addiction and his spiritual rebirth. There's also a video of him doing one of his original songs, "Will I Still Have Tomorrow?"

I called him. "Robin Wartell?"

"This is Robin."

"Have you ever heard of a woman named L. V. Thomas?"

"Auntie L. V.?" he said, emphasizing the V, the way she did. "That's my auntie!"

I told him we'd heard that she used to bring a little boy with her to church.

"That was me!"

He had lived with her, off and on, it turned out. His mother had been a "party girl." His father walked out on them. He and his brother Randy (who later died of AIDS) were often dropped at Aunt L. V.'s house in Acres Homes for safekeeping. "She was a big influence on me," he said. He remembered that she smoked a lot and that she wore pants and that (tantalizingly) she kept a guitar in the house. "She always encouraged me," he said, "when other people didn't take me seriously." His mother, Dally Mae Wilkerson, was one of the closest with Aunt L. V. and became her caretaker. "She's really the missing link here," he said. She inherited a box of pictures from L. V.—the ones Mack had seen, no doubt, of L. V. (and maybe Geeshie?) from younger days—but those were lost when his mother died and they paid someone to clean out her house (too painful): That person probably threw everything away.

I got a text from him one night when I was in Cincinnati, visiting my mother. It had a little picture attached.

I opened it and looked into the eyes of L. V. Thomas.

A Polaroid. Robin had put the image on the sofa and taken a picture of it with his own phone.

She was in a wheelchair, it appeared. I looked at the mouth—thin-lipped, pursed—that had sung "Motherless Child Blues."

I tried forcing myself, through an almost physical mental exertion, not to project momentousness onto the picture. People's faces often get caught in weird moments. But there was no doubt that her eyes were full of profound melancholy. The other thing you see immediately are her strikingly long fingers.

She has them folded in her lap. Her skin is reddish-brown, precisely the color of the stain on the wooden lectern that Pastor Randle had pointed to in telling us what color she was. Her straight white hair flowed back from her high forehead in a small mane. It is not a flattering picture. She was already dying when it was taken. But it is a very moving picture of an important woman and our only photograph of a great American artist (again provisional on what Mack has in the Monster).

A month later we worked with Robin to organize a little family reunion in Shepherd, Tex., at the home of one of L. V.'s great-great-grandniece's nieces. The hostess's name was Holly Bennett. Her husband was a retired firefighter. She very generously opened up her house for the afternoon, at the last minute, and invited a bunch of family in, people who remembered L. V. We sat in a circle in the Bennetts' living room. Robin's sisters, Pauline and Charlene, were there, and another woman of their generation, a cousin named Mary Alice. We played them the songs. "Pick Poor Robin Clean" came on, with its curious opening, eight seconds of minstrel-show banter, possibly part of a stage act Geeshie and L. V. had perfected.

The Reunion

At that last line, three of the women sitting there did a sudden jump forward in their seats. "That's her voice!" Pauline, Robin's sister, insisted. The other two nodded. They were mostly silent for the songs and shook their heads afterward, murmuring. I was at first disappointed, having hoped in some reptilian journalistic way for tears, but something more interesting was happening. They were unsettled. They said, "Beautiful." They'd known L. V. She wasn't a phantom artist to them but a woman, not always an easy woman to get along with, and she was their blood. These were some of the people who helped care for her when she was dying. And here I was, presenting them with a hologram of a creature named Elvie, who sang and played on these piercing blues, and I was saying, "Same woman!"

Our interviews at the church had given us a silhouette. Her family filled it in with bold, bright strokes. They told us that she rolled her own tobacco—Kite brand, in a green pouch—but that she also sometimes smoked a corncob pipe. She carried a pistol under her apron, a long-barreled "old type" of pistol. Robin stood and up and did an impersonation of her locking up the house at night. Staggering stiffly around in the nightgown, with the long pistol dangling in her hand. She would sing while doing the dishes and cleaning. Her house had no running water. She didn't trust banks and kept her money in the outhouse, under the planks. She liked to hunt possums and chopped her own wood. She was "almost a man," they said. Had I heard that she used to jump trains? She was turning back into a folk figure, only all of it was apparently true.

In the middle of our talk, Patricia Ware tapped me on the shoulder and said there was someone on the phone who wanted to speak with me, her cousin Gwen. I went into the dining room. She first told me some of the things the others had said. Then she changed her tone. "L. V. was a strange person," she said.

I told her that, yes, I'd gathered that she was a loner.

"Better word," she said, "hermit." She told me that when she'd gone with her father, Tommy Grant, L. V.'s nephew, to drop off groceries there sometimes, they didn't go past the gate.

"L. V. estranged herself from our family," she said. "Because of her lifestyle."

What did she mean, lifestyle?

"She dressed like a man," she said. "Do I have to say anything more?"

I said I didn't think so. But did she know anything more about it? Had she ever known L. V. to be with a woman?

"I never saw it, no," she said, "but I wasn't allowed in her yard!"

She added, "But I'm sure about that. . . . I'm absolutely sure about that."

I ran it past a few other members of the family, not that day but later. All pronounced some variation on, "Well, we always sort of figured."

There is a woman, whose identity I had wondered about at length but made no headway on, a woman named Sarah. L. V. was living with her in 1920, when she worked at the oil mill. They are listed as cousins, but Sarah's family had come from another part of Texas than L. V.'s, and they shared no family names. In the 1940 census, the one Alex van der Tuuk found, they're together again, listed as cousins again. Her name is Sarah Goodman Cephus or Sephus now. In the intervening years, she married a man with that name, but he abandoned her (very publicly—there was a trial, over his debts). Now she and L. V. were living together again in the Fourth Ward. No one in the family or at the church had ever heard of this woman. So that's twenty years of her life, minimum, that they knew each other, and L. V. had lived with her for at least two stretches. There was a place for lesbians in the blues world. Ma Rainey, Alberta Hunter, Gladys Bentley, Ethel Waters, many others—you can't tell the story of the early blues without the lesbians. And according to the music historian and gospel producer Anthony Heilbut, whose *The Fan Who Knew Too Much* gets into these questions, there was a place for lesbianism in the gospel world as well. I wrote to Heilbut and asked him what he thought about L. V. He knew "Motherless Child Blues" well and said he was confident that any black person listening to it in the late 1920s would have recognized her delivery as "butch."

But would the church have made a place for her? Could you be both?

I got a message from him a few weeks later. "In the last two weeks," he wrote, "I've asked seven or eight gospel old-timers (late 70s, early 80s) about Those Hard Baptist Women with their 'sisters' and 'daughters' and received such replies as 'Forever.' 'Shaddap' . . . and 'You know it, baby.' In other words, yes."

Sarah Goodman Cephus died in 1967. L. V. Thomas was the informant on the death certificate. She signed it, in a clear but ever-so-trembly hand. That's about fifty years that we know they knew each other.

L. V. and Geeshie? Is that why she had to kill Thornton, had he found them together? It is interesting that, as Greil Marcus said to me, Geeshie doesn't change the line in the "Pick Poor Robin" song, "Gamblin' for Sadie, she is my lady." A slender clue! Anyway, whether or not she was a lesbian is the least of Geeshie's withholdings. L. V. comes out of it all an indelible character, but Geeshie we don't know.

Does Mack know more? It's the biggest burning question for me, the one that I wake up once a month in the middle of dreaming about. There are intimations that he does. He mentioned to me, that night a year ago, that he had picked up rumors of Geeshie in Oklahoma, and several years ago he told the writer Ted Gioia that he "visited Wiley's home, and met with members of her immediate family while doing fieldwork in Oklahoma." McCormick told me that she had Cherokee blood. In those letters to Paul Oliver, he also says that he has "been to see L. V." again, and "managed to get on a lot better ground with her." So, there may be more on Sister Thomas, too. Pictures, tapes. The only thing sure is we don't have it all.

I don't know if Mack will be angry. Certainly, during the months we worked on this, there were times when I felt angry at him. It would happen every time we heard (and we heard it over and over): "I wish you'd gotten here"—fill in a number—"years ago! So-and-so could have told you all about her." I would shake my fist at Mack a little inside. Thief of souls! If we had known about this discovery in 1961—or in '71, '81, '91, '01, or even 2011—our knowledge of these two artists would be larger by an order of magnitude, and we might have a real notion of Lillie Mae, instead of coordinates. And yet Mack was the only reason we found any of it. The dualism of the man was defeating, finally. It can't have been easy for him to carry.

Also—the truth I forget more often than any other, in thinking about this—L. V., too, wanted it hidden. Or at least part of her did.

A few weeks ago, Caitlin got in touch with a woman in Houston named Jana, who hadn't been invited to the family reunion (by oversight, not intention). She lived with her father, John D. Wilkerson, who goes by Don, and her mother, Elnora, taking care of them. Don, she said (the family confirmed it) had known L. V. better than about anyone, but his mind was mostly gone. Just in the last two years, it had slipped precipitously. But he enjoyed passing windows of clarity, during the day.

Jana allowed Caitlin to come out, and Caitlin went back to Houston one last time (she was re-enrolled in school in Arkansas). Mr. Wilkerson was foggy, as warned, but he did something very important, the moment Caitlin walked into the room. His daughter told him that this young woman was here to ask about L. V. Thomas. "You want to talk about Slack?" he said.

Caitlin hadn't played him any of the songs yet. There was no way for him to know that, at the beginning of "Pick Poor Robin Clean," Geeshie calls her that. He said he gave her the nickname. Couldn't remember what it meant.

With that single word from his mouth, "Slack," Wilkerson sets falling an interesting chain of dominoes. This establishes beyond doubt, you see, that it's L. V. playing with Geeshie on "Pick Poor Robin Clean." Which proves in turn that the song was recorded in 1930—because L. V. is emphatic about there having been only one session, or series of sessions ("[We] made all of our records at that time")—and not recorded in 1931, as has been discographic wisdom since the 1950s.

That wasn't all Don Wilkerson said. He told Caitlin that he was once a Texan saxophone player and that he always considered L. V. to have been his "musical mentor." Jana watched them all play together, when she was a girl, she said. Don's mother, "Big Mama," would play piano, Don would play the sax, L. V. would play the guitar. And they did play blues.

Jana went into another room and got a 45 that her father made, in Los Angeles, on the unknown Tomel label, a song called "Low Down Dirty Shame." She gave it to Caitlin, who, when she got home, put it on the turntable. She held her phone to the speaker. Don Wilkerson's voice burst out. "It's a low, it's a low low, it's a low down dirty shame." It was her! It was her in him. The first line of "Eagles on a Half." Almost the exact same stuttered delivery. They must have played it together one of those nights.

He remembered Geeshie. He is in his nineties, his memory is mostly gone and there is a very good chance that he is the last man on earth who can say that he remembers Lillie Mae (Geeshie) Wiley, knows who she is and has seen her face (unless Mack found her). He implied that there was something funny about her background. He said that she'd been "maybe Mexican or something." That was it. But he saw her, he remembered. He was someone we almost didn't talk to because people had said it was too late.

Chicago

FINALIST—REPORTING

This, said the Ellie judges, is "old-fashioned, idealistic reporting at its best: a piece of journalism that exposes clear and consequential wrongdoing by public officials"—the underreporting of murder and other crimes by the Chicago Police Department. Chicago *was also nominated for the Reporting Ellie two years ago for another story—"Lawbreakers, Lawmakers," about the sordid relationship between street gangs and Chicago pols—by the same team. David Bernstein is the features editor at* Chicago; *Noah Isackson a contributing editor.* Chicago, *like many city magazines, is largely devoted to service journalism but also has a distinguished record of Ellie nominations in literary-journalism categories such as Feature Writing, Essays and Criticism, and Fiction.*

David Bernstein and
Noah Isackson

The Truth
About Chicago's
Crime Rates

I. Dead Wrong

It was a balmy afternoon last July when the call came in: *Dead body found inside empty warehouse on the West Side.*

Chicago police officers drove through an industrial stretch of the hardscrabble Austin neighborhood and pulled up to the 4600 block of West Arthington Street. The warehouse in question was an unremarkable-looking red-brick single-story building with a tall barbed-wire fence. Vacant for six years, it had been visited that day by its owner and a real-estate agent—the person who had called 911.

The place lacked electricity, so crime scene technicians set up generators and portable lights. The power flickered on to reveal a grisly sight. In a small office, on soggy carpeting covered in broken ceiling tiles, lay a naked, lifeless woman. She had long red-streaked black hair and purple glitter nail polish on her left toenails (her right ones were gone), but beyond that it was hard to discern much. Her face and body were bloated and badly decomposed, her hands ash colored. Maggots feasted on her flesh.

At the woman's feet, detectives found a curled strand of telephone wire. Draped over her right hand was a different kind of wire: thin and brown. The same brown wire was wrapped around each armrest of a wooden chair next to her.

The following day, July 24, a pathologist in the Cook County medical examiner's office noticed something else that had been obscured by rotting skin: a thin gag tied around the corpse's mouth.

Thanks to some still-visible tattoos, detectives soon identified this unfortunate woman: Tiara Groves, a twenty-year-old from Austin. She was last seen walking alone in the wee hours of Sunday, July 14, near a liquor store two miles from the warehouse. At least eight witnesses who saw her that night told police a similar story: She appeared drunk and was upset—one man said that she was crying so hard she couldn't catch her breath—but refused offers of help. A man who talked to her outside the liquor store said that Groves warned him, excitedly and incoherently, that he should stay away from her or else somebody (she didn't say who) would kill him too.

Toxicology tests showed she had heroin and alcohol in her system, but not enough to kill her. All signs pointed to foul play. According to the young woman's mother, who had filed a missing-person report, the police had no doubt. "When this detective came to my house, he said, 'We found your daughter. . . . Your daughter has been murdered,'" Alice Groves recalls. "He told me they're going to get the one that did it."

On October 28, a pathologist ruled the death of Tiara Groves a homicide by "unspecified means." This rare ruling means yes, somebody had killed Groves, but the pathologist couldn't pinpoint the exact cause of death.

Given the finding of homicide—and the corroborating evidence at the crime scene—the Chicago Police Department should have counted Groves's death as a murder. And it did. Until December 18. On that day, the police report indicates, a lieutenant overseeing the Groves case reclassified the homicide investigation as a noncriminal death investigation. In his write-up, he cited the medical examiner's "inability to determine a cause of death."

That lieutenant was Denis Walsh—the same cop who had played a crucial role in the alleged cover-up in the 2004 killing of David Koschman, the twenty-one-year-old who died after being punched by a nephew of former mayor Richard M. Daley. Walsh allegedly took the Koschman file home. For years, police officials said that it was lost. After the *Sun-Times* reported it missing, the file mysteriously reappeared.

But back to Tiara Groves. With the stroke of a computer key, she was airbrushed out of Chicago's homicide statistics.

The change stunned officers. Current and former veteran detectives who reviewed the Groves case at *Chicago*'s request were just as incredulous. Says a retired high-level detective, "How can you be tied to a chair and gagged, with no clothes on, and that's a [noncriminal] death investigation?" (He, like most of the nearly forty police sources interviewed for this story, declined to be identified by name, citing fears of disciplinary action or other retribution.)

Was it just a coincidence, some wondered, that the reclassification occurred less than two weeks before the end of the year, when the city of Chicago's final homicide numbers for 2013 would be tallied? "They essentially wiped away one of the murders in the city, which is crazy," says a police insider. "But that's the kind of shit that's going on."

·　　·　　·

For the case of Tiara Groves is not an isolated one. *Chicago* conducted a twelve-month examination of the Chicago Police Department's crime statistics going back several years, poring through public and internal police records and interviewing crime victims, criminologists, and police sources of various ranks. We identified ten people, including Groves, who were beaten, burned, suffocated, or shot to death in 2013 and whose cases were reclassified as death investigations, downgraded to more minor crimes, or even closed as noncriminal incidents—all for illogical or, at best, unclear reasons.

This troubling practice goes far beyond murders, documents and interviews reveal. *Chicago* found dozens of other crimes, including serious felonies such as robberies, burglaries, and assaults, that were misclassified, downgraded to wrist-slap offenses, or made to vanish altogether. (We'll examine those next month in part 2 of this special report.)

Many officers of different ranks and from different parts of the city recounted instances in which they were asked or pressured by their superiors to reclassify their incident reports or in which their reports were changed by some invisible hand. One detective refers to the "magic ink": the power to make a case disappear. Says another: "The rank and file don't agree with what's going on. The powers that be are making the changes."

Granted, a few dozen crimes constitute a tiny percentage of the more than 300,000 reported in Chicago last year. But sources describe a practice that has become widespread at the same time that top police brass have become fixated on demonstrating improvement in Chicago's woeful crime statistics.

And has there ever been improvement. Aside from homicides, which soared in 2012, the drop in crime since Police Superintendent Garry McCarthy arrived in May 2011 is unprecedented—and, some of his detractors say, unbelievable. Crime hasn't just fallen, it has free-fallen: across the city and across all major categories.

Take "index crimes": the eight violent and property crimes that virtually all U.S. cities supply to the Federal Bureau of Investigation for its Uniform Crime Report. According to police figures, the number of these crimes plunged by 56 percent citywide from 2010 to 2013—an average of nearly 19 percent per year—a reduction that borders on the miraculous. To put these numbers in perspective: From 1993, when index crimes peaked, to 2010, the last full year under McCarthy's predecessor, Jody Weis, the average annual decline was less than 4 percent.

This dramatic crime reduction has been happening even as the department has been bleeding officers. (A recent *Tribune* analysis listed 7,078 beat cops on the streets, 10 percent fewer than in 2011.) Given these facts, the crime reduction "makes no sense," says one veteran sergeant. "And it makes absolutely no sense that people believe it. Yet people believe it."

The city's inspector general, Joseph Ferguson, may not. *Chicago* has learned that his office has questioned the accuracy of the police department's crime statistics. A spokeswoman confirmed that the office recently finalized an audit of the police department's 2012 crime data—though only for assault-related crimes so far—"to determine if CPD accurately classified [these categories of] crimes under its written guidelines and if it reported related crime statistics correctly." (The audit found, among other things, that the department undercounted aggravated assaults and batteries by more than 24 percent, based on the sample cases reviewed.)

Meanwhile, the see-no-evil, hear-no-evil pols on Chicago's City Council have mostly accepted the police department's crime numbers at face value. So have most in the media. You can hardly turn on the news without hearing McCarthy or Mayor Rahm Emanuel proclaiming unquestioned: *Murders down 18 percent in 2013! Overall crime down 23 percent! Twelve thousand fewer crime victims!* "These days, everything is about media and public opinion," says one longtime officer. "If a number makes people feel safe, then why not give it to them?"

•   •   •

If you want proof of the police department's obsession with crime statistics, look no further than the last few days of 2012. On the night of December 27, a forty-year-old alleged gang member named Nathaniel Jackson was shot in the head and killed in Austin. The next morning, newscasters proclaimed that Chicago's murder toll for the year had hit 500—a grim milestone last reached in 2008, during the Great Recession.

By lunchtime, the police department's spinmeisters at Thirty-Fifth and Michigan had challenged the reports. The actual total, they said, was 499. A murder case earlier in the year had just been reclassified as a death investigation.

Critics howled. The bloggers behind *Second City Cop* declared: "It's a miracle! The dead have risen!!!"

By late afternoon, police had backed down; Jackson was, indeed, the 500th homicide of 2012. Chicago would end the year with 507 recorded murders, more than in any other city in the nation.

Many inside the police force, as well as many outside criminologists, saw the spike in violence in 2012 as a statistical anomaly. Crime tends to go in cycles, they pointed out; the city topped 500 killings not only in 2008 but also in 2003, 2002, and 2001, to name a few.

Still, it looked bad for Mayor Emanuel. His disapproval rating in the polls was rising sharply, particularly among black voters. Behind closed doors, according to a City Hall insider, Emanuel told his police chief that the department had better not allow a repeat performance of 2012 or McCarthy's days in Chicago would be numbered. (Through a spokeswoman, the mayor declined to comment for this article.)

McCarthy called 2012's homicide total a "tragic number" and vowed that things would be different in 2013. The mindset inside police headquarters, recalls one officer: "Whatever you gotta do, this can't happen again."

The chief felt even more pressure than his rank and file may have realized. For the former New Yorker to prove that his policing strategies worked in Chicago, he would need to keep the number of murders not just below 2012's total but also below 2011's: 435.

To do so, McCarthy leaned even more heavily on a tool that has proved wildly successful in his hometown: CompStat. Borrowing performance-management principles from the business world, CompStat collects, analyzes, and maps a city's crime data in real time. These statistics help police track trouble spots more accurately and pinpoint where officers are needed most. The department's number crunchers can slice and dice the stats all sorts of ways, spitting out reports showing percentage changes in various crimes by neighborhood over different time frames, for example: month to month, week to week—heck, hour to hour.

Armed with those statistics, the police brass turn up the pressure in weekly meetings, grilling field commanders about crime in their areas. The statistics are widely said to make or break a career. "The only evaluation is the numbers," says a veteran sergeant. "God forbid your crime is up. If you have a 20 percent reduction this month, you'd better have a 21 percent reduction the next month."

The homicide numbers are especially important, says one cop: "You should see these supervisors, like cats in a room filled with rocking chairs, afraid to classify a murder because of all the screaming they will hear downtown."

If the numbers are bad, the district commanders and officers get reamed out by McCarthy and the other bosses at headquarters. These targets frequently leave the meetings seething. Even McCarthy concedes that such meetings can get ugly. "When I was a commander in New York, it was full contact," he told *Chicago* in 2012. "And if you weren't careful, you could lose an eye."

• • •

Unfortunately for all concerned, January 2013 could not have started out worse. Five people were murdered in Chicago on New Year's Day. The number hit seventeen by the end of the first full week. "This is too much," Al Wysinger, the police department's first deputy superintendent, told the crowd in the January 17 CompStat meeting, according to a memo summarizing it. "Last October and November, I kept saying we have to start 2013 off on the right foot. Wrong foot! We can't reiterate this much clearer."

As the month wore on, the death toll kept rising. Among the victims were headline grabbers Ronnie Chambers, thirty-three, the last of his mother's four children to die from gun violence, and Hadiya Pendleton, fifteen, the honor student who was shot in a park about a mile from President Obama's house.

And then there was twenty-something Tiffany Jones from the South Side. (To protect the identity of her family, we have given her a pseudonym.)

In January, Jones got into an argument with a male relative that turned into a "serious physical fight," according to the police report. Her sister later told police that she saw the enraged man punch Jones in the head. Police and paramedics arrived to find Jones's siblings struggling to keep him out of the family's apartment.

Inside, Jones was sitting on the couch, gasping for breath. When officers asked her if she wanted to press battery charges, she could only nod yes, the police report shows. She tried to stand but collapsed to the floor, no longer breathing. Rushed to the hospital, Jones was soon pronounced dead.

The attending doctor noted head trauma and bleeding behind Jones's left eye. Seeing fresh bruises on her left cheek, left eye, and both arms, the investigating officers were leaning toward recommending a first-degree murder charge against the male relative, according to the police report. First-degree murder—willfully killing or committing an act that creates a "strong probability of death or great bodily harm"—carries more severe penalties than any other homicide charge.

The next day, however, a pathologist with the Cook County medical examiner's office came to the surprising conclusion that

Jones had died from a blood clot that was unrelated to the fight. "Because of the embolism," the pathologist noted to detectives, according to the police report, Jones "would have died 'from just walking down the street.'"

Disagreements between police and medical examiners are rare but not unheard of. When they do occur, the rule for police is clear. The FBI's *Uniform Crime Reporting Handbook* expressly states that a police department's classification of a homicide should be based solely on a police investigation, not on the determination of a medical examiner or prosecutor's office.

But the officers did not ask for a lesser homicide charge, such as involuntary manslaughter, against Jones's relative. Nor did they even charge him with battery. The reason, the report states: "the lack of any complaining victim or witness to the domestic battery incident." Never mind that a dead victim cannot complain.

Police sent the man on his way. And that was that. Search for this case in the police department's public database of 2013 crimes and you won't find it. It's as if it never happened.

By the end of January, forty-four people had been murdered in Chicago, more than in any first month since 2002. That big number—and the national attention brought by Pendleton's killing—set off more public furor about the inability of McCarthy and Emanuel to stem the bloodshed. A spokesman for the Fraternal Order of Police said that their strategies had "failed miserably."

Even aldermen who had heaped praise on McCarthy in the past started to criticize. "If this isn't dealt with soon," warned the Twenty-First Ward alderman Howard Brookins, chairman of the City Council's black caucus, "the mayor is gonna be forced to do something about McCarthy, or this could potentially become his snow issue." It was a reference to Mayor Michael Bilandic's mishandling of the Blizzard of '79, one of the most infamous career killers in Chicago political history.

After January 2013, the number of homicides in Chicago began falling dramatically. February ended with just fourteen. March ended with seventeen. That compares with twenty-nine and fifty-two, respectively, in 2012.

Emanuel and McCarthy were giddy. The policing changes they had made in the past three months had worked! Those changes included, a day after Pendleton's death, moving 200 officers from desks to the streets and bringing back the roving units Emanuel and McCarthy had disbanded when they first took over. What's more, in February, McCarthy started sending officers into twenty "impact zones" deemed the most dangerous in the city. In March, some 400 cops began patrolling these zones daily, racking up about $1 million in overtime per week.

McCarthy was frustrated that the media was giving most of the credit for the murder reduction to the cold weather rather than to his policing strategies. The city called a news conference. "We are clearly having an impact on the homicides," Emanuel told reporters on April 1. He declared that the number of murders in the first quarter of 2013 was lower than in any other first quarter in the past fifty years.

The mayor didn't mention that the department's own records show that Chicago had the exact same number of homicides in the first three months of 2009 as it did in the first three months of 2013. Nor did he remind his audience that Chicago's population has shrunk by nearly 1 million people since 1960. Look at murder *rates*—homicides per 100,000 people—and you get fifteen today. That rate is one-third higher than in 1960. And it's nearly four times New York City's current rate.

April Fool's Day marked the unofficial start of a new city tactic: inundate the public with crime-decline statistics, carefully choosing time periods that demonstrated the biggest possible drops from the same period in 2012 or beyond, whatever sounded best. "Between the time of 8:36 am 32 seconds and 8:39 am

15 seconds . . . crime went down an amazing 89%!!! compared to the same time last year," one wag posted on *Second City Cop.*

.   .   .

Turns out the low March homicide numbers were made possible in part by curious categorizations of two more deaths. One is the case of Maurice Harris.

On March 15, the fifty-seven-year-old Harris—an older man playing a young man's game—teamed up with a crew selling heroin near the corner of Cicero and Van Buren on the West Side. It was a sliver of turf that belonged to a street gang, the Undertaker Vice Lords.

Midmorning, Harris saw about five men walking up the block. His crew scattered. Harris got a tap on the shoulder, then a punch in the face, according to the police report. Moments later, he was on the sidewalk, taking repeated punches and kicks and blows to the head with a metal pipe. When the beat-down finally ended, Harris told a witness that he couldn't feel his legs.

He was rushed to Loretto Hospital, then transferred to two other hospitals—Mount Sinai and Rush—as his condition worsened. On March 19, Harris began slurring his words, and his arms went numb. Doctors put in a breathing tube; they also diagnosed a spinal cord injury. On March 21, six days after the beating, Harris died.

Police recorded the Maurice Harris case as a battery, which is indisputably true. But not as a homicide.

At first, the Cook County medical examiner's office said that an autopsy was inconclusive. The pathologist, according to the police report, "deferred the cause and manner of death pending further studies."

Eight months later, on November 13, the same pathologist made a final ruling—a head scratcher to every police source we spoke to who reviewed the case. Harris, the doctor determined, died from a pulmonary embolism, diabetes, and drug abuse. The police report summarized the pathologist's findings: "The victim showed no significant evidence of injuries sustained from the battery [and] that in no way did it appear that the battery contributed to the cause of his death and therefore ruled his death as natural."

That's all detectives needed to close their death investigation. But they still had to wrap up the battery case. They declared it solved, reporting that they knew what had happened, knew who beat up Harris, and had enough evidence to "support an arrest, charge, and [turn] over to the court for prosecution." But because the victim was dead and "there is no complaining witness to aid in the prosecution," there was no reason to move forward. Harris's attackers were therefore never apprehended.

On March 28, three weeks after *Chicago* filed a Freedom of Information Act request to the Cook County medical examiner's office about the case of Maurice Harris, the office changed its death ruling from "natural" to "undetermined." The ruling cited new information from medical records that, a spokesman for the medical examiner says, the office had requested "some time ago" but had only just received.

The current chief medical examiner, Stephen Cina, was appointed by Cook County board president Toni Preckwinkle in July 2012. That was shortly after the previous examiner, Nancy Jones, retired following an avalanche of negative publicity about bodies stacking up at the city morgue.

It was also a few months after Preckwinkle and the county's board of commissioners had passed ordinances giving themselves more power over the office—for example, imposing a five-year term limit and making it easier to fire the medical examiner by a simple majority vote. Previously, the medical examiner's tenure could last a lifetime: a Supreme Court–like term meant to insulate the position from the political and police pressures so notorious in "Crook County."

As the former deputy medical examiner of Broward County in famously corrupt South Florida, Cina was plenty used to politics. "If I get an inordinate amount of pressure, I don't intend to buckle or break under it," he vowed to the *Sun-Times.*

Cina says he has made numerous changes to the office to bring it more in line with national standards. "We've rewritten every standard operating procedure in the place," he says. He also says that he has "tweaked" how his office assigns the cause and manner of a death. For example, he added the ruling "homicide by unspecified means"—the ruling that police used to shut down the Tiara Groves homicide investigation. "Some people may not be familiar with the term, but it's an acceptable cause of death," Cina insists.

Might changes under Cina help explain the perplexing findings in other 2013 cases, such as those of Maurice Harris and Tiffany Jones? There is no evidence that the medical examiner's office intentionally issued misleading or inaccurate rulings to help the city keep its homicide count down. "I've never felt pressure one way or another to make my ruling," Cina says. "I'm pro–scientific truth more than anything."

But knowledgeable sources who reviewed these cases for Chicago say that the way the medical examiner's rulings were worded gave police the wiggle room they needed to avoid "taking a hit" on the statistics, as one detective put it. Says a source who used to work at the medical examiner's office: "I can see the powers that be in the police department saying, 'Here's our out.'"

•   •   •

On March 17, two days after Maurice Harris got pummeled, police were called to the top floor of a red-brick three-flat in Pilsen. A man who had just returned home from a trip smelled a "foul odor" coming from a plastic air mattress in the bedroom of a roommate he hadn't seen in weeks. When he started pulling debris from the mattress, he saw a grotesquely decomposed human head. The rest of the body was cocooned in garbage.

Investigators opened the bag to find that the corpse was a woman's, wrapped in a blood-soaked blanket. She was wearing turquoise jogging pants, a black camisole, a hoodie, and boots. Police identified her as Michelle Manalansan, twenty-nine, a student at Harold Washington College. She had last been seen at her downtown apartment on February 9. The police report adds that investigators were told by witnesses that the absent roommate "was the last person seen with [Michelle]."

The roommate, police learned, was wanted by the Cook County sheriff for a probation violation. They also learned that a relative had bought him a ticket to Los Angeles on a train that left Chicago six days after Manalansan disappeared.

Despite the circumstances, police classified the case as a non-criminal-death investigation. A detective soon made it an even lower priority: He suspended the case until the roommate could be "located and interviewed."

Manalansan's death certificate on file with the Cook County clerk's office says that she died by homicide—specifically, blunt head and neck trauma. But at press time, her case had still not been classified as criminal. The roommate was still at large.

With a hint of disgust, one retired veteran detective who reviewed the cases of Michelle Manalansan, Maurice Harris, Tiffany Jones, and Tiara Groves for *Chicago* called all four "counters." That is, cases that he believes the police should have counted as homicides. "I'm not surprised that these cases have not come to light, based on who the victims are," he says. "However, it is a travesty that the cases are not being investigated." (While all cases are technically ongoing until they are closed, detectives say that death investigations are much lower priorities than homicide investigations.)

·　　·　　·

As the spring of 2013 wore on, Mother Nature delivered a blessing: a deluge. That April would be the wettest on record and was relatively quiet; bad weather tends to keep criminals off the streets.

Murders began ticking up again in May. And June ended with forty-five, only three below 2012's total. Still, when the Chicago Police Department added up the homicides for the first half of the year, they got 184—a whopping 30 percent fewer than the year-ago period. "Fewer murders than in any year since 1965," McCarthy told reporters.

One factor, as the *Tribune* first noted, was that the department excluded from the count three homicides that occurred within city limits but on expressways patrolled by state police. (There would be another expressway homicide before the end of the year.) Before McCarthy's arrival, the department did not exclude such crimes from its homicide total, according to longtime police sources.

The second half of the year, of course, includes the dog days of summer, the high-crime period that really sends sweat down the backs of police leaders. And July exploded. Over the long Independence Day weekend alone, thirteen people were killed and more than seventy were shot in Chicago. The ensuing days weren't much better. "It's mayhem," declared one state lawmaker, Monique Davis, of the South Side. She called on Governor Pat Quinn to send the Illinois National Guard and the state police to Chicago to help keep the peace. By month's end, the murder count had hit fifty-three, versus fifty in July 2012.

In August—typically Chicago's hottest month—the stress inside Chicago Police Department headquarters was palpable. That's when several police insiders first told *Chicago* about what they called "the panel."

Said to be made up of a small group of very high-level officers, the panel allegedly began scrutinizing death cases in which the victims didn't die immediately or where the circumstances that led to the deaths couldn't be immediately determined, sources say. Panel members were looking for anything that could be delayed, keeping it off the books for a week, a month, maybe a year. "Whatever the case may be, it had to wait until it came back from the panel," says a well-placed police insider. "All this was to hide the murder numbers, that's all they are doing." (How many cases did get delayed, if any, is unknown.)

By the end of August the department had counted 286 homicides since January—80 fewer than in 2012.

With the summer all but behind them, the police brass pretty much knew that, barring some extraordinary crime wave, the year's homicide count would not eclipse 2012's. But 2013's total this far was still eight more than recorded during the same period in 2011. For McCarthy, beating the 2011 number was starting to look like an elusive goal.

•　　　•　　　•

On September 19, two gun-toting gangbangers opened fire on a crowded pickup basketball game in Cornell Park, in the Back of the Yards neighborhood. One of them used an AK-47. When the bullets stopped flying, thirteen people had been wounded, including a three-year-old boy. But no one died. A "miracle," McCarthy said. (In the stats book, the shootings counted as only one "shooting incident" in CompStat. Read more about that in part 2 of this story.)

Two days after gunfire lit up Cornell Park, an extra-alarm fire erupted in a three-story apartment building at 112th Street and King Drive, in the Roseland neighborhood. When firefighters arrived just before two a.m., much of the building and the stairwell was engulfed in flames.

Inside, they found Millicent Brown-Johnson, twenty-eight, in a purple nightgown, her body covered in black soot, unconscious on the floor of her third-floor apartment. Her eight-year-old son,

Jovan Perkins, was passed out in the stairwell, ravaged by second- and third-degree burns, according to the police report.

Ambulances rushed them to the hospital. Brown-Johnson, who had been working at the American Girl Place store on Michigan Avenue as she pursued a degree in physical therapy, did not survive. Perkins, a second grader, died later that night.

Firefighters and police immediately determined the fire to be suspicious. The next day they found a plastic gas container inside a garbage can in Palmer Park, across the street from the charred building.

On September 28, the medical examiner's office ruled that both mother and son had died of smoke inhalation and that, based on the police and fire department investigations, their deaths were homicides.

However, the case was classified as a death investigation, not a murder investigation, and the police did not include the two deaths in their year-end homicide count. Nor have police caught the arsonist. "How will I ever get justice if the case is not even categorized the right way?" asks Austin Perkins, the boy's father, a truck driver from Hammond, Indiana.

Excluding Brown-Johnson and Perkins from Chicago's homicide statistics helped the September numbers clock in at forty-two rather than forty-four. At this point, the 2011 numbers were actually beginning to look beatable. Through the first nine months of 2013, the department's murder tally was 322, versus 317 for the same period two years before.

The breakthrough happened in October. On the last day of the month, the 2013 year-to-date total was 352, versus 353 in 2011, by the department's count. McCarthy had edged out 2011 by just one number.

October 31 also marked Superintendent McCarthy's annual budget hearing before the Chicago City Council. He positioned himself in front of three giant charts: a set of blue bars illustrating how murders had dropped 20 percent over the past ten months; a fever line plunging toward "40-year lows" in index crimes, particularly murders; and another blue bar chart highlighting a 15 percent drop in overall crime for 2013, again labeled the "lowest level in 40 years."

Aldermen, some wearing Halloween costumes, gave these numbers about as much scrutiny as they had the epically disastrous parking-meter deal. The daylong session was essentially a love fest. "You've done excellent work, and those charts say it all," cheered Ariel Reboyras, alderman of the Thirtieth Ward, on the city's Northwest Side. "I say, numbers don't lie."

Latasha Thomas, of the Seventeenth Ward, which includes high-crime Englewood on the South Side, encouraged McCarthy to dial up the good news. "I just think your PR needs to be a lot better," she said. "We need to be shouting about what you are doing and not just throwing up these stats."

"No doubt about it," McCarthy replied.

•　　　•　　　•

But it wasn't until the end of November that police leaders could breathe more easily. The official year-to-date homicide count was now 376. With just one month of 2013 remaining, it now seemed a safe bet that the total wouldn't top 2011's count of 435.

But why settle there? According to police insiders, McCarthy and his deputies now hungered to reach a new goal: to keep 2013's number of homicides below 400, the lowest level since before Americans first landed on the moon. "They wanted to really have the big headline," says a detective. Every homicide mattered. Including Patrick Walker's.

Just after five a.m. on November 29, the day after Thanksgiving, a 2012 Chevy sedan with four men inside sped along a residential street in the Pill Hill neighborhood on the city's Far South Side. Driving conditions were good: clear, no ice, no snow. Yet the car suddenly veered off the road near the intersection of Ninety-Third and Constance, sliding into the opposite lane, clipping a parked vehicle, sailing over the curb, and bashing into a light pole. It stopped only after hitting a tree.

When police got to the car, they found that the three passengers had suffered only minor injuries. However, the driver, a twenty-two-year-old named Patrick Walker, was unresponsive, according to the police report. Officers assumed that he had suffered serious head trauma in the accident. An early case report from the medical examiner's office said that "brain matter" was found on the steering wheel.

The young man was taken to Advocate Christ Medical Center in Oak Lawn, where he died two hours later. Police told the *Tribune* that "alcohol was suspected as a factor in the crash."

Later that day, however, an autopsy showed that Walker had not died from the accident. He had been killed by a single gunshot to his right temple.

Interestingly, the *Sun-Times* had already reported that police found one of Walker's passengers, Ivery Isom, twenty-two, with a loaded Glock 9 mm and a twenty-round ammunition clip at the accident scene. Police also found a bullet shell in the back seat, according to the police report. (Isom was charged with two counts of aggravated unlawful use of a weapon. He pled not guilty; at press time, his next court appearance was scheduled for April 28.)

On November 30, a pathologist deferred the cause and manner of Walker's death "pending police investigation." That means the autopsy is inconclusive until the police further investigate the circumstances of his death.

Walker's death certificate, filed with the Cook County clerk's office, says that he was murdered. No one disputes that he died from a bullet in his brain. But at press time—four months after the shooting—the public record shows Walker's case inexplicably classified not as a homicide but as a death investigation.

That means, according to the department's own records, Walker's killing is not included in the city's 2013 homicide total.

.   .   .

In mid-December, McCarthy and Emanuel called a news conference to highlight the release of a report from a professor at Yale University. It had found that Chicago was on track to have its lowest homicide rate since 1967 and its lowest violent-crime rate for nearly as long. "This is not just 2013 against 2012," Emanuel told the *Sun-Times*. "This is 2013 against the last 40 years. That is what is significant."

Standing in front of a poster-size map showing the drops in overall crime in all of the city's twenty-two police districts, the mayor and the superintendent then took questions.

"Have you changed the way you measure statistics?" one reporter asked.

"I don't buy the premise of the question," Emanuel answered and quickly moved on.

The reporter persisted: "Has the police department changed the way they measure it?"

"The answer is no," McCarthy jumped in. "There's something called a Uniform Crime Report, which is the national standard by which we record crime. So that's the answer, no."

Well . . . not exactly. Two weeks earlier, in fact, various media outlets had reported details of an odd change in how Chicago's police department was counting "delayed homicides"—those in which there is a time lag between injury and death. "To meet federal and state guidelines," the *Sun-Times* said, police reviewed all murders in 2013 and 2012. "Under those guidelines, a murder should be classified in the year the person was injured, and not in the year the person died."

Huh? There were never any changes to federal guidelines, a FBI spokesman told *Chicago*. The standards of the FBI's Uniform

Crime Reporting program make it crystal clear that a homicide should be reported in the year of the victim's death.

Next we called the Illinois Uniform Crime Report—a one-person office within the state police department that collects statistics from law enforcement agencies in Illinois—to check whether the state rule on delayed homicides had changed in 2013. The staffer told us that it hadn't; that delayed homicides in Illinois have *always* been counted in the year of injury.

Confused? So were we. So we e-mailed Adam Collins, the director of news affairs for the Chicago Police Department. He e-mailed back: "In late 2013 . . . CPD began working to bring the city into stricter adherence with federal reporting standards. The Unified Crime Reporting System dictates each agency follow their state reporting procedures for federal reporting. According to Illinois reporting procedures, murders where the injury and death occurred in different years are to be tracked to the year of the incident, and CPD had for years been including these incidents in the wrong year."

However, every Chicago police leader, officer, and administrator with whom we spoke says that hasn't been the department's practice. It's not a murder until the injured person dies, they point out. Before then, it's an aggravated battery. "CPD is interpreting the state guidelines incorrectly," says an expert source on Chicago Police Department statistics. "It's a numbers game."

Welcome to the Dali-esque world of Chicago crime reporting.

No matter who you believe, it's clear that the department did change the way in which it counts delayed homicides—but only for the years in which McCarthy has been in charge. It subtracted four murders from the 2013 total, according to Collins. And it subtracted seven murders from 2012, five in which the injuries occurred in 2011.

Did the department add back those five murders to 2011? It doesn't appear so. Remember that there were 435 homicides in 2011, according to the 2012 year-end CompStat report. But at presstime, the City of Chicago's own public data portal listed only 434 homicides in 2011.

How is it fair to compare 2013's homicide totals with those of years before the department changed the rules of the game? It's not, according to John Eterno, a former NYPD cop and Comp-Stat expert, now a professor of criminal justice at Molloy College in Long Island. "You can't compare over the years when you do things like that," he says.

All of this creative number crunching, former police officials say, is a radical departure from past practices. Veteran members of the force blame McCarthy. Muddling murder statistics "benefits no one but the superintendent," says the retired high-level detective. "Not the citizens, not the investigators. It only benefits him."

It certainly doesn't benefit the victims' families. "I cry many days and many nights," says Alice Groves, whose daughter Tiara has been dead for eight months. "It makes me feel like they are trying to sweep this under the covers. They want to look good. They want the city to look good. But they ain't thinking about the family who lost their loved one."

•   •   •

New Year's revelry was still in full swing on January 1, 2014, when the Chicago Police Department sent out an e-mail blast just after two a.m. The subject line: "Chicago Ends 2013 at Historic Lows in Crime and Violence, More Work Remains."

Despite the measured tone of that last phrase, the chest thumping was deafening: "fewest murders since 1965"; "lowest murder rate since 1966"; "lowest overall crime rate since 1972"; "fewest robberies, burglaries, motor vehicle thefts and arsons in recorded history." And on and on, percentage after percentage, statistic after statistic after statistic.

But try this: Add back the ten cases *Chicago* found that, if classified as sources say they should have been, would have counted as homicides. (There may be more.) Add back the four homicides that occurred on Chicago's expressways. Add, too, the four delayed homicides that the department had stripped out in December. What you get is not 414 murders in 2013, but at least 432.

What you also get is the kind of public record that every Chicagoan deserves. Not to mention the knowledge that police are doing their jobs. The killers of Tiara Groves, Tiffany Jones, Maurice Harris, Michelle Manalansan, Millicent Brown-Johnson, Jovan Perkins, and Patrick Walker may remain on the streets. As long as their deaths are not considered homicides, that's unlikely to change, detectives say.

Saddest of all, perhaps, the victims' grieving families and friends are left with the belief that the system is profoundly unjust. "I wake up every day and I know my son and my son's mom were murdered," says Austin Perkins, Jovan's father. "I just don't understand how police can categorize it the way they are categorizing it. I just want answers. I just want justice.

"You can't go around setting buildings on fire and killing people and not be held accountable."

II. Getting Washed

In the first half of 2013, as the thermometer began to rise, so did the anxiety of those living in the Chicago Police Department's Nineteenth District. The district's neighborhoods—Lake View, Boystown, Wrigleyville, and North Center, plus portions of Uptown and Lincoln Square and the north part of Lincoln Park—are among the most desirable in the city. But residents were increasingly sharing horror stories about robberies, beatings, drug deals, and bloodstains on previously safe sidewalks. "I moved here in 1981, and I have never felt as unsafe as I do now," Lake View resident Michael Smith, fifty-six, an art director at a marketing firm, told *Chicago* last fall.

In fact, in the months of May, June, and July, one of the police beats within the Nineteenth District—a small area bordered by Belmont Avenue, Addison Street, Halsted Street, and Southport Avenue—notched more robberies than any other beat in Chicago, according to the police's own statistics. The beat also ranked among the ten worst, citywide, for violent crime. "Does it compare to what's happening on the South and West Sides of the city? No," says Craig Nolden, a forty-five-year-old marketing manager who lives with his wife and two children in the beat. "But it was out of control."

Last summer, Nolden says, he called 911 four times: to report someone breaking in to his wife's car, a couple brawling in a park, a fight outside his home, and someone dealing drugs nearby. In every case, by the time police arrived, the bad guys had departed. In the case of the drug deal, twenty minutes passed before cops showed up, Nolden says. When he asked them what took so long, the officers said they were answering another call, for an attempted apartment burglary. "I said, 'With all due respect, are we in a take-a-number situation?' And the officer said, 'It's such a colossally bad issue, I can't give you an explanation.'"

But even as Nineteenth District residents remained on high alert for a roving group of thugs who were threatening victims with a hammer, police leaders were assuring them that all was well. In fact, according to reports posted by the Chicago Police Department on its website each week, crime was consistently down nearly 20 percent in the district compared with the same weeks in the previous summer.

Frightened and frustrated residents started packing formerly quiet community-policing sessions. "You would go to these meetings with the [police] commander and alderman, and there was a complete denial that anything was happening," Smith says incredulously. "They would tell us it was all our perception and point to statistics. . . . You have no idea how furious that makes people."

By the time 2013 ended, according to the police department's count, the number of "index crimes"—the key crimes that virtually all cities report to the Federal Bureau of Investigation—had dropped 17 percent for the year. "You can say your statistics are down," says Sarah Gottesman, thirty-six, a food-company brand manager who moved to Lake View three years ago, after which one friend got her wallet snatched, another had a bike stolen, and a neighbor's apartment was burglarized. "But that doesn't mean the crime didn't happen."

North Siders aren't the only ones worked up about the disconnect between what Mayor Rahm Emanuel and Police Superintendent Garry McCarthy have claimed about falling crime and what they believe has actually been happening in their neighborhoods. Carrie Austin, the alderman of the Thirty-Fourth Ward on the Far South Side—which includes Roseland, one of the city's highest-crime neighborhoods told a *Sun-Times* reporter in January: "Don't tell me about no statistics of McCarthy's. You say, 'Well, statistically, we're down.' That means crap to me when I know that someone else has been shot."

·   ·   ·

Murders grab the headlines. But they make up less than 1 percent of the total number of crimes committed. So when Emanuel and McCarthy talk about the huge drop in crime since they took over in May 2011, they're referring mostly to reductions in the number of break-ins, car thefts, muggings, sexual assaults, and the like—the kinds of crimes much more likely to befall the typical Chicagoan.

"You can have a 100 percent reduction in murders, and as sad as this may sound, it won't have anywhere near the effect [on the overall statistics] of a 25 or 30 percent drop in burglaries," says Jody Weis, Chicago's police chief from 2008 to early 2011. "If you're looking at driving down crime, property crimes are the ones that are going to make a big difference."

And as far as public perception is concerned, no property crimes are more important than those tracked by the Federal Bureau of Investigation for its Uniform Crime Report. Of the hundreds of crimes on the books, the FBI compiles data from virtually every U.S. city on just four property crimes (burglaries, thefts, motor vehicle thefts, and incidents of arson) and four violent crimes (homicides, criminal sexual assaults, aggravated batteries/assaults, and robberies).

The level of index crime in a city is widely viewed as a gauge of its safety—essentially, its crime report card. "[Low crime] figures serve a political end," says Eli Silverman, a professor emeritus at John Jay College of Criminal Justice in New York City. "It brings in tourism; it's good for business."

As mentioned in part 1 of this report, which focused on homicides, from 1993 through 2010 the average annual decline in the number of index crimes in Chicago was less than 4 percent. If you go to the police department's website and compare the index crime totals for 2010 (found in that year's annual report) with the totals in the 2013 year-end CompStat report (more on that later), you'll see a drop of 56 percent, or 19 percent per year on average. It's akin to a chronically mediocre student all of a sudden earning straight As.

The plunge hasn't happened in just a few parts of the city, either. Index crimes have dropped sharply in all 22 police districts. In 20 of them, in fact, the total number committed in 2013 was a mere one-half to one-third the number committed in 2010, according to police figures.

Of all index crimes, motor vehicle thefts have plunged most. Over the past three calendar years, they're down 35 percent, again according to the department's own statistics. (They fell 23 percent last year alone.) Over that same three-year period, burglaries fell 33 percent; aggravated batteries, 20 percent; robberies, 16 percent.

Current and former officers and several criminologists say they can't understand how a cash-strapped and undermanned department—one that by its own admission has been focusing most of its attention and resources on combating shootings and murders and protecting schoolchildren in a few very violent neighborhoods—could achieve such astounding results. "God Almighty! It's just not possible," opines a retired high-ranking officer who reviewed the department's statistics.

To get to the bottom of the numbers, *Chicago* studied police reports and court documents, examined the department's internal and publicly available crime data, and interviewed more than seventy crime victims, neighborhood activists, criminologists, and former and current police sources. (Officers agreed to speak only if their names were withheld, some citing fears of retaliation.) We also reviewed a recently released audit by the city's office of the inspector general that found the police department failed to report nearly a quarter of aggravated assaults and aggravated batteries in 2012, based on the cases surveyed.

Together, this information shows what Smith, Gottesman, and countless Chicagoans have been saying all along: The city's crime numbers seem too good to be true. One former lieutenant has a name for the system: the washing machine. "They wash and rinse the numbers," the lieutenant says.

Documents and interviews reveal how this may be happening. First, on McCarthy's watch, the department quietly changed several bedrock crime-reporting and scoring policies. For example, in the statistics it compiles and shares with the public on its website each week, it stopped including certain crimes that had been counted in the past.

Second, many police sources say they have been pressured by superiors—explicitly and implicitly—to underreport crime. There are, according to an expert source on the department's statistics, potentially "a million tiny ways to do it"—including misclassifying and downgrading offenses, counting multiple incidents as single events, and making it more difficult for people to report crimes or actively discouraging them from doing so.

Finally, some of the drop is simply a byproduct of reduced manpower. Many officers say that their ranks have become so depleted that they can't respond to all 911 calls. It's like the proverbial tree falling in the empty forest: no victim, no report, no crime.

Since *Chicago* published part 1 of this special report, many current and former police officers have contacted us to share "washing machine"–like stories. Crime victims, too, have come forward to describe Kafkaesque dealings with police. And two aldermen—Scott Waguespack, from the North Side's Thirty-Second Ward, and Willie Cochran, from the South Side's Twentieth Ward—have introduced resolutions in the City Council calling for hearings on the reliability of the department's crime counting and reporting practices. At press time, more than a third of Chicago's fifty aldermen had signed.

"The allegations [in part 1 of the special report] are false, and built on information that is factually incorrect, misleading, and unsubstantiated," police department spokesperson Adam Collins said in a statement. "We take the tracking, compiling, and reporting of crime data extremely seriously . . . and [it] is shared with the public to provide an accurate understanding of crime conditions." (While Superintendent McCarthy did not agree to an interview, Collins sent McCarthy's answers to a few of our questions via e-mail on May 2, just before press time for this article. Mayor Emanuel did not respond to repeated requests for comment.)

.   .   .

Such allegations are far from new. Police departments around the country didn't start collecting and reporting crime statistics until the 1920s. And it didn't take long for accusations to arise that the numbers were being manipulated. A 1926 *Chicago Daily Tribune* investigation revealed that the police department was "covering up on the real crime situation" by "doctoring the books." The paper found that only 60 percent of the burglaries, thefts, and "stickups" made it into the department's public report.

So the scandals went, flaring up and then dying down every two or three decades. By 1958, the Chicago Crime Commission was accusing police of "minimizing" the city's crime numbers. Timothy Sheehan, a former Republican congressman who ran for mayor in 1959 against Richard J. Daley, described the numbers as a "farce": "What man with brains can believe [them]?"

In 1982, Channel 2 investigative reporter Pam Zekman unearthed evidence that the department had been "killing crime" for years by dismissing legitimate crime reports as unfounded. She reported that it undercounted robberies and burglaries by one-third or more and rapes by nearly one-half. The ensuing scandal led to an FBI review, which concluded that Chicago police were fourteen times more likely to deem crime reports "unfounded" than were police in at least thirty other big cities.

Admitted Richard Brzeczek, Chicago's police chief at the time: "There were, in fact, problems in the integrity of our reporting system." Lo and behold, when the department released its new figures for the first four months of 1983, the numbers shot skyward: burglaries and robberies up 23 percent, thefts up 30 percent, rapes up nearly 50 percent.

Inaccuracies are hardly a Chicago-specific phenomenon. In the recent past, police departments in many other big cities—Atlanta, Dallas, Milwaukee, New York, Philadelphia, Phoenix, and Washington, D.C., to name a few—have admitted to fudging the numbers. Each of those cases can be traced to the pressures of various versions of one system: CompStat.

A comprehensive method of mapping and recording crime patterns and data, CompStat was rolled out in 1994 in New York City by its police commissioner, William Bratton. The process involves weekly meetings in which top brass grill field commanders about what they're doing to solve crime problems in their areas. Garry McCarthy, a Bronx-born detective's son, would eventually run the NYPD's CompStat meetings as the deputy commissioner of operations, holding commanders' feet to the fire at any sign that crime in their districts wasn't heading downward.

After CompStat's launch, New York's crime numbers plummeted. Copycat systems quickly sprang up across the country. Police Superintendent Terry Hillard introduced a CompStat-like system in Chicago in early 2000; his successors Phil Cline and Jody Weis put in place their own variations. Nearly two decades after CompStat was born, about 80 percent of the nation's major police departments had adopted some variation of the system, according to a survey by the Police Executive Research Forum, a Washington-based think tank.

But New York's CompStat program was dogged by talk that its numbers weren't all that they seemed. In May 2010—four years after McCarthy left the NYPD to become the top cop in Newark, New Jersey—the *Village Voice* published excerpts of transcripts from hundreds of audio recordings of station-house roll calls from 2008 and 2009 made by an officer in the Eighty-First Precinct, in Brooklyn's tough Bedford-Stuyvesant neighborhood. NYPD bosses were caught on tape pressuring street cops to downgrade crimes and discourage victims from reporting offenses, among other things, to bolster the precinct's stats. An outside report ordered by former police commissioner Raymond Kelly would confirm that manipulation went well beyond one precinct and "may have an appreciable effect on certain reported crime rates."

In their 2012 book *The Crime Numbers Game: Management by Manipulation*, Silverman and John Eterno, a former NYPD captain who is now a professor of criminal justice at Molloy College in Rockville Centre, New York, describe how over time data-driven policing turned the NYPD to the dark side. "Initially, they started off with all the good intentions in the world, but then the political pressures and the pressures from the top became so great that they changed," explains Eterno. "When the pressure comes from the political powers, it is very difficult for honest working police officers to battle that."

At first, Eterno and Silverman say, producing steep declines is easy. Silverman compares the process to squeezing an orange. "It's very easy to extract the juice when the orange is new," he says. "But there is a point where it's more and more difficult. So you have to be more creative."

.   .   .

In early 2011, Mayor-elect Emanuel went hunting for a new top cop who would help him fulfill his campaign promise of reducing crime. He selected McCarthy, extolling his numbers-driven approach to policing. McCarthy brought to Chicago both Comp-Stat and his friend and former NYPD colleague Robert Tracy to run it.

Before McCarthy's arrival, the Chicago Police Department classified and reported incidents in just one way. The numbers that it shared with the public—for example, in clear, detailed annual reports—were the same ones it gave to the state of Illinois and the FBI every month for their Uniform Crime Reporting programs. (Very slight variances between those numbers can exist if the department reclassified cases after it released the annual report but before it submitted the year's numbers for the UCR.)

Now the department essentially keeps two sets of books. One follows FBI rules for what crimes to count and how to count them. The other—in CompStat—doesn't always. "CompStat is created by the administration for their own purposes, to do their own analysis," explains the expert source on the department's statistics. "They collect whatever data they want, they use it however they want to use it, and they don't have to tell anybody [what data they're collecting or how they're doing the counting]."

For example, McCarthy's administration doesn't include arson in CompStat reports. Spokesman Collins did not directly answer repeated requests as to why but did tell us that the department supplies arson figures for the Uniform Crime Report. The FBI's 2011 and 2012 UCR reports, however, have blank spaces where Chicago's arson figures should be. "Chicago arson counts were incomplete for those years," explains an FBI spokesperson.

Now take the assault-related crime category. It includes thirty-four classifications, from aggravated domestic batteries to non-fatal shootings, based on the severity of the injury (or threat of injury), the kind of weapon, and the location. The UCR programs for Illinois and the FBI require all types to be recorded and counted. But the police department doesn't count all types in CompStat.

Look at theft, too. For decades, the department counted a theft as a theft. Stealing $1 was the same as stealing $1 million. That practice follows Uniform Crime Report guidelines, which clearly state: "Agencies must report all larceny offenses regardless of the value of the property stolen."

But CompStat counts only felony thefts—that is, thefts of more than $500. The difference between the number of felony and non-felony thefts is huge. In 2010, the last full year before McCarthy took over, the department reported 74,764 thefts for the UCR. In 2011, under the CompStat system, the department's year-end report listed just 15,665 thefts.

That same year, the department gave the FBI a theft number of 72,373. That works out to a theft reduction of a little over 3 percent from 2010 to 2011, right around the long-term annual average reduction before McCarthy arrived. But look at the CompStat numbers and you'd see almost 60,000 crimes effectively subtracted. Poof!

You don't need to be a rocket scientist to realize that not counting nearly 60,000 index crimes can do wonders for a city's overall crime rate. This accounting change helped drive the total number of index crimes from 152,031 in 2010 (according to the department's annual report) to 86,174 in 2011 (according to CompStat).

Collins told *Chicago* that CompStat "is an internal tactical analysis and crime reduction strategy" and "is not a reporting mechanism in the way that UCR is." However, McCarthy and Emanuel have used CompStat as the source of official statistics they give the press and the public, even elected officials.

For example, on October 31, when the superintendent appeared before the City Council for an annual budget hearing, Cochran asked him for crime statistics by ward. On November 22, McCarthy sent a memo to budget committee chairman Carrie Austin stating, "Crime statistics are not available by ward. They are available by district." In an attachment, he included one week's worth of CompStat reports for the city's twenty-two districts and three areas, plus a citywide report. That's right: He didn't send UCR statistics. He sent CompStat statistics.

Emanuel and McCarthy have also compared CompStat crime data with pre-2011 crime data, a practice that Eterno says is "comparing apples and oranges." Consider the department's January 1 press release declaring, "Chicago Ends 2013 at Historic Lows in Crime and Violence." It states, among other things, that "felony thefts were at the lowest level since 1972" and "both criminal sexual assaults and aggravated battery/assault [*sic*] were at the lowest level since 1982." The year-over-year drops cited in the press release—down 23 percent in motor vehicle theft, 22 percent in burglary, and 18 percent in murder, for example—exactly mirror those in the 2013 year-end CompStat report. (The FBI has not yet made final UCR data available for 2013.)

By the way, the year-end CompStat report is one of the few that remains on the department's website longer than seven days. Each week, the department typically replaces that week's CompStat report with a new one, removing the old one from public view for good.

And what about those easy-to-understand annual reports that the department had been issuing since 1965? McCarthy discontinued them. Collins says there's no longer a need for them, given that "we've increased data available to the public and put it right on our website."

Well, not exactly. On the department's home page (http://chicagopolice.org/; click on "Crime Statistics" in the News tab and what you'll see are CompStat data. The numbers are helpfully crunched to show percentage changes in the frequency of seven crimes (representing all of the index crimes except for arson) over the past week, four weeks, one year, two years, and three years.

There *is* a more detailed public source of crime stats—not on the department's website, but on the city's. This data portal contains raw crime numbers in enormous spreadsheets—not exactly user-friendly. What's more, nowhere will you find numbers of arrests, numbers of murders solved, or data on offender and victim gender, race, and age, for example, all of which had been included in the annual reports.

Finally, another significant discrepancy between CompStat data and FBI data is due to how the department counts cases in which there are multiple victims. Imagine that a group of thugs armed with baseball bats beats up three people walking along the street. Three victims, three incidents, according to state and federal guidelines. The inspector general's audit found that the Chicago Police Department was counting such cases as only one incident. The result: The department had underreported assault cases by 24 percent in 2012, based on the sample cases reviewed.

Collins seemed to imply that McCarthy didn't realize there was any problem: "The issue was brought to this administration's attention during the course of [the] audit." Noting that the previous administration failed to follow the guidelines, the department pledged to review all of the aggravated assault and battery cases from 2012 and 2013 to correct them.

Incidentally, McCarthy's administration records data for shootings—a category he created in Chicago's CompStat system—exactly the same way: by incident rather than by victim. For example, when thirteen people got shot in last September's mass shooting at a pickup basketball game on the South Side, the department counted the shootings only once.

No wonder many in the police rank and file don't trust the CompStat numbers. Just read some of the grousing on the widely read blog *Second City Cop* about "Con-stat," "Compost," and "Comcrap."

$$\bullet \qquad \bullet \qquad \bullet$$

Last winter, as the polar vortex hunkered down for a bone-chilling stay, an elderly woman heard a knock on the front door of her house on the Northwest Side. (She requested that her name be withheld, saying that she was afraid of angering police.) The woman peered out and saw a young man "who looked like Justin Bieber," she says.

He seemed harmless enough, so she opened the door. "He asked me if I had seen his dog." The woman told the Bieber doppelgänger she hadn't seen the lost animal. But he kept standing there. "He wouldn't go away," she says. So she closed and locked the door and went upstairs to do some chores.

Soon after, she heard a loud noise coming from the first floor. She went downstairs to investigate and saw three men wearing black hoodies, their faces covered by scarves, creeping down her hallway. When the intruders saw her, they fled. "I went upstairs and called 911," she says.

A few minutes later, the shaken woman heard two cops. They had come in through the back door, which the men had broken open. (The front door was still locked.)

The officers handed her a police report and left. Relieved that the whole thing was over, the homeowner tried her best to fix the back door. The men had ripped the frame from the wall, knocking off a metal plate. Wood chips littered the floor. "I got a mallet and a hammer and some wood putty, and it held pretty good," she says.

On the report, police had recorded the incident as a case of criminal trespassing (which state law defines as entering private or public property after being told not to, either verbally or in a written notice). But a family friend pointed out that "they didn't just walk in; they broke in." That's burglary: a forced or unlawful entry into a home, business, or garage with the intent to steal. It's both a felony and an index crime. Trespassing isn't either one.

Days later, when she called police to follow up, the woman reminded the officer that the three masked men had broken in through her locked back door. "I told them my report wasn't complete, that there was nothing about the broken door," she recalls. "He told me that it didn't make a difference and just kept telling me to make sure my doors were locked."

Sure enough, a second report mailed days after their conversation still read criminal trespassing, not burglary. At press time, that had not changed.

Veteran detectives who reviewed this case for *Chicago* were not surprised. "It's become standard operating procedure," says one sergeant. "Cops are being told by their supervisors to change things and change classifications. We have a lot of cases where a neighborhood is experiencing a rash of burglaries and the cases are basically being eliminated."

Because the current Chicago Police Department culture is built on a wink-and-nod axiom that crime must only go down—and because careers are made or broken by good or bad "performance"—pressure to reduce crime numbers in this way has become acute at all levels. Patrol officers have to please sergeants; sergeants have to please lieutenants; lieutenants have to please captains; they all have to please district commanders; district commanders have to please the chiefs with the gold stars; and, of course, the superintendent has to keep his boss, the mayor, happy.

Much of the daily pressure lands on the beat cops on the bottom and the sergeants and lieutenants supervising them. Officers say the punishments for reporting numbers their supervisors don't like can include denying time due, splitting up longtime partners, and changing shift times so that officers can't make it to, say, their children's Little League games.

Multiple officers have the power to downgrade a crime at just about any stage of the process. "It happens all the time," says one detective. "It's so easy." First, the responding officer can intentionally misclassify a case or alter the narrative to record a lesser charge. A house break-in becomes "trespassing"; a garage break-in becomes "criminal damage to property"; a theft becomes "lost property." The former lieutenant mentioned earlier calls this the "speed wash cycle": Major crimes are immediately rinsed out of the stat books.

If the officer's supervisor won't accept the initial classification, the officer almost always has to change it. "What are you going to do?" says one patrol officer. Meaning: That's how top-down command works.

Victims usually don't find out about the reclassifications until later. Like the man we spoke to whose garage was set on fire but who later discovered that his case had been classified not as arson but as simple criminal damage to property—which is not an index crime. Or the college student who was knocked to the sidewalk and robbed of his phone and laptop, only to be told afterward by his insurance company that police reported his case as lost property. (The result: His insurer refused to cover it.)

Or the professor whose wallet was snatched out of her purse last winter when she was leaving a concert at Symphony Center with her husband, headed to their car in the underground garage at Grant Park. Her 911 call was routed to someone who "said he could not take a report until we first alerted the credit card company," her husband says. "It sounded bizarre and, to us, irrelevant."

But the couple did as they were told, then again called police. Weeks later, the department sent them a report categorizing the incident as lost property. "That struck me as very strange," he continues. "It was clearly a criminal case."

Later, their bank statement revealed that someone had somehow withdrawn $2,000 from their account. Now the original case report was becoming a serious issue. So the husband headed to the police district office and asked a desk officer to correct the original report, which the officer did. A copy provided to *Chicago* leaves little room for misunderstanding: "This was a theft, not a loss, and should be classified as such."

Four months later, though, nothing has changed. At press time, the city's data portal shows no such theft case.

•　　　•　　　•

While jogging near Montrose Beach on a beautiful day last fall, a twenty-something woman took a path to the bird sanctuary, a secluded area shrouded by trees, bushes, and brush. (Because of the nature of the crime, we are withholding her name.) Once she was out of sight of other parkgoers, a man appeared. Clutching his crotch, he lunged toward her and shoved his hand between her legs, grabbing her genitals.

Adrenaline surging, the woman punched him and then chased him as he ran away. "Stop him!" she yelled. But no one did. So she kept after the man until he reached the street, jumped into his car, and sped off. She called 911 on her cell phone and told the dispatcher everything, including the man's license plate number. And she waited.

Half an hour went by, she says, before a Nineteenth District police officer arrived. "I told him my story," she says. "And the officer says, 'I want to catch this guy.' And I said, 'It's been thirty minutes already. He's gone.'"

That same fall, during a heated community meeting in which residents blasted the police department for failing to respond to crimes quickly enough, the Nineteenth District's commander, Elias Voulgaris, gave an unusually candid speech that lasted nearly half an hour. Yes, Voulgaris said, he was short on cops. The district now had sixty-nine fewer beat cops than when he took over in August 2012. "I don't think there is any district commander in this city who doesn't want more officers," he said.

Yes, on some days the district got so overwhelmed by 911 calls that his officers couldn't get to crime scenes in a reasonable amount of time. "It's a major concern," he said. "It's a major concern citywide and, yes, part of the issue is manpower."

It was such an issue, Voulgaris told the group, that he had to prioritize. Given the shortage of officers, he didn't want his cops making arrests for minor crimes that would take them off the streets. "I'm being totally frank and honest with you, and I hope you appreciate that," he said, adding, "I'll probably be fired tomorrow."

The group responded with a nervous laugh. The shortage of patrol officers was no secret—according to an analysis by the *Tribune*, the city had 779 fewer beat cops in December 2013 than it did in the fall of 2011, a decline of 10 percent—but it was rare to hear a senior official be so specific about what sorts of problems that shortage was causing.

Officers say that in busy districts, it can take hours for anyone to show up in response to a 911 call. "It sucks, but it's true," says a patrol officer on the South Side. "There may be only one car freed up for the entire district that can answer jobs."

According to a 2012 federal study, only 44 percent of violent crime victims (and 34 percent of property crime victims) report the incidents anyway. The longer victims wait for police to arrive, the greater the chance they will leave the scene. No victim, no report. "If people are waiting around for a squad car to show up because you don't have enough manpower, your reported crime is going down," a detective says.

The problem is especially acute in minority neighborhoods, says Harvey Grossman, legal director of the American Civil Liberties Union of Illinois. The ACLU has a pending case against the city, on behalf of a West Side community group, alleging that the city failed to deploy police equitably across communities. The case is currently in the discovery phase.

On top of that, if you call 911 these days, you may wind up getting shunted off to the city's nonemergency 311 call center. As of February 3 last year—days after the headline-grabbing murder of teenager Hadiya Pendleton—citizens who call 911 to report garage burglaries, vehicle thefts, thefts, simple assaults, and similar crimes in which the suspect is no longer on the scene and no one is in danger are directed to 311. (Under Weis, only 911 calls about lost property and a few other minor issues were rerouted.) McCarthy called the change "the best use of our resources," a move that would free up 44 officers a day and absorb 137,000 hours of case reporting that was once handled by patrol officers.

Sounds reasonable in theory. But cops say the pushing of calls to 311—the line Chicagoans use to, say, report potholes or rats in their alley—has worsened the underreporting of crime. That's because the typical wait for someone to pick up a 311 call is much longer than for a 911 call, according to both victims and officers interviewed. And when a police officer does answer, the report is almost always taken by phone. Says one cop: "Victims get frustrated because they are talking to someone on the phone [instead of in person], and they just say, 'To hell with this.'"

·   ·   ·

None of this is to say that crime in Chicago hasn't gone down since Emanuel and McCarthy arrived. It almost certainly has. After all, the city saw a steady drop in index crimes over the preceding seventeen years.

That kind of modest decline was the norm in 2013 for the ten biggest U.S. cities. Preliminary FBI statistics show that index property crimes (burglaries, thefts, auto thefts, and arsons) declined by an average of less than 3 percent last year in those cities. Of those, burglaries and motor vehicle thefts fell the most: by just under 7 percent each, on average. In contrast, Chicago recorded seismic drops of 22 and 23 percent, respectively, for those two crimes in 2013.

If Chicago has indeed succeeded in slicing property crime by such huge amounts—especially when most of its manpower has been devoted to preventing shootings—then you'd think Emanuel and McCarthy would have been touting their winning strategies. The two have never been bashful about their accomplishments. But when was the last time you heard them describe their strategies to prevent burglaries? Or robberies? Or auto thefts? (When *Chicago* asked Collins for those details, he gave a four-point response that basically boils down to: The decreases shown in CompStat are due to CompStat.)

It would be easy enough for an independent authority to make sure that crime statistics are accurate. But none do. The Illinois Uniform Crime Reporting program—a one-person office within the state police department—merely submits the department's numbers to the FBI after checking for data-entry errors, not for accuracy, according to a state police spokeswoman.

And the FBI? Its Uniform Crime Reporting program leaves the counting and reporting to the police. (The departments can refuse to participate, by the way.) Which essentially means the departments police themselves. Audits are rare: From 2009 to 2013, the FBI audited just 451 of the nation's nearly 18,000 law enforcement agencies that report crime data to the bureau. The last time the FBI audited the Chicago Police Department, the FBI spokesman said, was April 2006.

Here's the capper: Even if the FBI finds problems, it cannot impose any penalties. "It's an absolute joke," says Eterno.

Even the recent audit by the office of Inspector General Joseph Ferguson was quite limited. It examined only 383 of the 83,480 assault-related incidents reported by the department in 2012. And it didn't check to make sure the facts in the reports matched the victims' original complaints.

When we asked Collins what safeguards the department has to prevent or catch the manipulation of crime reports, he pointed to the department's Quality Assurance Unit. It randomly checks case reports for accuracy, Collins said, and reviews every report that has been reclassified. In 2012, the department's Robert Tracy told *Chicago*: "I have quality assurance . . . ensuring that the numbers we put out publicly are accurate. Nothing worse can happen than not having the right numbers."

Tracy, as you'll recall, also runs the CompStat program. It's the old fox and hen house dilemma.

Changes to how crimes get recorded and counted. Allegations by cops of rampant downgrading and underreporting. Lack of transparency. All this has a familiar ring to Silverman, the criminologist, who has studied police data practices in numerous U.S. cities for years. His opinion: "It's like they wrote the script here [in New York], and you guys [in Chicago] took it."

·　　·　　·

Since part 1 of this special report was published on April 7, strange things have happened to the department's crime data. On April 11, *RedEye* reported that eight homicide cases were missing from the 2014 year-to-date murder total on the city's public data portal. Collins called the problem a "temporary technology glitch." An online vendor, he added, would "re-sync" the data that same day.

But three weeks later, the problem hadn't been fixed. Also, when we checked the portal a week after part 1 of this story ran, 364 murders were listed for 2013, though the department's widely reported official year-end tally was 414. That error persisted until at least May 1. Also on May 1, the department announced 95 murders for the first quarter of 2014, but the portal showed just 72 for that period. (It has since been corrected.) The data for 2011 and 2012 are consistent with previously reported totals.

At the end of April, another odd thing happened. A blog called *Crime in Wrigleyville and Boystown* found that the data portal was missing at least 22 percent of all reported crimes in Lake View between March 15 and April 14. When we asked Collins about it, he said "the issue should be completely correct by the end of the day [May 5]."

Just as puzzling, a week before part 1 of our story was published, the department stopped its usual practice of posting CompStat reports on its website each week. It did not resume posting until May 2, at which time it put up a report covering the week ending April 27. What about data for the weeks ending March 30, April 6, April 13, and April 20? Never posted. "The person who updates the CompStat data on our website was on vacation for several weeks," Collins responded, calling the lapse an "administrative oversight."

These issues, and others described in this story, aren't just academic. Reliable data are integral to virtually every police-budgeting and crime-fighting decision, from how many officers to hire to where to deploy them. Undercounting allows crimes to go unsolved and criminals to get lighter penalties. And it leaves victims—the real people who become the statistics—feeling betrayed, distrustful, and vulnerable.

Consider the unfortunate jogger mentioned earlier. According to veteran police sources, her attacker's behavior constitutes criminal sexual abuse, defined as sexual conduct by the use of force or threat of force. And that's exactly how the police report, filed a few days later, classified the incident.

Shortly afterward, however, a detective told the woman that the crime was not sexual abuse after all, but battery. The woman recalls the detective saying that "the man who attacked me would've had to have said something sexual or touched himself" for the crime to be sexual abuse. So she reiterated: "He grabbed his crotch and grabbed mine."

She says the detective told her, "To be honest, I don't think the state's attorney is going to do anything with this. . . . It's just not a big deal compared to all the other crime that's going on."

Maybe so. But according to the FBI, crimes are supposed to be classified and counted based solely on the police's investigation, not on what officers think prosecutors might do later in court.

Weeks later, the woman learned, to her dismay, that the police report had been changed anyway. It no longer contained any reference to the sexual nature of the attack, which was now classified a simple battery—the kind of charge given to a person who, say, slugs someone.

"It was a sexual attack," the woman insists. "He could do it again, and he could do it to someone who couldn't fight back, who couldn't get away. . . . It's not fair that the sexual nature of this wouldn't be on his record." (Because the victim captured the man's license plate number, the police caught a suspect; the case is working its way through the courts.)

"There's no reason to reclassify [this case] to a battery," agrees a veteran detective who reviewed the case at *Chicago*'s request. "Unless someone just wanted to make the lakefront seem a lot safer."

•   •   •

Before Commander Voulgaris and his officers closed last fall's meeting in Wrigleyville, the Nineteenth District's community policing sergeant, Jason Clark, urged the people gathered in the room to be aware of their surroundings. He reminded them to call police when they spot anyone suspicious. He added that the department had grant money coming in for "personal alarms" that they could attach to their key chains. The crowd gave him a blank stare.

Moments later, everyone stood up to leave. It was already dark. Toward the back of the room, an older woman gathered her things, including the packets of monthly police statistics distributed when the meeting began. She stopped for a minute and turned to a neighbor.

"Could I get someone to walk me home?" she asked.

Grantland

FINALIST—FEATURE
WRITING

One of two stories published by a digital-only publication to be nominated for the 2015 Ellie for Feature Writing (the other was the winner, The Atavist's *"Love and Ruin"), "The Sea of Crises" is, said the Ellie judges, "a daring, dreamlike narrative that weaves together reporting on the career of Hakuho, the great sumotori, and the suicide of the writer Yukio Mishima." Brian Phillips is a staff writer at* Grantland, *where he covers sports ranging from tennis to the Iditarod. Launched in 2011,* Grantland *is a sports and pop-culture website operated by ESPN. This year* Grantland *was also nominated for Ellies for film criticism by Wesley Morris and Jonathan Hock's video series on Steve Nash.*

Brian Phillips

The Sea of Crises

The White Bird

When he comes into the ring, Hakuho, the greatest *sumotori* in the world, perhaps the greatest in the history of the world, dances like a tropical bird, like a bird of paradise. Flanked by two attendants—his *tachimochi*, who carries his sword, and his *tsuyuharai*, or dew sweeper, who keeps the way clear for him—and wearing his embroidered apron, the *kesho-mawashi*, with its braided cords and intricate loops of rope, Hakuho climbs onto the trapezoidal block of clay, two feet high and nearly twenty-two feet across, where he will be fighting. Here, marked off by rice-straw bales, is the circle, the *dohyo*, which he has been trained to imagine as the top of a skyscraper: One step over the line and he is dead. A Shinto priest purified the *dohyo* before the tournament; above, a six-ton canopy suspended from the arena's ceiling, a kind of floating temple roof, marks it as a sacred space. Colored tassels hang from the canopy's corners, representing the Four Divine Beasts of the Chinese constellations: the azure dragon of the east, the vermilion sparrow of the south, the white tiger of the west, the black tortoise of the north.[1] Over the

---

1. Japanese mythology, like many aspects of Japanese culture, was heavily influenced by China.

canopy, off-center and lit with spotlights, flies the white-and-red flag of Japan.

Hakuho bends into a deep squat. He claps twice, then rubs his hands together. He turns his palms slowly upward. He is bare-chested, 6-foot-4 and 350 pounds. His hair is pulled up in a top-knot. His smooth stomach strains against the coiled belt at his waist, the literal referent of his rank: *yokozuna*, horizontal rope. Rising, he lifts his right arm diagonally, palm down to show he is unarmed. He repeats the gesture with his left. He lifts his right leg high into the air, tipping his torso to the left like a watering can, then slams his foot onto the clay. When it strikes, the crowd of 13,000 souls inside the Ryogoku Kokugikan, Japan's national sumo stadium, shouts in unison: "*Yoisho!*"—*Come on! Do it!* He slams down his other foot: "*Yoisho!*" It's as if the force of his weight is striking the crowd in the stomach. Then he squats again, arms held out winglike at his sides, and bends forward at the waist until his back is near parallel with the floor. Imagine someone playing airplane with a small child. With weird, sliding thrusts of his feet, he inches forward, gliding across the ring's sand, raising and lowering his head in a way that's vaguely serpentine while slowly straightening his back. By the time he's upright again, the crowd is roaring.

•   •   •

In 265 years, sixty-nine men have been promoted to *yokozuna*. Just sixty-nine since George Washington was a teenager.[2] Only the holders of sumo's highest rank are allowed to make entrances like this. Officially, the purpose of the elaborate *dohyo-iri* is to

2. There are two additional *yokozuna* who supposedly practiced before 1749, but it's only with the ascension that year of Maruyama Gondazemon, the third holder of the title, that we can be pretty sure about names and dates and whether people actually existed outside folklore.

chase away demons. (And this is something you should register about sumo, a sport with TV contracts and millions in revenue and fan blogs and athletes in yogurt commercials—that it's simultaneously a sport in which demon-frightening can be something's official purpose.) But the ceremony is territorial on a human level, too. It's a message delivered to adversaries, a way of saying *This ring is mine*, a way of saying *Be prepared for what happens if you're crazy enough to enter it.*

Hakuho is not Hakuho's real name. Sumo wrestlers fight under ring names called *shikona*, formal pseudonyms governed, like everything else in sumo, by elaborate traditions and rules. Hakuho was born Mönkhbatyn Davaajargal in Ulaanbaatar, Mongolia, in 1985; he is the fourth non-Japanese wrestler to attain *yokozuna* status. Until the last thirty years or so, foreigners were rare in the upper ranks of sumo in Japan. But some countries have their own sumo customs, brought over by immigrants, and some others have sports that are very like sumo. Thomas Edison filmed sumo matches in Hawaii as early as 1903. Mongolian wrestling involves many of the same skills and concepts. In recent years, wrestlers brought up in places like these have found their way to Japan in greater numbers and have largely supplanted Japanese wrestlers at the top of the rankings. Six of the past eight *yokozuna* promotions have gone to foreigners. There has been no active Japanese *yokozuna* since the last retired in 2003. This is a source of intense anxiety to many in the tradition-minded world of sumo in Japan.

As a child, the story goes, Davaajargal was skinny. This was years before he became Hakuho, when he used to mope around Ulaanbaatar, thumbing through sumo magazines and fantasizing about growing as big as a house. His father had been a dominant force in Mongolian wrestling in the 1960s and 1970s, winning a silver medal at the 1968 Olympics and rising to the rank of undefeatable giant. It was sumo that captured Davaajargal's imagination, but he was simply too small for it.

When he went to Tokyo, in October 2000, he was a 137-pound fifteen-year-old. No trainer would touch him. Sumo apprentices start young, moving into training stables called *heya* where they're given room and board in return for a somewhat horrifying life of eating, chores, training, eating, and serving as quasi slaves to their senior stablemates (and eating). Everyone agreed that little Davaajargal had a stellar wrestling brain but he was starting too late, and his reedlike body would make real wrestlers want to kick *dohyo* sand in his face. Finally, an expat Mongolian *rikishi* (another word for sumo wrestler) persuaded the master of the Miyagino *heya* to take Davaajargal in on the last day of the teenager's stay in Japan. The stablemaster's gamble paid off. After a few years of training and a fortuitous late growth spurt, Davaajargal emerged as the most feared young *rikishi* in Japan. He was given the name Hakuho, which means "white Peng"; a Peng is a giant bird in Chinese mythology.

Hakuho's early career was marked by a sometimes bad-tempered rivalry with an older wrestler, a fellow Mongolian called Asashoryu ("morning blue dragon"), who became a *yokozuna* in 2003. Asashoryu embodied everything the Japanese fear about the wave of foreign *rikishi* who now dominate the sport. He was hotheaded, unpredictable, and indifferent to the ancient traditions of a sport that's been part of the Japanese national consciousness for as long as there's been a Japan.

This is something else you should register about sumo: It is very, very old. Not old like black-and-white movies; old like the mists of time. Sumo was already ancient when the current ranking system came into being in the mid-1700s. The artistry of the *banzuke*, the traditional ranking sheet, has given rise to an entire school of calligraphy. Imagine how George Will would feel about baseball if he'd seen World Series scorecards from 1789. This is how many Japanese feel about sumo.

Asashoryu brawled with other wrestlers in the communal baths. He barked at referees—an almost unthinkable offense. He pulled another wrestler's hair, a breach that made him the first *yokozuna* ever disqualified from a match. *Rikishi* are expected to wear kimonos and sandals in public; Asashoryu would show up in a business suit. He would show up drunk. He would accept his prize money with the wrong hand.

The 600-pound Hawaiian *sumotori* Konishiki launched a rap career after retiring from the sport;[3] another Hawaiian, Akebono, the first foreign *yokozuna*, became a professional wrestler. This was bad enough. But Asashoryu flouted the dignity of the sumo association while still an active *rikishi*. He withdrew from a summer tour claiming an injury, then showed up on Mongolian TV playing in a charity soccer match. When sumo was rocked by a massive match-fixing scandal in the mid-2000s, a tabloid magazine reported that Asashoryu had paid his opponents $10,000 per match to let him win one tournament. Along with several other wrestlers, Asashoryu won a settlement against the magazine, but even that victory carried a faint whiff of scandal: The Mongolian became the first *yokozuna* ever to appear in court. "Everyone talks about dignity," Asashoryu complained when he retired, "but when I went into the ring, I felt fierce like a devil." Once, after an especially contentious bout, he reportedly went into the parking lot and attacked his adversary's car.

The problem, from the perspective of the traditionalists who control Japanese sumo, was that Asashoryu also won. He won relentlessly. He laid waste to the sport. Until Hakuho came along, he was, by an enormous margin, the best wrestler in the world. The sumo calendar revolves around six grand tournaments—*honbasho*—held every two months throughout the year. In 2004, Asashoryu won five of them, two with perfect 15–0 records, a mark that no one had achieved since the mid-1990s. In 2005, he became the first wrestler to win all six *honbasho* in a

3. Sample lyrics: "Built to last, like an Energizer bunny / Pushin' 700, and still makin' money."

single year. He would lift 400-pound wrestlers off their feet and hurl them, writhing, to the clay. He would bludgeon them with hands toughened by countless hours of striking the *teppo*, a wooden shaft as thick as a telephone pole. He won his twenty-fifth tournament, then good for third on the all-time list, before his thirtieth birthday.

Hakuho began to make waves around the peak of Asashoryu's invulnerable reign. Five years younger than his rival, Hakuho was temperamentally his opposite: solemn, silent, difficult to read. "More Japanese than the Japanese"—this is what people say about him. Asashoryu made sumo look wild and furious; Hakuho was fathomlessly calm. He seemed to have an innate sense of angles and counterweights, how to shift his hips a fraction of an inch to annihilate his enemy's balance. In concept, winning a sumo bout is simple: either make your opponent step outside the ring or make him touch the ground with any part of his body besides the soles of his feet. When Hakuho won, how he'd done it was sometimes a mystery. The other wrestler would go staggering out of what looked like an even grapple. When Hakuho needed to, he could be overpowering. He didn't often need to.

The flaming circus of Asashoryu's career was good for TV ratings. But Hakuho was a way forward for a scandal-torn sport—a foreign *rikishi* with deep feelings for Japanese tradition, a figure who could unite the past and future. At first, he lost to Asashoryu more than he won, but the rivalry always ran hot. In 2008, almost exactly a year after the Yokozuna Deliberation Council promoted Hakuho to the top rank, Asashoryu gave him an extra shove after hurling him down in a tournament. The two momentarily squared off. In the video, you can see the older man grinning and shaking his head while Hakuho glares at him with an air of outraged grace. Over time, Hakuho's fearsome technique and Asashoryu's endless seesawing between injury and controversy turned the tide in the younger wrestler's favor. When Asashoryu retired unexpectedly in 2010 after allegedly breaking a man's nose outside a nightclub,[4] Hakuho had taken their last seven regulation matches and notched a 14–13 lifetime record against his formerly invincible adversary.

With no Asashoryu to contend with, Hakuho proceeded to go 15–0 in his next four tournaments. He began a spell of dominance that not even Asashoryu could have matched. In 2010, he compiled the second-longest winning streak in sumo history, sixty-three straight wins, which tied a record set in the 1780s. He has won, so far, a record ten tournaments without dropping a single match. When I arrive in Tokyo, in early January 2014, Hakuho has twenty-seven championships, two more than Asashoryu's career total and within five of the all-time record. That he will break the record is a foregone conclusion. He is in his prime, and since winning his first *basho* in May 2006, he has won more than half of all the grand tournaments held in Japan.

·   ·   ·

Watching Hakuho's ring entrance, that harrowing bird dance, it is hard to imagine what his life is like. To have doubled in size, more than doubled, in the years since his fifteenth birthday; to have jumped cultures and languages; to have unlocked this arcane expertise. To be followed on the street. To be a non-Japanese acting as a samurai incarnate, the last remnant of a fading culture. At the time when I went to Tokyo, there was one other *yokozuna* in Japan, Harumafuji, another Mongolian. He was widely seen as a second-tier champion, and when I arrived he was out with an ankle injury. Hakuho is everything. How do you experience that without losing all sense of identity? How do you remember who you are?

4. After chasing him into the street and into a taxi, allegedly.

But it's time, here at the Kokugikan, for his first match of the *hatsu basho*, the first grand tournament of the year. *Rikishi* in sumo's top division wrestle once per day during the fifteen-day derby; whoever has the best record at the end of the final day wins the Emperor's Cup. Hakuho opens against Tochiozan, a Japanese *komusubi*—the fourth-highest ranking, three tiers below *yokozuna*. Tochiozan is known for outmuscling his opponents by gripping their loincloth, the *mawashi*. The wrestlers squat at their marks. The referee stands between them in shining purple robes, holding his war fan up. The crowd calls Hakuho's name. There's a roar as the fighters lunge for one another. Nothing Hakuho does looks difficult. He spins slightly out of the way as Tochiozan grabs, unsuccessfully, for his *mawashi*. Then he uses his rotation as a windup to smash the other wrestler in the chest. Tochiozan staggers back, and Hakuho presses the advantage—one shove, two, three, and now Tochiozan is over the barrier, the referee pointing his war fan toward Hakuho's side to indicate victory. The entire match lasts four seconds.

He doesn't celebrate. He returns to his mark, bows to Tochiozan, and squats as the referee again points to him with the fan. Win or lose, sumo wrestlers are forbidden from betraying emotion. That was the sin Asashoryu used to commit; he'd raise a fist after winning or snarl a happy snarl. Hakuho is not so careless. Hakuho is discreet. There are many crimes a *sumotori* can commit. The worst is revealing too much.

The Disappearing Sword

Some Japanese stories end violently. Others never end at all but only cut away, at the moment of extreme crisis, to a butterfly or the wind or the moon.

This is true of stories everywhere, of course: Their endings can be abrupt or oblique. But in Japan, where suicide is historically woven into the culture,[5] where an awareness of life's evanescence is the traditional mode of aesthetics,[6] it seems truer than in other places.

For instance: my second-favorite Japanese novel, *Snow Country*, by the twentieth-century writer Yasunari Kawabata. Its last pages chronicle a fire. A village warehouse where a film has been playing burns down. We watch one of the characters fall from a fiery balcony. The protagonist runs toward her, but he trips in the crowd. As he's jostled, his head falls back, and he sees the Milky Way in the night sky. That's it. There is no resolution. It's left to the reader to discover how the pieces fit together, why Kawabata thought he had said everything he needed to say. Why he decided not to give away more than this.

The first time you read a story like this, maybe, you feel cheated, because you read stories to find out what happens, not to be dismissed at the cusp of finding out. Later, however, you might find that the silence itself comes to mean something. You realize, perhaps, that you had placed your emphasis on the wrong set of expectations. That the real ending lies in the manner of the story's turning away from itself. That this can be a kind of metamorphosis, something rich and terrifying and strange. That the seeming evasion is in fact a finality, a sudden reordering of things.

5. The extent of Japan's suicide problem is sometimes overstated by the media, but Japan may be unique in the way that suicide has been historically celebrated and seen as an honorable rather than a shameful act.

6. E.g., the concept of *mono no aware*, which translates into something like "a pleasing sadness at the transience of beautiful things." The literary scholar Motoori Norinaga coined this idea in the mid-eighteenth century to describe *The Tale of Genji*, the great Heian-period novel whose author—perhaps deliberately—left it unfinished. When the protagonist dies late in the book, his death is never mentioned directly; instead, it's marked by a blank chapter called "Vanished Into the Clouds."

For instance: In January I flew to Tokyo to spend two weeks watching sumo wrestling. Tokyo, the city where my parents were married—I remember gazing up at their Japanese wedding certificate on the wall and wondering what it meant. Tokyo, the biggest city in the world, the biggest city in the history of the world, a galaxy reflected in its own glass. It was a fishing village barely 400 years ago, and now: 35 million people, a human concourse so vast it can't be said to *end*, only to fade indeterminately around the edges. Thirty-five million, almost the population of California. Smells mauling you from doorways: stale beer, steaming broth, charbroiled eel. Intersections where a thousand people cross each time the light changes, under J-pop videos ten stories tall. Flocks of schoolgirls in blue blazers and plaid skirts. Boys with frosted tips and oversize headphones, camouflage jackets and cashmere scarves. Herds of black-suited business-men. A city so dense the twenty-four-hour manga cafés will rent you a pod to sleep in for the night, so posthuman there are broth-els where the prostitutes are dolls. An unnavigable labyrinth with 1,200 miles of railway, 1,000 train stations, homes with no ad-dresses, restaurants with no names. Endless warrens of *Blade Run-ner* alleys where paper lanterns float among crisscrossing power lines. And yet: clean, safe, quiet, somehow weightless, a place whose order seems sustained by the logic of a dream.

It's a dream city, Tokyo. I mean that literally, in that I often felt like I was experiencing it while asleep. You'll ride an escala-tor underground into what your map says is a tunnel between subway stops, only to find yourself in a thumping subterranean mall packed with beautiful teenagers dancing to Katy Perry re-mixes. You will take a turn off a busy street and into a deserted Buddhist graveyard, soundless but for the wind and the clacking of *sotoba* sticks, wooden markers crowded with the names of the dead. You will stand in a high tower and look out on the reason-defying extent of the city, windows and David Beckham billboards and aerial expressways falling lightly downward, toward the Ferris wheel on the edge of the sea.

All that winter I had been forgetful. No one who knew me would have guessed that anything was wrong, because in fact nothing was wrong. It was only that things kept slipping my mind. Appointments, commitments, errands. My parents' phone number. Sometimes, and for minutes at a time, what city I was in. There is a feeling that comes when you open a browser window on a computer and then realize you have lost all sense of what you meant to do with it; I felt that way looking out of real windows. Some slight but definitive shift in my brain had separated me from my own thoughts. The pattern had changed and I could no longer read it; the map had altered and I could no longer find my way.

There was a reason for this, but instead of confronting it I was evading it, I was refusing to name it to myself. I would come up to the point and then trail off in the middle of the sentence. I kept myself in the margins of a safe semioblivion, around whose edges things kept erasing themselves. Of course I would go to Tokyo, I said when I was asked to write about sumo wrestling. Inwardly, I was already there.

I drifted through the city like a sleepwalker, with no sense of what I was doing or why. Professionally, I managed to keep up a façade of minimum competence, meeting with photographers, arriving on time for the first bell at the Kokugikan, taking notes. (I have: "arena French fry cartons made of yellow cardboard with picture of sumo wrestler printed on it." I have: "bottle openers attached to railings with string, so fans can open beer." I have: "seat cushions resting on elevated platforms, so fans can slide their shoes underneath.") Early one morning I stood in a narrow side street between a bike rack and a pile of garbage bags, spying on a sumo practice through windows steamed over from the heat of the bodies within. Occasionally a wrestler would come out and stand in the doorway (it was a sliding glass door, motion sensitive), sweat-slick and naked but for his brown *mawashi*, to let the winter air wash over him. We would look at each other and not smile.

I wandered through Ryogoku, the neighborhood near the Kokugikan, past run-down *chanko* joints peddling the high-calorie protein stew that *rikishi* guzzle to gain weight. I followed wrestlers who were out running errands, crossing the street on the way to or from their stables: soft kimonos and wooden sandals, working their iPhone touchscreens with big thumbs or bopping their heads to whatever was playing in their earbuds. One afternoon I spied on a young *rikishi* who was sitting alone on a park bench, 375 pounds if he was an ounce, watching some tiny kids play soccer. He was sitting on the left side of the bench, and he was very careful not to let his kimono spread onto the other half of the seat, as though he were conscious that his bulk might impose on others. Every once in a while a mother would approach and give him her child to hold, and he would shake the little baby, very gently.

Most of the time, though, I was lost in Tokyo, and if I wound up anywhere I was supposed to be, anywhere I had agreed to be, it felt like a fortuitous accident. The disorientation I had experienced all winter latched onto Tokyo's calm madness and found a home in it, like one of the silent water buses—glass beetles from a science-fiction film—that glide up the Sumida River.

Part of this had to do with another Japanese story, one I found myself increasingly preoccupied with, even though it had nothing to do with the wrestling culture I'd come to Japan to observe. This story fit into mine—or maybe the reverse—like the nesting sumo dolls I saw one afternoon in a *chanko* shop window, the smaller fighters enclosed in the larger, tortoises in a strange shell. It was a distraction, but unlike almost everything else during those weeks, I couldn't get it out of mind.

.   .   .

On the flight to Tokyo, I brought a novel by Yukio Mishima. *Runaway Horses*, published in 1969, is the second book in his Sea of Fertility tetralogy, which was the last work he completed before his spectacular suicide in 1970. What happened was that he sat down on the floor and ran a dagger through his abdomen, spilling twenty inches of intestine in front of the general whom he had just kidnapped, bound, and gagged. He had taken the general hostage in his own office in the headquarters of the Japan Self-Defense Forces (SDF) in a failed attempt to overthrow the government of Japan. If you tour the building today, you can see the gouges the writer's sword left in the doorframe when he fought off the general's aides.

Mishima was a contradiction. Handsome, rich, a perennial contender for the Nobel Prize, he was at forty-five a national celebrity, one of the most famous men in the country. He was also possessed by an increasingly charismatic and death-obsessed vision of Japanese culture. After its defeat in the Second World War, Japan had accepted severe restraints on its military, had turned away from martial values. The SDF was the shadow of an army, not really an army at all. Mishima not only rejected these changes but found them impossible to bear. As a child, he had been sickly and sheltered. Now he worshiped samurai and scorned the idea of peace. He fantasized about dying for the emperor, dying horribly: He posed in an artist's photo shoot as the martyred St. Sebastian, his arms bound to a tree, arrows protruding from his sides.

In 1968, horrified by the scale of left-wing protests in Tokyo, Mishima founded a private army, the Tatenokai, advertising for soldiers in right-wing student newspapers. A married father, he had long haunted Tokyo gay bars. He fell in love with the Tatenokai's second-in-command, a young man called Masakatsu Morita, and began to imagine a coup attempt that would double as a kind of erotic transfiguration, an all-consuming climax of the sort that sometimes fell at the end of kabuki melodramas.

And so in 1970 Mishima made an appointment to visit the headquarters of the Self-Defense Forces accompanied by four young Tatenokai officers. He wore his brown Tatenokai uniform, sword in a scabbard at his belt. When the general asked to see the blade, a seventeenth-century weapon forged by the Seki no Magoroku line of swordsmiths, the writer requested a handkerchief to clean it. This was the signal for the four Tatenokai officers to seize the general and barricade the door.

Here is what I see when I picture this scene: the orange tassel hanging from the hilt of Mishima's sword. The twin rows of metallic buttons on the brown tunics of the Tatenokai officers. The polite smile on the general's face in the moment before he felt himself grabbed from behind.

Mishima went onto the general's balcony and delivered a fiery speech to the soldiers, around 1,000 of them, assembled below. He urged the members of the SDF to take their place as a true national army, as warriors devoted to the emperor—a move that, had it succeeded, would have shattered the social structure of postwar Japan. He was asking the men to stage a coup. The soldiers jeered him. There is broad consensus among scholars that Mishima never expected the coup to succeed, that his only aim was to die gloriously. But he had planned to speak for half an hour, and he gave up after seven minutes. "I don't think they even heard me," he said as he climbed in through the window. Back in the general's office, he unbuttoned his uniform jacket. The young officers could hear helicopters circling outside, police sirens wailing. Mishima sat down. He screamed. Then he drove the dagger with both hands into his stomach.

Here is what I think about when I envision this scene: the moment earlier that morning when the Tatenokai officers, none older than twenty-five, stopped to wash their car on the way to Mishima's house. Mishima joking on the drive about what sort of music would play in a yakuza movie at that moment (he began to sing a song from the gangster flick *A Lion Amid Peonies*;

the younger men joined in). The gagged general's eyes bulging as one of Japan's most celebrated writers committed seppuku on his floor.

"Please," Mishima gasped, "do not leave me in agony too long." He was speaking to his lover, Morita, the student leader of the Tatenokai, whose role in the ritual was to cut off Mishima's head. In a formal seppuku, the *kaishakunin* decapitates the dying man, sparing him the prolonged anguish of death by disembowelment. Morita hacked at Mishima's neck but missed, slicing into his shoulder. He tried again and left a wound across his back. A third stroke cut into the neck but not deeply enough. Finally another Tatenokai officer, a law student named Hiroyasu Koga, took the sword from Morita—the writer's sword, the sword with the orange tassel—and beheaded Mishima in one blow.

Morita, as planned, then knelt and tried to commit seppuku. He was too weak. At his signal, Koga beheaded him too.

In the confusion afterward, as Koga and the other officers surrendered, as reporters struggled to piece together the sequence of events,[7] Mishima's sword was taken into custody by police. Some time later, it went missing.

Here is what I wonder when I try to imagine this scene: *What did this feel like for Koga?* To have followed Mishima into that place and then, unexpectedly, to have been called on to cut off his head? To have lived the rest of his life with that memory?[8] To have drifted out of the center of the story, drifted into obscurity, carrying those moments with him? At his trial, where he was sentenced to four years in prison for (among other things) "murder

7. There had been no public instances of seppuku in Japan since the war era; incredulous editors concluded that their writers were getting the story wrong. One newspaper's late-afternoon edition ran with the headline "Injured Mishima Rushed to Hospital."

8. Koga, too, was prepared to commit seppuku—all the young men were—but shortly before the coup attempt, Mishima ordered them to live, charging them to explain his actions to the world.

by agreement," Koga said that to live as a Japanese is to live the history of Japan, that the experience of each Japanese person is the experience of the nation in microcosm. What a history he must have conceived, I thought, to have said that, having done what he had.

On my third day in Tokyo I discovered that he was alive.

The Floating World

Watch the slow, sad figure of the *yobidashi* with his broom, endlessly sweeping the edges of the ring. For the long minutes between bouts, while the wrestlers move through their preparations, this slight man circles gravely and patiently, smoothing sand, erasing footprints. No mark can be allowed beyond the line because the judges must be able to tell, from a glance, whether a toe has landed outside the *dohyo*, whether a heel has slipped. Each *rikishi* is called into the ring by a singer, then announced over the stadium loudspeakers by a voice that sounds strangled and furious, like an oboe filtered through the dive alarm on a submarine. Through this, the *yobidashi* sweeps.

The wrestlers face off at their marks, not once but twice, three times, squatting and flexing, glaring intimidation at each other. Then they break and walk to their corners, where they scoop salt out of a bowl and hurl it across the clay—another Shinto purification ritual. The *yobidashi* sweeps the salt, mixing it into the sand. Tall silk banners, representing sponsors' bonus prizes— extra money guaranteed for the winner of the bout—are carried around the ring on poles. The *yobidashi* sweeps around the banners. The wrestlers slap their bellies, slap their thighs, signaling massiveness to their enemies. The spectators, who know the routine, chat lightly, snap pictures, reach out to receive bags of snacks from the tea-shop waiters who circulate through the aisles. At the center of the ring, the referee poses and flits his fan, a luminary in silks; the hilt of his knife, which he wears as a reminder of the days when one wrong decision meant his immediate seppuku, peeks out from the sash at his waist. Through all this, the *yobidashi* sweeps.

Then the atmosphere changes. The crowd grows quiet. The *rikishi* toss one last handful of salt and stamp back to their marks, fat torsos shining. The referee's fan hangs in the air between them. And in the last split second before the combatants launch at one another, the *yobidashi*, who has never changed his pace, who has never at any point moved without perfect deliberation and slow, sad care, lifts his broom and steps down from the *dohyo*.

And here is something you should register about sumo: how intensely hierarchical it is. It is not only the *sumotori* who are ranked. Referees are ranked, too. So are *yobidashi*.

Hakuho glides through his first five matches. On day 2, he lets the diminutive and root-vegetable-like Toyonoshima—five feet six inches tall and maybe five-foot-eight from rump to navel—push him almost to the edge of the ring, only then, when Toyonoshima lunges in with what looks like the winning shove, Hakuho just *isn't there*; Toyonoshima does an arms-flailing slapstick belly flop over the line. On day 3, Hakuho gets a grip on the *mawashi* of Okinoumi, a wrestler known for his movie-star looks. Okinoumi outweighs the *yokozuna* by twenty pounds, but Hakuho lifts him half off the clay and guides him out of the ring; it's like watching someone move an end table. On day 4, against Chiyotairyu, a wrestler whose leg he once snapped in a match, Hakuho slams his adversary with the first charge, then skips aside; Chiyotairyu drops; the bout lasts one second. On Day 5, he grapples with Ikioi, a physically strong wrestler known for controlling his opponent's *mawashi*. Hakuho ducks out of Ikioi's grasp, plants a hand on the back of his adversary's neck, and thrusts him to the floor. It takes a sumo novice perhaps ten seconds of match action to see that among the top-class *rikishi*, Hakuho occupies a category of his own. What the others are doing in the ring is fighting. Hakuho is composing little haiku of battle.

There is a feeling of trepidation in the crowd over these first five days, because the Yokozuna Deliberation Council has come to the stadium to observe Kisenosato, a wrestler of the second rank, *ozeki*, who is being considered for promotion. This is a rare event. Unlike a *sumotori* of any other rank, a *yokozuna* can never be demoted, only pressured to retire, so the council must make its recommendation with great care.[9] It has fifteen members, all sumo outsiders, professors and playwrights, dark-suited dignitaries from various backgrounds. For five days they tilt their heads back and scrutinize the action. They are austere and haughty, their lips as shriveled as bacon. The crowd is anxious because Kisenosato is Japanese, his country's best hope for a native-born *yokozuna*, and he has already failed in one promotion attempt.

After sumo's scandal-torn recent past, the desire for a native-born *yokozuna* is palpable.[10] The council has recently announced that if Kisenosato wins thirteen matches here, he could be promoted even if he does not win the tournament. In fact, Kisenosato has never won a tournament, and the number of *yokozuna* of whom that could be said at the time of their promotion is very small.

The hope of Japan is sour-faced and prim, a six-foot-two, 344-pound maiden aunt in a crimson loincloth. His stomach protrudes inflexibly straight in front of him; his soft breasts hang to either side. When he enters the *dohyo*, his posture is erect. When he swings his arms before the fight, he does so with a strange,

9. The advice of the Yokozuna Deliberation Council carries immense weight, but the Japan Sumo Association has final say in all promotions.

10. Although in fairness, Japanese *rikishi* have been involved in their share of controversy; of Hakuho's first five opponents, two were among the more than a dozen wrestlers suspended in 2010 for illegally betting on baseball.

balletic slowness. On the first day, with the council looking on, he wrestles Toyonoshima, the root vegetable.

The crowd is afraid because Kisenosato is thought to be weak under pressure. The smack as their bellies collide is thunderous. Toyonoshima drives his stubby legs into the clay, trying to force Kisenosato backward. Kisenosato gets a right-handed grip on Toyonoshima's pale green *mawashi*, but he fails to lift Toyonoshima, his hand slips off, and his fallback attempt to throw his opponent also fails. Now he is in trouble. Toyonoshima is a little locomotive, churning forward. The wrestlers' guts grind together. Muscles leap in their thighs. With a huge effort, Kisenosato grunts his way back to the center of the *dohyo*, gets Toyonoshima in check. Toyonoshima twists his torso hard to divert the larger man's momentum, and the throw works; Kisenosato's knee folds, and he goes over onto his back, then rolls over the edge of the clay platform and into the photographers' trench. He rests on his hands and knees, defeated, surrounded by flashbulbs.

On the fifth day, Kisenosato goes over the edge again, this time battered out by the frenzied shoves of Aoiyama, a gigantic Bulgarian. The frowns of the Yokozuna Deliberation Council go right to the pit of your stomach. There is talk later that Kisenosato has suffered a toe injury. Regardless, he will lose more than he wins at the *hatsu basho*, finishing 7–8, falling to Hakuho on day 13, and there will be no Japanese *yokozuna* in the sport that most embodies the history of Japan.

·　　·　　·

I thought about Hiroyasu Koga.

The drummer in the tower outside the Kokugikan started pounding his *taiko* at eight o'clock each morning of the grand tournament, but the elite wrestlers, like most of the crowd, didn't arrive till late afternoon, when the *makuuchi* division made its formal ring entrance. For a day or two it was fun to watch the skinny teenagers and midlevel hopefuls who wrestled first. But if I spent all day in the stadium, I started to feel like the *yobidashi* was sweeping around the edges of my brain rather than the edges of the *dohyo*.

So I wandered, lost, around Tokyo. I went to the shrine of Nomi no Sukune, the legendary father of sumo, who (if he lived at all) died 2,000 years ago. I went to the food courts in the basements of department stores. I thought I should look for the past, for the origins of sumo, so early one morning I rode a bullet train to Kyoto, the old imperial capital, where I was yelled at by a bus driver and stayed in a *ryokan*—a guest house—where the maid crawled on her knees to refill my teacup. I climbed the stone path of the Fushimi Inari shrine, up the mountain under 10,000 vermilion gates. I visited the Temple of the Golden Pavilion, rebuilt in 1955 after a mad monk burned it to the ground (Mishima wrote a novel about this), and the Temple of the Silver Pavilion, weirder and more mysterious because it is not actually covered in silver but was only intended to be. I spent one hundred yen on a vending-machine fortune that told me to be "patient with time."

As of 2005, I learned from Wikipedia, Koga was a practicing Shinto priest on Shikoku, the smallest of Japan's main islands. I pictured him in his white robes, standing in a cemetery behind a dark gate.

Back in Tokyo, I thought the city was a river, the urban element somehow changed to liquid form. In New York, the storefronts come and go but the shape of things stays relatively stable, which is why you can, say, lay a photograph from the 1940s over a neighborhood scene from today. You marvel at the difference, but the edges connect. War, earthquakes, fire, and human ingenuity have annihilated Tokyo over and over again; the city never stops building because it never stops rebuilding. Change comes like a crash, like a wave, the crowd parting and then re-forming around whatever new reality has fallen from the sky. We were shopping for sunglasses, now we're eating ice cream, let's listen to music, let's take pictures with our phones.

The way you remember things in a dream is not precisely like remembering, yet anything you've experienced can come back to you in a dream. Under the shoguns, sumo wrestlers often appeared in *ukiyo-e*—meaning "pictures of the floating world"—woodblock prints from the pleasure districts whose other great subjects were courtesans and kabuki actors, musicians and fishermen, archers and demons and ghosts. I went to an *ukiyo-e* exhibit and noted the wrestlers intermixed among the geisha, among the snarling samurai. Their bellies were rendered with one or two curved brushstrokes, their navels cartoon X's. Their eyes were oddly placid and I thought: *It will be a miracle if I can ever finish a thought.*

And I thought about Koga. I'm not sure why. I didn't know how I'd find him. I didn't know how I'd speak to him. But I priced tickets to Shikoku. I looked at the sumo schedule to figure out when I could get away. To be honest, Mishima's suicide had always struck me as somewhat absurd—in bad taste, at the very least. But I thought: *It is a small island. If I can get to the train station, I can walk to the shrine, and I will find him there.*

Then I looked at a map of Shikoku. "The smallest of Japan's main islands" covers 7,300 square miles, is home to 4.1 million people, and contains dozens of Shinto shrines. I gave up.

But I found that I couldn't give up. Whenever I stepped onto a subway train, whenever I rode an escalator up into the light, the idea came back, and I thought: *If I can track down the shrine, I will find him there.* I tried to locate a directory of Shinto sites on Shikoku—but how to make contact with one, how to ask for him?

Hello, yes, are you familiar with this celebrated author? Wonderful. Now, did one of your priests by any chance decapitate him in the early 1970s using a 400-year-old samurai sword that has since vanished?

It was an impossible question to imagine putting in English, much less Japanese. And I spoke no Japanese. I pictured the look on the face of whomever I roped into being my interpreter.

One thing struck me, though: The only source for the "Shinto priest in 2005" line on Wikipedia was a copied-and-pasted *Sunday Times* article that mentioned Koga only in passing. Even that article was hard to find online. What if it was misinformation? Perhaps Koga was no longer in Shikoku, or had never gone there. Perhaps he was a priest someplace else.

Finally I wrote an e-mail to my friend Alex, a college professor who studies Japanese literature and film. "WEIRD JAPAN QUESTION" was the subject line. I asked if he had any thoughts about how I could track down Mishima's *kaishakunin*. I hit send. And I waited for an answer, wandering through the city, lost. I listened to jazz in blue doorways. I pulled my coat a little tighter. I watched the setting sun float in pale high glass.

The Mandarin Ducks

In the Kokugikan there are stories of ghosts, sounds with no sources, invisible hands that seize you from behind. Security guards are reluctant to enter a certain hallway at night. A reporter from the *Asahi Shimbun* recalls being shoved in the back by something large and round, "like a volleyball," only to turn and find that "no one was there." A clerk is pulled from behind while using a urinal. The clatter of sumo practice comes from an empty dressing room. Somewhere under or near the stadium is said to be a mass grave containing victims of the great fire of 1657, which razed two-thirds of Tokyo and killed 100,000. The shogun built a temple to commemorate the dead; the temple became the site of sumo matches whose popularity led to the construction of the first national arena in 1909.

Even to die in this country, you might say to yourself, is somehow to live the history of Japan. But this thought does not seem to weigh on the fans streaming through the gates under banners of watery silk, nor on the *gaijin* tourists lined up in the entrance hall to buy the little glitchy radios that offer audio commentary in English. The tourists talk about being tourists, and about the ¥1,000 deposit for the radios: Is it refundable or not? It is refundable. No one talks about ghosts.

Hakuho is frictionless, devastating. He wins his next eight matches. On day 10, Hakuho hits his fellow Mongolian, the thirty-nine-year-old Kyokutenho, so hard that the older man practically rolls out of the ring. On day 13, he wrestles Kisenosato, the Japanese *rikishi* who has flubbed his chance to be promoted to *yokozuna* and is fighting only for pride. The match is furious, Hakuho thrusting his open hand repeatedly into Kisenosato's neck; neither man can get a grip on the other's *mawashi*, so they simply bash one another, tactically berserk. Little violent nasal exhalations, the sound of a spray bottle's trigger being squeezed. Finally, with his foot braced on the edge of the rice-bale circle, Kisenosato twists to throw Hakuho and fails. The *yokozuna* loses his balance and lurches forward but Kisenosato also stumbles backward; Kisenosato's foot touches out of bounds a fraction of a second before Hakuho's hand. The *yobidashi* sweeps up the marks.[11]

On day 14, Hakuho wrestles Kotoshogiku, an *ozeki* from Fukuoka who specializes in bodying his opponents with his torso. Kotoshogiku seems to have grappled Hakuho to a standstill, the two men bent at the hips and clinging to one another in the middle of the *dohyo*, and then Hakuho slaps his left hand against Kotoshogiku's knee. Kotoshogiku crumples; the move is so unexpected and counterintuitive—and the end so sudden—that the match almost looks fixed. Hakuho shows no emotion.

---

11. In the four tournaments since his losing effort in January, Kisenosato has gone 9–6, 13–2, 9–6, and 9–6. He has yet to win a championship and has not been promoted to *yokozuna*.

On the second-to-last day of the tournament he is 14–0 and one win away from a perfect championship—a *zensho yusho*.

His body is strange, Hakuho's. It's smooth, almost unformed, neither muscled like a boxer's nor bloated like that of many *rikishi*. Gagamaru, the Georgian wrestler who is currently the largest man in top-division sumo—440 pounds and a little over six feet tall—looks like a canyon seen from the air, all crevasses and folds. Hakuho, by contrast, is a single large stone. His face is vague, broad so that his eyes look small and rimless, but also inexpressive, self-contained. Once in a while he will glance to one side with what looks like critical intelligence. Then he blurs again. The sources of his strength, whether physical or psychological, are almost totally hidden from view.

Another Mongolian, the *ozeki* Kakuryu, has fought his way to a 13–1 record, making him the only *rikishi* with a chance to tie Hakuho and force a playoff. Kakuryu is the son of a university professor who, unlike Hakuho's father, had no background in Mongolian wrestling. With the championship at stake, he and Hakuho are scheduled to meet on the tournament's final day.

·　　·　　·

"Re: WEIRD JAPAN QUESTION" dinged into my inbox in the middle of the night. "Sounds like a cool piece," Alex wrote. He had looked into the Koga question, and as far as he could tell, Shikoku was a red herring. Koga had never lived there. Nor was he a Shinto priest. He had indeed joined a religious group, but it was Seicho-no-Ie, "the House of Growth," a spiritual movement founded in the 1930s. Seicho-no-Ie fuses Christianity with Buddhism and Shintoism. After prison, Koga became the head of its branch in Hokkaido, the snowy island in northern Japan where he had been born and raised. He married the daughter of the group's leader and changed his name to reflect that he'd been adopted into her family: Hiroyasu Arechi. "Arechi" was an unusual Japanese name, formed from characters that meant *wild land* or *barren ground*. "If you want to get really literary," Alex told me, "Arechi" was also a Japanese translation of the title of T. S. Eliot's poem "The Waste Land." But that was only a coincidence.

Seicho-no-Ie struck a chord, so I looked it up in one of the Mishima biographies. There it was: The writer's grandmother had been a member. When Koga said at his trial that to live as a Japanese is to live the history of Japan, he was quoting one of the group's teachings.

Then Alex sent me a link that made me cover my mouth with my hand. Koga/Arechi retired in 2012 and moved to the other end of the country, to the city of Kumamoto, on the southern island of Kyushu. The link led to a video from the website of an apartment complex in Kumamoto. In it, a sixty-five-year-old man named Hiroyasu Arechi answers questions about being a new resident. He mentions at the beginning that he is from Hokkaido. He wears a black V-neck sweater over a red-and-white gingham sport shirt. His features match those of the young Koga in a photograph I'd seen of him posing with fellow Tatenokai conspirators, looking fierce in their ridiculous faux-military uniforms.

The older man in the video has warm eyes. As he speaks, we see a bit of his apartment in the background. Flowers hanging on a light-flooded balcony. A cream-colored curtain, tied back. An inset picture on the website shows a console table that holds framed photographs of what look like children and grandchildren. A couple holding hands in front of a landscape. Young people at a wedding. A man or woman in a parka, smiling, surrounded by snow.

He does not mention decapitation or suicide or Mishima. He says that the bus is very convenient to the building. The sales representatives are compassionate and polite. The park nearby is a good place to take walks. There is a MaxValu store across the street, open twenty-four hours, a handy place to shop. There is a roof garden. He has a wide balcony. There are beautiful views at night.

.　　　　.　　　　.

I remember the auditorium of the Kabuki-za Theater, warm and high and tinted by lights reflecting off the lavish pictorial curtains—herons in a stream, Mount Fuji, a hummingbird breaking out of a tangle of cherry blossoms. Tiny old ladies in surgical masks sat with bento boxes resting on their knees, looking pleased; packs of theater kids sprawled in fishnet tights. Old men slept in their chairs with both hands balanced on their canes. The kabuki play I had come to see was about sumo or involved sumo; I was not entirely sure. The English-language audio guide I had rented was unclear about the details. The play's story was fantastically complex and was itself only a tiny peripheral fragment of a larger story about two brothers seeking revenge for the murder of their father, a revenge that spanned decades and flowed inexorably from an equally long back story. The story when the curtain opened, however, was simple. It was a story about love.

A beautiful young woman was adored by two men. She herself loved the handsome youth with the impossibly sad white face, but the burly cross-eyed villain with the orange-red face was determined to win her hand. The villain (I learned from the voice in my ear) had never lost a sumo wrestling match. So the youth with the sad white face and the wrestler with the orange-red face wrestled to decide who would marry the woman. They danced this, spinning slowly and not quite touching their hands. At last the youth with the sad white face won the match. But the cross-eyed villain explained in an evil aside to the audience that he would yet betray the lovers. Spotting a pair of Mandarin ducks in the lake, he threw his dagger and killed the male (a little wooden duck turned upside down, like a prop in a parking-lot carnival). The villain explained that if he could trick the youth into drinking the duck's blood, it would drive him mad. And he did so.

But the Mandarin duck is a symbol of marriage, of fidelity, and now, in some mystical way, the two young lovers began to swirl. They swirled until they became the ducks. They became, by magic, the souls of the ducks. They took to the air on bright wings. They had become transcendent, timeless. On the same ground where the sumo match was fought, the duck-souls attacked the wrestler. They danced this, darting and bending their backs. The ducks drove the cross-eyed villain to the ground, making him even more cross-eyed. Then the lovers' costumes turned inside out, revealing brilliant plumage, plumage like an illustration in a children's book, feathers as vivid as fire. Then they all froze in place and the curtain dropped.

The Reconstrcuted Castle

Yukio Mishima's novel *Runaway Horses* tells, in part, the story of a samurai rebellion. In 1868 the reign of the shoguns ended and power reverted back to the emperor of Japan or (because nothing is ever as simple as the official story) to a group of powerful men acting in his name. One of the consequences of this event, which is called the Meiji Restoration, was that the large samurai class that had governed Japan for hundreds of years was stripped of its power and dissolved.[12] Imperial edicts forced members of the former warrior caste to stop styling their hair in topknots, to stop carrying swords.

---

12. The twentieth-century Western idea of the samurai as an armored warrior, a kind of Japanese knight, is not particularly accurate. Some samurai were warriors, and samurai were licensed to carry swords. But by the nineteenth century the samurai class had evolved into a kind of hereditary government bureaucracy. Many were officials whose roles had nothing to do with war.

In 1876, a group of 200 reactionary ex-samurai called the League of the Divine Wind launched a surprise nighttime attack on the castle in the city of Kumamoto, on the southern island of Kyushu. As the barracks burned, they drove back the conscript soldiers of the Imperial Army, wounding hundreds and killing the wounded. Fires broke out everywhere. "Even his garments, drenched in enemy blood, glowed crimson in the flames," Mishima writes of one samurai. At last the soldiers regrouped and reached their guns and ammunition. The League, whose aim was to eradicate all traces of Westernization and return Japan to its feudal past, had chosen to fight with swords. With no firearms, the samurai were decimated. The leader of the attack, gravely wounded, called on a follower to cut off his head. Most of the survivors committed seppuku.

Old buildings in Japan are seldom really old. A country that builds with wood instead of stone runs the constant risk of losing its monuments to fire. Ancient shrines are really copies of ancient shrines. The Imperial Palace in Kyoto has been rebuilt eight times, and its current layout would make no sense to any emperor who lived there. The main keep of Kumamoto Castle, which burned to the ground in another samurai uprising in 1877, was reconstructed from concrete in 1960. The forms return again and again. They end violently, and they never end at all. To live as a Japanese, Koga said, is to live the history of Japan.

His building is there. Koga's, I mean. In Kumamoto. Just down the hill from the castle. I found him a few hundred yards from the scene of the battle in the book that made me think of him in the first place.

A trip on the Shinkansen train from Tokyo to Kumamoto takes about six hours. You change in Osaka. The train passes just below Mount Fuji at the start of the trip and stops near the end at Hiroshima, where it looks out on the baseball stadium. As it hurtles south, you pass into a misty country where hills drift toward you like ghost ships. If it's raining when you get out at Kumamoto Station, you can buy a clear plastic umbrella for ¥350 from a bucket in the station shop. If you have time and don't mind getting wet, you can walk into town along the river, the Shirakawa, which lies in a wide, ugly basin.

The castle is on a hill in the center of the city. There is a tiny parking lot at the base of the hill with a vending machine that sells Boss-brand hot coffee. The castle's fortifications merge with the hillside just behind the parking lot, a tortoiseshell of large, dark stones too steep to climb.

His building is down the hill. A five-minute walk, if that. Come around the slope and you will see the complex, a series of squat, identical gray blocks, each maybe eleven stories tall. Cars speed by on a busy street. A security guard in a gray jacket and white motorcycle helmet stands beside the gate, near some orange traffic cones. The complex's sign, printed in English on a black stone fence, is intersected at intervals by purple neon bars.

There is a bus stop very convenient to the building. There is a MaxValu just across the street.

·   ·   ·

So this is where I am. I am standing in the parking lot of the Max-Valu. It is four o'clock in the afternoon. The air is drizzly and cool. The cars that turn in to the lot are blunt, compact hatchbacks, little modern microvans in gold and pale blue and white. They are shaped like sumo wrestlers, I think, and it hits me that sumo is essentially a sport of refusing to die, refusing to be swept away, refusing to accept the insolidity of the dream. It was a street entertainment, really, until the early twentieth century. Then the samurai tradition burned down and had to be rebuilt.

And soon I will think about this while I watch Hakuho wrestle Kakuryu on the TV in my hotel room, on what is supposed to be the last match of the last day of the tournament: Hakuho missing his chance to seize Kakuryu's *mawashi* just as Kakuryu wins a two-handed grip on his. Kakuryu literally leaping forward with spasmodic sliding jumps, backing the *yokozuna* to the edge of the rice-bale circle, where Hakuho's knees and then his ankles will flex frantically, until he goes toppling, the greatest wrestler in the world, off the edge of the clay, twisting onto his stomach as he falls. When he gets to his feet, Hakuho will offer no reaction. A few minutes later, in the playoff match to break their identical 14–1 records, he will grapple Kakuryu in the middle of the ring and then drop his hips and lift Kakuryu halfway off the sand and force him backward. They will both fall out of the ring at the same moment, but Kakuryu's foot will touch first, giving Hakuho the Emperor's Cup and his twenty-eighth tournament championship. The *yobidashi* will sweep the marks away.[13] Hakuho will smile slightly, not a smile that is meant to be read.

But that will happen later. Now I am leaning on a railing in the parking lot of the MaxValu, thinking about endurance at four o'clock in the afternoon. I am looking across a busy street at the apartment complex of the man who beheaded Yukio Mishima and then lived a whole life afterward, lived another forty years. I think: *He is in there*. I think: *It is time to decide what to do*.

I get up and move toward the crosswalk. The wind is damp. It's January, so I don't see any butterflies. It is a cloudy day, so I do not see the moon.

---

13. In the Osaka tournament two months later, Kakuryu beat Hakuho, won the championship, and earned a promotion to *yokozuna*. Hakuho being Hakuho, however, he won the next three tournaments, including last month's fall *basho* in Tokyo. He now has thirty-one championships, one short of the record.

New York

"Even those who know little about art will find Jerry Saltz' work fascinating," wrote the judges who awarded his art criticism the National Magazine Award for Columns and Commentary. *"Knowledgeable yet unpretentious, Saltz wins the trust of the reader with writing that is itself painterly."* Formerly an art critic for the Village Voice, *Saltz joined* New York *in 2007. His work was also nominated for the Columns and Commentary award in 2011. Since Adam Moss was named editor in chief of* New York *in 2004, the title has established new standards for magazine making. Just this year,* New York *received ten Ellie nominations, including its fifth for Magazine of the Year, and won three awards.*

Jerry Saltz

Zombies on the Walls: Why Does So Much New Abstraction Look the Same? *and* Taking in Jeff Koons, Creator and Destroyer of Worlds *and* Post-Macho God: Matisse's Cut-Outs Are World-Historically Gorgeous

Zombies on the Walls: Why Does So Much New Abstraction Look the Same?

For the past 150 years, pretty consistently, art movements moved in thrilling but unmysterious ways. They'd build on the inventions of several extraordinary artists or constellations of artists, gain followings, become what we call a movement or a school, influence everything around them, and then become diluted as they were taken up by more and more derivative talents. Soon younger artists would rebel against them, and the movement would fade out. This happened with impressionism, postimpressionism, and Fauvism, and again with abstract expressionism after the 1950s. In every case, always, the most original work led the way.

Now something's gone terribly awry with that artistic morphology. An inversion has occurred. In today's greatly expanded art world and art market, artists making diluted art have the upper hand. A large swath of the art being made today is being driven by the market and specifically by not very sophisticated speculator-collectors who prey on their wealthy friends and their friends' wealthy friends, getting them to buy the same look-alike art.

The artists themselves are only part of the problem here. Many of them are acting in good faith, making what they want to make and then selling it. But at least some of them are complicit, catering to a new breed of hungry, high-yield risk-averse buyers, eager to be part of a rapidly widening niche industry. The ersatz art in which they deal fundamentally looks the way other art looks. It's colloquially been called modest abstraction, neo-modernism, MFA abstraction, and crapstraction. (The gendered variants are chickstraction and dickstraction.) Rhonda Lieberman gets to the point with "Art of the One Percent" and "aestheticized loot." I like dropcloth abstraction, and especially the term coined by the artist-critic Walter Robinson: zombie formalism.

Galleries everywhere are awash in these brand-name reductivist canvases, all more or less handsome, harmless, supposedly metacritical, and just "new" or "dangerous"-looking enough not to violate anyone's sense of what "new" or "dangerous" really is, all of it impersonal, mimicking a set of preapproved influences. (It's also a global presence: I saw scads of it in Berlin a few weeks back, and art fairs are inundated.) These artists are acting like industrious junior postmodernist worker bees, trying to crawl into the body of and imitate the good old days of abstraction, deploying visual signals of suprematism, color-field painting, minimalism, postminimalism, Italian arte povera, Japanese mono-ha, process art, modified action painting, all gesturing toward guys like Polke, Richter, Warhol, Wool, Prince, Kippenberger, Albert Oehlen, Wade Guyton, Rudolf Stingel, Sergej Jensen, and Michael Krebber. I've photographed hundreds of examples this year at galleries and art fairs.

This work is decorator-friendly, especially in a contemporary apartment or house. It feels "cerebral" and looks hip in ways that flatter collectors even as it offers no insight into anything at all. It's all done in haggard shades of pale, deployed in uninventive arrangements that ape digital media or something homespun or dilapidated. Replete with self-conscious comments on art, recycling, sustainability, appropriation, processes of abstraction, or nature, all this painting employs a similar vocabulary of smudges, stains, spray paint, flecks, spills, splotches, almost-monochromatic fields, silk-screening, or stenciling. Edge-to-edge, geometric, or biomorphic composition is de rigueur, as are irregular grids, lattice and moiré patterns, ovular shapes, and stripes, with maybe some collage. Many times, stretcher bars play a part. This is supposed to tell us, "See, I know I'm a painting—and I'm not glitzy like something from Takashi Murakami and Jeff Koons." Much of this product is just painters playing scales, doing finger exercises, without the wit or the rapport that makes music. Instead, it's visual Muzak, blending in.

Most zombie formalism arrives in a vertical format, tailor-made for instant digital distribution and viewing via JPEG on portable devices. It looks pretty much the same in person as it does on iPhone, iPad, Twitter, Tumblr, Pinterest, and Instagram. Collectors needn't see shows of this work since it offers so little visual or material resistance. It has little internal scale, and its graphic field is taken in at once. You see and get it fast, and then it doesn't change. There are no complex structural presences to assimilate, few surprises, and no unique visual iconographies or incongruities to come to terms with. It's frictionless, made for trade. Art as bitcoin.

Almost everyone who paints like this has come through art school. Thus the work harks back to the period these artists were taught to lionize, the supposedly purer days of the 1960s and 1970s, when their teachers' views were being formed. Both teachers and students zero in on this one specific period; then only on one type of art of this period; then only on certain artists. It's art-historical clear-cutting, aesthetic monoculture with no aesthetic biodiversity. This is not painting but semantic painterbation—what an unctuous auction catalogue, in reference to one artist's work, recently called "established postmodern praxis."

Apologists offer convoluted defenses, saying that certain practitioners differ from all the others. Lucien Smith uses fire extinguishers to make his little drips; Dan Colen uses M&Ms for his; Adam McEwen deploys chewing gum; Parker Ito paints fields of hazy colored dots. There are many artists who make art that looks printed but is handmade; others make it look handmade when it's printed. We're told that a painting is made by cutting up other paintings, or that it was left outdoors or in a polluted lake or sent through the mail, or that it came from Tahrir Square. We hear that the artist is "commenting on" commodity culture, climate change, social oppression, art history. One well-known curator tried recently to justify the splattered Julian Schnabel–Joe Bradley–Jean-Michel Basquiat manqué of Oscar Murillo—the hottest of all these artists—by connecting his tarp- or tentlike surfaces to the people living under makeshift canvas shelters in Murillo's native Colombia. Never mind that he was educated in England and largely grew up there. At twenty-eight, obviously talented, Murillo's still making his student work and could turn out to be great. Regardless, so many buyers and sellers are already so invested in him that everyone's trying to cover his or her position. In one day at Frieze last month, three major art dealers pulled me aside to say that, although they agreed that we're awash in crapstraction, their artist was "the real deal." I told each dealer what the other had said to me, and that each had named a different hot artist.

I'll admit that I don't hate all of this work. Frankly, I like some of it. The saddest part of this trend is that even better artists who paint this way are getting lost in the onslaught of copycat mediocrity and mechanical art. Going to galleries is becoming less like venturing into individual arks and more like going to chain stores where everything looks familiar. My guess is that, if and when money disappears from the art market again, the bottom will fall out of this genericism. Everyone will instantly stop making the sort of painting that was an answer to a question that no one remembers asking—and it will never be talked about again.

Taking in Jeff Koons, Creator and Destroyer of Worlds

It's all helixed into this: something fantastic, something disastrous. "Jeff Koons: A Retrospective" is upon us. One can't think of the last thirty years in art without thinking of Koons, a lot. I've witnessed this career from very close range. I have seen him transform himself into the Koons hologram we know now; him polishing sculptures late at night in galleries before and during his shows; not selling his work; almost going broke; charging less for a sculpture than it cost to produce. In a Madrid club in 1986, I watched him confront a skeptical critic while smashing himself in the face, repeating, "You don't get it, man. I'm a fucking genius." The fit passed when another critic who was also watching this, the brilliant Gary Indiana, said, "You are, Jeff." I agreed.

No, Koons is not "our Warhol," as so many claim. Warhol's complex aura changed everything, whereas Koons is cheery, centerless, more of a bland Mitt Romney Teletubby than a mysterious force of nature. But once upon a time, it was thrilling to live though the undeniable challenging newness and strangeness of his art, the novelty and luxury of watching money pour into the art world and focus on him, seeing Koons twist all this for art's purposes while providing respite from older, much more doctrinaire appropriation artists and conceptualists. It's hard to see it now, but he did break some ice. Watching Koons between 1985 and 1992 was like being on a roller coaster, beholding the ready-made crossed with greed, money, creepy beauty, and the ugliness of our culture. We witnessed this squirrelly celebrity as he was born out of a small East Village gallery. Everything about him was played out in public: the hype, the high prices, the collector love, the critical cringing, his Twinkie-like quotes, like "It's like I have God on my side or something," and the almost-career-killing spectacle he put up in 1991, the show of enormous photographic paintings of himself with waxed chest and having anal sex with his porn-star ex-wife, Ilona Staller. In part owing to Koons, art in general regained the power to show us what Wallace Stevens called "the possible nest in the invisible tree." Koons helped art reenter public discourse while also opening up the art world. A generation of artists and gallerists who had similar aspirations took the stage to excellent effect in the 1990s. That's when their world began to mutate into what it is today.

Which is what? The very environment he did so much to re-engineer, followed by the mad amplification of the luxury economy, has meant that Koons's art now seems to celebrate the ugliest parts of culture. The rich and greedy buy it because it lauds them for their greediness, their wealth, power, terrible taste, and bad values. Just as Koons was a positive emblem of an era when art was reengaging with the world beyond itself, he is now emblematic of one where only masters of the universe can play.

This isn't shooting the messenger. Few artists have ever exercised such precision targeting of an audience. Koons's ideas about his work—even if they have never made any sense to me (likening his art to a "sacred heart of Jesus")—are always stated up front. His notion of how to behave as an artist is crystal clear. I love the weird, sick, fascist undertones of that pose he struck, naked and lifting weights, for an Annie Leibovitz picture in this month's *Vanity Fair*. It's impossible to imagine any other artist doing this. Especially a male one.

Can we look at Koons at all with the ever-present knowledge of how the feeding-frenzied art market enables him? He and other superstars are able to employ huge teams of assistants to make high-production art that sells like crystal meth for obscene prices to megacollectors and museums with atria that need filling. Moreover, his retrospective arrives at a moment when museums themselves are at a tipping point, getting ever bigger and more obsessed with newness—often at the expense of their permanent collections. Most curatorial decisions today come off as predictable. Even a massive earnest undertaking like this will strike many as simply the ratification of the inevitable—or worse, an afterthought.

Which leaves one to wonder if there's any way a Koons show can enlighten or surprise, let alone shock. Before even seeing "A Retrospective," I knew that there are whole bodies of Koons's work I have never related to. I've loved a handful of paintings for looking like they've never been touched by living beings but have been made by scores, maybe hundreds, of hands, almost transcending human touch, for their mutilating of ambiguities. Most of the others, though, strike me as hyper-anal-retentive Pop collages peppered with cartoon creatures and vulvas. I don't like his work when it's all about technical prowess, shininess, cuteness, or replication of an everyday object or children's toy. Except for the giant *Balloon Dog* (oddly, only the red one) and a few of the other huge, shiny baubles for billionaires, I don't like much that he made between 1994 and 2007. Nor does much of the work from the "Statuary" series, from 1986, transcend its buzz of fun: These nifty, simple casts of everyday objects or works of art have density and surface, but little more. And I don't get much from the carved polychromed wood and porcelain sculptures of bears, Buster Keaton, and St. John the Baptist from the 1988 "Banality" series. They are all curio, empty idea, obviousness, control, and kitsch. The big exception from this series is the large porcelain Michael Jackson cradling his beloved pet monkey, Bubbles, in which both figures have painted white faces—a sculpture that should remain uncanny as long as the memory of this pop star lasts. Otherwise, though, this work never changes or displaces thought. (*String of Puppies* is riveting, too, even though it got Koons in trouble for supposedly stealing the image from a postcard. He lost the case, even though his work has no resemblance to the so-called stolen one. Absurd.)

The Whitney's show shocked me—by catching me completely off guard. Ingeniously organized by Scott Rothkopf to entirely bypass hysteria and spectacle, "A Retrospective" is as near to a great show of this colossally controlling artist as will be possible as long as Koons is alive. For one thing, it's well installed. Koons installs his shows like crowded showrooms, but the roughly 150 objects in "A Retrospective" all have space, pacing, placement. The show looks great. In Rothkopf, Koons has met his almost-equal obsessive, but without the artist's showboating. Haters will hate, but "A Retrospective" will allow anyone with an open mind to grasp why Koons is such a complicated, bizarre, thrilling, alien, annoying artist.

Koons has always worked in very distinct series, and the show is installed thus. This allows viewers to track his development, concerns, material hunger, peaks, plateaus, and valleys. Start your tour on the museum's second floor, and you'll instantly be confronted by two rows of vacuum cleaners stacked in acrylic vitrines, internally lit by exposed fluorescent lights. These are from

"The New," made beginning in 1980. The installation discourages walking around these aberrant things, but that doesn't diminish the work's undeniable optical power. It's hard to overstate how different this work was from everything else being made at the time. Anywhere. The works weren't—aren't—the snazzy cross-breedings of Donald Judd, Dan Flavin, Duchamp, and Warhol, or only about commodity culture or post-Pop. You're seeing Koons's ability to tease anthropomorphic meaning from everyday objects. These works have a totemic quality, like high-tech Neolithic stones or temple sentinels. The vitrines are space-age Egyptian sarcophagi and canopic jars for preserving these industrial-age machines for the afterlife. Breath, breathing, making things vividly visible, placing objects in suspended physical states, visual theatrics executed with meticulousness: These are ongoing concerns for this artist. The objects are visual anomalies, exuding hollowness. You look in, and nothing happens. Here is Koons's great creepy beauty.

Before you continue, I'd advise making a quick detour into the small gallery on your right, which contains work from the late 1970s and 1980. Almost every idea Koons has ever investigated is already here, played out in primitive inflatable flowers and bunnies set on plastic or mirrors, or toasters and teapots mounted on fluorescent lights. Then turn around and proceed through the vacuum cleaners to one of my favorite Koons works, *One Ball Total Equilibrium Tank (Spalding Dr. J 241 Series),* from 1985. A single orange basketball hovers miraculously in a vitrine filled with clear liquid. The thing looks less like art than a high-school science experiment or something from a magic museum. Here are Koons's obsessions with balance, entropy, and drop-dead honesty. Forget the trick—chemicals in the ball and water create this almost- impossible stasis—and consider instead Damien Hirst's enormous shark in a tank of formaldehyde. Unlike Koons, the Englishman employs clearly visible monofilament line to hang the shark in this state. That isn't "art"—it's a stage-prop device that produces gee-whiz. Whereas Koons is interested in the poly-centric mysteries of inside-ness, of objects in space, not surface effects. The ball is like some alien zygote hovering in a dormant state in embryonic fluid.

Rothkopf opens the third floor with a bang, a gallery with the 1986 "Statuary" series that centers on Koons's summa, *Rabbit*. The manifest presence of this oscillating object, originally ex-hibited in a 1986 four-person show at Sonnabend Gallery in Soho, took Koons into the very heart of hollowness—and made him. A highly polished stainless cast of an inflatable bunny with crinkly phallic ears holds a carrot, giving off the mien of a golden calf, an idol of the id, an icon for something not yet made, a kalei-doscopic looking-glass that creates cracks in meaning. We're psychically aware how Koons has captured his breath inside this and made it last forever. In all his attempts to end entropy, *Rab-bit* comes closest—even if it's doomed, like all things, to become Shelley's Ozymandias. The cacophony of clarity that is *Rabbit*'s reflective, undulating surface turns the world into parabolas of distortion. Rabbit is simultaneously a camera seeing you as you see yourself in its twisted topography. It's like an anamorphic mirror placed in the center of space that organizes the world around itself. It's a family tree of one, a shadow of doubt.

In this part of his career, Koons was ruling the roost. Then ev-erything fell apart on November 23, 1991, when "Made in Heaven" opened at Sonnabend Gallery. I remember that day, in front of the painting of Staller straddling and being penetrated by Koons, when I saw Jeff with the legendary gallerist Leo Castelli and noted the look of horror and awe on the dealer's face. Koons looked at me and said, "Jerry, don't you think that Ilona's asshole is the center of the universe?" The paintings appeared among marble self-portrait busts, polychrome sculptures of dogs and cherubs, small glass works depicting Koons getting a blow job or performing cunnilingus. The gallery was packed every day for a month. Few male artists in the history of art have shown themselves with an erection, let alone having sex. Koons had found a point in taste lower than pornography. Then the axe dropped. The village turned on him.

In an art world that said it wanted people to be free, at the exact moment everyone rallied to defend artists like Robert Mapplethorpe and Karen Finley for their forays into sexuality, Koons had gone too far. He became the pariah that many see him as today, a sort of American Taliban. Rosalind Krauss called him "repulsive"; Yve-Alain Bois went with "crude"; Benjamin Buchloh wrote that Koons is among the "neurasthenic victims of opportunistic assimilation" (whatever that means). The local art writer John Yau later sniffed that he boycotted a Koons public sculpture because "some things you shouldn't do." So pure; so tenured. Whatever. I still say it's thrilling to see this work in a museum—even if the objects are better than the paintings.

Since then, Koons has never been in a Whitney Biennial or Documenta. He's continually accused of cynicism. I think that only a cynic could see cynicism in this cosmically, freakishly sincere true believer: The forty-foot-high topiary sculpture of a West Highland terrier that Koons created the following year in Arolsen, Germany, isn't here, but another equally great topiary work, *Split Rocker*, now stands in front of Rockefeller Center. I'm still ruminating on this work, but I appreciate its disruption of scale, standing as it does like a squat monument to schizophrenia, the mysteries of childhood, and inner rites of passage.

I was certain the fourth floor would just be silliness, shininess, filled with flops and fatuous paintings. They're all here, yes. A big bronze Liberty Bell, a life-size granite gorilla, polychrome aluminum casts of lobsters and inflatable pool toys, and other similar works come off as glitzy doodads and gewgaws. Yet, and most shocking of all, the fourth floor of this show took my breath away. Off the elevator is a complete unknown, a work that took him twenty years to complete. *Play-Doh* (1994–2014) is a ten-foot-high multicolored polychromed aluminum hill. It makes its debut here. I don't know what to make of this imploded rainbow, except that I flashed on Koons as a modern mound builder, making sculpture that is instantly archaeological, mystical, able to mark a future burial of contemporary culture. (That the most recent piece in an artist's retrospective might be one of his/her best is beyond remarkable.) Then, in the last gallery on this floor, are three mirror-polished high-chromium-stainless-steel giant figures: the so-so sapphire *Metallic Venus* (2010–2012); the gigantic canary-colored remake of Bernini's *Pluto and Proserpina*; and my favorite, the tangerine *Balloon Venus (Orange)*—Koons's super-strange-sexy version of the Venus of Willendorf. All exist in a state of absolute-zero frozen liquidity. They are monstrosities brought to beautiful Frankenstein life.

Even the three plaster-and-glass-gazing-ball sculptures in the lobby gallery took on a new presence as I left the show. But it may all come to naught. We live in an art world of excess, hubris, turbocharged markets, overexposed artists, and the eventocracy, where art fairs are the new biennials. Shows like this cost millions of dollars to mount; once they're up, mass audiences will gawk at the "one of the world's most expensive living artists." It becomes a giant ad, and the spectacle of more of Koons's work up at auction awaits.

Today, he's the most reviled artist alive. A few days ago, I posted a photo of one of his paintings on Facebook, and hundreds of artists expressed strong antipathy toward him. It was akin to what de Kooning reportedly said to Warhol: "You're a killer of art, you're a killer of beauty . . . you're even a killer of laughter." We live in a starker, harder art world than we did before Koons. As perfectly executed as "A Retrospective" is, it's also a culmination, a last hurrah of this era—even as the era keeps going. It is the perfect final show for the Whitney's building. Artists in Koons's category no longer even belong to the art world. In fact, "A Retrospective" confirms that the art world doesn't belong to the art world anymore.

Post-Macho God: Matisse's Cut-Outs Are World-Historically Gorgeous

Nothing readied me for the visual thunder, physical profundity, and oceanic joy of "Henri Matisse: The Cut-Outs" at MoMA. In The Cut-Outs, Matisse found the artistic estuary he'd always been looking for, a way to concretize and make physical the painted flat space of his own early-twentieth-century invention, Fauvism—color used to describe form, its fatness, fullness, and where it's located in space, while being almost abstract, voluptuously colored, radically simplified, or elaborated. With The Cut-Outs, Matisse crosses a mystical bridge. One of the true inventors of modernism, he stands at the precipice and points to a way beyond it, to a pre-digitalized space, where pixels and separate segments of color and line form images, where painting seems to exist even where there is no paint and no canvas. With The Cut-Outs, Matisse goes beyond the romantic notion of the self-mythologizing agonized male genius. With The Cut-Outs, all we see is the work; only process is present; process and something as close to pure beauty in all of Western art.

Matisse made these works in a prolonged fever-dream that lasted from the early 1940s to the week he died in 1953, at the age of eighty-four. Combining drawing, painted paper cut with scissors and shears, and pinning and pasting this tactile pliant material to flat surfaces, Matisse collapsed boundaries between painting, sculpture, drawing, architecture, bas-relief, pattern, decoration, and art. This is Matisse locked in tight. The Cut-Outs are a new form of poetry that come at us like a flotilla of visionary barges on an imaginary Nile.

Two giant, mural-like works in the show's third gallery from 1946, *Oceania, the Sky* and *Oceania, the Sea* (both on loan from Paris for the first time ever), are just white paper on a wide expanse of raw canvas. Huge, minimal, monochromatic, and reduced to essentials, the works are so sensual, it's like we're looking at them with our kundalini. Flying fish fill empty skies, birds dive under invisible waters, surf splashes, seaweed and shells float along some primordial tide. Vantage points toggle from above the waters to below to inside this mystic sea. Continual perceptual shifts between micro- and macro-scales occur; pinholes and minute surface changes loom large; a pucker on paper takes on the presence of a sun spot; immense forms like the ocean feel intimate. I began to see winged sharks, protozoa, creatures from Pleistocene seas, things that move like eels. Skip The Cut-Outs at the peril of your deepest viewing pleasures and expanded capacities for appreciating great art. Book your timed tickets today; they're already selling out.

The first work in the first gallery, *Two Dancers*, rattled the walls of my perception. *Two Dancers* is a medium-size design for a stage curtain from 1937–38—I hadn't quite known Matisse was this far along in the process this early. Nearby images confirm that he was already experimenting with cutting and pasting paper as early as 1933. By 1937, he had already developed an intensely meticulous, canny practice—a process so simple, it's shocking no one had gone all-out with it in this way before. Look closely at *Dancers*. See the gouache-covered paper cut and pasted and mounted on board. Notice the inconsistencies in the color coating, brushstrokes, and barer spots. Multiple pinholes and tacks evince how each piece of paper was shifted in space until it fell into compositional place. An aesthetic photosynthesis is revealed. Paper ripples, indents, bends; cuts overlap, are smooth, jagged. Everything is abstract yet palpable. There's no illusion at all; every move is revealed; no tracks are covered or smoothed over. In just one work, we're immersed in a different notion of touch—cutting into paper as drawing, tacking as sculpture, surface and color as blocks of paint. Already present in *Dancer* are the phosphorescent colors, multiplying shapes, kaleidoscopic composition, incantational beauty, and camouflaged forms that will mutate into unforeseen objects that mark almost everything else here. Even though it's titled *Two Dancers*, I see a fabulous firebird rupture in the upper ultramarine waters of the picture.

Few artists reward prolonged scrutiny more than Matisse, and in scrutinizing him, a beautiful paradox arises: The Cut-Outs are some of the easiest great works to love in the history of Western art. Yet they contain some of the most complex spatial architectonics in all of art. Without any kind of shading, rendering, or cross-hatching, Matisse is layering space without illusionism; the eye is always savoring surface and different internal juxtapositions. In addition to the physicality of the surface, Matisse gets different-colored paper to conjure tiny changes in spatial depth. Shades of color on similar shapes might be reversed to make one shape come forward and the other go back. He gets lighter colors and larger forms to go back into space and darker colors and smaller shapes to come forward. This should not work according to our laws of perspective and color theories. New visual ordinances form. Whole careers have sprung in some part from The Cut-Outs, notably those of Robert Motherwell, Ellsworth Kelly, and Richard Tuttle. The Egyptian levels of optical clarity, blocky shapes, and opaque color have helped form contemporary artists as varied as Gary Hume, Wangechi Mutu, Huma Bhabha, and Joe Bradley. And I surmise this show, too, will exert a pull on artists everywhere, now and in the future.

Yet despite all this visual firepower and radical experimentation, many persist in dismissing Matisse as a painter interested only in prettiness and making art "a comfortable armchair." The unspoken charge is that "He's not as powerful as Picasso." Or macho. Just last month, an *Artforum* writer decried The Cut-Outs as "sensuous distraction." This has been a party line since 1908, when Gertrude Stein recorded that "the feeling between the Picassoites and the Matisse-ites became bitter." In 1925, "Picassoite" Jean Cocteau wrote that Matisse painting in the sun-drenched

South of France had "turned into one of Bonnard's kittens." This prejudice goes beyond the need for heroes and powerful male figures; it comes from the fear of art being too beautiful, girly, gay-looking, ornamental, or decorative and can be traced back to the proscriptions against pleasure, sensuality, and sex in Judeo-Christian tradition. Similar arguments were used against geniuses like Boucher and Fragonard and all of the Rococo, which was seen as too feminine and frilly to be taken seriously. Interestingly, these proscriptions never existed in Asia, Oceania, or Africa. It has never been explained why pure beauty, form, color, comfort, or even kittens are any less visceral than a picture of a bull with a naked lady being raped in the background. Part of what makes The Cut-Outs feel especially electric today is that few artists buy the old bogus arguments.

Plus, there is pain in them. Lots of pain. In fact, the kitty-cat Matisse said that before working, he wanted "to strangle someone," and that making art was like "slitting an abscess with a penknife." Nearly everything you're seeing was made while Matisse was confined to bed or in a wheelchair. Unable to walk, he chose colors for assistants to paint on paper, directed them to place shapes, and pointed at or drew on surfaces with a long stick. He'd already suffered a colostomy and pulmonary embolism. Knowing the end was near, suffering all day, he was unable to sleep for more than a few hours, sometimes waking up in cries of physical agony that could be heard a quarter-mile down the road.

The Cut-Outs are Matisse's long good-bye to painting—but not a bitter one. He never painted again after 1948, saying "Painting seems to be finished for me now." He saw that the four sides and semirigid surface of painting was holding him back; the processes of painting itself could not create the tangible real surface he longed for. In paintings, he said, "I can only go back over the same ground," while The Cut-Outs allowed him to "cross into a different dimension." The Cut-Outs, he noted, were "beyond me, beyond any subject or motif, beyond the studio . . . a cosmic space."

Which brings us back to Picasso. After looking over their shoulders at one another's work for decades, Matisse just went his own way. But Picasso knew a new "cosmic space" was in the offing. Accompanied by Francois Gilot, he visited the ailing Frenchman often. Gilot recorded seeing The Cut-Outs: "We were spellbound, in a state of suspended breathing." After one visit, Matisse wrote of Picasso, "He saw what he wanted to see. He will put it all to good use in time."

As for what we can see—our eyes can only stand so much, but gather your forces for the mind-bending extended crescendo to come. In the last four or five galleries are what I think of as the masterpieces in this show. The huge gaga dreamboats that alternatively have the majesty of Gericault's *Raft of the Medusa*, the marbleized flying power of Giotto's Scrovegni Chapel frescos, the shimmering lightness of being of the Blue Mosque, blues as blissful as those in Fra Angelico. Chinese fish mutate into heraldic underwater beings, a beautiful bathing nude is looked at from deep within a candy-colored canopy of palm fronds by a parakeet that must be the dying Matisse. A wraparound frieze of splashing bathers is part swimming pool, part Greek temple, and part Zen garden of delight. The enormous abstract *Snail* turns history painting into prehistory painting. Seeing all these visual facts beyond facts, we witness a mighty tree falling in art's forest. And we beguiled are transformed into things that move forward like eels, mouths forever agape in this Sea of Love.

Vogue

WINNER—MAGAZINE
OF THE YEAR

Vogue, *said the judges who chose it as the 2015 Magazine of the Year, "has proved that there is no limit to its hold as the absolute fashion and style authority"— further testament to the talent of Anna Wintour, the title's long-time editor in chief and a member of ASME's Hall of Fame. This piece, which profiles the model Kate Upton as it explores the growing importance of social media to fashion and its -istas, was published in the celebrated Kim Kardashian–Kanye West issue. The writer, Jonathan Van Meter, is a veteran magazine journalist whose work, including the definitive profile of Joan Rivers, was nominated for Ellies in 2010 and 2011.*

Jonathan Van Meter

Follow Me

Kate Upton Leads the Charge of Models Who've Gone Crazy for Social Media

Have you met Kate? Kate who? Upton! This is how it all begins, in Paris, way back in October (an eternity on Planet Fashion)—spring 2014 Chanel ready-to-wear, Grand Palais, ten a.m. The show has not yet begun, editors are staring into their smart phones, and I am standing *this close* to Kate Upton but have somehow failed to recognize her. To be fair, not only is she *not* in a bikini, but she is totally covered up! The honey-blonde hair is coiffed; the assets disappeared beneath a classic Chanel tweed jacket. The only thing missing is a briefcase. Trust me, you wouldn't have recognized her either.

Well, hello, lady. I'm the guy who's writing about you, I say. "Then I guess I shouldn't say anything too offensive," she says, four inches from my face, eyelashes aflutter. And that is when I notice: Her Miami-blue eyes are yellow at the center, like an egg yolk. "I have sunflowers in my eyes," she says in a this-old-thing voice. She stares for a second to see if I am in on the joke yet. "My favorite flowers are in my eyes! I can't help it!" and then lets out one of her loud giggle-honks.

In an instant, I get it: She is a modern-day Mae West–meets–Marilyn Monroe, the perfect larger-than-life avatar for our exhilarating (and vexing) social-media moment. Suddenly the lights dim and Upton, who is here as a front-row celebrity, scurries to her seat. Among the many peculiarities of this Instagram era is that one of the most famous models in the world almost never gets invited to walk the runway. When the music kicks up—bleep! bleep! bleep!—it's like the sound of a million tweets going off at once. Around the perimeter of the football-field-length room are send-ups of bloated, supersize modern art. The Jay Z song "Picasso Baby" booms from the speakers, and the procession begins. An editor sitting next to me leans over and says, "The art world is so horrifying right now—this is perfect." One girl after another, robots in identical wigs and makeup, marches past, all but indistinguishable from each other.

I know that Joan Smalls and Liu Wen, whom I will chase after for this story, are in there somewhere, but I cannot make them out in the clone parade. Is fashion, at least as it is presented on the runway, really still doing this? The no-personality, samey-samey thing? Is it any wonder so many models have taken to Twitter and Instagram and Facebook and Tumblr to establish themselves as actual humans, with quirks, style, and interests all their own? No one should be the least bit surprised that Upton, who looks nothing like most models, has stormed the gates. The hunger for personality—for stars—in the modeling world is just that great.

On the runway, the women are carrying Chanel bags covered with graffiti, which puts me in mind of a time before the ubiquity of cell phones—the eighties—when the way for a model to become super was by dating a famous man (rock star, handsome actor) or by showing up at every A-list party and misbehaving. Or she could just be sassy and louche and say outrageous things to writers, like *We don't wake up for less than $10,000 a day,* which, come to think of it, would have made the perfect tweet. Well under 140 characters, it was the quote heard round the world. Evangelista, Campbell, and Turlington were household names back then—and they did it all without posting a single selfie.

As the models make their laps, I grow distracted by the editor next to me, who is by now manipulating her phone with such intensity that she may as well be juggling chainsaws: Snap the look, type a description, post the look. *Snap, type, post!* Fully half of the faces in the front row are lit glow-stick blue from below by their iPads, which only heightens the sense that, like so many of us, the audience is torn between watching what's happening right in front of them and participating in it in real-time, via their interweb machines.

The next day I catch Marc Jacobs's spooky-great farewell to Louis Vuitton, where he reprises the carousel staging from his spring 2012 collection. (Back then, Kate Moss was the last model to dismount her horse and stalk the circular runway. Today, it is Kate Upton who rides round and round, the cherry at the center, although she never gets off.) Seeing the carousel again, this time in all black, reminds me of something Jacobs said to me back then: "This merry-go-round idea is such a simple thought. It's like, you get on it, it's a pleasure, and it just kind of never ends—as long as you're enjoying it."

The carousel—Planet Fashion—has been spinning at pretty much the same rate for as long as there have been Fashion Week schedules, which began in earnest by the 1930s. And while social media hasn't sped up the wheel, exactly, it has caused the ride to be a lot more hectic. *Snap, type, post!* Once upon a time, Linda and Naomi could at least have a moment backstage after a show (and a glass of champagne and a cigarette) and share in the designer's triumph: Genius! *May*-jah! Today, as Karlie Kloss puts it, models are required to be "almost like reporters," documenting the scene with their iPhones. "Everything gets posted right away," says Kloss, who has more than 700,000 followers on Instagram, where you might see her smiling in the Seahawks' end zone during the Super Bowl or posing with Diane von Furstenberg after the designer's fortieth-anniversary-of-the-wrap-dress show. "You can post what's happening before something even happens!" she adds.

"When I was live-tweeting the Victoria's Secret show, I think I gained 60,000 Instagram followers in a matter of hours. It's shocking, the power of having a presence on these platforms."

Having a presence on these platforms may now be de rigueur, but, like the rest of us, most fashion designers did not immediately grasp the way social media were going to change everything. Prabal Gurung was an exception: He was one of the first designers on Twitter, which really caught on shortly before his career began in 2009. Demi Moore, another early adopter of social media (thanks, no doubt, to her ex-husband the Twitter enthusiast Ashton Kutcher), wore one of Gurung's dresses to her perfume launch in Paris. "In a tweet she said, 'Wonderful young designer to look out for Prabal Gurung!'" he remembers. "I signed up just to say thank you, and I went from eighteen followers to 500. So I talked to my very small team. 'There's something here. We don't have the budget for marketing or PR, but I think this is at our disposal.'"

Four years later, when Gurung's fall 2013 digital ad campaign featuring Bridget Hall was teased on Instagram in advance of his runway show, it sent a ripple through the fashion world. "It was just one piece at a time," he says. "Twelve photos, and then finally we showed her face." Other blue-chip brands have been catching on. Oscar de la Renta also rolled out his fall 2013 campaign on Instagram, thanks largely to his senior vice president of global communications, Erika Bearman, a.k.a. @OscarPRGirl. "She started her Instagram account a long time ago," says Sara Wilson, who oversees fashion companies and public figures for both Instagram and Facebook. "She is the living, breathing embodiment of the Oscar lifestyle—but you also get this really amazing backstage view." As Burberry's Christopher Bailey, who's celebrated for, among other things, the clever social-media spin he's put on the classic English brand, points out, "Digital is part of the way we live, and it would be counterintuitive to pretend that it's not—to do one thing in real life, and then have a business that didn't reflect that behavior."

For John Demsey, the group president at Estée Lauder Companies, it was Lady Gaga who t-t-t-telephoned with the wake-up call. Thanks to Gaga tweeting to her fans, MAC's Viva Glam campaign raised $33 million for the company's AIDS charity. "It was unprecedented," Demsey says, which is why "today when we look to sign a modeling contract, it's a prerequisite that our models are on social media." Vicky Yang, who works for Elite, explains, "Brands are recognizing that models are the true middlemen between a young girl who might buy a bag and the brand itself. The models are communicating on social media: 'Oh, I have this bag, and it's cool.'"

Given the frenzy around the possibilities of social media, models, and branding, it should come as no surprise that Demsey sounds positively Donald Trump–like in his enthusiasm about some big . . . news: In July, Kate Upton will follow Katie Holmes as the face of Bobbi Brown, a mash-up that he sees as near-perfect brand-to-celebrity synergy. Brown herself has a huge social-media following, a persona that is "earthy and no-nonsense," says Demsey, and embraces "all shapes and sizes." Likewise, Upton "has capitalized on the medium like no one has ever done before," has a "big personality," and is not "überthin." He goes on, "She took a risk by putting herself out there in a fun, sexy way while always looking bombshell gorgeous and yet still somehow like the girl next door—we love the notion of Bobbi Brown and the Bombshell."

By the time I finally catch up with the Bombshell again, it's early December in Los Angeles. We meet at the Four Seasons in Beverly Hills and find a table in the lounge. It's freakishly cold outside, so once again, Upton is all covered up: black Viktor & Rolf jacket, big scarf, leggings, and buckle-y black riding boots.

You may not be able to tell from her Twitter feed, a high-low mix that occasionally veers dangerously close to soft-core, but social media's favorite pinup girl used to be a serious equestrian, competing at a national level on the paint-horse circuit. "It definitely relates to what I'm doing now," she says. "At a very young age I was traveling the country. It was our life. You have to be so dedicated. And that's exactly what I did with modeling. I had a goal, and it's a passion, and it's become my life."

Thanks in large part to her canny use of social media, Upton, twenty-one, is probably the closest thing that fashion has to a supermodel right now, and she's done it with her own distinct body type and in her own distinct way. Though she'd signed with Elite at fifteen and made a splash in *Sports Illustrated*, it wasn't—as everyone knows by now—until dippy videos appeared on YouTube of her doing the Dougie and the Cat Daddy that she truly became a sensation. ("A booby-star," as a friend of mine likes to say.) When I ask about her unusual route to the top of the fashion heap, she insists that it was not calculated. "I had no clue," she says. "I wasn't the target audience. I grew up in Florida, where you walk around in flip-flops and jean shorts. I didn't know the fashion world. It really happened in an organic way, wanting to do jobs that I loved."

Given her 1.26 million Twitter followers, I had assumed that Upton had been a kid who always had a phone in her hand. "Who would I call?" she says. "I was out at the barn every day. I barely watched TV. People think I am an expert on social media, but I am still trying to figure it out, too. How much do you want to put yourself out there?" She lets out a honk. "Well, I am *out* there. There's no turning back for me."

Upton sometimes worries that one of the things that made her a star—her refreshingly unfiltered voice on Twitter—is being compromised by the success that her social-media persona has brought her, especially now that she is about to become the face of a major cosmetics brand. "Now I overthink it. Like, 'Ugh, are people going to understand this joke?' Before, I had no filter because I had, like, a hundred followers."

From her self-deprecating humor to her game-for-anything spirit, Upton radiates an authenticity that has clearly struck a nerve. Despite the fact that she was raised in Florida and now has an apartment in New York, she has a very pronounced Midwestern aspect—that "nice" thing. Sure enough, her big extended family all now live in the same neighborhood in the same town in Michigan. Kate's uncle, Fred Upton, a Republican congressman, lives next door to her parents, Jeff and Shelley. It's hard not to think about all of that when one watches some of her more notorious YouTube videos, not least of all the banned Carl's Jr. ad in which she appears to be making love to an extra-spicy patty melt.

When I ask her point-blank how Jeff and Shelley feel about that stuff, she stammers for a bit. "Hold on, let me think," she says. "Well, they never sit there and say, 'Why did you do that?' Because I always talk about things with them before I take a job. I don't really ask for their *permission*." She laughs. "But I will say, 'I really want to do this.' And they understand. It's just part of my personality, and maybe some things I took too far, but . . . I like being sexy." Is there anything she won't do? "Yes, I definitely have limits. But I never like to say never because I feel like I'm setting myself up. There's a line between becoming, you know, a little cheap and cheesy versus being sexy. And I try to be very careful of that line."

Historically this hasn't been an easy thing to pull off. Earlier we had walked by the famously weird statue of Marilyn Monroe outside the hotel in which she is shown at the peak of her wily-airhead-bombshell glory. I bring it up to Upton and suggest that, as a culture, we are still puzzling over whether or not it was Monroe's volcanic sexuality that destroyed her—and if, as consumers of it, we were complicit. Upton leans in and looks me square in the eye: "Maybe it was drugs and alcohol that destroyed her. Maybe having no family support destroyed her." She leans back. "What I try to do—and it took me a little while to learn—is to only do things I really believe in so that it's more of a collaboration. That way, I'm not pretending to be someone I'm not. I'm not putting out this, Look at me! I'm sexy! and then feeling like a fake, which would lead to feeling depressed and empty inside."

Making a movie that trades off her smokin'-hot goofiness would certainly appear to be a sign that, having conquered media old and new, Upton is ready to take her career to the next level. She's had cameos in a couple of small films, but later this month, she will star in the Nick Cassavetes comedy *The Other Woman,* alongside Cameron Diaz and Leslie Mann, in which all three women discover they are being cheated on by the same man and plot revenge against him. When I saw the trailer in a packed theater over the holidays, the air got sucked out of the room as Upton, in a bikini, came bouncing down the beach in slow motion. It's not exactly the role of a lifetime—more Bo Derek in *10* than Cher in *Silkwood*—but it's a start. After all, Monroe had to take a lot of laughing-at-me-not-with-me dumb-blonde parts before she got to *Some Like It Hot.*

Let's admit it: Not everyone can be Kate Upton. So many of the girls who go into modeling are plucked from obscurity when they are very young, and most of them never make it anywhere near the top. As Elite's Vicky Yang put it to me, "I think she's an outlier. The group you are interviewing are 0.1 percent of the business." Having written about the supermodels in the early nineties and then having looked at the industry again in 2007, I have sometimes worried that modeling was turning into a glamorous form of indentured servitude, with so many nameless, faceless women from the Czech Republic or southern Brazil walking show after show, with no real role other than to look exactly the same: mannequins, the worst cliché of the business.

For models these days, social media offer the promise of a different kind of career: one that is more connected, more fulfilling, and, if they are lucky (and want it), lasts longer than three or four years. And while there's nothing surprising about the fact that this new crop feels comfortable on social media—they are part of the generation that's grown up on them—it still takes a certain mastery of the form (your own jargon, an irresistible personality) to really stand out. Even then, the top models might have only one million followers, as opposed to the tens of millions that actors and pop stars have.

In the wake of Kate Upton's social-media-fueled rise, models are grappling with exactly how to present themselves. "It's a really interesting opportunity for them," says Lara Cohen, Twitter's head of TV and film talent, "because it gives them a voice and makes them more three-dimensional. There's no shortage of pictures of Coco Rocha out there, but to know that she likes watching *New Girl* humanizes her."

Everyone agrees that Rocha was the first high-fashion model to embrace social media across every platform. And you can tell from one look at her constantly updated Tumblr or Instagram feed that she unequivocally loves it. So does Liu Wen. "It's just part of my life," she says. Liu is not only China's first supermodel, she is America's first Chinese supermodel—the first Chinese woman to walk the Victoria's Secret runway, the first to become a global face of Estée Lauder, and also, along with Kloss, the current face of Coach. With 6.8 million followers on Weibo (China's answer to Twitter), Liu also has, by far, the biggest social-media audience of any model—and, perhaps uncoincidentally, she seems to be the least conflicted about it: "Before, on Instagram, only a thousand people like me. Right now it's 280,000. I am very happy about that. Chinese people have a word. We say, Not *you* happy— you have to make *everyone* happy. To share the happy. That is very important."

Not every model finds it so simple. Perhaps the most in-demand model in the world, Joan Smalls is ranked number one on models.com but had only 170,000 Instagram followers when I met her in Paris at Hôtel Costes during Fashion Week. Many of her adoring fans have no idea that she is Puerto Rican, the daughter of an accountant and a social worker who grew up in rural Hatillo. Smalls, wearing a camouflage button-down, a black trucker's cap, supertight jeans, and a pair of boyish Céline shoes, tells me she is determined to change all of that with her presence on social media (and in fact her number of followers has since grown to more than 340,000). Like most of the models I spoke with, she resisted Twitter at first. "Some people are so good at it, and I kind of envy that," she says. "How are you so cheeky?"

It is true that Twitter is not for the faint of heart—or the less verbally inclined. "There's a reason why comedians and musicians have been the early adopters," says Cohen. "They're the ones who are most comfortable in front of an open microphone, which is basically what Twitter is." Putting yourself out there as a model now means exposing yourself to an unprecedented level of scrutiny and criticism. Many models no longer read the comments on their feeds. And can you blame them? Scroll through and see if you feel better about humanity. "You have to kind of detach from what people think of you," says Smalls, "because sometimes it's just too hurtful. Opinions are like belly buttons: Everybody has one."

Especially when it comes to in-your-face sexuality. If Upton is a potent reminder that Sex Still Sells, not every model feels entirely comfortable with that equation. "You see some models' profiles and what they post," says Smalls, "and it can be oversexualized to get more followers—and more jobs. I'm like, Now, was that necessary?" Thanks to social media, models have a whole new set of lines to draw. "I will do topless in pictures but not topless in video," says Smalls. She gestures toward her breasts and mentions the ever-popular GIF memes. "I do not want to see these in motion!" But video is now often part of the fashion picture, literally. As Stuart Vevers, who recently left Loewe to be executive creative director at Coach, explains, social media has allowed for "campaigns to be much more 360," he says. "It's important now to tell a story, whether it's with video or a hashtag or an Instagram post." Models are often the lead characters in these stories.

To tell their own stories, Instagram really has become the Twitter feed for those who prefer to say it with pictures. So whether it's Cara Delevingne showcasing her new grillz and posting fifteen-second videos of herself partying on New Year's Eve with Rihanna, Karlie Kloss and her boyfriend visiting shrines in Myanmar, or Joan Smalls relaxing with her mother in Puerto Rico, Instagram offers a glimpse of these models' peripatetic lives—and a hit of the voyeuristic thrill that is the strange pleasure of social media. "I follow all these girls," says Prabal Gurung, "and when you see them together backstage or at an after-party, it brings you back to that glamorous world of fashion."

There's no such thing as living in the moment anymore. Thanks to social media, every event, from the Super Bowl to the State of the Union, from the Olympics to your best friend's wedding, now happens in real time and "real" time. It certainly has completely transformed our experience of fashion. As Zac Posen says, "I think the big transition started almost a decade ago, with the realization that fashion had gone beyond the industry and had become fashion-tainment." Posen, of course, is a judge on *Project Runway*, a show whose success has served to point out that, surprisingly enough, untold millions are fascinated by how dresses are made—and how someone from Kalamazoo gets to Fashion Week.

Last fall, things felt palpably different at New York Fashion Week by virtue of the fact that a giant screen at the tents at Lincoln Center "surfaced beautiful Instagram images from across the city," says Instagram and Facebook's Wilson, who is part of a whole new cadre of tech-savvy fashion people who make the rounds during the shows interfacing with brands, bloggers, and models. "The idea was to bring what was happening inside the tents, these rarefied places of fashion, outside to the public and vice versa. It was like this giant beautiful feedback loop." The Instagram screen at Lincoln Center during Fashion Week this February was twenty-seven feet wide.

Along with lifting the curtain on fashion, social media have fundamentally altered its process. Jason Wu cast Christy Turlington in his last campaign after "getting to know her" on Instagram. They didn't actually meet in the flesh until the day of the shoot. "She's the kind of model I'm attracted to," he says, "women who have a story behind them. It brings something to the clothes." Designers are also responding to social media as a source of inspiration—Instamuse! "You see things that you wouldn't have been privy to before," Wu says. "It's like you get to flip through everyone's photo albums constantly." All of these midcareer designers are having to adapt, learning by necessity to work with the tools of this new era. "When I was younger, the only thing I went to were magazines," says Thakoon Panichgul. "I'd go through them and see these beautiful images from Bruce Weber or Avedon. But the way that I absorb information now is through Instagram. And that is sort of translating to the way that I'm designing. The clothes are a bit more reflective of that attitude of the street because of it."

There's no doubt that social media have opened fashion up to new influences—and influencers, as stylish people are now called. But do selfies sell clothes? So far, the answer seems to be, not so much. Last August, the social-media-news website Mashable posted a piece with the headline "Social Media Fails to Drive Sales for Fashion Brands. Now What?" Based on a study of nearly 250 "prestige" fashion brands over the last four years, the article revealed abysmal numbers: "Less than 0.25 percent of new customers have been acquired through Facebook and less than 0.01 percent from Twitter."

How to monetize fashion content on social media is a big topic these days at all the social-media platforms, where fashion represents no small percentage of their content. Of the more than

170 million blogs on Tumblr, for instance, posts tagged #fashion have generated 23.7 million notes in a single month. But so far, no one seems to have found an exact correlation between chatter and sales. As Twitter's Cohen tells me, there's a lot of talk around the halls about "what tweeting signifies in terms of 'intent to buy.'" Indeed, there are now tech companies like ShopSense and RewardStyle that are focusing all their code-writing know-how on figuring out how to turn tweets and likes into dollars and cents. Amber Venz created RewardStyle with her partner, Baxter Box. The nut they seem to have cracked is how to bring a "like" one step closer to a "buy" through an instantaneous e-mail of a product that has been liked. If the "liker" buys the product, the blogger or the magazine where it originally appeared gets a percentage of the sale. It's a big *if.*

Which also raises the question: Are models actually moving merchandise? "Interestingly enough, no," says Venz. "It's really the personal-style bloggers. And we're talking about a twenty-two-year-old girl from Utah who's excelling as far as driving revenue for the brands."

One of the many strange paradoxes that the collision of fashion and social media has created is the so-called democratization of something that has for so long been built on exclusivity. "It's kind of cool to be nice right now," says social-media-ist and *Lucky* editor in chief Eva Chen. "Look at Prabal Gurung and Alex Wang. Everyone feels like they can be part of their cool-girl clique. If you look at the brands that everyone's talking about—Warby Parker, Toms shoes—there's a sense of openness and transparency. It's the Obama generation."

When it comes to modeling, this new mood has left room not only for Kate Upton to begin to grab magazine covers and beauty contracts back from pop and movie stars but for other outliers to dare to dream as well: girls like Charlotte Free, a.k.a. "Tumblr girl," who has hot-pink hair; Soo Joo Park, a platinum-blonde Korean American who just hit 100,000 followers on Instagram;

and Kelly Mittendorf, who updates her Tumblr seemingly every fifteen minutes. "It's usually girls with a really striking look," says Chen. "You see pictures of them at Coachella; they answer questions on Tumblr. They're relatable. "

But even in this social-media-besotted world of ours, mystique still has value, doesn't it? If, when it comes to models, Kate Upton is the bodacious—and gravity-defying—Marilyn Monroe and Cara Delevingne is the let-it-all-hang-out Lena Dunham, Kate Moss is the never-let-'em-see-you-sweat Greta Garbo. She has not once tweeted or "liked" a single thing in her fabulous life, and yet she is, arguably, the most intriguing person modeling has ever known. "Kate is Kate," as one fashion person put it to me. "She can do whatever she wants." Like that pitch-perfect cover of *Playboy* that seemed to sell out on New York newsstands in one day. When I took my seat at Marc Jacobs's Louis Vuitton farewell show back in October, I picked up the requisite folder off my chair and flipped through the list of models and looks. Included among the sheaf of exquisite black stationery was a letter from Jacobs. Its theme: "the showgirl in all of us." Among the list of the thirty-four women who inspire him, Kate Moss was the only model who made the cut.

National Journal

FINALIST—PUBLIC
INTEREST

Described as "wrenching" and "thorough" by the National Magazine Award judges, "Jackie's Goodbye" is both Tiffany Stanley's personal account of caring for an aunt suffering from Alzheimer's disease and an indictment of our failure as a nation to provide assistance not only to the victims of the disease but also to those burdened with its emotional and financial costs. Stanley is the managing editor of Religion and Politics, the online journal of the John C. Danforth Center on Religion and Politics at Washington University in St. Louis. Founded in 1969, National Journal is published weekly by the Atlantic Media Company for a readership largely consisting of Washington policy makers.

Tiffany Stanley

Jackie's Goodbye

I became an Alzheimer's caregiver the week of my twenty-ninth birthday. It was August 2012, and I was standing at my kitchen counter in Washington when I got a call from a family friend telling me, "We have a problem." My father had been hospitalized with congestive heart failure. For seven years, he'd been the primary caregiver for his older sister, who had Alzheimer's disease. Without his oversight, she had followed his hospitalization with one of her own after collapsing in her bedroom from dehydration or low blood sugar or both. My sixty-six-year-old aunt was a widow with no children. My father was a divorced bachelor, and I was an only child. They were my responsibility.

I had thought I would drive the eight hours to my hometown in South Carolina to get my aunt, Jackie Belcoe, settled back at home, and perhaps hire a nurse to come help out during the day. But when I got there, I found a much graver situation than I had expected.

Tucked into her hospital bed at Lexington Medical Center, Jackie looked so frail and sick that it was heartbreaking. She had been a hairdresser for many years and once owned her own salon. She was the woman who taught me to wear lipstick, who never left the house without her mascara on and her blond bob perfectly styled. Now, her hair was matted and unkempt. She needed a bath and her teeth brushed.

In the emergency room, a nurse had cut the urine-soaked T-shirt off her body. When the paramedics found her, she told them she was nineteen and lived at home with her parents.

Though her parents were no longer alive, it was true that she lived in the house where she had grown up. I soon learned that conditions there were as deplorable as the state she was found in. Her bed and sheets were soiled, and dirty laundry had been left beside the washer. A trail of feces stained the carpet from the bed to the bathroom. It was clear that Jackie, like many late-stage dementia patients, had become incontinent—a fact that perhaps a caregiver who was also a brother was too ashamed to admit. Full trash bags were piled in the kitchen. Shards of broken cups were scattered on the floor. The mess had attracted pests, and mice and flies had invaded the brick ranch house.

I traced the chaos to my father's own declining health. That spring, after years with a weak heart, he took leave from work. He tried to stay upbeat and not worry me. I had stopped by to see them in recent months but kept my visit short. It was so hard, seeing Jackie the way she was. Now, I wondered, how had I missed that something was terribly wrong? Or had I just not wanted to see?

For years, I had been pressuring my dad to think about the long-term plan. What would we do if Jackie needed more support than we could provide at home? Should we decide on a facility where we could place her if the time came?

We had to consider a nursing home, I assumed. My hand had been forced. Naïvely, at first I didn't think about the money involved. It had been a relief when Jackie reached age sixty-five, with all its attendant public benefits. Surely, I thought, Medicare would cover the kind of care she needed.

"There is nothing medically wrong with her," the hospital social worker told me.

I was incredulous. "What do you mean nothing is wrong with her?" I implored. "Her brain is decaying. If she was left alone, she would die."

The social worker informed me that there was nothing wrong with Jackie that warranted a longer hospital stay or a transfer to a skilled nursing home. What she meant was that Jackie needed custodial care—help with eating, dressing, and bathing. She needed a watchful eye, the adult equivalent of day care. She did not need the assistance of a registered nurse or another medical professional who could administer IVs or monitor complicated equipment and treatments.

Medicare pays for hospital stays and short-term, skilled nursing care for older Americans. It does not cover the kind of custodial care Jackie required, and it generally does not pay for long-term stays in a nursing home or a dementia-care unit, a fact nearly 40 percent of Americans over forty don't fully realize, according to a poll from the Associated Press–NORC Center for Public Affairs Research. Medicaid, designed to provide health care to the poorest Americans, can pay for nursing-home residence and long-term care. However, in some states, such as South Carolina, it cannot be used to cover room and board in assisted living or an assisted-living facility's dementia-care unit—that is, the kinds of places that provide custodial care to those who don't qualify for nursing homes. Medicaid supports some at-home services, but only if states apply for waivers. (There is also a program in South Carolina and other states that can supplement payments to assisted-living facilities for Medicaid-eligible residents, but Jackie, like many other seniors, did not meet its stringent income and resource limits.)

Jackie did not qualify for Medicaid outright: Her assets and her monthly Social Security income of $1,223 disqualified her from South Carolina's basic 2012 Medicaid limits of $2,000 in resources and a monthly income of just over $900 (the limit is now $973). Given her needs, she could have possibly qualified for some in-home benefits—such as visits from a nursing aide—through the state's Medicaid programs, some of which have higher income thresholds. But it would have taken months to get through the paperwork, and even with some Medicaid supports, I knew she needed full-time caregiving, a role my father could no longer fulfill.

My dad fought me when I first suggested moving Jackie to an assisted-living facility. He didn't want to institutionalize her. He also didn't know how we were going to pay for it.

I soon learned what my father already knew: Brochure after brochure in his files showed glossy photos of luxury dementia-care units in our area with twenty-four-hour supervision, secured access to prevent patients from wandering, and life-enrichment programs for the memory-impaired. I called them. A family member toured many of them. Most cost between $4,000 and $6,000 a month out-of-pocket. My dad made just under $29,000 a year working as a welder in the maintenance department at the University of South Carolina. His house was on the brink of fore-closure. Years of health crises had left him and Jackie with very little savings. The annual cost of an assisted-living facility with dementia care was more than double what my father made annually and nearly four times Jackie's income. What I had assumed was procrastination or denial on my father's part was really paralysis.

Hospitals, though, do not like you to overstay your welcome, and Jackie had not been a model patient. More than once, she had gotten out of bed and wandered down the hall and into other patients' rooms. She got agitated, and the staff had to physically restrain her, wrapping her in a vest so she could no longer move. She grew so fitful that a doctor prescribed her a regimen of anti-anxiety drugs, hoping she would just go to sleep.

On the day Jackie was discharged, it was nearly impossible to wake her. The combination of medication and a new environment had made her sleeping patterns even more erratic than usual. She appeared lethargic to the point of being catatonic.

Soon, however, she became more aggresive. She gripped the sheets tighter each time I tried to remove them. When I finally had her sitting up, she didn't want to put on the pair of pants I had brought her. I lifted her hospital gown to put them on her myself. "Stop! Stop!" she yelled. "What are you doing?" In a flash of anger, she pulled her fist back to hit me. She relented when I grabbed her hand.

"What are you doing?" she kept repeating, as we fought over getting dressed. "*What are you doing?*"

The truth was I didn't know what I was doing. And I didn't know what we were going to do.

·　　　·　　　·

The first diagnosed Alzheimer's patient was a woman named Auguste Deter, who entered a German mental hospital in 1901, at the age of fifty-one, after her family could no longer care for her at home. Her memory and language skills were poor, she had not been sleeping, and she seemed delusional. "I have lost myself," she told Dr. Alois Alzheimer, the physician who examined her. Deter spent the next four and a half years institutionalized, as her mind and body functions deteriorated. She died in 1906, and afterward, when Alzheimer examined her brain tissue under a microscope, he spotted the atrophy, tangles, and plaques that still signify the disease.

Memory loss has been associated with aging for millennia, but it was not until after Dr. Alzheimer's discovery that scientists really began to wonder whether senility was an abnormal part of growing old. Until the twentieth century, life expectancy for Americans was relatively low by today's standards (around forty-seven years in 1900). But as more and more people lived into their seventies and eighties, to the years when dementia most often strikes, the disease became much more common. In 1974, Congress passed a law establishing the National Institute on Aging to deal with the burgeoning elderly population's needs. Within a decade of its launch, NIA had established ten Alzheimer's disease research centers. At the same time, there was a growing public awareness of the condition. President Reagan designated National Alzheimer's Disease Week in November 1982, only to reveal his own struggle with the illness a dozen years later.

Today, as the baby boomers age, Alzheimer's has reached epidemic proportions. More than 5 million Americans currently have the disease, with more than 400,000 new cases each year—numbers that are expected to at least double by 2050. While Alzheimer's is the most common cause of dementia, there are dozens of related disorders, including Parkinson's, dementia with Lewy bodies, vascular dementia, and fronto-temporal dementia.

The rhetoric around Alzheimer's advocacy in recent years has been focused on finding a cure. But the U.S. government spends less than $600 million annually on Alzheimer's research—compared with $3 billion for HIV/AIDS and more than $5 billion for cancer. And of the ten leading causes of death in the United States, Alzheimer's is the only one without a means to prevent or treat it. Although decades of research have yielded important discoveries, Alzheimer's largely remains a mystery. "Anybody who says we're getting close to a cure is lying," says Howard Gleckman, a senior fellow at the Urban Institute and an elder-care expert.

Lost too often in the discussion about a cure has been a much more basic, more immediate, and in many ways more important question: How can we better care for those who suffer from the disease? Dementia comes with staggering economic consequences, but it's not the drugs or medical interventions that have the biggest price tag; it's the care that dementia patients need. Last year, a landmark Rand study identified dementia as the most expensive American ailment. The study estimated that dementia care purchased in the marketplace—including nursing-home stays and Medicare expenditures—cost $109 billion in 2010, more than was spent on heart disease or cancer. "It's so costly because of the intensity of care that a demented person requires," Michael Hurd, who led the study, told me. Society spends up to $56,000 for each dementia case annually, and the price of dementia care nationwide increases to $215 billion per year when the value of informal care from relatives and volunteers is included.

Most of the care provided to Americans with dementia comes from unpaid family members. "Family caregivers really are the backbone of long-term care in this country," says John Schall of the Caregiver Action Network. A majority of dementia patients live and die at home—which saves taxpayers in the long run but forces caregivers to sacrifice work and wages. Caregiving can be a long, grueling task: Alzheimer's patients live, on average, eight to ten years after diagnosis, and they eventually need round-the-clock care. There are more than 15 million unpaid dementia caregivers in the United States, according to the Alzheimer's Association. Most of them are women, though a growing number are men; nearly 1 million are between the ages of eighteen and twenty-nine; some are seniors themselves, caring for a disabled spouse; and many are in their forties and fifties, still working, and sometimes caring for children and an aging parent. At the same time, family systems are changing, with fewer children born to help older adults, and more mobile populations, meaning families live hundreds of miles apart, severing the support networks that traditionally helped spread the burden of care.

"We have no rational policy to support caregivers," says Dr. Joanne Lynn, director of the Altarum Institute's Center for Elder Care and Advanced Illness. Public supports such as Medicare and Medicaid do not adequately cover the care dementia patients need at home. There are not appropriate Medicare reimbursements for a family member to meet with medical personnel about care plans and ongoing supports. State programs for relief services—such as respite care or adult day programs that allow family members to take a break—are sporadic. Meanwhile, the average cost of caring for a patient in a skilled nursing facility is more than $80,000 a year. As Dr. Bruce Chernof of the SCAN Foundation, which advocates for better care of older adults, puts it: "We need to move beyond saying family caregivers need to be 'supported,' and we need to begin to really think about what that means."

For years, the go-to public-policy stance has been to recommend that more people buy long-term-care insurance, but very few do. According to the Robert Wood Johnson Foundation, less than 8 percent of Americans have purchased long-term-care insurance policies that could be drawn on in the case of cognitive impairment. These policies can be expensive, and the price only goes up for individuals as they age and their health worsens. Moreover, the financial burden may be compounded when they move onto fixed incomes. In recent years, companies have been pulling out of the long-term-care market, finding the policies unsustainable. Some now only offer policies that provide three to five years of care—about half of the time a typical Alzheimer's patient needs support.

The Affordable Care Act tried to remedy the dearth of options. Enacted as part of the health-care legislation, the CLASS Act offered voluntary, public long-term-care insurance. But in 2011, the Obama administration canceled the program before it ever got started, saying that it was not financially feasible. "It was not structured in a way that would get enough participation among the healthy to support the populations that would be served," says Judy Feder, a public-policy professor at Georgetown University who researches long-term care.

Without an insurance safety net, the other option is for Americans to save enough for retirement to cover expenses out-of-pocket, but, again, very few do. The median amount that working-age American households have saved for retirement is $3,000, according to a National Institute on Retirement Security survey, and the Robert Wood Johnson Foundation reports that less than 10 percent of Americans save specifically for long-term care. "The full risk and caregiving burden and financial burden falls on the people who unpredictably get hit with long-term-care needs," Feder says. "The money and the service is coming from somewhere—

it's coming at enormous cost, personal as well as financial, for families."

These long-term-care costs were certainly a crucial factor for my family. In those first days in South Carolina, as I sifted through Jackie's financial records, I found a copy of her old long-term-care policy. A few years before, my dad had begun to fill out a claim, only to find that Jackie had recently canceled the policy. We still don't know why she stopped the plan—the cost, maybe? By the time we thought to ask, her mind was too far gone to know.

Without that slip of paper, our options were limited and the prices were high. So it seemed like a boon when we came across Lexington Gardens, an assisted-living facility two miles from my dad's house. He could visit her whenever he wanted. It was clean and bright and had the feel of an upscale apartment building. It did not have a dementia-care unit, but the staff assured me that many residents had dementia and the staff was experienced in caring for residents with memory impairment. At $2,350 a month, it was by far the most affordable option we found. A staffer even mentioned that the cost might go down after Jackie had settled in and needed less help. They put her in a private room on the second floor. At our request, they painted the walls a happy shade of yellow. Extended family helped me haul pieces of her furniture upstairs, and we hung artwork from her home, all meant to give the space some sense of familiarity.

On her first night in the new room, I hesitated to leave her. I couldn't decide whether to shut her door—what if she needed something? Who would hear her call? As I left, I kept the door open a crack and, walking away, hoped for the best.

·　　·　　·

There is a story told in my family about a defining moment in the lives of my father and aunt. My dad was eighteen, the last child living at home, when his mother collapsed in the den, likely from a stroke. He ran to her, and she died in his arms. Her death, while sudden, was not unexpected. From the time my father was born, his mother's body was riddled with diabetes, in an era when the disease meant a certain, steady decline. She suffered a series of debilitating strokes, and by the time he was twelve, she had gone blind. Jackie was the only girl in the family and became a surrogate mother. She cooked and she cleaned and she took care of her younger brother.

When I think of Jackie's relationship to my father, John, it is this: part sister, part mother. Their bond puts his eventual care of her into sharper focus. After he and my mother divorced, my father moved back to his family homestead, to the house next to Jackie's. My aunt decorated my room with a floral bedspread and matching curtains. I was nine at the time, and most of the weekends I spent with my dad were really spent next door at Jackie's house, on her screened-in back porch or sitting with her in the den. She was the keeper of our family stories, the one with all the photo albums and recipes. Every holiday and most Saturdays, I was there in her kitchen, eating at her table.

My aunt was married then, and had been since 1971. Her marriage to my Uncle Gerry was not a happy union. He was a stern man and often absent, away working shifts as a security guard and later as a police officer. Though they never divorced, he finally left while I was in college. He took their savings, opened a line of credit on their house, and moved to Costa Rica. I suspect now that, as her spouse, he saw what we would later learn: that her mind was failing and falling further into dementia. He came home once, but after seeing Jackie's diminished state, he told my father, "I'm not ever coming back again." He died in 2011 of a heart attack, leaving Jackie none of his assets. My father and I arranged through the embassy in San Jose to have his body cremated and his ashes scattered off the coast.

By then, it had been six years since I had first noticed something was wrong with Jackie. In 2005, on a trip to my college graduation, she forgot her insulin—a mistake so unlike her, given her mother's history. A relative had to drive her to a twenty-four-hour pharmacy in the middle of the night. Three months later, when my father was having another round of heart surgery, Jackie was with me in the waiting room, but she seemed confused and incapable of helping me make important decisions. Later that summer, she would call me at odd hours, in tears. She wasn't sleeping, she said. Soon she stopped calling me altogether.

That fall, after a battery of tests, we had an answer: dementia. Later, it was labeled probable early-onset Alzheimer's. A lawyer prepared a living will and power-of-attorney papers, which I signed along with my dad. I had always known I would take care of Jackie in her old age. But dementia at age fifty-nine was not what any of us had imagined.

In the initial stages of the disease, my dad and aunt managed quite well. He would walk the well-worn path between their yards, waking her in the morning, cooking her meals, and putting her to bed at night. His job was just a six-minute drive away from their homes, so he could drop by to check on her during the day. She wasn't a wanderer then, and she easily handed over the keys to her car.

My dad kept a burgundy binder for Jackie with hand-drawn charts, where she recorded her daily activities, keeping a log for doctors' visits. She could note which medicines she took at what hour, how she was sleeping and feeling. "I've just gotten up. Boy, do I feel rested," she wrote in May 2007. In the early years, she could busy herself around the house. "Thursday morning, worked in yard, pulling weeds and creating a new flower bed." But still she knew she wasn't well. "It's 3:16 a.m. and I'm still up," she wrote. "I must remember to set an alarm. . . . I've got to get back to a normal, day-and-night schedule."

My father became increasingly worried about their futures, and he fretted especially about money. The truth was that Jackie had always been a spender, not a saver. She was terrible with money and had only gotten worse with it as her Alzheimer's progressed, which is typical of those with the disease. Once, my dad came home to find a pile of boxes from a home-shopping network filled with expensive orders she didn't remember. She racked up more than $30,000 on her credit cards before he realized it. He closed the accounts and started working with the companies to pay off her debt. The disease seemed to age him alongside her.

Alzheimer's places a heavy toll on family caregivers. Their own health suffers. Dementia caregivers report higher rates of depression and stress than the general population. Some studies show they have an increased risk for heart disease and stroke as well as higher mortality rates. Their own use of medical services, including emergency-room visits and doctors' appointments, goes up, and their yearly health-care costs increase by nearly $5,000, according to research from the University of Pittsburgh and the National Alliance for Caregiving. "Caring for a person with dementia is particularly challenging, causing more severe negative health effects than other types of caregiving," reads an article in the *American Journal of Nursing.*

When I brought my father home from the hospital, his heart and kidneys were failing. There was talk of more surgery, but only to give him a better quality of life, not to cure him. His body was breaking down, and his own hold on life, we both knew, was tenuous.

.   .   .

After Jackie had lived at Lexington Gardens a few months, I wondered if I had made a mistake. The staff did not seem well trained to handle Alzheimer's after all. They would try to administer her medication in the early evening, even though this was the time of day she was most agitated—a very common syndrome in dementia patients, called sundowning. After an inspection from the state health department, Lexington Gardens informed me that they had been told to move Jackie from the second to the first floor because she couldn't walk well. She was getting frequent urinary tract infections. Staffers didn't seem to keep her on a schedule. Several times when I stopped by after eleven a.m. she was still in bed, not dressed or fed or toileted, which I felt only made her night outbursts more frequent.

I got calls from Lexington Gardens in the middle of the night and at the office. I had trouble sleeping. My job suffered. I barely wrote anything. I took days and weeks off. I answered work calls from the assisted-living parking lot. I tried to work in waiting rooms.

In some respects, it felt hard to complain about the facility, though. Many of the staffers were nursing aides and medication technicians making low wages—on average these jobs pay between eight and twelve dollars an hour—and they labored long hours doing the work I deemed too difficult.

Some incidents were more dangerous than others. One night, a staff member called to let me know that Jackie had walked out the back door unnoticed and wandered over to a nearby building. Another time, the facility notified me that Jackie had gone out the front door and was found sitting on the sidewalk. How long she was out there, I don't know. Lexington Gardens sits on a frontage road where cars speed past. Just over a grassy hill is a busy interstate. All I could think about was what would have happened if she had walked a little farther.

Jackie was also falling frequently. She was found in the kitchen on the floor; she was found repeatedly on the floor of her room, according to her medical records. Each time, the facility would send her unaccompanied to the emergency room to be examined. (This is not an unusual practice for some assisted-living facilities.) Jackie went to the ER eleven times in nine months for mostly routine examinations. My mother often became the proxy for her former sister-in-law when I wasn't in town. She would meet her at the hospital and keep me posted if I needed to catch the next flight home.

The hospital seemed like the least efficient place to treat Jackie. "You go in hospital emergency departments and they're filled with patients with dementia who are there because they fell, because they got bedsores or urinary tract infections, because they wandered," Gleckman explains. Says Carol Steinberg of the Alzheimer's Foundation of America: "Because there is a lack of medical-school training in dementia care, sometimes I think there's a lack of understanding on the part of the hospital staff. If you think of a typical ER—massive confusion, crowds of people—then think of an Alzheimer's patient who has confusion already and limited communication skills, that environment can be very frightening at a time when a person's health is at risk already."

Health-care providers often didn't know what to tell me. I couldn't seem to find an expert who could really help me navigate the system. "I don't want to blame my primary-care colleagues, but they haven't been trained," says Dr. Pierre Tariot, an internist and psychiatrist who runs the Banner Alzheimer's Institute. Only "a very small minority of patients with dementia" are treated appropriately for their diagnosis, he explains. Meanwhile, "more than half of dementia patients receive grossly inappropriate treatment that actually makes symptoms worse," including drugs to calm agitation that make patients more prone to falling.

After one of my aunt's more harrowing trips to the hospital, a kind emergency-room doctor wrote the name of a neurologist she trusted on a slip of paper. We had an appointment the following month, and that specialist was the closest I ever came to coordinating Jackie's care. But aside from removing extraneous drugs from Jackie's regimen, there wasn't much she could do. It was hard to tell where Jackie fit in the Alzheimer's staging process. Given her youth and her relatively good physical health, the neurologist advised me to prepare for the long haul: She could live with the disease another ten years.

To prepare financially for the impending decade, I began selling off Jackie's possessions. I hired an auction house to sell anything of value—her china, her furniture, her silver. A veteran bought her used car. A local jeweler offered cash for her gold bangles and necklaces. For a few months, checks began showing up, in amounts of $100 and $500 and $2,000. But the money was gone to the assisted-living facility almost as soon as it arrived.

By chance, I also discovered that there was one bright spot in Jackie's marriage to Gerry: Through him, she was entitled to monetary military benefits. Gerry had been a decorated Vietnam veteran and served in the army for more than twenty years, and Jackie should have been receiving a pension since his death. She was also due funds from the underused and little-known Aid and Attendance program, which supplements the pensions of veterans and their spouses to meet needs including custodial care. Both benefits together could have given Jackie an additional income of at least $2,500 per month. I filled out the paperwork with the Veterans Benefits Administration. We were told to sit tight. The process for Aid and Attendance can take up to nine months or more. So we waited.

.   .   .

My father died on a Saturday morning at the end of October 2012. I was underground on the New York City subway when I found out. A family member had been trying to reach me and couldn't because of the lack of cell service, so in her own state of shock she frantically texted, "911 911 please call johnny passed!"—which went through. At the next stop I rushed out of the station and up the stairs, exiting somewhere on the Upper West Side. I called my mom. I started crying hysterically. A man digging through a garbage can asked if I was OK. Two women saw me from the corner and rushed to my side. "My dad died," I told them. "My dad just died." They hailed me a taxi, which whisked me off to the airport and onto a flight to South Carolina.

The day my father died, he had gotten up and showered. He was freshly shaven when he was found. He had the radio on, and his lunch was cooking in the oven. Somewhere in the midst of this routine, he sat down on the sofa and closed his eyes and didn't wake up. In a way, it was the ending he had wanted. He died at home, not in a hospital. He was sixty-three.

I decided to tell Jackie the news, against the advice of some clinicians and on the advice of others. No one seemed in agreement on whether it would inflict undue pain, and I felt a compulsion to let her know, even if she didn't remember. Perhaps it was selfish; she was the only other person who would have mourned him like I did. When I told her, she said she couldn't believe it. She didn't cry. We sat in silence for a few minutes. Then she said, "My mother will be here soon." "She will?" I asked. "We're going to Georgia for a funeral," she said, and began to recall in barely coherent phrases the death of a relative who had passed some sixty years ago.

For months afterward, when we got into the car or were sitting at the doctor's office, Jackie would ask, "Where is Johnny? Have you seen Johnny?" And I would reply, in the calmest voice I could muster, "He's not here right now," as if at any moment he would walk through the door.

· · ·

In January 2013, Jackie's primary-care doctor, whom she saw through Lexington Gardens, spotted a sore on the bottom of her toe. Such lesions can be dangerous for the ill or elderly, especially those with a history of diabetes; they can lead to infection, gangrene, or possible amputation. Lexington Gardens had just hired a new resident-care director, who called to let me know that the situation was being handled. She said Jackie needed to see a wound-care specialist as soon as possible and that she would make the arrangements. But in late March, I learned that Jackie had not been to the specialist at all over the past two months.

In a meeting the next day with the executive director and another staffer, I was told the care director responsible for that lapse had left some weeks before for unrelated reasons. I also learned there were limits to how long a resident can stay in assisted living with a wound like Jackie's. Her foot was noticeably worse. She would now need home-health nurses to come in several times a week to change bandages, and she would need weekly appointments at a local wound-care center.

She would also need more-intensive care at the facility—including added assistance getting to and from meals, more frequent safety checks, and extra help with hygiene. For these tasks and others, we would need to pay Lexington Gardens a higher rate of $3,220 per month, which I signed off on. One of the most dedicated staffers took to keeping Jackie in the office with her, to make sure she didn't fall. I wanted the arrangement to work. I knew that transferring her to another facility with more supports would be twice the cost. I kept thinking if I could just get her veterans' benefits, if I could just sell her house, if I could just get my feet under me, we could find a better situation.

Ultimately, the decision wasn't mine to make. Three weeks after my meeting with the executive director, I received a letter in the mail from Lexington Gardens. "In review of Ms. Belcoe's incidents and her daily care needs, it appears that Ms. Belcoe has reached her maximum benefit from residing in an assisted living environment," the executive director wrote. "Ms. Belcoe has had some type of unsafe event every month consistently since August 2012. She remains an extremely high fall risk and her cognition has declined to the point where she has become a threat to herself."

Jackie was being kicked out. In hindsight, it was the responsible thing for Lexington Gardens to do: The home simply wasn't capable of taking care of a patient at her stage of dementia. The problem was that the types of homes which could provide this care all seemed out of our price range. Still, I had no choice: I had thirty days to find her a new place to live.

Assisted-living facilities are regulated by the states, unlike nursing homes, which are regulated by the federal government. Assisted living has become a booming industry over the last twenty years and provides many Americans with stopgap care that is less intensive than the skilled medical assistance provided by nursing homes. Despite the lower level of care, these facilities often house very ill people, including those with advanced dementia. (At least 42 percent of assisted-living residents have dementia, according to the Centers for Disease Control and Prevention.) The definition of what constitutes an assisted-living facility is murky, and the quality of care varies. These facilities can range from dementia care units for late-stage Alzheimer's patients to rooms that a health-care worker rents out of his or her private home. "Some of these places are absolute hellholes," Gleckman says. "They're frankly dangerous, and you need to have enough regulation to prevent that."

Lexington Gardens was part of Emeritus Senior Living, the largest chain of assisted-living facilities in the country. Two months after Jackie was discharged from Lexington Gardens, *ProPublica* and *Frontline* released an investigative series alleging a host of problems and neglect at Emeritus residences. Reporters A. C. Thompson and Jonathan Jones wrote that in 2004 a woman with Alzheimer's in a Texas Emeritus facility had wandered outside and frozen to death. At an Emeritus home in Georgia in 2009, a man with dementia died after swallowing dishwashing liquid that was supposed to be in a secured cabinet. In 2012, a woman in a Pennsylvania Emeritus facility died in a locked bathroom, and it took the staff thirty-six hours to notice. In some of the reported incidents, families had already brought lawsuits against

Emeritus; one case involved a woman who died after her wounds were not properly treated, resulting in a $22.9 million verdict against the company.

In an employee memo at the time (which *ProPublica* published), Emeritus characterized the series as an account of "some isolated and unfortunate incidents." The company encouraged staff members to post positive comments about Emeritus through social media "to offset the potential negative backlash created." Its public-relations team created a website called "Emeritus Facts" to counter twenty-nine negative claims in the report. Recently, company spokeswoman Kristin Puckett told me via e-mail, "The incidents that *Frontline/ProPublica* featured happened years ago and were exceptions to the quality care that takes place in our communities. We continue to make sure that our associates are well trained and our company has policies and procedures in place that promote quality care."

In February 2014, Thompson broke the news that Emeritus was under federal investigation for its billing and business practices. Puckett told me that the company is "cooperating fully with this ongoing investigation." (Lexington Gardens was not mentioned in the original *ProPublica/Frontline* series, or in Thompson's February report.) On July 31, 2014, Emeritus merged with another large company, Brookdale Senior Living. The merger means the new company—to be known as Brookdale Senior Living—will now care for more than 112,000 seniors in forty-six states.

Less than a year after we left Lexington Gardens, but before the merger with Brookdale, there was a complete turnover in the facility's management staff, except for maintenance, according to the home's online newsletter—a shift the company confirmed. Lexington Gardens did not comment for this article, referring questions to Brookdale, though it did send me a copy of Jackie's records. Due to privacy concerns, Brookdale would not comment on the specifics of Jackie's care.

Last year, I sent a letter to the South Carolina Department of Health and Environmental Control, detailing our family's experiences at the facility. An official called me after he received my note and said the department would be looking into the case. When I followed up recently, I received a letter from the department stating that inspectors made an unannounced visit to Lexington Gardens in June 2014. They found that the facility was in violation of state laws and rules "in the areas of enforcing regulations, record maintenance, resident care/services and resident physical examination." According to Puckett, "A plan of correction was submitted to the state within the required 15 days after receiving the citation." She added, "The community has implemented the corrective action and is awaiting the state's annual inspection."

·   ·   ·

Last Summer, I began reaching out to other families dealing with Alzheimer's. I wondered whether my family was alone in our struggles. What began as a personal endeavor quickly became a reporting project as I called people from local support groups, online networks, and regional chapters of the Alzheimer's Association. Most of the family caregivers I found were as lost as I was.

I talked to a seventy-five-year-old man taking care of his eighty-two-year-old wife with Alzheimer's. He had to keep working to support them, so he left her home during the day. "We've got a gas stove, and I've got to make sure the burners are off," he said. Nights had so far been calm, but she wandered sometimes. "A couple of neighbors have caught her down at the end of the street. What kind of locks do I have to put on the door?" he asked me.

In Northern Virginia, I sat at Sarah Harris's kitchen table and listened to her describe the night she decided to institutionalize her husband, who eventually died from Alzheimer's. "He didn't sleep at all. He walked around the house. He would walk and walk," she said. "It was probably the one time that I was fearful. I was afraid to go to sleep because I didn't know what he was going to do." He cycled through three different facilities during the last two years of his life. "The first home, I hate to say it, but they were abusing him." She said she found him soiled and tied down in restraints. The next assisted-living facility kicked him out because they were afraid he would injure another resident.

Joan Gershman, who lives in Florida, detailed her battles with Medicaid to get help for her husband in the months before he qualified for a nursing home. "You have to fight for every single thing. They deny, deny, deny. I asked for help at night because I couldn't shower and change him by myself. 'We'll give you three days a week.' When I said I needed more, they said, 'You have to put him in assisted living.' 'I can't afford assisted living.' They said, 'That's too bad.'"

In a support group I attended as a reporter, a woman about my age cried over putting her early-onset mother in a facility. For years, through college and after, she had shared an apartment with her mother so she could take care of her, but eventually she no longer could.

I began to think about bringing Jackie home to live with me. I was spending so much time with her and beginning to know her again and see the parts of her that had not disappeared. She was still funny. She tried to tell jokes. She liked riding in the car and eating ice cream. But the prospect of being her at-home caregiver was also terrifying. I would likely have to quit my job and leave behind my career, which I didn't want to do. It was also unclear how we would make ends meet if I did. Some states have programs that pay family caregivers out of Medicaid funds, but the District of Columbia, where I live, does not. In South Carolina, I could have been paid as a caregiver if I was related to Jackie but not if I was her legal guardian, which I was. Then there was the matter of duration. I could imagine taking care of Jackie for a year, maybe two—but ten?

MaryAnne Sterling's story resonated. An only child, she had been caring for her aging parents, both of whom developed dementia, since she was thirty. Last year, after she turned forty-seven, she and her husband realized they needed to start thinking about their own futures. She said, "We don't have children. We don't want to be a burden on anybody. If we don't begin saving earnestly for retirement, who's going to look after us?"

On an NBC broadcast with Maria Shriver, I heard Jim Crabtree's experience, which was particularly chilling. His wife was diagnosed with Alzheimer's at fifty-seven. "I was looking at ten years of care at six grand a month. Who has the money to do that?" he said to the camera. His ailing parents often looked after his wife while he was at work. In 2013, his eighty-four-year-old father, who also had dementia, shot Crabtree's wife and mother before killing himself. "It sounds like a horrible, violent end, but in actuality it was a euthanasia that my father did," Crabtree said. He called the triple murder-suicide a "mercy killing."

. . .

Jackie still did not qualify for skilled nursing care under Medicare, so her next assisted-living placement was at Agapé Senior in West Columbia, which was one of the few organizations in our area that had "continuum of care" options, meaning that Jackie could advance from assisted living to specialized dementia care, then through nursing care to hospice. She wouldn't have to change homes again.

Agapé assessed Jackie as eligible for its enhanced-care assisted-living facility, which was a step before their dementia care unit. We couldn't afford the monthly payments of $5,595, and we could barely afford the $3,500 application fee, but Agapé had a foundation, and we were admitted on scholarship. The deal was I had to pay them back any money borrowed from the foundation once I sold Jackie's house or her VA benefits came through. The day I moved her in, though, I found out that in order for her to be eligible for foundation support, I would need to spend the rest of the $5,000 I had set aside in a savings account. I quibbled with an administrator, because I still had outstanding hospital bills and pharmacy payments for her. "What are you worried about? Her credit?" he said. "Let me ask you this: What's the worst that can happen if you don't pay those bills?"

In a sense, he was right. He also knew we were in the process of "spending down," which meant we were using all of Jackie's assets until she qualified for Medicaid. She would likely be eligible once she had only $2,000 in resources left. In the best worst-case scenario, by the time we ran through her remaining assets, she would also be ill enough to be admitted to a skilled nursing home, where the government would be more likely to pick up the tab through Medicaid. Agapé's foundation might also aid us. Otherwise, I would have to fund the bulk of her care on my own—a daunting financial burden many caregivers face.

Medicaid pays for almost two-thirds of U.S. long-term-care costs. But not all nursing homes accept Medicaid, and there are waiting lists around the country for Medicaid in-home services and for spots in facilities that do accept the program's funds. Critics say the system is artificially impoverishing the middle class and overburdening itself. Judy Feder calls Medicaid "an enormously valuable safety net," but notes that "it's only available to you when you are either poor or have exhausted all your resources. It clearly doesn't protect people from financial catastrophe. It protects you only after catastrophe strikes."

Agapé at least proved to be a safer home for Jackie. It wasn't as nice-looking as Lexington Gardens—it was older with dank hallways—but the staff was better trained. They kept Jackie cleaner, in matching clothes and combed hair. There were fewer falls and almost no urinary tract infections or hospital visits. A nurse taught me how to safely help Jackie stand after she went to the bathroom. Most days, Jackie seemed happier and more alert.

But, of course, her Alzheimer's was still progressing. In August, she was found in another resident's room, hitting her in the head and screaming. She was moved to the Vista, Agapé's specialized dementia-care unit, which had individually locked rooms and increased supervision at $930 more a month.

Agapé helped me find a realtor. I sold Jackie's house to a man who flipped it. Last July, he proudly showed me around the house my grandfather built, which he had gutted to put in a sunroom and a breakfast nook. The money from the sale paid off Jackie's remaining debts, leaving her with around $38,000. At the rate we were going, that amount would cover six months of her care.

. . .

In many developed countries, long-term care for citizens with dementia is a priority. In Finland, access to long-term care is enshrined in the nation's equivalent of the Bill of Rights. The Netherlands has created a specialized dementia village for residents, to improve their quality of life. In 2001, France became the first European country to launch a national plan to deal with Alzheimer's and related dementias. The policy emphasizes improving dementia care, including educating families about services and residential-care options. In several other countries, it's a family's right to have ongoing help with coordinating care and services, according to Laura Gitlin, who directs the Johns Hopkins Center for Innovative Care in Aging. "With a diagnosis of dementia in our country," she says, "the family gets the diagnosis, and that's it."

There are pockets of the United States that are creating innovative solutions for Alzheimer's long-term care, but they vary enormously by state, and access to them is largely a matter of chance and geography. Minnesota ranks first on AARP's state rating system for long-term-care options. The state enacted an early, exemplary Alzheimer's plan in 2011 to increase detection, quality care, and awareness; Minnesota could save nearly $1 billion over the next fifteen years if the plan's enhanced supports for caregivers are fully applied across the state. New Jersey is one of several states that piloted a Medicaid program to allow people to hire an at-home personal aide, who can be a family member. Florida has fifteen Memory Disorder Clinics to diagnose conditions and coordinate care. There are experiments happening at universities and big research centers to find more cost-effective ways to provide better dementia care. And throughout the country, small group homes are popping up that provide more hands-on assistance for the same price as larger facilities.

In 2010, in an effort to better coordinate U.S. efforts, Congress unanimously passed the National Alzheimer's Project Act, which authorized the creation of a national action plan to combat the disease and related dementias. In 2012, the Obama administration released its National Plan to Address Alzheimer's Disease with the ambitious goal to "prevent and effectively treat Alzheimer's disease by 2025." The plan has many worthy initiatives; but while advocates applaud the heightened awareness it has brought to the issue, they also are quick to note it isn't a panacea. "The National Plan is a beginning, and that's all it is," Gitlin says. "It does not go far enough and it has to go further."

"It does focus too much on a cure," Gleckman says of the plan. Others agree. "We obviously need to find a cure to stop the pipeline of people getting this disease," says Steinberg, of the Alzheimer's Foundation of America. "But, in the meantime, there are still people coming down the pipeline who need care. Both sides of this disease need to be addressed." Says Gitlin, "The issue with the National Alzheimer's Project Act is striking the right balance between cure and care. We're all for the cure, but the emphasis on care must be, in terms of dollars and policy, equivalent, if not more so, than the cure."

Many care-oriented goals in the plan offer well-intentioned but superficial fixes. Short-term webinars by various government agencies for health-care workers and providers appear throughout as evidence of training people about dementia, and the document cites the distribution of instructional videos as proof of strengthening the direct-care workforce. "A series of videos, 'Hand in Hand,' were developed and disseminated to every nursing home in the country," the plan says. The dozens of strategies in its eighty-three pages range from convening Alzheimer's research summits to assessing family-caregiver needs, but the document—which has been updated yearly since its release—does not offer concrete steps to pay for its initiatives, leaving that up to government agencies. The plan is still a work in progress, and many of its action items are forthcoming, such as a survey on attitudes toward long-term care and a panel on advanced dementia. One vague and bureaucratic-sounding goal promises: "Through a learning collaborative process, a tool will be created to help states measure whether they are improving the dementia capability of their systems."

Even if Congress hoped to jump-start the search for an Alzheimer's cure with the plan, lawmakers have shirked fully funding that effort. The 2014 federal budget included an increase of $122 million for Alzheimer's research, the largest hike ever—but still a far cry from what's needed. Congress's own advisory group, put in place by NAPA, has recommended that the federal government spend $2 billion per year on research for Alzheimer's and related dementias over the next decade, which would put it on par with other major diseases. Federal Alzheimer's research funding is headed in the right direction, but it still does little to meet the ambitious goal that the administration's National Plan promised: an effective treatment by 2025.

Earlier this year, Robert Egge, who directed the study group that spurred the government to create a national plan, wrote in the journal *Health Affairs* that strides had been made nationally on Alzheimer's, but the disease was not yet "a top priority either for the administration or for Congress as a whole." Last November, Sens. Susan Collins and Amy Klobuchar introduced a reso-lution that would specify that treating and preventing Alzheim-er's by 2025 was "an urgent national priority." It hasn't come up for a vote.

Alzheimer's remains a winning topic for policy makers to ad-dress, even if tangible reforms are hard to find. That ethos was on display this past February, when the comedian Seth Rogen testified in front of a Senate subcommittee about his mother-in-law's early-onset Alzheimer's. The hearing was sparsely attended—not a rarity on Capitol Hill—and a few lawmakers left before Rogen's speech, in which he implored Congress to help ordinary people deal with the financial and emotional strain the disease causes. Afterward, Rogen tweeted, "Not sure why only two senators were at the hearing. Very symbolic of how the Gov-ernment views Alzheimer's. Seems to be a low priority."

The single biggest help to many families coping with demen-tia would be to reform the long-term-care market. According to an AP-NORC poll, 58 percent of Americans forty and older now favor a government-backed, long-term-care insurance plan simi-lar to Medicare. After the Affordable Care Act's version of long-term-care insurance was canceled, Congress formed a bipartisan commission to review next steps. From the start, there were prob-lems. The effort was understaffed, underfunded, and short on time to meet its deadline. Feder, one of the commission's mem-bers, calls the group "a consolation prize" that was tacked onto last year's fiscal-cliff legislation. The commission's final report ended with a stalemate on how to pay for long-term care. "It es-sentially avoided the biggest problem of all—the financing," Feder says. Some members believed private insurance would not be suf-ficient, but they couldn't decide what public supports were rea-sonable. "There are problems with the long-term-care products out there," Chernof, the commission's chair, told me, adding, "I think we need a new generation of planning tools for working families."

Feder argues that the only way to truly make long-term-care insurance affordable is to mandate it for everyone. That may be a quixotic goal in a divided Congress with fatigue over the Affordable Care Act's individual mandate. "It's not realistic to expect we're going to get a big, new government entitlement program to pay for this from the beginning to end. We saw what just happened with the Affordable Care Act and with the current political environment," Gleckman says. "But providing some sort of solution that includes a more attractive insurance program, perhaps with subsidies, and then a better Medicaid program—that is something that is possible."

In the end, it may be more about instituting commonsense reforms across the board nationally than about pushing for entitlement reform. What I thought I needed most as an Alzheimer's caregiver was relatively simple: access to an expert to help me navigate the system, whether that was a doctor, a nurse, or a social worker. And that is one simple recommendation that both the National Plan and the Commission on Long-Term Care have explored. My dad spent years caring for someone without any support, without knowing that she qualified for veterans' benefits and for some Medicaid services, or that there was adult day care and respite care that could have helped them both. By the time I found out these services were available, it was too late.

Gitlin notes that researchers like her are aware of more than fifty interventions—from training family members to home modifications to therapies for curbing behavioral issues—that are known to improve the lives and care of people with Alzheimer's and those who are looking after them. They're just not widely available or integrated into our health care system. "There is a lot we can do, and there is a lot we know we can do," Gitlin says. "But we just haven't done it because that's not where our priorities are from a societal and policy perspective."

.   .   .

Last October, Jackie woke up struggling to breathe. A facility staffer called me a little after six a.m. to let me know she was being taken to the hospital, just in case, just as a precaution. This time was different, though. It wasn't a false alarm.

When I arrived at the hospital, Jackie no longer recognized me. She was listless and nonresponsive. Worse yet, she had lost the ability to swallow, a sign of end-stage Alzheimer's. In her advance directives, Jackie had been clear that she did not want a feeding tube or artificial hydration as her Alzheimer's worsened. Typically the human body can live a month without food, a week without water. If Jackie could not swallow, she could not live for long.

She went into hospice care, and we moved to the skilled nursing side of Agapé. Even as she was dying, I struggled to get her the proper care. Hospice nurses circled us during the day, but at night, we were on our own with the regular nursing staff who typically managed rehabilitation services, not dementia patients or palliative care. It was a large and busy place, and nearly every shift I had to explain to a new face that Jackie had Alzheimer's and couldn't push a call button or tell them what she needed. I bonded with an experienced nurse who understood. When she was on night duty, I could go home. Otherwise, I spent two weeks sleeping in a recliner by Jackie's bed. I was with her when she died on a Tuesday morning.

It is only in looking back almost a year later that I can begin to grapple with the decisions I made and the ones I wish I had made instead. Now I think that if I had only known she had so little time left, I would have gone all out, broken the bank, and poured the rest of my savings into putting her up in the nicest facility I could find. Or, better yet, I would have rented us a two-bedroom apartment and an army of nursing aides so I could have kept her at home and been the one to wash her hair, sit with her at meals, and pick out her clothes. A year of that I could have managed, I sometimes think.

I often remember the days right before her death, when her delirium and discomfort were amplified, but she still had flashes of lucidity. One afternoon, as I bent over her hospital bed to turn her over, she looked up at me with what I took to be a glimmer of recognition. "I know I am cared for," she said. I only hope that was true.

The New Yorker

WINNER—ESSAYS AND
CRITICISM

"Roger Angell has written a brilliant account of life at the age of 93," said the judges who awarded "This Old Man" the National Magazine Award for Essays and Criticism. "His tone is unsentimental, almost brusque, as he recalls his past and anticipates his death. The result is a piece of tremendous honesty and poignancy." This was Angell's first Ellie, and his acceptance speech, posted on YouTube, helps to explain the respect his fellow magazine journalists feel for him. The New Yorker, *where Angell has been a contributor since 1944, is the most honored publication in the history of the National Magazine Awards. This year alone the magazine received six nominations and won three Ellies, including the award for General Excellence.*

Roger Angell

This Old Man

Check me out. The top two knuckles of my left hand look as if I'd been worked over by the KGB. No, it's more as if I'd been a catcher for the Hall of Fame pitcher Candy Cummings, the inventor of the curveball, who retired from the game in 1877. To put this another way, if I pointed that hand at you like a pistol and fired at your nose, the bullet would nail you in the left knee. Arthritis.

Now, still facing you, if I cover my left, or better, eye with one hand, what I see is a blurry encircling version of the ceiling and floor and walls or windows to our right and left but no sign of your face or head: nothing in the middle. But cheer up: if I reverse things and cover my right eye, there you are, back again. If I take my hand away and look at you with both eyes, the empty hole disappears and you're in 3-D, and actually looking pretty terrific today. Macular degeneration.

I'm ninety-three, and I'm feeling great. Well, pretty great, unless I've forgotten to take a couple of Tylenols in the past four or five hours, in which case I've begun to feel some jagged little pains shooting down my left forearm and into the base of the thumb. Shingles, in 1996, with resultant nerve damage.

Like many men and women my age, I get around with a couple of arterial stents that keep my heart chunking. I also sport a minute plastic seashell that clamps shut a congenital hole in my heart, discovered in my early eighties. The surgeon at Mass General who fixed up this PFO (a patent foramen ovale—I love to say it) was a Mexican-born character actor in beads and clogs, and a fervent admirer of Derek Jeter. Counting this procedure and the stents, plus a passing balloon angioplasty and two or three false alarms, I've become sort of a table potato, unalarmed by the X-ray cameras swooping eerily about just above my naked body in a darkened and icy operating room; there's also a little TV screen up there that presents my heart as a pendant ragbag attached to tacky ribbons of veins and arteries. But never mind. Nowadays, I pop a pink beta-blocker and a white statin at breakfast, along with several lesser pills, and head off to my human-wreckage gym, and it's been a couple of years since the last showing.

My left knee is thicker but shakier than my right. I messed it up playing football, eons ago, but can't remember what went wrong there more recently. I had a date to have the joint replaced by a famous knee man (he's listed in the Metropolitan Opera program as a major supporter) but changed course at the last moment, opting elsewhere for injections of synthetic frog hair or rooster combs or something, which magically took away the pain. I walk around with a cane now when outdoors—"Stop *brandishing!*" I hear my wife, Carol, admonishing—which gives me a nice little edge when hailing cabs.

The lower-middle sector of my spine twists and jogs like a Connecticut county road, thanks to a herniated disk seven or eight years ago. This has cost me two or three inches of height, transforming me from Gary Cooper to Geppetto. After days spent groaning on the floor, I received a blessed epidural, ending the ordeal. "You can sit up now," the doctor said, whisking off his shower cap. "Listen, do you know who Dominic Chianese is?"

"Isn't that Uncle Junior?" I said, confused. "You know—from *The Sopranos*?"

"Yes," he said. "He and I play in a mandolin quartet every Wednesday night at the Hotel Edison. Do you think you could help us get a listing in the front of *The New Yorker*?"

I've endured a few knocks but missed worse. I know how lucky I am and secretly tap wood, greet the day, and grab a sneaky pleasure from my survival at long odds. The pains and insults are bearable. My conversation may be full of holes and pauses, but I've learned to dispatch a private Apache scout ahead into the next sentence, the one coming up, to see if there are any vacant names or verbs in the landscape up there. If he sends back a warning, I'll pause meaningfully, duh, until something else comes to mind.

On the other hand, I've not yet forgotten Keats or Dick Cheney or what's waiting for me at the dry cleaner's today. As of right now, I'm not Christopher Hitchens or Tony Judt or Nora Ephron; I'm not dead and not yet mindless in a reliable upstate facility. Decline and disaster impend, but my thoughts don't linger there. It shouldn't surprise me if at this time next week I'm surrounded by family, gathered on short notice—they're sad and shocked but also a little pissed off to be here—to help decide, after what's happened, what's to be done with me now. It must be this hovering knowledge, that two-ton safe swaying on a frayed rope just over my head, that makes everyone so glad to see me again. "How great you're looking! Wow, tell me your secret!" they kindly cry when they happen upon me crossing the street or exiting a dinghy or departing an X-ray room while the little balloon over their heads reads, "Holy shit—he's still vertical!"

·   ·   ·

Let's move on. A smooth fox terrier of ours named Harry was full of surprises. Wildly sociable, like others of his breed, he grew a fraction more reserved in maturity and learned to cultivate a separate wagging acquaintance with each fresh visitor or old pal he came upon in the living room. If friends had come for dinner, he'd arise from an evening nap and leisurely tour the table in imitation of a three-star headwaiter: Everything OK here? Is there anything we could bring you? How was the crème brûlée? Terriers aren't water dogs, but Harry enjoyed kayaking in Maine, sitting like a figurehead between my knees for an hour or more and scoping out the passing cormorant or yachtsman. Back in the city, he established his personality and dashing good looks on the neighborhood to the extent that a local artist executed a striking head-on portrait in pointillist oils, based on a snapshot of him she'd sneaked in Central Park. Harry took his leave (another surprise) on a June afternoon three years ago, a few days after his eighth birthday. Alone in our fifth-floor apartment, as was usual during working hours, he became unhinged by a noisy thunderstorm and went out a front window left a quarter open on a muggy day. I knew him well and could summon up his feelings during the brief moments of that leap: the welcome coolness of rain on his muzzle and shoulders, the excitement of air and space around his outstretched body.

Here in my tenth decade, I can testify that the downside of great age is the room it provides for rotten news. Living long means enough already. When Harry died, Carol and I couldn't stop weeping; we sat in the bathroom with his retrieved body on a mat between us, the light-brown patches on his back and the near-black of his ears still darkened by the rain, and passed a Kleenex box back and forth between us. Not all the tears were for him. Two months earlier, a beautiful daughter of mine, my oldest child, had ended her life, and the oceanic force and mystery of that event had not left full space for tears. Now we could cry without reserve, weep together for Harry and Callie and ourselves. Harry cut us loose.

A few notes about age is my aim here, but a little more about loss is inevitable. "Most of the people my age is dead. You could look it up" was the way Casey Stengel put it. He was seventy-five at the time, and contemporary social scientists might prefer Casey's line delivered at eighty-five now, for accuracy, but the point remains. We geezers carry about a bulging directory of dead husbands or wives, children, parents, lovers, brothers and sisters, dentists and shrinks, office sidekicks, summer neighbors, classmates, and bosses, all once entirely familiar to us and seen as part of the safe landscape of the day. It's no wonder we're a bit bent. The surprise, for me, is that the accruing weight of these departures doesn't bury us and that even the pain of an almost unbearable loss gives way quite quickly to something more distant but still stubbornly gleaming. The dead have departed, but gestures and glances and tones of voice of theirs, even scraps of clothing—that pale-yellow Saks scarf—reappear unexpectedly, along with accompanying touches of sweetness or irritation.

Our dead are almost beyond counting, and we want to herd them along, pen them up somewhere in order to keep them straight. I like to think of mine as fellow voyagers crowded aboard the *Île de France* (the idea is swiped from *Outward Bound*). Here's my father, still handsome in his tuxedo, lighting a Lucky Strike. There's Ted Smith, about to name-drop his Gloucester home town again. Here comes Slim Aarons. Here's Esther Mae Counts, from fourth grade: hi, Esther Mae. There's Gardner—with Cecille Shawn, for some reason. Here's Ted Yates. Anna Hamburger. Colba F. Gucker, better known as Chief. Bob Ascheim. Victor Pritchett—and Dorothy. Henry Allen. Bart Giamatti. My elder old-maid cousin Jean Webster and her unexpected, late-arriving Brit husband, Capel Hanbury. Kitty Stableford. Dan Quisenberry. Nancy Field. Freddy Alexandre. I look around for others and at times can almost produce someone at will. Callie returns, via a phone call. "Dad?" It's her, all right, her voice affectionately rising at the end—"Da-ad?"—but sounding a bit impatient this time. She's in a hurry. And now Harold Eads. Toni Robin. Dick Salmon, his face bright red with laughter. Edith Oliver. Sue Dawson. Herb Mitgang. Coop. Tudie. Elwood Carter.

These names are best kept in mind rather than boxed and put away somewhere. Old letters are engrossing but feel historic in numbers, photo albums delightful but with a glum after-kick like a chocolate caramel. Home movies are killers: Zeke, a long-gone Lab, alive again, rushing from right to left with a tennis ball in his mouth; my sister Nancy, stunning at seventeen, smoking a lipstick-stained cigarette aboard *Astrid*, with the breeze stirring her tied-up brown hair; my mother laughing and ducking out of the picture again, waving her hands in front of her face in embarrassment—she's about thirty-five. Me sitting cross-legged under a Ping-Pong table, at eleven. Take us away.

My list of names is banal but astounding, and it's barely a fraction, the ones that slip into view in the first minute or two. Anyone over sixty knows this; my list is only longer. I don't go there often, but, once I start, the battalion of the dead is on duty, alertly waiting. Why do they sustain me so, cheer me up, remind me of life? I don't understand this. Why am I not endlessly grieving?

.   .   .

What I've come to count on is the white-coated attendant of memory, silently here again to deliver dabs from the laboratory dish of me. In the days before Carol died, twenty months ago, she lay semiconscious in bed at home, alternating periods of faint or imperceptible breathing with deep, shuddering catch-up breaths. Then, in a delicate gesture, she would run the pointed tip of her tongue lightly around the upper curve of her teeth. She repeated this pattern again and again. I've forgotten, perhaps mercifully, much of what happened in that last week and the weeks after, but this recurs.

Carol is around still, but less reliably. For almost a year, I would wake up from another late-afternoon mini-nap in the same living-room chair, and, in the instants before clarity, would sense her sitting in her own chair, just opposite. Not a ghost but a presence, alive as before and in the same instant gone again. This happened often, and I almost came to count on it, knowing that it wouldn't last. Then it stopped.

People my age and younger friends as well seem able to recall entire tapestries of childhood and swatches from their children's early lives as well: conversations, exact meals, birthday parties, illnesses, picnics, vacation B&Bs, trips to the ballet, the time when . . . I can't do this and it eats at me, but then, without announcement or connection, something turns up. I am walking on Ludlow Lane, in Snedens, with my two young daughters, years ago on a summer morning. I'm in my late thirties; they're about nine and six, and I'm complaining about the steep little stretch of road between us and our house, just up the hill. Maybe I'm getting old, I offer. Then I say that one day I'll be really old and they'll have to hold me up. I imitate an old man mumbling nonsense and start to walk with wobbly legs. Callie and Alice scream with laughter and hold me up, one on each side. When I stop, they ask for more, and we do this over and over.

·   ·   ·

I'm leaving out a lot, I see. My work— I'm still working, or sort of. Reading. The collapsing, grossly insistent world. Stuff I get excited about or depressed about all the time. Dailiness—but how can I explain this one? Perhaps with a blog recently posted on Facebook by a woman I know who lives in Australia. "Good Lord, we've run out of nutmeg!" it began. "How in the world did that ever happen?" Dozens of days are like that with me lately.

Intimates and my family—mine not very near me now but always on call, always with me. My children Alice and John Henry and my daughter-in-law Alice—yes, another one—and my granddaughters Laura and Lily and Clara, who together and separately were as steely and resplendent as a company of marines on the day we buried Carol. And on other days and in other ways as well. Laura, for example, who will appear almost overnight, on demand, to drive me and my dog and my stuff five hundred miles Down East then does it again, backward, later in the summer. Hours of talk and sleep (mine, not hers) and renewal—the abandoned mills at Lawrence, Mass.; Cat Mousam Road; the Narramissic River still there—plus a couple of nights together, with the summer candles again.

Friends in great numbers now, taking me to dinner or cooking in for me. (One afternoon, I found a freshly roasted chicken sitting outside my front door; two hours later, another one appeared in the same spot.) Friends inviting me to the opera or to Fairway on Sunday morning or to dine with their kids at the East Side Deli or to a wedding at the Rockbound Chapel or bringing in ice cream to share at my place while we catch another Yankees game. They saved my life. In the first summer after Carol had gone, a man I'd known slightly and pleasantly for decades listened while I talked about my changed routines and my doctors and dog walkers and the magazine. I paused for a moment, and he said, "Plus you have us."

Another message—also brief, also breathtaking—came on an earlier afternoon at my longtime therapist's, at a time when I felt I'd lost almost everything. "I don't know how I'm going to get through this," I said at last.

A silence, then: "Neither do I. But you will."

I am a world-class complainer but find palpable joy arriving with my evening Dewar's, from Robinson Cano between pitches, from the first pages once again of *Appointment in Samarra* or the last lines of the Elizabeth Bishop poem called "Poem." From the briefest strains of Handel or Roy Orbison, or Dennis Brain playing the early bars of his stunning Mozart horn concertos. (This Angel recording may have been one of the first things Carol and I acquired just after our marriage, and I hear it playing on a sunny Saturday morning in our Ninety-fourth Street walkup.) Also the recalled faces and then the names of Jean Dixon or Roscoe Karns or Porter Hall or Brad Dourif in another Netflix rerun. Chloë Sevigny in *Trees Lounge*. Gail Collins on a good day. Family ice-skating up near Harlem in the 1980s, with the Park employees, high on youth or weed, looping past us backward to show their smiles.

Recent and not so recent surveys (including the six-decades-long Grant Study of the lives of some 1940s Harvard graduates) confirm that a majority of us people over seventy-five keep surprising ourselves with happiness. Put me on that list. Our children are adults now and mostly gone off, and let's hope full of their own lives. We've outgrown our ambitions. If our wives or husbands are still with us, we sense a trickle of contentment flowing from the reliable springs of routine, affection in long silences, calm within the light boredom of well-worn friends, retold stories, and mossy opinions. Also the distant whoosh of a surfaced porpoise outside our night windows.

We elders—what kind of a handle is this, anyway, halfway between a tree and an eel?—we elders have learned a thing or two, including invisibility. Here I am in a conversation with some trusty friends—old friends but actually not all that old: they're in their sixties—and we're finishing the wine and in serious converse about global warming in Nyack or Virginia Woolf the cross-dresser. There's a pause, and I chime in with a couple of sentences. The others look at me politely, then resume the talk exactly at the point where they've just left it. What? Hello? Didn't I just say something? Have I left the room? Have I experienced what neurologists call a TIA—a transient ischemic attack? I didn't expect to take over the chat but did await a word or two of response. Not tonight, though. (Women I know say that this began to happen to them when they passed fifty.) When I mention the phenomenon to anyone around my age, I get back nods and smiles. Yes, we're invisible. Honored, respected, even loved, but not quite worth listening to anymore. You've had your turn, Pops; now it's ours.

I've been asking myself why I don't think about my approaching visitor, death. He was often on my mind thirty or forty years ago, I believe, though more of a stranger. Death terrified me then because I had so many engagements. The enforced opposite—no dinner dates or coming attractions, no urgent business, no fun, no calls, no errands, no returned words or touches—left a blank that I could not light or furnish: a condition I recognized from childhood bad dreams and sudden awakenings. Well, not yet, not soon, or probably not, I would console myself, and that welcome but then tediously repeated postponement felt in time less like a threat than like a family obligation—tea with Aunt Molly in Montclair, someday soon but not now. Death, meanwhile, was constantly onstage or changing costume for his next engagement—as Bergman's thick-faced chess player; as the medieval night-rider in a hoodie; as Woody Allen's awkward visitor half-falling into the room as he enters through the window; as W. C. Fields's man in the bright nightgown—and in my mind had gone from specter to a waiting second-level celebrity on the Letterman show. Or almost. Some people I knew seemed to have lost all fear when dying and awaited the end with a certain impatience. "I'm tired of lying here," said one. "Why is this taking so long?" asked another. Death will get it on with me eventually and stay much too long, and though I'm in no hurry about the meeting, I feel I know him almost too well by now.

A weariness about death exists in me and in us all in another way, as well, though we scarcely notice it. We have become tireless voyeurs of death: he is on the morning news and the evening news and on the breaking, middle-of-the-day news as well—not the celebrity death, I mean, but the everyone-else death. A roadside-accident figure, covered with a sheet. A dead family, removed from a ramshackle faraway building pocked and torn by bullets.

The transportation dead. The dead in floods and hurricanes and tsunamis, in numbers called "tolls." The military dead, presented in silence on your home screen, looking youthful and well combed. The enemy war dead or rediscovered war dead, in higher figures. Appalling and dulling totals not just from this year's war but from the ones before that and the ones way back that some of us still around may have also attended. All the dead from wars and natural events and school shootings and street crimes and domestic crimes that each of us has once again escaped and felt terrible about and plans to go and leave wreaths or paper flowers at the site of. There's never anything new about death, to be sure, except its improved publicity. At second hand, we have become death's expert witnesses; we know more about death than morticians, feel as much at home with it as those poor bygone schlunks trying to survive a continent-ravaging, low-digit-century epidemic. Death sucks but, enh—click the channel.

$$\bullet \qquad \bullet \qquad \bullet$$

I get along. Now and then it comes to me that I appear to have more energy and hope than some of my coevals, but I take no credit for this. I don't belong to a book club or a bridge club; I'm not taking up Mandarin or practicing the viola. In a sporadic effort to keep my brain from moldering, I've begun to memorize shorter poems—by Auden, Donne, Ogden Nash, and more—which I recite to myself some nights while walking my dog, Harry's successor fox terrier, Andy. I've also become a blogger and enjoy the ease and freedom of the form: it's a bit like making a paper airplane and then watching it take wing below your window. But shouldn't I have something more scholarly or complex than this put away by now—late paragraphs of accomplishments, good works, some weightier op. cit.'s? I'm afraid not. The thoughts of age are short, short thoughts. I don't read Scripture and cling to no life precepts, except perhaps to Walter Cronkite's rules for old men, which he did not deliver over the air: Never trust a fart. Never pass up a drink. Never ignore an erection.

I count on jokes, even jokes about death.

> TEACHER: Good morning, class. This is the first day of school, and we're going to introduce ourselves. I'll call on you, one by one, and you can tell us your name and maybe what your dad or your mom does for a living. You, please, over at this end.
>
> SMALL BOY: My name is Irving and my dad is a mechanic.
>
> TEACHER: A mechanic! Thank you, Irving. Next?
>
> SMALL GIRL: My name is Emma and my mom is a lawyer.
>
> TEACHER: How nice for you, Emma! Next?
>
> SECOND SMALL BOY: My name is Luke and my dad is dead.
>
> TEACHER: Oh, Luke, how sad for you. We're all very sorry about that, aren't we, class? Luke, do you think you could tell us what Dad did before he died?
>
> LUKE (seizes his throat): He went *"N'gungghhh!"*

Not bad—I'm told that fourth graders really go for this one. Let's try another.

A man and his wife tried and tried to have a baby but without success. Years went by and they went on trying, but no luck. They liked each other, so the work was always a pleasure, but they grew a bit sad along the way. Finally, she got pregnant, was very careful, and gave birth to a beautiful eight-pound-two-ounce baby boy. The couple were beside themselves with happiness. At the hospital that night, she told her husband to stop by the local newspaper and arrange for a birth announcement, to tell all their friends the good news. First thing next morning, she asked if he'd done the errand.

"Yes, I did," he said, "but I had no idea those little notices in the paper were so expensive."

"Expensive?" she said. "How much was it?"

"It was eight hundred and thirty-seven dollars. I have the receipt."

"Eight hundred and thirty-seven dollars!" she cried. "But that's impossible. You must have made some mistake. Tell me exactly what happened."

"There was a young lady behind a counter at the paper, who gave me the form to fill out," he said. "I put in your name and my name and little Teddy's name and weight, and when we'd be home again and, you know, ready to see friends. I handed it back to her and she counted up the words and said, 'How many insertions?' I said twice a week for fourteen years, and she gave me the bill. OK?"

I heard this tale more than fifty years ago, when my first wife, Evelyn, and I were invited to tea by a rather elegant older couple who were new to our little Rockland County community. They were in their seventies, at least, and very welcoming, and it was just the four of us. We barely knew them, and I was surprised when he turned and asked her to tell us the joke about the couple trying to have a baby. "Oh, no," she said, "they wouldn't want to hear that."

"Oh, come on, dear—they'll love it," he said, smiling at her. I groaned inwardly and was preparing a forced smile while she started off shyly, but then, of course, the four of us fell over laughing together.

That night, Evelyn said, "Did you see Keith's face while Edie was telling that story? Did you see hers? Do you think it's possible that they're still—you know, still doing it?"

"Yes, I did—yes, I do," I said. "I was thinking exactly the same thing. They're amazing."

This was news back then but probably shouldn't be by now. I remember a passage I came upon years later, in an op-ed piece in the *Times*, written by a man who'd just lost his wife. "We slept naked in the same bed for forty years," it went. There was also my splendid colleague Bob Bingham, dying in his late fifties, who was asked by a friend what he'd missed or would do differently if given the chance. He thought for an instant, and said, "More venery."

More venery. More love; more closeness; more sex and romance. Bring it back, no matter what, no matter how old we are. This fervent cry of ours has been certified by Simone de Beauvoir and Alice Munro and Laurence Olivier and any number of remarried or recoupled ancient classmates of ours. Laurence Olivier? I'm thinking of what he says somewhere in an interview: "Inside, we're all seventeen, with red lips."

This is a dodgy subject, coming as it does here from a recent widower, and I will risk a further breach of code and add that this was something that Carol and I now and then idly discussed. We didn't quite see the point of memorial fidelity. In our view, the departed spouse—we always thought it would be me—wouldn't be around anymore but knew or had known that he or she was loved forever. Please go ahead, then, sweetheart—don't miss a moment. Carol said this last: "If you haven't found someone else by a year after I'm gone I'll come back and haunt you."

．　　　．　　　．

Getting old is the second-biggest surprise of my life, but the first, by a mile, is our unceasing need for deep attachment and intimate love. We oldies yearn daily and hourly for conversation and a renewed domesticity, for company at the movies or while visiting a museum, for someone close by in the car when coming home at night. This is why we throng Match.com and OkCupid in such numbers—but not just for this, surely. Rowing in Eden (in Emily Dickinson's words: "Rowing in Eden— / Ah—the sea") isn't reserved for the lithe and young, the dating or the hooked-up or the just lavishly married, or even for couples in the middle-aged mixed-doubles semifinals, thank God. No personal confession or revelation impends here, but these feelings in old folks are widely treated like a raunchy secret. The invisibility factor—you've had your turn—is back at it again. But I believe that everyone in the world wants to be with someone else tonight, together in the dark, with the sweet warmth of a hip or a foot or a bare expanse of shoulder within reach. Those of us who have lost that, whatever our age, never lose the longing: just look at our faces. If it returns, we seize upon it avidly, stunned and altered again.

Nothing is easy at this age, and first meetings for old lovers can be a high-risk venture. Reticence and awkwardness slip into the room. Also happiness. A wealthy old widower I knew married a nurse he met while in the hospital but had trouble remembering her name afterward. He called her "kid." An eighty-plus, twice-widowed lady I'd once known found still another love, a frail but vibrant Midwest professor, now close to ninety, and the pair got in two or three happy years together before he died as well. When she called his children and arranged to pick up her things at his house, she found every possession of hers lined up outside the front door.

But to hell with them and with all that, OK? Here's to you, old dears. You got this right, every one of you. Hook, line, and sinker; never mind the why or wherefore; somewhere in the night; love me forever, or at least until next week. For us and for anyone this unsettles, anyone who's younger and still squirms at the vision of an old couple embracing, I'd offer John Updike's "Sex or death: you take your pick"—a line that appears (in a slightly different form) in a late story of his, "Playing with Dynamite."

This is a great question, an excellent insurance-plan choice, I mean. I think it's in the Affordable Care Act somewhere. Take it from us, who know about the emptiness of loss and are still cruising along here feeling lucky and not yet entirely alone.

The New Yorker

WINNER—FICTION

From its 200-word first sentence, Donald Antrim's "The Emerald Light in the Air" immerses the reader in a short but fable-like trip through the lush countryside of the Virginia Piedmont. "Antrim," wrote the Ellie judges, "guides the reader with seeming effortlessness on an affecting journey from despair to something close to hope." A collection of Antrim's stories, bearing the name of this piece, was published late last year. While the short story is central to the editorial mission of dozens of smaller magazines, especially literary journals, The New Yorker is one of the few large-circulation titles that still publish fiction—a commitment that has earned the magazine fourteen National Magazine Awards for Fiction since 1974.

Donald Antrim

The Emerald Light in the Air

In less than a year, he'd lost his mother, his father, and, as he'd once and sometimes still felt Julia to be, the love of his life; and, during this year, or, he should say, during its suicidal aftermath, he'd twice admitted himself to the psychiatric ward at the University Hospital in Charlottesville, where, each stay, one in the fall and one the following summer, three mornings a week, Monday, Wednesday, Friday, he'd climbed onto an operating table and wept at the ceiling while doctors set the pulse, stuck electrodes to his forehead, put the oxygen meter on his finger, and then pushed a needle into his arm and instructed him, as the machines beeped and the anesthetic dripped down the pipette toward his vein, to count backward from a hundred; and now, another year later, he was on his way to the dump to throw out the drawings and paintings that Julia had made in the months when she was sneaking off to sleep with the man she finally left him to marry, along with the comic-book collection—it wasn't a collection so much as a big box stuffed with comics—that he'd kept since he was a boy. He had long ago forgotten his old comics; and then, a few days before, he'd come across them on a dusty shelf at the back of the garage, while looking for a carton of ammo.

It was a humid Saturday morning. Thunderstorms had come through in the early hours after dawn, but now the rain and wind had passed, and sunlight lit the puddles on the road and the silver roofs of the farmhouses and barns that flickered into view between the trees, as he steered the ancient blue Mercedes—it had been his father's, and his grandfather's before that—across the county he'd grown up in. Maybe on his way back home he'd stop at Fox Run Farm for a gallon of raw milk. Or no. He'd drink a glass or two and then, in a month, have to dig the rest out of the refrigerator and pitch it. He reminded himself to vacuum the living room and clean the downstairs toilet. His name was Billy French, and he was carrying a Browning .30-06 A-bolt hunting rifle in the trunk of the Mercedes. He wasn't a gun nut, and he didn't hunt. He was a sculptor and a middle-school art teacher. Every now and then, he liked to stop on his way home from school and shoot cans off the rotting fence posts that surrounded the unused cow pasture where, at sixteen, in the grass and weeds, he'd lost his virginity to Mary Doan. He hadn't thought about Mary in ages, and then, recently, he'd run into her—surprise, surprise, after all these years—at a bar in the Valley. He'd recognized her right away—he remembered her limp—but it had taken her a couple of tries to remember his name. They'd had a laugh over that, and he'd bought her a drink, and she'd bought him one, and now she was coming across the mountain, she was coming that night for dinner.

He'd told her seven-thirty.

Ahead on the road, a tree limb was down. He was on a small rural route, a cut between two lanes, not much used. He stopped the Mercedes, unbuckled his seat belt, and got out. A locust bough had sheared off in the wind. The bough was long and twisting, green with crooked branches and smaller, thorny stems. His tree saw and his axe were back at the house, but it might be possible to drag the bough from the tip and more or less swing the whole thing—swing wasn't the right word, maybe—over and around and off the road, enough at least for the car to pass. He reached through the leaves and grabbed a narrow stem that stuck up in the air. There were no flowers—it was late in the season for that—but the locust's seedpods had begun to sprout, and many of these were scattered across the asphalt.

He swatted a mosquito and got the branch in both hands. The wood was damp, and the end of the bough flexed and bent when he pulled. He moved down to a thicker part, planted his feet, and leaned back. After four or five difficult heave-hos, he'd opened enough clearance, he thought, to steer the car through. He was out of breath and his shirt was wet and sticky. He got in the driver's seat and eased the Mercedes onto the oncoming side of the road. The ground sloped down from the road's edge and the soil had taken on rain. As he was working his way around the branch, wheels partly on the shoulder, the car tipped to the left and then shifted further, and a piece of ground seemed to fall away underneath. It was startling: a little slide and the Mercedes plunged. Then the tires dug in, and, abruptly, a distance off the road and at a steep angle, the car settled and stopped. Billy pushed his foot against the brake. He gripped the steering wheel. When he took his hands off, he saw that he'd scraped his palms on the locust. He was bleeding.

"Shit, fuck. Shit," he said aloud.

He turned off the engine. He hadn't slept the night before. It wasn't the thunder and lightning that had kept him up—he'd been going through the art works that Julia had left rolled in tubes or stacked against the wall in the upstairs bedroom that had been her studio. They were piled in the back seat now. The paintings, he thought, while sitting in the car perched on the berm, were not as strong as the drawings, which, though more or less precise studies for their oil counterparts, all rural Virginia scenes—trees in a field, a dying pond, a rotting house in a mountain hollow— nonetheless had about them, with their bold erasures and smudges and retraced pencil lines, the feeling of something abstract and, in comparison with the worked and reworked paintings, complexly three-dimensional. The paintings seemed to exist as strangely flat fields—they put Billy in mind of Early American naïve art—and, in looking at them and, back in the day, talking to Julia about them, he'd come to see how purposefully she distorted light and shadow. "I'm searching for something that isn't quite there," she'd once said.

He was fearful of shifting his weight and starting another slide—the car had gone four or five feet already, and the embankment fell maybe ten more. He could hear running water. Was there a creek off in the woods? He knew this country, or thought he did, but it was always surprising him, just the same.

He wiped his hands on his pants. Gently now, he ratcheted down the brake. He eased open the driver's-side door.

Anyway, her drawings and paintings—he knew better than to throw them out, but the fact of them in his house was terrible. He'd meant for some time to do something about them. At first, of course, he'd tried to get them back to her, but she'd told him—this was during one of their five or six phone conversations since her departure, two years earlier—that her old work was no longer meaningful or important to her. "I'm not doing that kind of painting anymore," she'd said. "I'm engaged with a more total realism."

"Photo-realism?" he'd asked.

"No, nothing like that."

He was standing in the kitchen in his socks and underwear, drinking bourbon and Coke—his mother's drink. Ice rattled in the glass. The floor was brown and dirty, in need of mopping.

Julia said, "Billy, you're drinking."

Oh, God, how to get out of the Mercedes safely? The hillside was steep and the grass was wet. And what if he made it, with both feet firmly on the ground, and the car slid down on top of him?

He pushed the car door open all the way and, clutching the doorframe for balance, tumbled out onto the incline. Fuck Julia. He could take her pictures and toss them into the woods right now.

He had weed in the glove compartment. Might there be a stray Ativan or two in there as well? The thing to do was slog around to the uphill side, the passenger side, reach through the window, and feel around in the glove compartment for whatever he could find. But wouldn't you know it? He got partway around the Mercedes, and the whole car seemed to shudder and tremble. Billy watched it start into another drop—it was as if the car were shaking its wheels free of the mire—and then down the grade it rumbled, through the mud and across the grass, sliding to a rest at last in a patch of milkweed at the foot of the hill.

He felt a raindrop, and another. The clouds were not in sight yet, but Billy could sense the weight of low pressure bearing down. An emerald light was in the air. The birds and other animals had gone quiet; the world was still, as it can be when bad weather is coming. He was thinking of Mary. By the time he'd managed to have sex with Mary, back in high school—she was a senior and he was a junior, and that fact alone was thrilling—she'd already had one abortion and one marriage proposal.

He half walked, half slid down the hill. The Mercedes was sitting in a gulch between the woods and the embankment. He heard running water again—the creek had to be close. He reached gently into his pocket and took out his phone. His hands were a cut-up mess. The garage he used for the Mercedes was on the other side of Charlottesville, close to Julia and Mark's farm, and, anyway, too far away for a tow truck to come. Could he drive back up to the road? It didn't look to Billy as if there'd be much room to maneuver.

Daily life's frustrations, even the big ones, no longer ruled him, not the way they had for a long time in his life. He'd been psychotic with agitation that had grown from his grief, and it was hard for him to remember what that had been like, exactly: not the grief—he had plenty of that still—but the urge to die. He'd got all but there. He'd had the Browning loaded. He'd had it ready and at hand, a few times.

He smelled storm. He might be able to drive for a while beside the road. The sun was high. Billy put his phone in his pocket and got back in the Mercedes. The car seemed all right. He drove slowly. He was in a wide but navigable trench. It wasn't bad driving. The trench curved slowly around to the right, and then came to a straight section that reminded Billy of the Roman road that he and Julia had walked a length of during that difficult vacation in Italy, the winter before she left.

They'd gone to see the paintings and frescoes of Tiepolo. Billy had become vocal about Tiepolo after seeing *Bacchus and Ariadne* in Washington, and Julia had got into him, too. After Christmas in Rome, they had taken the train north to Venice, and had spent a week walking around in the cold, searching out churches and palazzos and wandering the Gallerie dell'Accademia, where they had both become enchanted, though for different reasons, with *The Rape of Europa*. Julia got excited over the distant meeting of clouds and sea in the picture's right-hand corner, while Billy fixated on the encroaching cloud plume to the left, the spire of pink and gray—it looked to him like a mushroom cloud—exploding upward from behind the rocky outcropping on which Zeus, transformed into a bull, seduces the Phoenician princess Europa, dressed in white and attended by ladies-in-waiting. The cloud threatens to wipe them all out, but Europa and her entourage seem either unconcerned or unaware. She sits enthroned on the back of Zeus. Two other bulls wait nearby. A maid tends to Europa's hair, and another bathes her feet; shepherds and an African are on hand, and putti fly about and urinate from on high, and a black bird perches on a strange little cumulus cloud that has floated in over the princess's head.

There was the creek. It came out of the woods and flowed into a concrete drainpipe that tunneled under the road. A stretch near the trees looked fordable. He could angle the car just so, over and between the rocks. Once he got to the other side, though, where was he going to go? Trees pushed against the embankment, and the way was overgrown. Billy nosed the car forward anyway. He felt a curiosity. The undercarriage of the Mercedes was not high, and when the wheels dropped into the water Billy heard and felt the bumper scrape the rocks. He jerked the car, not across but up the creek—maybe he could follow it out into a field or a yard somewhere upstream. The retirement home where his parents had ended their lives was up the way he'd come that morning, not on the little lane but on the bigger road at the end of it, heading down from the hills toward town. He saw lightning in the distance, and peered through the windshield at the dark clouds now crossing the sky over Afton Mountain.

He turned on the headlights and the wipers.

In the hospital, he'd had hallucinations. He remembered looking in his bathroom mirror—it was made of metal, not glass—and seeing his face deformed. He'd known better than to believe what he saw, but, on the other hand, he hadn't known better, far from it: there it had been in front of him, his bent, misshapen skull. Now, as he drove into the forest, Billy recalled that, for a long time, the time of the locked ward and his sick brain and the torn-up suicide notes to Julia, he'd felt the burning. He'd felt it in his temple. It was, somehow, he knew, both imaginary and real, a beckoning, an itch, a need for a bullet. Of course he'd thought always of the Browning, of loading it and getting into position on the living-room floor, or maybe out back in the barn, maybe laying down a tarp first.

The barn on the hill behind his house—that was where he made his art. When he wasn't teaching seventh graders how to draw, he made big untidy installations that he referred to as his trash heaps. Along with the rifle and the comics and Julia's art, he had in the back of the Mercedes a canvas bag with about two dozen cans that he'd saved from trips to the shooting pasture. He was planning to include them in a piece. He needed more, but he didn't eat much canned food, and his personal use of the materials in his work was crucial to him.

The thing about Mary was that her limp looked good. It wasn't a very noticeable limp. One of her legs was shorter than the other. Billy remembered her swaggering down the hall in high school, thirty years before. Her father had been a country doctor, the sort who got out of bed and drove into the hills at all hours to treat people who couldn't pay or get down the mountain to town. Mary was a year older than Billy, but she'd let him put his hands down her pants. He'd ridden his bike up Route 250, past the Episcopal church, to her house. There was never anyone home but her. She'd been provocative and graceful and unembarrassed. He remembered her standing on her short leg, the other leg propped out at an angle, toes touching the floor, a dancer's pose.

What he needed to do was fix up the car. It was a 1958 220S with a white roof and a gray interior, and there had been rust on the body and the chrome and underneath, on the chassis, for a long time. Billy wasn't a car buff, and didn't know what this one might be worth cleaned up. People had offered to buy it. He remembered riding in it with his grandfather, who never drove faster than twenty-five miles per hour. His grandfather had told stories, actually, of driving his old Ford up creek beds, back in the thirties.

Billy urged the car up a mossy rise and over a little waterfall. Branches scraped the roof.

After Julia left, in his worsening he'd walked and moved as if crushed by some stronger form of gravity. The air had pressed him down, and he could not get out from under it. Some days, he'd curled in a ball on the floor and promised himself that soon, soon, soon—it would be his gift to himself—he'd walk up to the barn and lie down with the rifle.

The car was swamped. Or it wasn't, exactly, but the creek had risen and the tires now made a wake. The Mercedes didn't have much acceleration, and the steering felt loose. Billy powered over a high rock, or maybe a tree root—it was hard to see—then, suddenly, precipitately, the wheels dropped in front and the car slammed down and stopped.

Billy pressed the gas. The motor raced and the car shook but didn't move. He gave the engine gas again, and the rear wheels spun, churning the creek and throwing mud. He put the lever in park. Lightning hit, close and loud. Billy reached across the seat, opened the glove compartment, and felt around for the pot. There was the registration paperwork, and there was a pill bottle, his Ativan; and there were his pliers (he'd recently begun preparing the cans, tearing and disfiguring them before shooting), and the joint and the lighter, and the driving gloves that his grandfather had worn and that Billy's father had kept in the car after Billy's grandfather died, and that Billy had left there after his own father died. He took the gloves out and felt how old they were, then worked his hands into them.

On or off—he wasn't sure what felt better.

He put the pills in his shirt pocket, turned off the ignition and the wipers and the lights. He remembered how the misery had bowed him over: he'd gone everywhere, in those days, with his head down, barreling rigidly forward, compounding the pain by moving at all; but when he touched himself to find where the pain was coming from he couldn't find the spot.

It was dark in the woods without the headlights. He lit the joint and the car glowed inside. Julia's paintings were in back. She worked with tiny brushes, and he'd wondered, sometimes, when he saw her at it, what she was thinking while she slowly built up the paint on the canvas. He exhaled smoke and watched the saplings at the edge of the creek bend in the surge.

She'd talked to him, as they stood together at the Accademia, gazing at *The Rape of Europa*, about the singular cloud hovering over Europa, its complete nonrelation to the more natural-seeming clouds that dominate the painting as a whole, the delicate, pale clouds on the horizon, the spire of darker cloud rising up behind the rocks. "Everything is off in Tiepolo," she'd said. "Spatial relations don't cohere. It isn't simply that people fly with angels through the air. What world are we looking at? The paintings at all points lead the eye toward infinity." She might have been anticipating his own predicament, his own crisis of perception, when, nine months later, and again the following year, he'd lain on the operating table, crying and holding the nurse's hand, while the doctors got him ready. The hospital ceiling was white foam tile with fluorescent lights, and the doctors had looked to Billy as if they were levitating beneath them, beneath the lights—as if they, the doctors, had descended from heaven to perform electroconvulsive therapy.

Someone was coming toward the car. A figure moved between the trees beside the creek. It was a boy carrying an umbrella. He was skinny and wore jeans and no shirt. He stepped down to the bank and splashed across to the car with the umbrella over his head. Billy rolled down the window, and the rain swept in, drenching him.

"Are you the doctor?" the boy said.

"Doctor?" Billy said.

"Luther said he saw car lights. We prayed you'd come. Are you smoking pot?"

"I'm stuck on this rock," Billy said.

"I see that," the boy said.

"I was making good progress, and the next thing I knew the wheels were spinning."

"Creeks aren't the best for driving in a storm," the boy said.

Billy rolled up the car window. He opened the door and put out his foot. The rock was massive and slick; the creek was about to overtake it. He eased himself out and stood clear of the car. He was still wearing his grandfather's driving gloves, and holding the joint. He lowered one foot into the creek, leaped in, and lunged toward the bank, where his feet sank into the wet earth. "I'm fine," he said. "I made it."

"Don't you have your doctor's bag?" the boy asked.

He looked to be twelve or thirteen, the age of Billy's students, but Billy didn't recognize him.

"It's our mother," the boy said.

"Your mother?"

"She's up that way." He held the umbrella over Billy, who said, "What's wrong with her?"

"It's cancer."

"I'm sorry," Billy said.

"She's up here," the boy said.

There was no need to lock the car or take the key. Billy put the joint in his shirt pocket with the pills—it would get soaked; he should have left it in the car, but there was nothing he could do about that now—and said, "I doubt I'll be able to help her. I want you to know that," and then followed anyway, a few steps behind the boy, to the place where the boy had crossed the creek on his way down. Billy watched the boy wade through the water, and then slogged in after him. The creek here was deep and fast. The car would be all right or not. Billy leaned against the torrent and struggled up onto the bank, and then he and the boy pushed ahead, slipping in the mud and on the mossy ground, pushing branches away from their faces. Once, Billy stumbled, and the boy held the umbrella over him while he got up. The umbrella was torn and bent, and water poured down it onto Billy's neck.

They went over a rise, and then walked down along what looked like a lane—maybe the land had been cleared at one time—a grassy, open promenade between the trees. The lane led into a hollow. There was a cabin, a shed, really, with a sinking roof and small square windows and a chimney overtaken by ivy. The cabin featured a porch, though not much was left of that, only a few boards elevated on piled stones, with no steps leading up from the yard to the door. The cabin had two front doors, oddly—one beside the other. Billy didn't see an actual road, or a car parked nearby, but there was trash littering the ground.

The boy hopped onto the porch, closed and shook the umbrella, and stomped clay from his shoes. Billy climbed onto the porch—he had to heave himself up—and kicked the red mud off his own heels. The boy pushed open the door on the left. "I brought the doctor," he called inside.

"Show him in," a man answered.

The boy held the door. Billy had to duck under the frame. Water ran from every part of him. The floor inside was missing in places, and the air felt cold, like a draft from underground. Water dripped through the roof. Two windows, one in the rear and one on the side of the cabin, let in faint light—their panes, if they'd ever had any, were gone.

Billy's eyes were adjusting. The cabin seemed bigger from inside than from out. As he came in, he saw, to the left of the door, a tumble of bags and suitcases. A dividing wall ran down the middle of the cabin, splitting the space—that explained the two front doors—and there was an interior door, partway down the dividing wall, leading to the cabin's right-hand side. The room on the left, the one he was in, might have been ten feet wide by thirteen or fourteen feet deep. The fireplace and the chimney were over in the other half.

Billy saw a bed pushed up under the window at the back of the cabin. A woman was lying in it, and a man stood over her. The man spoke to the boy on the porch, "Caleb, put down that umbrella and get the doctor something to dry himself."

Billy heard the other front door open and close, and he heard the sounds of the boy moving behind the dividing wall. Billy could feel his footfalls traveling through the floorboards.

"She's struggling," the man said to Billy.

The bed was an old iron thing with a mattress on top. The woman had a coat draped over her, and a bundle of clothes for a pillow. Rain spattered the windowsill above the bed but didn't seem to be getting on her.

"We've moved her from corner to corner, all night, except where the floor's out. The water follows her," the man explained.

"It's been quite the storm," Billy said.

He picked his way across the damaged floor to the bedside. His shoes squished.

"Don't fall through," the man said.

The man was bald and hadn't shaved—he wore the shadow of a beard. It was hard to tell if he was old, or maybe just Billy's age, and he spoke with an accent that reminded Billy of the Appalachian mountain speech he'd heard when he was a boy, but which, even so, he couldn't place—it wasn't local.

"I'll be careful," Billy said. He felt as if he were seeing through a fog. The splashing rain on the windowsill made a mist in the air, but it was also the pot, deranging his balance, his sense of perspective.

At the bedside, Billy leaned down and saw the woman shudder beneath the coat that was covering her. Then she was still. The door in the dividing wall opened, and the boy appeared and handed him a damp, dirty piece of cloth, a towel, of sorts.

"Thank you," Billy said.

The man said to the boy, "Go find your brother and tell him the doctor's arrived." The boy left the room through the front door. To Billy, the man said, "We didn't mean to be staying here."

They stood over the woman on the bed. Why were there no chairs? Everything looked wrecked and rotten.

Billy went down on his knees. The man said, "I know there's nothing to be done," and knelt, too.

The woman's eyes were closed and her mouth was open. Her skin seemed stretched, and her lips were parched. The man told Billy that she'd taken neither food nor water for some time. He and Billy faced each other over her. There was a moment when Billy's heart raced. The man studied him. Billy looked down. The man said, "You're not a doctor, are you?"

"No, I'm not. I'm sorry."

"But you're here."

Billy explained, "I teach junior high over in Crozet. I was on my way to the dump to throw some things out."

"The dump's not up here."

"The road was blocked. I took the creek and wrecked on the rocks."

Billy heard footsteps on the porch. The door opened and the cabin shook as Caleb and his brother came in. The brother was bigger than Caleb, older, and wore a dark shirt. They stood dripping side by side at the foot of the bed, and Billy remembered sitting at his own mother's deathbed, feeding her a mixture of morphine drops and Ativan, squeezing her hand, and telling her he would miss her, while her breaths came farther and farther apart.

The woman on the bed inhaled. Her dark hair was fanned out around her head.

The man told the boys, "I want you two to go down to the creek and bring the doctor's car."

"It's stuck," Caleb said.

"That's what the doctor told me," the man said, and added, "The doctor and I will stay with her."

"The flood may have washed it away," Caleb said.

"Go see. Go on."

The brothers backed away from the bed.

The man asked Billy his name, and, in that moment, Billy could not say—he felt too dizzy to speak. He raised one hand and pulled the coat more neatly and more fully across the woman, tucking the collar around her neck; the tail reached almost to her feet. He saw that she was wearing socks. Her feet were tiny. He was shaking.

He tried to take a deeper breath. He felt his grandfather's gloves shrinking and tightening as they dried on his hands.

"I can help her," he said finally.

Light came dully through the window, and seemed to drip down between the beams overhead. Billy listened to the softening rain. He reached inside his shirt pocket and clumsily got hold of the pill bottle. He said, "This will help her rest."

It took him some time to open the cap. He peered down into the bottle. There was a handful of pills. He thought to take one himself, maybe more than one. But there were so few; he didn't. Instead, he asked the man, "Do you have any water?"

"Water?" the man said.

"Is there a tap?"

"No," the man said. "There's a pump out back."

Billy held the open bottle in one hand. With his other hand, he reached up to the window. He stuck his hand out to catch the rain in the bottle cap. He said to the man, "I want you to watch what I'm doing." Then he held the bottle cap over the woman's mouth. He let a drop, and another, fall.

He shook a pill from the bottle.

"Like this," he said.

He leaned over the woman. He held the pill unsteadily between his thumb and forefinger, between the raised seams at the fingertips of his glove. He tucked the pill beneath the woman's lower lip, near her cheek, and then reached up and caught more rain. "Give her water with the pill."

He shook the cap dry, then put it back on the bottle and told the man to give her four or five a day. "There should be enough here to get her through," he said.

"Thank you for your kindness," the man said.

After a moment, Billy left the bedside. He stepped across the broken floor planks and opened the front door. Thunder rolled in the far distance. He stood on the porch, in the drizzle, and tried to stop trembling.

It isn't the shock. It's the brain seizure, brought on by the shock. Atropine goes in, to keep the heart working. The anesthetic follows, and, after that, succinylcholine, which paralyzes the body. Life support is necessary. A blood-pressure cuff inflated tightly around one ankle keeps the succinylcholine out of the foot, which, when the shock is given, shows the seizure as twitching toes. The head and the heart are wired: electroencephalograph to scalp; electrocardiograph to body. A bite plate goes between the teeth, and an oxygen mask covers the face. The anesthetic has a sweet smell; the patient loses consciousness ten or fifteen seconds after it enters the blood. That done, the doctor places the paddles against the forehead. Optimally, the seizure, the convulsion, should last twenty, thirty, forty seconds. Shorter or longer is less effective. There must be enough anesthetic in the blood to keep the patient unconscious but not so much that it soaks the brain and dampens the seizure. The anesthetic is short-lived, and the procedure is over in minutes. The anesthetic goes in, blackness comes, and then, suddenly, as if nothing had taken place, the nurse's voice asks, "Can you tell me where you are?"

He heard a noise and saw lights. It was the Mercedes, coming toward him along the avenue of trees.

He stepped down off the porch, into the mud.

The boy was driving. His brother sat beside him. The boy parked in front of Billy, like a valet at a restaurant. He rolled down the window and called, "We brought the car."

"You brought the car," Billy said.

"The flood almost took it down the mountain."

"I thought it surely would have."

"We got it in time," the boy said, and Billy said, "Your mother is sleeping."

The boy got out, leaving the door open for Billy. "Come on," he said to his brother.

The hood and the roof were covered with leaves, and scratches and dents ran along the body of the car, where it had crunched onto the rock.

The boy pointed. "Drive between the trees and don't cross the creek. Follow the side of the mountain. Turn left at the train tracks. There's a busted fence. Go through it and drive across the field. There's an empty house and a pond. Go past the house to the gate. The road is on the other side."

"OK," Billy said.

He watched the brothers climb onto the porch, kick the mud off their shoes, and go through the right-side door into the cabin.

Billy swept the leaves off the car with his hand—first the roof, then the hood—and pulled more from under the wipers. He got in the car. The rain had about stopped. He rolled up the window, just in case. His scraped hands hurt beneath the gloves, but he could hold the wheel.

He drove out of the hollow, and the gray sky opened to view. He heard the rushing creek on his left, and kept going. It wasn't long before he had to thread between trees and under branches. He saw only glimpses of sky. A deer jumped in front of the car and scared him, and several times he had to back up and redirect the Mercedes around fallen logs. He didn't know how far he'd come, but he could feel the slope of the mountain rising beside him on his right.

He was on the tracks before he saw them. They were ancient and broken, buried in the weeds. He turned left and followed them. The Mercedes bumped along over the crooked ties. After a mile or so, he saw the field and the fence that the boy had told him to look for, and, beyond the field, the empty house and the pond. He relaxed his grip on the wheel and took his time crossing the waterlogged grass. He stopped at the gate, put the lever in park, and got out. The gate was chained and locked. He yanked on the lock. "Fuck me," he said, and walked back to the car.

He opened the trunk and retrieved the Browning, unzipped the case, and removed the rifle. He took a bullet from the box and loaded the gun. He walked over and stood about ten feet from the gate, raised the rifle to his shoulder, and aimed. It took one shot. The lock jumped and settled. Billy expelled the shell, walked up to the gate, removed the shattered lock from the chain, unwrapped the chain from the fence, and pushed open the gate. He carried the gun, the chain, and the lock to the car. He put the Browning into its case, and the lock and the chain into the canvas bag full of cans. Before shutting the trunk, he walked back to where he'd fired the gun. It took him a minute to find the shell. He picked it out of the grass, then tossed it into the bag with the other things. Before closing the trunk, he opened his box of comic books. He didn't take any out. He knew what they were, pretty much. He should have given them to the boys. He closed the trunk, took his phone from his pocket, got into the driver's seat, pulled off one of his gloves, and dialed 911. The operator, a woman, said, "What is your emergency?"

"I want to report a dying woman, a woman who's dying," he said.

"Can you tell me your name, sir?"

"My name is Billy French."

"Where are you located?"

Billy looked about. He said, "I thought I was below Afton Mountain, but things don't look right. I'm in a field. There's a vacant house near a pond."

"Can you be more specific, sir?"

Billy said, "She's in a cabin on the mountain. There's a man and two boys. You go through a field and along some rusted tracks. There's a kind of lane or alley or something in the woods."

"I'll need an address, sir."

"There is no address."

"I need to know where the woman is, sir," the operator said.

"I don't know," he said.

"Sir?"

"I'm not sure."

He hung up.

He turned off the phone and put it in the glove compartment. He put the driving glove back on his hand. He buckled his seat belt, steered up to the road, and looked both ways.

It was too late to make the trip to the dump. Mary was coming, and he had to get ready. He'd thought of braising rabbit. Did he still have time for that?

Left or right? He turned the car to the left.

As he drove, he decided that he would keep Julia's paintings a while longer. He could clear some space in the attic, or stow them under a tarp in the barn.

He went over and down a hill. He had the mountains on one side and a cow pasture on the other. The sky above the mountains glowed. Soon the sun would come out and the day would be blue again. He was certain that the road would lead him somewhere familiar if he drove long enough. He rolled down the window and felt the breeze on his face. The damp, shining road curved over the gentle foothills, and the trees alongside seemed to become greener and lusher in the growing light, and before long a car passed him going the other direction; and, a little farther down the road, he did in fact come upon a house that he recognized. He slowed the car and pulled into the driveway. How had he got so far from home? He was all the way up past White Hall.

Soft white clouds and a few birds were in the air. The thunder and lightning were over at last.

Billy circled the drive, eased the Mercedes to the road, checked both directions, and went back the way he'd come.

Permissions

Contributors

ROGER ANGELL has contributed to *The New Yorker* since 1944. He is a senior editor and a staff writer. Since 1962, Angell has written more than one hundred "Sporting Scene" pieces, mostly on baseball but also on tennis, hockey, football, rowing, and horseracing. In addition, he has written film reviews, stories, casuals, "Notes and Comment" pieces, and, for many years, the magazine's Christmas verse, "Greetings, Friends!" His writing has appeared in many anthologies, including *The Best American Sports Writing*, *The Best American Short Stories*, *The Best American Essays*, and *The Best American Magazine Writing*. His work has also been collected in nine of his own books, among them *The Stone Arbor and Other Stories*, *A Day in the Life of Roger Angell*, and, most recently, *Let Me Finish*. His baseball books include *The Summer Game*, *Five Seasons*, *Late Innings*, *Season Ticket*, *Once More Around the Park*, *A Pitcher's Story*, and *Game Time*. *Nothing but You: Love Stories from* The New Yorker is an anthology of fiction selected by him. He has won a number of awards for his writing, including a George Polk Award for Commentary, a Kenyon Review Award for Literary Achievement, and the Michael Braude Award for Light Verse, presented by the American Academy of Arts and Letters. He is a member of the American Academy of Arts and Letters and a fellow of the American Academy of Arts and Sciences, and in 2011 he was the inaugural winner of the PEN/ESPN Lifetime Achievement Award for Literary Sports Writing. In 2014, Angell received the J. G. Taylor Spink Award, the highest honor given to writers by the Baseball Hall of Fame.

DONALD ANTRIM is the author of the novels *Elect Mr. Robinson for a Better World*, *The Hundred Brothers*, and *The Verificationist*, as well as a memoir, *The Afterlife*. He is a regular contributor to *The New Yorker* and an associate professor in the writing program at Columbia University. He is a 2013 MacArthur Fellow.

DAVID BERNSTEIN is the features editor at *Chicago* magazine. This year and in 2013 he and coauthor Noah Isackson were finalists for a National Magazine Award in the prestigious Reporting category. He has received numerous other awards, including from the Nieman Foundation for Journalism at Harvard University, the Medill School of Journalism at Northwestern University, the Society of Professional Journalists, the City and Regional Magazine Association, the Chicago Bar Association, and the Chicago Headline Club. Previously, Bernstein was a freelance writer, contributing frequently to the *New York Times, Chicago,* and *Crain's Chicago Business.* His work has also appeared in *The Best Technology Writing 2006* (Digital Culture Books) and *The Best American Crime Reporting 2007* (Harper Perennial). He has a master of science in journalism from Medill.

TA-NEHISI COATES is a national correspondent for *The Atlantic.* He is the author of *The Beautiful Struggle* and *Between the World and Me* (forthcoming September 2015).

AMANDA HESS is a *Slate* staff writer and a contributor to the *New York Times Magazine.* She has written about Hollywood, sex, teenagers, and the Internet for places like *ESPN the Magazine, T: The New York Times Style Magazine, Details,* the *Village Voice,* the *Los Angeles Times,* and *Pacific Standard.* She cowrote the *Book of Jezebel: An Encyclopedia of Lady Things* and was featured in the anthology *The Best American Sports Writing 2014.* She lives in New York but left her heart scattered across several western states.

NOAH ISACKSON is a magazine writer based in Chicago. A contributing writer at *Chicago* magazine, his work has also appeared in *Time, People,* the *Chicago Tribune Magazine, Time Out Chicago,* the *Boston Globe,* and *Men's Health,* among other publications. His work has received awards from the Nieman Foundation for Journalism at Harvard, the Medill School of Journalism at Northwestern University, the Society of Professional Journalists, the City and Regional Magazine Association, the Chicago Headline Club, and the Chicago Bar Association and has been recognized as a notable selection in the anthology *The Best American Sports Writing*. In 2015 and in 2013, he and coauthor David Bernstein were finalists for a National Magazine Award in Reporting. Previously, Isackson was a general assignment reporter for the *Chicago Tribune* and the Associated Press, assigned to the Chicago and Sacramento, Calif., bureaus. He began his journalism career in 1997 after graduating from Northwestern University's Medill School of Journalism.

MONICA LEWINSKY is a social activist, public speaker, writer, and consultant. As ambassador and strategic advisor to the antibullying organization Bystander Revolution, she has advocated for a safer social-media environment and has battled online harassment. A contributor to *Vanity Fair*, Lewinsky has a master's degree in social psychology from the London School of Economics and has recently spoken at the *Forbes* 30 Under 30 Summit, the annual TED conference, and the Cannes Lions International Festival of Creativity.

BRIAN PHILLIPS has been a staff writer for Grantland since 2011.

JERRY SALTZ is the senior art critic at *New York* magazine and its entertainment site Vulture.com, a leading voice in the art world at large, and an innovative user of social media. He joined the magazine's staff in 2007, and his writing ranges from cover stories to reviews to quick online commentaries. He won a National Magazine Award for Columns and Commentary in 2015 and was a finalist for the same award in 2011. Saltz was previously the senior art critic at the *Village Voice*, where he was twice a finalist for the Pulitzer Prize in criticism (in 2001 and 2006) and was the recipient of the 2007 Frank Jewett Mather Award in Art Criticism from the College Art Association. A frequent guest lecturer at major universities and museums, Saltz was also the sole advisor on the 1995 Whitney Biennial. Saltz has written for *Frieze*, *Modern Painters*, *Parkett*, *Art in America*, *Time Out New York*, *Flash Art*, *Arts* magazine, and many others. His *Village Voice* columns were compiled into a book published by Figures Press, *Seeing Out Loud: The* Village Voice *Art Columns, 1998–2003*. A second volume of his criticism, *Seeing Out Louder*, was published by Hardpress Editions. Saltz appeared as a judge on Bravo's *Work of Art: The Next Great Artist* for the show's two seasons and has been a guest on CNN, *CBS This Morning*, NPR, and other news outlets.

JEFF SHARLET is the best-selling author of *The Family*, *C Street*, and *Sweet Heaven When I Die*. His edited books include *Radiant Truths* and *Believer, Beware*, and he is coauthor, with Peter Manseau, of *Killing the Buddha*. He is a contributing editor for *Harper's*, *Rolling Stone*, and *Virginia Quarterly Review* and a frequent contributor to *GQ*. Sharlet is an associate professor of creative writing at Dartmouth College. Among his distinctions is belletrist Ann Coulter's designation of him as one of the stupidest journalists in America.

TIFFANY STANLEY is a contributing writer at *National Journal*. She lives in Washington, D.C., where she is managing editor of *Religion and Politics*, the journal of the Danforth Center on Religion and Politics at Washington University in St. Louis. She has also written for *The New Republic*, *The Daily Beast*, and *Paste*, among other publications.

JOHN JEREMIAH SULLIVAN was born in 1974 in Louisville, Kentucky. He now lives with his wife and two daughters in North Carolina, where he writes books and essays. "The Ballad of Geeshie and Elvie" is part of a larger project having to do with the origins of the blues.

REBECCA TRAISTER is a journalist who covers women in politics, media, and culture from a feminist perspective. Currently a senior editor at *The New Republic* and a contributing editor at *Elle*, she spent ten years at *Salon* and has also written for the *New York Times Magazine*, *The Nation*, the *Washington Post*, the *New York Observer*, *Glamour*, *Marie Claire*, and elsewhere. Her first book, *Big Girls Don't Cry*, about women in the 2008 election, was a *New York Times* Notable Book of 2010 and the winner of the Ernesta Drinker Ballard Book Prize. Her second book, about unmarried and late-married women in the United States, will be published by Simon and Schuster in early 2016.

JONATHAN VAN METER is a contributing editor at *New York* and *Vogue* as well as the founding editor of *Vibe*. He is the author of *The Last Good Time: Skinny D'Amato, the Notorious 500 Club, and the Rise and Fall of Atlantic City*.

JAMES VERINI is a writer based in Africa.

EMILY YOFFE is a *Slate* contributor who has written the magazine's "Dear Prudence" advice column since 2006. She also writes for *Slate* about culture, health, politics, and science. Her writing has appeared in many publications, including *Esquire*, the *Los Angeles Times*, the *New Republic*, the *New York Times*, *O the Oprah Magazine*, and the *Washington Post*. She is the author of the book *What the Dog Did: Tales from a Formerly Reluctant Dog Owner*. She was a senior editor at *Texas Monthly*, where she won the Press Club of Dallas Investigative Reporting award for her story "The Deadly Doctor." She was a John S. Knight Journalism Fellow at Stanford University. She is a graduate of Wellesley College.